D0939954

The Last of the Fathers

THE
LAST
OF THE
FATHERS

The Cistercian Fathers of the Twelfth Century

A Collection of Essays

M. Basil Pennington, OCSO

Studies in Monasticism   I

St. Bede's Publications
Still River, Massachusetts

152|90

Permissu Superiorum Dom Paschal Skutecky, OCSO

1452

LIBRARY OF CONGRESS CATALOGING IN PUBLICATION DATA

Main entry under title:

The Last of the Fathers.

Bibliography: p.
1. Cistercians—Europe—History—Addresses, essays, lectures.
2. Church history—Middle Ages, 600-1500—Addresses, essays, lectures. I. Pennington, M. Basil.
BX3415.L37   1983   271'.12   82-24098
ISBN 0-932506-24-0

*This volume is dedicated to my community
and to our abbot, Thomas Keating, who,
by the way they live, teach the
Cistercian way far more effectively
than any words can ever hope to*

Contents

Introduction

A return to our roots—this is for many a very real concern. The Second Vatican Council, using another typology, urged a return to our "sources." The Cistercian Fathers are my roots, one of the sources of life that enlivens the currents of my spirit—and not only mine and that of other Cistercian monks and nuns, but that of the whole of Western Christian culture. For Bernard of Clairvaux stood, for a quarter of a century, in one of the most important and formative centuries of Western civilization, as the Spiritual Father of the Christian community. It is difficult for us today to conceive of such universal impact on the part of one man. Perhaps the nearest modern example would be Gandhi and the role he played on the Indian subcontinent. In his day, Bernard determined who was accepted as pope and king, Bernard called forth men to war and to peace, Bernard defended the widow, the poor, the orphan, the Jew. So dynamic was his appeal that when he spoke at the University of Paris half of the students are reported to have withdrawn to flock to the monasteries. When he was heard to be coming, wives hid their husbands, mothers their sons. As a youth, when he decided to enter the monastery, he did not go alone. He went at the head of a band of thirty relatives. Any young man who can inspire his older brothers, knightly warriors, to lay down their arms and send their wives to nunneries to follow him through the forbidding marshes to an obscure monastery certainly has an extraordinary charism for leadership.

The other Cistercian Fathers we speak of here were among those who followed Bernard most closely, in spirit if not in actual presence—though they would have clung to his physical presence if he would have allowed them. These are the men history and Bernard's correspondence indicate to have been dearest to him, most influenced by him, extensions of himself and, in one case perhaps, greatly influencing him.

William of St. Thierry wanted desperately to cling to Bernard. And Bernard did favor him with a special closeness at periods, most notably when they lay side by side in the infirmary for a long period and produced their joint commentary on the Song of Songs. But Bernard was adamant in sending William from him to be a presence among the Black monks, setting his reforming spirit at work from within the ranks of his most formidable critics.

Aelred of Rievaulx has always been referred to as the "Bernard of the North." Bernard never crossed the Channel, but in the person of this great Christian humanist he had a marked influence on the life of England and Scotland. For Aelred was to the kings and peoples of Britain what Bernard was to the whole of the Continent.

Guerric was Bernard's own most dear novice, eventually his prior, and then his choice for abbot of Igny, to be a presence in northern Europe, close to the important see of Reims—the area of Guerric's origin. Isaac of Stella would carry Bernard's influence to another generation. But by then that influence was waning. Isaac's forced resignation and exile are a most striking witness to that diminution.

This volume certainly has no intention of presenting even the merest lineaments of this great Spiritual Father of Christendom, nor of his disciples. Capable historians and biographers have been and are working at that. It is hoped that the monk of our times closest to Bernard, Dom Jean Leclercq of Clervaux Abbey, who has brought forth the critical edition of Bernard's writings and hundreds of articles on him, will yet grace us with the definitive biography.

The importance of these Fathers and their influence has been renewed in our times by what Dom Leclercq speaks of as "the closing of the scholastic parenthesis." The rationalistic approach toward theology which saw its first significant expression in the eleventh century with St. Anselm and reached a high water mark with Thomas Aquinas in the thirteenth, drove a wedge between theology and spirituality. When the Queen of the Sciences lost her solid grounding in the Sacred Page and the Fathers (how well Aquinas knew his sources, but this was not so for many of his successors), she devolved into a sad sterility on the one hand and a less than stable vigor on the other. But today we again have men who think and write in the style of the Fathers of the Church, men like Henri de Lubac, Jean Daniélou, Hans Urs von Balthasar. These men have picked up where the Cistercian Fathers and the other great and less known writers of the twelfth century left off.

With the development of the more rationalistic attitude toward the basic truths of life, a tendency universalized by the proliferation of the printed word, a more and more conceptual stance dominated the Western approach to life and spirituality. The power of thought—sometimes totally divorced from the heart—prevailed. But today's world is less and less dependent on the written word. Multi-media communications, rich in imagery and touching all the senses, evoke a holistic response which gives prominence to the heart, to that which is beyond thought, to the transcendental. The heart, the whole person, has its reasons of which the mind knows nothing. The evolution of the global village, increased communications with the Far East, its religions and its cultures, have challenged the Christian West and are making it acutely aware of its need to get in touch with all the dimensions of its rich heritage. There is a great need to reach back to the other side of the scholastic parenthesis and pick up those currents of life which were more integrally and fully human, open to the divine and to the divinization of the human. One who is experiencing with some liveliness the currents of global spirituality, an ecumenism beyond ecumenism, in these last years of the twentieth century, finds himself surprisingly at home with these very existential, personalist and transpersonal Fathers of the twelfth century.

I present here but a random collection of essays, each touching on a single facet—a ripple in the stream close to its original source. I do not think I have to apologize for a collection of occasional essays on these men for their own writings are almost exclusively occasional writings: the sermons they were called upon to give in their roles as abbots in service of their communities or on special occasions outside the abbeys, letters written in response to those received from every level of church and society or in response to the unfolding events that evoked concerned intervention, treatises unremittingly required by scholars and hierarchs. I believe these studies have a particular value—apart from their reflecting something of the recent scholarship in more popular form—in their coming from a monk who has sought to live fully in the current of life that flows from these Fathers. Until the very decisive General Chapter of 1969 the Cistercians of the Stricter Observance were literally living even in details (right down to their twelfth-century underdrawers) a regulated life that was set by the *Usages* of the 1130s. However, this should not be exaggerated, for not only were there obviously some significant changes, but no twentieth-century person could expect to approach, understand, and live out particular regulations in the same way as did his twelfth-century brother. Yet it is true that at times a lived experience of particular details is the key to understanding certain passages in the Fathers' writings. I have seen this in my contact with scholars, sometimes smiling as unwitting professors or graduate students wove an elaborate and totally unwarranted theory to explain a text that was patently clear to one who was familiar with the detail of life to which the Cistercian author was alluding. But far more significant is the shared spiritual current which prevails within the Cistercian communities even after the sweeping reforms of 1969. Living within that current for a quarter of a century and more, in daily contact with the Fathers and their life-form one develops a certain connatural sensitivity to what they are seeking to communicate in their writings. At times Bernard, William, or Guerric will say: If you have experienced this you will know what I am talking about; if not, then seek the experience and you will understand. When I first encountered such statements, I thought them rather snobbish. Time has proven their validity.

In sharing these essays it is my hope that they will be of assistance to young monks and nuns, to students and to those who would not consider themselves students but are yet seekers, in their first meetings with these men. I think hearing the Fathers a bit in their own words, with the help of some exegesis, can better facilitate an initial introduction than an exhaustive biographical journey. It would be my hope that these rather familial introductions will entice the reader to seek a fuller acquaintance with one or the other of these great, loving, and lovable Fathers. To facilitate this I have included an English language bibliography of my favorite Father, the one who I think speaks most directly to our times and who wrote mostly for young people, the very existential, open, and sharing Abbot of St. Thierry. The extensive notes will offer ample leads for pursuing contact with the other Fathers.

In 1973 I had the privilege of chairing an international symposium at Oxford University which brought together Spiritual Fathers and Mothers of the Cistercian and Orthodox traditions. At one point in the program a western participant decried the fact that there are so few Spiritual Fathers available today. The Orthodox reechoed this lament. Knowing the key role the Spiritual Father plays in the life of a monk in the East, I inquired how they supplied for this devastating lacuna. Bishop Antonie of Rumania responded that when a monk or nun or a pious lay person cannot find a Spiritual Father or Mother he or she turns to the Fathers, and learns from them through their writings. These Fathers are alive now in the Lord and can speak directly to us.

It is my humble hope that as the reader peruses these pages Bernard and his disciples will speak to him or her, and as most loving and God-filled Fathers, open out to him or her new vistas of life, new depths of joy, new hope for a renewed tomorrow. In their lifetime these abbots spoke not just to their own monks. We have their writings today because they were constantly copied and widely diffused among the literate. Within each one of us there is something of the monk. Perhaps some of the emptiness we experience at times is due to the fact that we leave that cell in our hearts uninhabited so much of the time. We need, each one of us, to be in touch with our own contemplative dimension and the sources within our own tradition that can feed that dimension. The mystical tradition of the West is a current that has never ceased to flow. Like the silent peaceful waters of Siloe it has ever been flowing beneath the surface and needs but to be tapped, to be brought again to the surface, and allowed to flow over a parched land to bring new freshness, life, and hope.

M. Basil Pennington, OCSO

The Founders

Toward Discerning the Spirit of
the Founders of the Order of Citeaux

It is difficult to define exactly what is meant by "the spirit." The term is used analogically, or, more precisely, metaphorically.

In a living organism the spirit is the life principle—that which animates it. Though it is distinct from the body, it is united intimately with it. In an institution the spirit is what makes it "alive," able to fulfill its functions with vitality. In the final analysis, this spirit lives in the men who constitute the institute. In our present context, it is that driving inspiration which moved the Founders of Citeaux as they brought a new monastic order into existence.

When this spirit has been embodied in writing, often it is later set in opposition to its very body, the "letter." In reality, the spirit will be found deep within the letter. We have to consider then the writings and the actions of the Founders to discern their spirit; we have to probe these to their very heart and discover the ultimate criteria for the choices they made. These ultimate criteria are what constitute the spirit.[1]

Father Claude Piefer brings out how well the renewal of the Cistercian Founders corresponds to present-day concerns. For he sees it as that mentality which "examines the structure itself and the value of the system upon which it is based and undertakes to revise and reformulate the theory and to rebuild the structure in a form which will effectively communicate the theory to the contemporary world."[2]

One of the greatest problems we have in trying to discern the spirit that guided the renewal of the Cistercian Founders is in truly discerning their attitude toward the Rule of St. Benedict. The *Little Exordium,* the documentary account of the founding of Citeaux, emphasized their great desire to live the Rule which they had professed, their sorrow at seeing it transgressed, their attempt to abandon everything that was contrary to the Rule or superfluous to its observance.[3] The Rule was to be obeyed in everything just as it was in the New Monastery,[4] as Citeaux was then called.

While it is true that they do not speak in these early documents of a literal (*ad litteram*) observance of the Rule,[5] they are nonetheless preoccupied with precision and intensity in returning to the purity of the Rule. When confronted with this great emphasis on the careful observance of the Rule we sometimes attempt to water it down by pointing to as many exceptions as we can, e.g. the sweeping simplicity in the liturgical accouterments that is found in Chapter Seventeen of the *Exordium,* the institution of the lay brothers, the omission of deans and oblates, and the confederation of the monasteries. However, in all frankness it has to be admitted that these are at most *praeter regulam* rather than *contra regulam.* Nevertheless, they are realities and they do show some real adaptation to the social and economic conditions of the times. This cannot be denied. Yet neither can it be denied that in the mind of the Founders these innovations were directly ordered to a fuller living of the Rule.[6]

This desire to live the Rule of St. Benedict more integrally and fully was not unique to Citeaux. It was an inspiration common to many of the monastic foundations being made in that period. We might note in particular the foundation of Savigny, which was one day to affiliate with the Cistercians, and Bernard de Abbeville's foundation at Tiron.[7] More notable is the earlier foundation of Molesme in the Alps. In its Foundation Charter, drawn up in 1087, we find terminology which will again appear in the *Little Exordium:* "Under God's inspiration, we were adhering in our actions to the precepts of our Father, St. Benedict."[8]

The most distinctive innovation and perhaps the greatest departure from the Rule was the federation of the monasteries, worked out and established in the Charter of Charity. The Cistercians rightly pointed to the centralized Cluniac system as being something contrary to the Rule of St. Benedict, which made the local abbot very much the lord and master of his monastery.[9] They asserted as part of their renewal the reestablishment of the autonomy of the local community.[10] However, in practice, while safeguarding to a great extent the juridic and economic independence of the monasteries, they formed a bond of social charity which to some degree restricted the full autonomy of the local abbot.

THE FOUNDERS OF THE ORDER OF CITEAUX

Here it might be opportune to raise the question, who *in concreto* are the Founders of the Order of Citeaux?

There can be no doubt that Robert of Molesme, Alberic, and Stephen Harding, along with their companions, are the Founders of the New Monastery which in a short while came to be called the Abbey of Citeaux.[11] But if they had in mind that the New Monastery should become the center of a federation of abbeys they nowhere expressed this. Nor did Robert's early return to Molesme leave him much time to develop such an idea. Alberic, too, passed quietly off the scene in death while the very survival of the dwindling group was still in question.[12] If the title of Founder of the Order of Citeaux can be claimed for any single man, that man would be Stephen Harding.[13]

However, I do not think any one man can be the subject of such a claim. The actual Founders of the Order of Citeaux were the abbots gathered in the General Chapter of 1123. When they ratified the Charter of Charity, they created "a new society endowed with a democratic authority, having its own proper end and laws which were to be established by a supreme authority within the Order, the General Chapter."[14] With this, the Order of Citeaux was born.

When these abbots abdicated some of the autonomy which was natively theirs as superiors of *sui juris* abbeys, to establish a corporate body, they brought into existence a true Order. Up to this time, the Order of Citeaux was an order only in an earlier sense of the word. It signified a particular mode of life or discipline. It was at the Chapter of 1123 that the Order of Citeaux became a true institute within the Church. And the abbots there assembled were the Founders of this institute, the Founders of the Order of Citeaux as an institute.

SAINT BERNARD: ONE OF THE FOUNDERS

If the Founders of the Order of Citeaux were the twenty abbots assembled for the General Chapter of 1123, then there were included among the Founders a number of the so-called "second generation" Cistercians, and most significantly Bernard of Clairvaux.[15] However, the fact that Bernard and the other great leaders of the "second generation" are technically Founders does not make a great difference. For certainly their doctrine and example pertain to the constitutive tradition of the Order of Citeaux and are the fullest expression of the spirit of the Founder.[16] As Dom Salmon has well put it:

> Although St. Bernard is not one of the Founders of Citeaux (sic) *he is the incarnation of its spirit.* He entered the monastery fifteen years after its foundation and received his formation from St. Stephen Harding. With Bernard the new Order matured and entered a new era of unprecedented fruitfulness. In him, the new-born institute received a genius and a saint who would give the Cistercian ideal its definitive form.[17]

St. Stephen recognized in Bernard the flowering of his own spirit and ideal. After Bernard had been only a few years under his guidance he did not hesitate to send him as the spiritual father and guide of his third foundation. With his great gifts of mind and heart and his unsurpassable art of expression, Bernard has incarnated for us in written word the spirit of Citeaux.[18]

Some have proposed that there is a marked difference between the outlook of the actual Founders of the New Monastery and that of the "Second Generation" and of St. Bernard in particular. In support of this, they point to ideas on art,[19] music,[20] and to a number of their particular provisions of the early General Chapters. These enactments have a certain strictness or narrowness about them which, they say, are due to Bernard's influence.[21]

I do not know to what extent we can attribute different decisions of the General Chapter to St. Bernard's influence. I would agree with Dom Salmon that "Bernard's ideas on the problem we are dealing with are not easy to assess because they are usually expressed in connection with the dispute with Cluny in which feeling and eloquence had a greater role than objective description."[22] In any case, it may well be asked whether these particular and relatively minor observances really do reflect the basic spirit of the man or the institute. Certainly, in approaching the question of the observance of the Rule no one was more benign and discreet than Bernard:

> He who thinks it perjury not to observe the Holy Rule in its purity has, I think, paid scant attention to what he has actually promised. No one at profession really promises "the Rule," but specifically, that he will act "according to the Rule" in the inception and pursuit of his holy undertaking. This sort of profession formula has, in our day, been adopted by almost all monks. However, God is served in many diverse ways in the various monasteries. So long as one carefully observes the good customs of his house, he is beyond any doubt living according to the Rule, for the Rule admits of variations in local customs. . . . Even if they do not keep it all "to the hair" (as the saying goes), and even if they change or omit certain details according to the customs of their house, as long as they are faithful to what is locally accepted as a sober, just, and pious life, they are truly living the Rule. Such conduct is, in fact, recommended by the Rule itself in the eighth degree of humility: "That a monk do nothing that is not sanctioned by the custom of the house or the example of the seniors."[23]

It is true, however, that St. Bernard holds up a particular ideal for his Cistercian brethren. He goes on to say in the same place:

> Of course, it is a different matter for the Cistercians and for those who, like them, have promised an integral and literal observance of the Rule, rather than a life according to the Rule, since such is their interpretation of monastic profession.[24]

PRIMACY OF CHARITY

However, this statement, strong though it may be, must be understood in the whole context of Bernard's thinking. In his famous *Apology* he very frankly says to his Cistercian brethren:

> If you think that all those who profess the Rule are bound to keep it literally (*ad litteram*) without any possibility of dispensation, then I dare say you yourself fail as much as the Cluniac.... On the other hand, if you admit that some things can be changed by dispensation, then it must be true that both you and the Cluniac are keeping the Rule, though each in his own way. You keep it more strictly (*districtus*); and he, perhaps, keeps it more reasonably.[25]

In the Book on *Precept and Dispensation*, Bernard expresses his thought more fully in regard to changing the Rule by dispensation. Speaking of the Rules of Sts. Basil, Augustine and Benedict, as well as those of the Canons Regular, he says:

> These Rules were devised or ordained, not because it is unlawful to live in a different manner, but because this manner of life was found to be expedient for the gaining or the preservation of charity.[26]

Bernard, then, places the end of all the Rules in charity. In this he is clearly giving voice to the thought of St. Benedict, who expresses the same idea in the Prologue to his Rule for Monasteries:

> But if a certain strictness results from the dictates of equity for the amendment of vices or the preservation of charity, do not be at once dismayed and fly from the way of salvation, whose entrance cannot but be narrow. For as we advance in religious life and faith, our hearts expand and we run on the way of God's commandments with unspeakable sweetness of love.[27]

Again, in the seventh chapter on humility, which is the heart and center of Benedictine spirituality, St. Benedict points toward the goal of this way of life: "Having climbed all these steps of humility, therefore, the monk will presently come to that perfect love of God which casts out fear."[28] As Dom Salmon sums it up: "In St. Benedict's mind, all the observances it [the Rule] prescribes have no other purpose than that of preparing for the expansion of charity and union with God."[29]

St. Bernard conceives the matter in no other way. The end of the life is love. The purpose of a return to the Rule, a fuller living of the Rule, is a fuller growth in charity. Therefore, St. Bernard very logically concludes:

> However, should they (the rules) ever be found contrary to charity by those to whom God has granted insight and entrusted with authority, is it not clearly just and fitting that they should be omitted, interrupted or

altered for the sake of the very charity which conceived them? It would certainly be blameworthy to hold in opposition to charity that which was ordained solely for charity.[30]

That this primacy of charity is a central facet in the spiritual heritage of the Founders of Citeaux hardly needs to be argued. The very name which they have given to their fundamental charter bespeaks it: Charter of Charity. And they themselves make it clear why they have chosen this name:

> ...the mode of their agreement, it was charity by which the monks in their abbeys, though separated in body in different countries of the world, would be indissolubly united in spirit. They had a good reason to name this decree the Charter of Charity because...it had for its object charity alone and the good of souls in regard to divine and human affairs.
> We wish to retain in the spirit of charity the care of their souls...that we may live united by one charity, one Rule....[31]

This theme is common in the writings of the Cistercian Fathers, but it is most eloquently developed in the book written at the request of St. Bernard by the novice master of Rievaulx, St. Aelred.[32]

THE ROLE OF OBSERVANCES

In establishing the primacy of charity the Cistercian Fathers did not seek to deny the importance to be placed on external observances, especially those outlined in the Rule of St. Benedict. The Fathers would not readily subscribe to the tendency which has been found in more recent centuries to spiritualize the Rule; to place all the stress on the inner spirit, maintaining that that is all that matters and giving little importance to the external.[33] Here we have another element of the spirit of Citeaux which we must readily admit, namely, a real importance is given to the observances of the monastic life, specifically to those of the Rule of St. Benedict, since this is the Rule the Cistercians profess. It is a ready and realistic acceptance of the fact of each monk's personal incarnation, that body and soul must work together. St. Bernard expressed it thus:

> I don't mean by this that external means can be overlooked, or that the man who does not employ them will quickly become spiritual.... Spiritual things are certainly higher, but there is littler hope of attaining them or of receiving them without making use of external excercises.... The man in the best position is he who makes use of both as occasion demands and with discernment.[34]

Today Cistercians may need quite different observances.[35] Monks today may need even greater simplicity than the Founders of Citeaux. But it pertains to the spirit of Christian life that it be wholly ordered to love, and that there be certain observances in a life which is lived with a certain intensity to foster growth in love. Then and today, a person is called to enter the Christian community to live together in community with observances structured to foster a disciplined human and Christian freedom for a maximum response to God and to one's brethren in love.

THE EXPERIENCE OF GOD

We see, then, that the central facet of the spirit of the Founders of Citeaux is that of giving a primal place to charity in a life which is structured according to the order (and I use *order* here in the older sense of a way of life, or discipline) of St. Benedict's Rule insofar as that order truly serves the primacy of love. Undoubtedly, other facets of the spirit of the Founders of Citeaux are to be explored in serious studies. They certainly set for themselves an ideal of poverty, to be "poor with the poor Christ,"[36] uniting it with a remarkable simplicity.[37] Solitude was important to them, and effective separation from the world.[38] Another aspect of Cistercian spirituality or asceticism was manual labor.[39] Indeed, this, if anything, seemed to be one of the distinguishing marks which set the Cistercian renewal apart from all the other renewals taking place contemporaneously with it. Another note which responds very much to our times was the Founders' authenticity.[40] They vowed to live according to the Rule of St. Benedict, and this they determined to do. They did not want to promise one thing and do another.[41]

But I would like to bring forward here only one other facet of the Cistercian spirit, one which is very closely connected with its central facet, the primacy of love, and that facet is the emphasis placed upon the experience of God. In a later terminology this might well be referred to as mystical experience of God, or the mystical element, mysticism; but as the idea of "mystic" has come to have many connotations, it is perhaps best for us to stay with the simple expression—the experience of God.

Father Amedeus Hallier, in his excellent work, *The Monastic Theology of St. Aelred,*[42] brings out clearly the fundamental and dominating role this element of experience plays in the thought and spirituality of St. Aelred. Examples can readily be drawn from many other early Cistercian Fathers.[43] Here I will content myself with indicating very briefly its presence in the writings of the "Theologian of the Cistercian Life."

St. Bernard, in tracing out the stages of the spiritual life, uses many and varied analogies. But whether his image be three kisses,[44] or three ointments,[45] or seven infusions of the Spirit,[46] or any other, it always leads to "the quiet of contemplation" after the painful fatigue of action, to the fullness of love where God is not so much perceived as vaguely felt and apprehended, and that in a passing way and by the light of a sudden and momentary blaze of glory, so that a great flame of love is enkindled in the soul.[47]

When he comes to the central theme of Benedictine spirituality in his commentary on Chapter Seven of the Rule, this characteristic thrust of the Cistercian spirit is much in evidence.[48] For Bernard, Benedict's ladder leads directly to perfect love, to the banquet of King Solomon, to the delights and joy of contemplation.[49] It leads to the chamber of the king where the soul rests securely in the king's embrace. While in this chamber the soul "sees things invisible and hears things unspeakable which it is not given man to utter."[50]

Here we see that this "mystical" element of the Cistercian spirit is nothing more than an explication of elements to be found in the Rule itself, the full flowering of the seeds sown by the Legislator of Monte Cassino. For he, too, would have his monks "run the way of God's commandments with unspeakable sweetness of love,"[51] and "come to that perfect love of God which casts out fear."[52] He would have them "attain to the loftier heights."[53]

From this we can perhaps glean this insight: When the Founders of the Order of Citeaux aspired to live the Rule in a fuller and more perfect way: *arctius, perfectius, pure, simpliciter, ex integro,* their concern was not only, and indeed not even primarily, to live all its particular observances. Their concern was to live the Rule in its fullness and to come to the fullness of the life of the Rule. A full observance for them meant truly striving to attain the ultimate goal which the Rule set before them, the perfection of love in the experience of God. It is the goal repeatedly proposed in the Rule of St. Benedict. While its thrust toward the ultimate makes the Cistercian spirit impatient of anything that does not truly contribute to its quest, intense realism makes it aware of the need of incarnational observances and the structures of an order bonded in charity. This leads it to seek an authentic living of the Rule professed, in simplicity and poverty, in solitude and effective separation from the ways of the world. None of these elements is exclusively or uniquely Cistercian, but a balanced blending of them has produced and can still produce a monastic life that is eminently attractive and fruitful.

NOTES

[1]Paul Molinari, S.J., "Religious Renewal and the Founder's Spirit," in *Review for Religious*, 27 (1968) p. 801.

[2]C. Piefer, "Monastic Renewal in Historical Perspective," in *American Benedictine Review*, 19 (1968) p. 2.

[3]This can be found expressed in almost every chapter of the *Little Exordium*, ed. J.-B. Van Damme, *Documenta pro Cisterciensis Ordinis Historiae ad Juris Studio* (Westmalle: Typis Ordinis Cisterciensis, 1959); trans. R. Larkin in L. Lekai, *The White Monks* (Okauchee, WI: The Cistercian Fathers, 1952).

[4]Charter of Charity (hereafter CC) c. 2, ed. J.-B. Van Damme, *Documenta pro Cisterciensis Ordinis Historiae ad Juris Studio* (Westmalle: Typis Ordinis Cisterciensis, 1959), p. 16, trans. D. Murphy in L. Lekai, *The White Monks* (Okauchee, WI: The Cistercian Fathers, 1952) p. 268.

[5]P. Salmon, "Monastic Asceticism and the Origins of Citeaux" in *Monastic Studies*, n. 3 (1965) pp. 131ff., n. 25.

[6]E.g., in the case of the lay brothers: "Since they realized that without their help they would be unable to fulfill perfectly the precepts of the Rule day and night, they decided to admit unlettered men as lay brothers with the approval of the bishop and treat them in life and in death as their own except for the rights reserved for monks." *Little Exordium*, c. 15, *op. cit.*, p. 13; Larkin, p. 263.

[7]P. Cousin, *Precis d'Histoire Monastique* (Paris: Bloud & Gay, 1956) pp. 287ff. We might indicate also St. Stephen's foundation at Grandmont and the foundation of Geraud at Sauve-Majeure, and the double monastery founded by Robert d'Arbrissel, Fontevrault. Cf. also, D. Meade, "From Turmoil to Solidarity: the Emergence of the Vallombrosan Congregation," in *American Benedictine Review*, 19 (1968) pp. 323ff., especially p. 330; R. Duvernay, "Vallombruse, Citeaux et Etienne Harding" in *Analecta S. O. Cisterciensis*, 8 (1958) pp. 428ff.

[8]*Documenta*, p. 3: "Deo inspirante Sancti Patris nostri Benedicti praeceptis actibus inhaerentes."

[9]St. Benedict's *Rule for Monasteries* (hereafter RB), cc. 2, 3, etc. (For citations of RB we use the division of chapter and verse of E. Manning [Westmalle: Typis Ordinis Cisterciensis, 1962] who follows Lantini).

[10]*Little Exordium*, c. 14, *op. cit.*, p. 14; Larkin, p. 264. Cf. J.-B. Van Damme, "Formation de la Constitution Cistercienne" in *Studia Monastica*, 4 (1962) p. 127: "Mais il y eut un statut arrêté par les moines venus de Molesme: les monastères qu'ils fonderaient un jour, devaient être tous des abbayes. C'était une position de principe, rien de plus, mais le principe était défini, et il était de grande importance!"

[11]See J. Marilier, *Chartes et Documenta concernant l'Abbaye de Citeaux 1098-1182* (Rome: Editiones Cistercienses, 1961) pp. 24ff.

[12]*Little Exordium*, cc. 14ff., *op. cit.*, pp. 14ff.; Larkin, p. 264.

[13]We could hardly consider the group as a whole to be the Founders of the Cistercian Order, for there was evidently a lack of unanimity among them as to their ideal and aims and some of them freely withdrew to return to Molesme with Robert. *Little Exordium:* "And some of the monks who did not love the desert returned with him (Robert)" c. 7, *op. cit.*, p. 9; Larkin, p. 257.

[14]J.-B. Van Damme, "Formation de la Constitution Cistercienne," p. 135; see also J. B. Mahn, *L'Ordre Cistercien et son Gouvernement*, 2nd ed. (Paris: Boccard, 1951) pp. 61ff.

[15]Aside from Stephen Harding, Bernard of Clairvaux and Arnold of Morimond, (who shortly after withdrew irregularly from his abbey) most of the names would be unfamiliar, e.g., Blessed Peter I of La Ferté and Hugh of Macon, Abbot of Pontigny.

[16]It is noteworthy that in the *Dialogue between a Cluniac and a Cistercian*, written in a Morimond filiation not long after the death of Bernard, it is Bernard who is most frequently cited to give expression to the Cistercian ideal. Cf. Idung of Prufening, *Dialogus inter Cluniacensem Monachum et Cisterciensem de Diversis Utrusque Ordinis Observantiis*, ed. Martene and Durand, *Thesaurus Novarum Anecdotarum*, V, 1569ff., also, W. Williams, *Monastic Studies* (Manchester: University of Manchester Press, 1938) c. 6, pp. 61ff.; trans. J. F. O'Sullivan, *Cistercians and Cluniacs*, Cistercian Fathers Series (hereafter CF) 33, (Kalamazoo, MI: Cistercian Publications, 1977).

[17]Salmon, "Monastic Asceticism," p. 133.

[18]Very aptly does Dom Jean Leclercq speak of him as the "Theologian of the Cistercian Life." J. Leclercq, "The Intentions of the Founders of the Cistercian Order" in *The Cistercian Spirit*, Cistercian Studies Series (hereafter CS) 3, (Spencer, MA: Cistercian Publications, 1969) p. 101.

[19]Cf. C. Oursel, *Miniatures Cisterciennes (1109-1134)* (Macon: Protat, 1960) pp. 19ff.

[20]Cf. S. Marosszéki, "Les origines du chant Cistercien" in *Analecta S. O. Cisterciensis*, 8 (1952) pp. 1-137; especially, c. 2, pp. 10-14, p. 23, p. 72, and the conclusion, pp. 129ff.

[21]E.g., *Instituta Generalis Capituli*, 13: no gold and silver clasps on liturgical books; 14: no white bread, not even on feasts; 20: no statues or pictures, only painted wooden crosses. (It must be noted that this is only a repetition of what is already found in the *Little Exordium* which in the seventeenth chapter prescribes very extensive austerity and simplicity in the liturgical ornamentation, just as in chapter fifteen it called for great simplicity and poverty in food and clothing. While some of the later prescriptions of the General Chapters seem to us to descend to too many details and to be perhaps petty, they do find a certain precedent in the basic prescriptions of the *Little Exordium*); 22: no pets, at least not unusual ones; 25: no cheese or eggs for guests on fast days; 27: only two externs with their wives may be buried in the monastery; 29: monks are not to baptize or be sponsors at Baptism (this has been incorporated into Canon Law); 52: monks are not to sell wine to taverns; 54: the measure of the bread and wine and also of vegetables is to be the same in all abbeys and granges; 58: the monks need permission of the General Chapter to write books; 59: detailed regulations for shepherds; 61: detailed regulations for bishops of the Order; 63: pepper and cinnamon and other imported spices are forbidden; 64, 65, 76, and 88: detailed penal regulations; 73: monks are to sing with manly voices; 80: the books are to be in one color and only white glass is to be used with no crosses or pictures; 83: the monks when riding are not to use leather chaps; 84: the monks are not to prostrate in prayer in church.—*Nomasticon Cisterciense*, ed. Paris-Séjalon (Solesme: St. Peter's 1892) pp. 212ff.

[22]Salmon, "Monastic Asceticism," pp. 133ff.

[23]*De Praecepto et Dispensatione*, n. 47ff., *S. Bernardi Opera Omnia* (hereafter OB) 3

(Rome: Editiones Cistercienses, 1963) p. 286; trans. C. Greenia. *Monastic Obligations and Abbatial Authority: St. Bernard's Book on Precept and Dispensation, The Works of Bernard of Clairvaux,* 1, Treatises 1, CF 1, (Spencer, MA: Cistercian Publications, 1970) pp. 140ff. Compare this with the Letter of Peter the Venerable to Bernard, among the letters of St. Bernard, Epistle 229, PL 182:398ff.

24*Ibid.,* n. 49.

25*Apologia ad Guielmum,* n. 14, OB 3:93ff.; trans. M. Casey, *Cistercians and Cluniacs: St. Bernard's Apology to Abbot William, The Works of Bernard of Clairvaux,* 1, Treatise 1, CF 1:50ff.

26*De Praecepto,* n. 5, OB 3:257; CF 1:108.

27RB, Prologue, 47ff.

28RB 7:67.

29Salmon, "Monastic Asceticism," p. 136.

30*De Praecepto,* n. 5, OB 3:257; CF 1:108-9.

31CC, Prologue and c. 1, *op. cit.,* pp. 15ff.; Murphy, pp. 267ff.

32*Speculum Caritatis,* PL 195:503-620; trans. A. Walker & G. Webb, *Mirror of Charity* (London: Mowbrays, 1962).

33Cf. Salmon, "Monastic Asceticism," pp. 119ff.

34*Apologia,* n. 14, OB 3:94; CF 1:51.

35"The manner of living, praying and working should be suitably adapted every-where...to the modern physical and psychological circumstances of the members, as required by the nature of each institute..." Second Vatican Council, *Perfectae Caritatis,* n. 3. "The special penitential practices of institutes should be revised insofar as it is necessary, so that taking into account traditions, whether of the East or the West, and modern circumstances, the members may in practice be able to observe them, adapting also new forms drawn from modern conditions of life." Pope Paul VI, *Ecclesiae Sanctae,* II, n. 22.

36*Little Exordium,* c. 15, *op. cit.,* p. 13; Larkin, p. 263. Duvernay has assembled several pages of texts showing this: *op. cit.,* pp. 397-404.

37Cf. *Little Exordium,* cc. 15, 17, *op. cit.,* pp. 13ff.; Larkin, pp. 262ff.

38*Ibid.* For other texts see Duvernay, *op. cit.,* pp. 389ff.

39*Ibid.,* c. 15. Cf. also Duvernay, *op. cit.,* p. 404.

40This word "authentic" had a somewhat different or more restricted meaning for the twelfth century Founders, primarily, conformity of texts. But I am using it in our present-day sense.

41This is evident throughout the documents.

42A. Hallier, *The Monastic Theology of St. Aelred; A Theology of Experience,* trans. C. Heaney, CS 2 (Spencer, MA: Cistercian Publications, 1969).

43E.g., William of St. Thierry, *Exposition on the Song of Songs,* nn. 4, 20, trans. C. Hart, *The Works of William of St. Thierry,* 2, CF 6 (Spencer, MA: Cistercian Publications, 1969) pp. 6, 15.

44Sermon 3, *Sermones super Cantica Canticorum* OB 1 (Rome: Editiones Cistercienses, 1957) pp. 14ff.; trans. K. Walsh, *On the Song of Songs, The Works of Bernard of Clairvaux,* 2, CF 4 (Spencer, MA: Cistercian Publications, 1969) pp. 16ff.

45Sermon 10, nn. 4ff., OB 1:50ff.; Walsh, CF 4:63ff.

46Sermon 18, OB 1:103ff.; Walsh, CF 4:133ff.

⁴⁷Sermon 18, n. 6, OB 1:107; Walsh, CF 4:138.

⁴⁸St. Bernard, *The Steps of Humility and Pride,* OB 3:15ff.; trans, M. Ambrose Conway, *Treatises II, The Works of Bernard of Clairvaux,* CF 13 (Washington, DC: Cistercian Publications, 1974).

⁴⁹*Ibid.,* c. 2, OB 3:18; CF 13:31ff.

⁵⁰*Ibid.,* c. 7, OB 3:33; CF 13:50.

⁵¹RB, Prologue, 49.

⁵²RB 7:67.

⁵³RB 73:9.

Three Early Documents

The Psalter of Saint Robert

The "Psalter of St. Robert" is the title given to a psalter of Saint-Vaast which is today in the Municipal Library of Dijon.[1] It is a psalter of the eleventh century which was adapted for the use of Citeaux. According to tradition, St. Robert himself brought it from Molesme. The note in the Psalter which interests us is accepted as having been written in the twelfth century.

This note is a witness to the consciousness of the early Cistercian Fathers of the role of the Holy Spirit in the founding of Citeaux. The pertinent passage of the note is the opening line:

> The blessed Father Robert, under the inspiration of the Holy Spirit, went forth from the Monastery of Molesme...

Our translation is based on the text which S. R. Marosszéki published in the *Analecta* of the Sacred Order of Cistercians in 1952.[2]

Note from the Psalter of St. Robert

The blessed Father Robert, under the inspiration of the Holy Spirit, went forth from the Monastery of Molesme which he himself had founded, and, as a bee laden with the sweetness of the Lord, came with his holy swarm of confreres to a place indicated to him by heaven, the place where stands the Monastery of Citeaux. This monastery was to become the head of a most excellent and devout Order. Among the things which he brought with him was this psalter. Through the agreement between Citeaux and Molesme, established by apostolic authority, it has remained at Citeaux. All the psalters of this whole sacred Order are to be taken from and amended in accord with its letter, accent, and punctuation. But the Order did not adopt the foregoing Calendar nor the appended Litany.

NOTES

[1] Ms. 30 (12), fol. 10.

[2] S. R. Marosszéki, S. O. Cist., "Les origines du chant Cistercien" in *Analecta Sacri Ordinis Cisterciensis,* VIII (1952) p. 164.

St. Stephen's Letter on the Use of Hymns

What is commonly called the Letter or Epistle of St. Stephen on the Use of Hymns is actually an introduction or preface to the hymnal of Citeaux. Father Chrysogonus Waddell, O.C.S.O., is presently making a study of this hymnal and we can hope that in his report he will bring out the full significance of this letter.[1]

The Letter is cited primarily for the witness it gives to the dedication of the Founding Fathers of Citeaux to living the Rule of St. Benedict:

> ...indeed, our blessed Father and Master Benedict, in his Rule, which we have decreed must be observed in this place with great care, prescribes that these hymns be sung by us.

In this very short Letter, St. Stephen Harding, the third abbot of Citeaux, originally St. Robert's subprior, seems to be even more concerned about living the Rule than about the hymns. The bulk of the Letter actually pertains to this very important element of the Cistercian reform:

> Wherefore, by the authority of God and by our own authority, we enjoin upon you that you never presume through levity to change or detract from the integrity of the Holy Rule which you know has been worked out and established by us in this place with no little labor....

The devotion of the Founders to the person of St. Benedict is also evident:

> ...living as lovers, imitators and defenders of our Holy Father...

One might ask whether it would be reading something into the mind of St. Stephen if one understood by the phrase: "...never presume through levity to change or detract from...," that the holy Father meant to allow for changes where there were serious reasons. Certainly as St. Stephen wrote the words, "by all our posterity," he could not have imagined the vast progeny which was to be his in the Spirit, a progeny which today is scattered throughout the globe. It would be hard, therefore, to say that his enactment is meant to be taken literally by today's Cistercians. Yet, as they struggle to get a fuller and deeper insight into the true spirit and aims of their Founders, the literalism evident in this Letter in regard to the living out of the Rule of St. Benedict is for them a challenging problem.

The translation given here is based on the text published by D. P. Blanchard in *Revue Bénédictine* in 1914.[2] It has been taken from a twelfth century manuscript which probably has its origins in the Abbey of Melleray. It is now preserved in the Municipal Library at Nantes.[3] Marilier dates the Letter between 1108, the beginning of the abbacy of St. Stephen, and 1115-1119, when the name "The New Monastery" ceased to be used.[4]

Letter on the Use of Hymns

The letter of Dom Stephen, the second Abbot of Citeaux, concerning the use of hymns, here begins:

Brother Stephen, the second superior of the New Monastery,[5] sends greetings to his successors. We command the sons of Holy Church that these hymns, which it is certain that the Blessed Archbishop Ambrose composed, and which were brought to this place, namely, the New Monastery, from the Church of Milan, where they are sung, *these alone and no others,* henceforth must be sung by us and by all our posterity; and indeed, our Blessed Father and Master Benedict, in his Rule, which we have decreed must be observed in this place with great care, prescribes that these same hymns be sung by us. Wherefore, by the authority of God and our own authority, we enjoin upon you that you never presume through levity to change or detract from the integrity of the Holy Rule, which you know has been worked out and established by us in this place with no little labor, but rather, living as lovers, imitators, and defenders of our holy Father, *you hold to these hymns inviolably.*

The Letter happily ends. Amen.

NOTES

[1] In particular, Father will bring out the true significance of Benedict's word *ambrosianum* (RB 9, 4; 12, 4; 13, 11; 17, 8) which St. Stephen in this Letter evidently interprets as meaning the hymns which Ambrose himself composed.

[2] D. P. Blanchard, "Un monument primitif de la Règle Cistercienne" in *Revue Bénédictine*, XXXI (1914) p. 38.

[3] Ms. 9, fol. 144a. Marosszéki reproduces this same text in his article (cf. *op. cit.*, p. 9) as does J. Marilier, *Charter et documents concernant l'abbaye de Cîteaux* (Rome: Editiones Cistercienses, 1961) p. 55.

[4] Marilier, *loc. cit.* The author, however, seems to contradict himself and his reasoning when in the Introduction he affirms emphatically "le premier (document 1, no. 31—our document) a été certainement écrit en 1109," p. 25.

[5]The enumeration here does not take into account St. Robert, who was required to return to Molesme after only a brief service as superior of the New Monastery, but only his successor, St. Alberic. However, the preceding document shows him, Robert, as the leader of the founding group. The *Little Exordium* makes it clear that St. Robert was truly superior of the New Monastery: "The Abbot (Robert) who has come here, upon the command of the above mentioned Legate received from the Bishop of the diocese the shepherd's staff together with the charge of the monks...."—The *Little Exordium* (hereafter EP), ch. 4; trans. R. Larkin in L. Lekai, *The White Monks* (Okauchee, WI: Cistercian Fathers, 1954), p. 254.

The Epistle of Thurstan of York

The Letter of Thurstan, Archbishop of York, to William of Corbeil, the Archbishop of Canterbury and Legate of the Apostolic See, gives a very colorful and sometimes amusing account of the events which set the stage for the founding of Fountains Abbey. The Letter was written in the last months of 1132. No less a person than Bernard of Clairvaux proclaims the merits of the author, Archbishop Thurstan:

> The splendor of your work and your reputation among men have combined greatly, as I know, to your credit. Your deeds prove that yours is no undeserved or empty reputation, for facts themselves bear out what hitherto has everywhere been reported of you...I admire you...[1]

Thurstan not only had a great understanding and appreciation of monastic life, as is seen in this letter, but also a personal desire to embrace it, as is evident from another letter addressed to him by St. Bernard.[2] Thurstan's Letter is brought forward as a witness to the fact that the Cistercian Fathers sought to live the evangelical life according to the monastic tradition expressed in the Rule of St. Benedict.

Thurstan repeatedly and explicitly states that this was the intent of the Founders of Fountains Abbey:

> ...men who were determined to correct their way of life according to the Rule of St. Benedict, or rather, according to the truth of the Gospel.(3)[3]
>
> These brethren with many tears sought nothing but...that they might not be impeded from living in evangelical peace and observing the Rule of the Blessed Father Benedict.(4)
>
> All of them are seeking full observance of the Rule and of their profession and likewise of the Gospel.(19)
>
> ...these men who wish truly to obey the Gospel of Christ and the Rule of St. Benedict...(20)

Moreover, in his Letter, Thurstan quotes Richard, the Prior of York, who was the leader of the Founders of Fountains Abbey and their first abbot.[4] Richard, as the leader of the reform movement, expresses to Abbot Geoffrey of St. Mary's Abbey, York, their precise intent:

> We must undertake with all our strength to observe by God's grace the true and age-old service of our blessed Father Benedict, or rather the more ancient Gospel of Christ which precedes all vows and rules.(4)

Richard had a very deep reverence for the Rule:

> Whatever the blessed Benedict established, the whole of it was designed by the providence of the Holy Spirit, so that nothing more useful, more happy or holy can be conceived.(4)

In conclusion, his plea to his Abbot was:

> St. Benedict acknowledges as his own only those who live in a monastery under a rule and an abbot, so, venerable Father, if you will allow, we will hasten back to the purity of the Gospels, to evangelical perfection and peace.(5)

Richard makes clear the source from which these monks drew: the spirit which animated the early Cistercians:

> We think of the monks of Savigny[5] and Clairvaux who recently came to us. The Gospel so clearly shone out in them that it would be more useful to imitate them than to recite it. When, indeed, their holy life is seen, it is as if the Gospel were relived in them. . . . Happy, indeed, are men such as these whose clothing, food, and whole way of life savor of the Gospel.(6)

Thurstan, too, gives his witness to the spirit and the aim which animated the early Cistercians. He does this not only by direct affirmation:

> The Cistercians went forth to establish and found the most perfect way of life. . . . They faithfully undertook a renewal of the Holy Rule and a total living of it. . . . Indeed, it is clearer than light that in their wonderful way of life the truth of the whole Gospel shines forth.(22)

He also noted that there was a real similarity between the monks who had gone forth from Molesme and the monks then going forth from York under the leadership of Richard:

> We ought to recall what happened in the affair of the Molesme monks, which is quite similar.(22)

As one reads through this account of the actions which led to the founding of Fountains Abbey, one is forcibly struck by the many similarities it has with the founding of Citeaux. There are the laments of some of the brethren about the observance of the Rule,[6] deep concern about their profession and vows,[7] and a desire for a stricter life.[8] At York as at Molesme the expression of this desire aroused strong indignation among the rest of the brethren.[9] In their renewal the reformers were concerned about the same matters: food and clothes,[10] revenues and tithes,[11] manual labor,[12] and above all, to be poor with the poor Christ.[13]

We have, then, both by similarity and by explicit affirmation, a strong witness in this Letter to the fact that the Cistercian Founders sought to live the life of the Rule, and primarily as an expression of a true evangelical life. Within a very short time after the founding of their abbey, Richard and his monks were incorporated into the Order of Citeaux as a daughter house of Clairvaux,[14] showing that Bernard and the other Cistercian Fathers readily acknowledged in them the true spirit and aims of the Cistercian renewal.[15]

The translation we present here is based on the text of Mabillon's edition of the works of St. Bernard.[16] Another version of the Letter which is much longer has come down to us, but in the matter which is our primary concern there is no substantial difference between the two versions. What the latter has by way of addition seems to be clearly a later interpolation with polemical intent.[17]

The Epistle of Thurstan, Archbishop of York

To William his most revered Lord in Christ's love, by the grace of God Archbishop of Canterbury and Legate of the Apostolic See, Thurstan, by the same grace, Archbishop of York, expresses the earnest desire that his Lord might grow in Christ and never fall away.

1. It is the highest honor of an ecclesiastical dignitary to give the best counsel to the finest sons of the Church when they are in most difficult situations. Wherefore, my venerable Lord and esteemed Father, we have decided to bring to the attention of your Paternity an unusual thing which has happened recently among us here at York.

2. Indeed, it is well known and certain to many men how great in the eyes of all is the goodness and virtuous renown of the outstanding Monastery of St. Mary's of York. Because it is without doubt true that when riches increase, virtue begins to wane and be less constant, some of the brethren of this monastery for the past half-year, moved by divine inspiration I believe, have begun to be very concerned about the manner and condition of their way of life. The gnawing of their consciences, as they have testified, has caused them much distress. For they fear that they would be wholly failing if they did not live out in a holy way their awesome vows. Whence, these brethren of York were struck with a very terrible fear in that they seemed to carry out their profession in nothing, or, at least, in very few

things.[18] They feared, indeed, lest they were running or had run, if indeed not to damnation itself, at least in vain because of the guilt that lay upon them for such great infidelity to their vows. They believed it to be a crime, or rather insanity, to bear the yoke of the Rule of St. Benedict not unto salvation but unto condemnation.

3. Therefore, disturbed by these things, these brethren undertook to make known the concern that was burning in their hearts to their Prior, Richard, revealing their fear concerning their transgressions. They sought his help to correct the situation; and lest he fear to be of help out of considerations of prosperity or adversity, they adjured him by the Spirit of God and the Name of Christ. He was alarmed at the novelty of the thing they offered. But although among his own his position was the best, once he heard the quiet call to a better life, he pondered seriously upon the doubtful promise of his transitory good fortune. For a short time he took counsel within himself, considering the alternatives, and then he made his decision. He promised not only to help, but, indeed, to ally himself with their desires. What then? Within a short time the number increased to fully thirteen who were determined to correct their way of life according to the Rule of St. Benedict, or rather, according to the truth of the Gospel.

4. Therefore, on the Vigil of the holy Apostles Peter and Paul, our beloved brother, Prior Richard, on whom almost the whole care of the monastery rested, taking with him his Subprior, Gervaise, who was well known among his brethren for his religious spirit, went to their Lord Abbot and frankly made known to him the whole matter as it had developed. The Lord Abbot, a man who, in his own way and according to his own lights, is decent and good, but, however, overly simple and unschooled, was terrified by the miracle of this new spirit. He denied that he could change in his monastery the ancient rites and the usual practices which generally obtained throughout the whole world. But the Prior, as a man well read, responded: "Father, we do not seek to introduce anything crude or new. We must undertake with all our strength to observe by God's grace the true and age-old service of our blessed Father Benedict, or rather, the more ancient Gospel of Christ, which precedes all vows and rules. We do not seek to detract in any way from the rest of the monks. We are not envious of their practices. We know that in every place one Lord is served. We fight under one King.[19] Both in the public square and in the cloister the same grace of God prevails and wins out. For Job is stronger on his dungheap than Adam in Paradise. Whatever the blessed Benedict established, the whole of it was designed by the Providence of the Holy Spirit, so that nothing more useful, more holy, or happy can be conceived. As he knew and taught that idleness was the enemy of the soul, he arranged that certain times should be given to reading and to fervent prayer and that certain

times be given to labor and to work,[20] in such wise that at one time the soul would be fruitfully employed, at another, the body, and thus both would be saved from weariness.[21] And, moreover, he added this, 'Coarse jests and idle words or words that move to laughter, these we exclude forever from every part of the cloister. For such speech we do not permit the disciple to open his mouth.'[22] And in another place he says: 'At all times a monk should be zealous for silence, but especially during the night hours.'[23] How diligently this decree has been observed is not unknown to anyone who knows our practices. For while some are going to church after collation, others step aside to jest and to exchange useless and garrulous talk, as if the evil of the day were not sufficient,[24] unless there were added to it that of the night."

5. He added many things, moreover, concerning the delicate food, the sweet and expensive variety of drinks, the expensive quality of the clothes. "This was not the taste of our blessed Father Benedict; it was not what he taught. He did not attend to the color of the clothes but to the needed warmth.[25] He did not look after the tastiness of the vegetables. Rather, necessity was hardly satisfied by frugality.[26] St. Benedict acknowledges as his own only those who live in the monastery under a rule and an abbot.[27] So, venerable Father, if you will allow, we will hasten back to the purity of the Gospel, to evangelical perfection and peace. For we see that nothing or very little shines forth in our conduct and in our actions which was taught by Christ. We are filled with concupiscence, we are angry, we quarrel, we steal from others, we go to court to get out goods back, we defend ourselves with fraud and lies, we follow the ways of the flesh and its desires, we live for ourselves, we please ourselves, we fear being overcome, we glory in overcoming others, we oppress others and seek to avoid being oppressed, we envy others and we glory in our own perfections, we take our pleasure, grow fat on the sweat of others, and the whole world does not suffice for our wickedness. It seems as if the Gospel had perished and become impossible for us.

6. "We think of the monks of Savigny and Clairvaux who recently came to us. The Gospel so clearly shone out in them that it must be said it would be more useful to imitate them than to recite it. When, indeed, their holy life is seen, it is as if the Gospel were being relived in them. They alone do not seek their own. They alone possess nothing by which they would seek to prefer themselves to their brethren. They alone do not seek the harm of their neighbors. They are content to cultivate a little land and to use some cattle.[28] And these things, indeed, they do not desire to have except insofar as God wills it. Because when God wills to take them away from them they do not seek to keep them. For them, if I be not mistaken, if is fitting to say: 'The world is crucified to us and we to the world.'[29] For them it is fitting to

say: 'Forgive us our trespasses as we forgive those who trespass against us,'[30] because they have no trespasser from whom they wish to demand anything. Happy, indeed, are men such as these whose clothing, food, and whole way of life savor of the Gospel. Their portion is God alone.[31] They know, insofar as it is humanly possible, how to be filled with the love of God and neighbor. Adhering to God alone, they so fully leave behind all temporal things except for a poor contemptible habit, they desire nothing over which a neighbor could become angry.

7. "Therefore, Father, never let it seem to be impossible to hold fast to the Rule of St. Benedict, as long as God gives us such examples as these who go before us in the way of holiness and virtue so that we may follow them. If, indeed, because of the nearness and the noisiness of the people we are not able wholly to follow them, let us at least advert to our way of life and profession according to our Rule, and moreover, to the fact that we are not monks but rather dead men."

8. In this manner, the Lord Prior, Richard, spoke with their Lord Abbot, Geoffrey, concerning the reformation of their monastery. The Lord Abbot did not receive these words with joy because it is difficult to change long standing practices.

9. Nevertheless, confessing himself to be unlearned and less perspicacious, he asked if he might be more fully informed in writing as to how such things could be accomplished in his monastery. Prior Richard willingly accepted this and was not slow in fulfilling it. He wrote that they ought to conform to what the Rule permitted in speech, clothes, and food. He so carefully explained the arrangement and order of the monastery that it seemed as if the Rule could be observed in the city hardly less perfectly than in a desert. Knowing secular affairs well, he arranged their temporalities with such fidelity that he in no way departed from evangelical justice. Everything concerning the incomes from churches and tithes, in regard to the investment of which monks are usually held to be more reprehensible, was to be undertaken and done with the legitimate and canonical advice of the bishops, and they were to be used only for the poor, the pilgrims, and for guests. He decreed that the monks were to live by agriculture and the rearing of cattle.[32]

10. When the rumor of all these things began to reach the others, the anger of the rest of the community burst forth in a jealous rage. They thought that this man and his companions should be sent into exile or thrown into prison.

11. After meeting with them many times in different places for friendly talks, the Lord Abbot saw that only with difficulty could he change what his predecessors seemed to have upheld. Nevertheless, wishing in this matter to use good counsel, he put off a full reply until after the Nativity of the

Blessed Virgin Mary. Meanwhile, some of the brethren, vainly fearing that they were to be constricted by more than the regular discipline, began, out of envy toward the Prior and the others, to plot like the Pharisees. If the benignity of some had not brought about a delay, immediate persecution would have burst out.

12. At the same time the rumor of the internal strife spread among the people outside. We heard this talk among the people, but the truth of the matter remained hidden. Then Prior Richard, bringing with him the Subprior and the Secretary of the monastery, came to make the truth of the situation known to us. They sought the clemency of St. Peter and of ourselves in order that they might begin without delay to undertake to observe what they had vowed. They said their need was pressing, especially because the brethren had so conspired that if any one of them said anything about his profession he would be excommunicated. Some of the companions of the Prior, shaken by fear or self-love or vanity, so turned back because they could not otherwise find peace, that they confessed it as a fault that they had said anything about observing their profession.

13. Therefore, I, Thurstan, by the grace of God, Archbishop of York, heard these servants of Christ who, according to the command of St. Benedict, wished to prefer nothing to the love of Christ.[33] I feared to offend in them Christ's grace if I did not receive their just petition with pastoral concern. It pertains to the primary responsibilities of a bishop to provide for monks a sacred peace and to comfort the oppressed in their need. Therefore, taking the advice of holy men, I convoked the Lord Abbot Geoffrey and the Prior Richard with his Subprior to a suitable place in order that with some other holy men I might peacefully receive the petition of the brethren and the reply of the Abbot.

14. These brothers, with many tears, sought nothing but what they had previously asked, namely, that they might follow the poor Christ in voluntary poverty,[34] that they might carry the Cross of Christ in their own bodies,[35] that they might not be impeded from living in evangelical peace and observing the Rule of the blessed Father Benedict. To do this, they earnestly sought the permission and the paternal help of their Lord Abbot. And, indeed, the Lord Abbot with tears confessed that their undertaking was something very much needed and he promised that he would not stand in the way of their desire, which was holy, but without the consent of his chapter he dared not promise anything in regard to the assistance they sought.

15. And so the Lord Abbot returned to the monastery with his monks. In the meantime there was peace and a day was established on which I would come to their chapter and, with some religious who would come with me, would treat with the Abbot on this matter. Meanwhile, the rest of the

brethren displayed their envy with increasing cruelty as these men sought more manifestly to carry out their desire. They called in some men from the Great Abbey and some monks of Cluny who were dwelling in the neighborhood. And in their presence and with their approval they deprived these monks, as men who had profaned and deserted the common order, of every dignity and responsibility in the monastery, for, after the Abbot, the greatest responsibility in the monastery had been in their hands. All of this happened in the interim.

16. On the established day, early in the morning, I prepared to come to the chapter of the monks. I had almost arrived at the very door—with me there were a number of wise and religious men: Hugh, the Deacon; William, the Prior of the Clerks Regular of Cisbarne; William, the Treasurer; Hugh, the Archdeacon; Serlo, the Canon; Alfred, my Chaplain and Canon; and Robert, the Chaplain of the Hospital. We had left our horses outside the inner gate with a few men.

17. Then, as I have said, as we were about to enter the door of the chapter, the Lord Abbot met us at the door with his monks, who fairly filled the chapter room. He forbade me to enter unless some of the clerics who were with me were sent away. I was scarcely able to reply that I ought not to enter upon such an affair without my clerics who were good and wise men and their friends, when, behold, the whole chapter resounded with shouting and terrible cries. It seemed that I was faced with the seditious outburst of drunken and debauched men rather than with the humility of monks, of which nothing was there. Many rose up, and swinging their arms as if they would charge to the attack, cried that they would leave if I entered. I said: "God is my witness, that I came as a Father, with no thought of inflicting harm on you, desiring only that there be peace and Christian fraternity among you. Now, in truth, because you have sought to take away from me what pertains to the episcopal authority and office, I, in like manner, take from you what you need. I place your church under interdict." Then one of them, Simon by name, said: "We would prefer to have our church a hundred years under interdict." To this all assented and cried in upraised voices: "Seize them!" Seizing the Prior and his companions, they began to pull them away, wishing, as they had decided among themselves, either to throw them into prison or to send them into exile. The latter, indeed, having no other hope of escaping their hands, clung to me, looking for the peace of Peter and our peace. So we ran to the church, and they, all the way, screamed and cried: "Seize the rebels! Apprehend the traitors!" Thus we escaped into the church. The Abbot and the rest of his monks returned to their chapter.

18. While this was going on, the men of the Abbey stood around the closed doors and the entrance gates as if lying in ambush. We (as I must

truly confess) fearing an attack from the monks, took care to bar, from within, the door of the church which opened on the cloister. Meanwhile, the news spread abroad and people gathered, but no untoward thing was said or done by them.

19. Since, therefore, nothing could be done to establish concord among the monks, we returned home, taking with us the group: twelve priests and a subdeacon. Several of them are learned men. All are seeking full observance of the Rule and their profession and likewise of the Gospel. And so they dwelt as guests in the house of St. Peter, our residence. They are in no wise deterred from their proposal by the violence they have suffered. However, the brethren of the abbey, on their part, carry on without restraint, and the Abbot—I know not for what reason—has gone off on a journey.

20. Wherefore, we beseech your paternity, in Christ, to defend with your authority the interests of these monks who desire to change to a stricter and more austere life. If, in fact, their Abbot comes to you, guide him back to peace with your God-given authority and wisdom, and warn him not to impede the holy resolution of his sons. If he has already come and gone, we ask that through the present messenger you send letters to him, exhorting him not to stand pertinaciously against these men, who wish truly to obey the Gospel of Christ and the Rule of St. Benedict, but rather to give them his assistance and the opportunity to do as they desire. The Abbot and his monks ought at least in this to imitate the Egyptians and the Babylonians, who allowed the Israelites to go in quest of the Land of Promise.[36] Indeed, when Jacob secretly fled from Laban's domination, Laban, after a cruel persecution, let him return to his fatherland.[37] In truth, they are not to be thought deserters but prudent men who wish to leave a place where there is greater liberty to sin, desiring one where they can live more safely in communion with God. Indeed, Christ himself threatens them! Did he not rebuke the Pharisees in that they themselves did not enter, and would not permit others to enter?[38] It is indeed known to all that the Rule of St. Benedict commonly, and it might be said almost everywhere in the world, has lost its proper place and observance in almost everything. Really, no one can be sufficiently amazed that some dare to promise before God and his saints with such solemnity that which they will daily neglect, or, if I might speak more truly, will be compelled not to observe. What the prophet says fits them perfectly: "This people honors me with their lips, but their heart is far from me."[39] And, as the Apostle says: "They confess with their voice to know God but in their deeds they deny him."[40]

21. Perhaps it is true that many act in this way. Frequency makes for audacity. Truly, I must say in sorrow, it is deceived, it is wholly deceived, this audacity of the monks, because a multitude of sins does not grant

impunity to the sinners. Wherefore, those who wish to observe the Rule of their profession are not to be impeded but to be protected. They are not to be reprehended when, for this reason, they hasten to change their place, for God is not chosen for the sake of a place. The place is chosen for the sake of God. St. Benedict clearly testifies that in every place it is the same Lord God who is served, the same King for whom the battle is fought.[41] In the Conferences of the Fathers, the hermit Joseph said very clearly that that man was more faithful to his profession who went where he could more fully live out the precepts of the Lord of faith.[42] And, indeed, "He who helps us in our needs and in our tribulations helps us to seek a holy situation."[43] If I be not mistaken, they should be considered Pharisees and heretics who do not fear nor permit others to fear what Truth himself has said: "Unless your justice exceeds that of the Scribes and the Pharisees, you will not enter the kingdom of heaven."[44] For, if an angel from heaven preaches other than that which must be preached, let him be anathema.[45] And he preaches a Gospel other than Christ's Gospel who tries to impede men who seek angelic peace and the observance of the Rule of their profession. Whoever he be, he must be totally refuted, as Truth himself says: "If your right eye scandalize you, tear it out and cast it from you."[46] Nothing in the body causes more pain when it is wounded, or is more carefully taken care of, than the eye. Nevertheless, when it becomes an impediment, it must be spiritually torn out. For this is the prudence of the serpent,[47] to free the head—that is, the mind—from all folly that can wound the soul.

22. Because of the scandal of the weak, who have less ability to discern the truth, we ask Your Holiness and all who wish to hear this petition of ours, to endeavor, insofar as it is possible, to restore peace between the Abbot of York and these brothers. We ought to recall what happened in the affair of the Molesme monks, which is quite similar. The Cistercians went forth to establish and found a most perfect way of life[48] which has set the whole Church at wonder. The Lord Hugh, of venerable memory, the Archbishop of Lyons, with true Christian piety praised the extraordinary purity of their life.[49] They faithfully undertook a renewal of the Holy Rule and a total living of it.[50] And then, when complaints of the jealous came to the knowledge of the Apostolic See, Pope Urban II issued a decree to the effect that as long as the Abbot returned to his duties as Abbot in his former monastery, none of the others who wished to persevere in a full living of the Rule should suffer any impediment or molestation.[51] Indeed, it is clearer than light that in their wonderful way of life the truth of the whole Gospel shines forth.

23. We have been very long, and perhaps tiresome, in this letter. But, although it will not please them, it seemed that the situation of the monks

remaining at St. Mary's should be clearly set forth, lest only the opinion of these jealous men be known, which should not be the case.

24. May Your Holiness prosper in Christ.

NOTES

[1]Epistle 95, PL 182:228ff.; trans. B. S. James, *The Letters of Saint Bernard of Clairvaux* (London: Burns & Oates, 1953), Letter 170, p. 240.

[2]Epistle 319, PL 182:524ff.; James, Letter 175, p. 244ff.

[3]The numbers in parentheses refer to paragraph numbers in the Epistle.

[4]St. Bernard had words of high praise for this good monk also: "What great things have I heard and known, and our brothers, the two Geoffreys, have told me of you! How you have been inflamed anew by the fire of God, how from weakness you have risen to strength, how you have blossomed afresh into holy newness of life!... Who will grant that I may come over and see this great sight? Your progress from the good to the better is no less wonderful, no less gratifying than a conversion from evil to good." Epistle 96, PL 182:229; James, Letter 171, p. 241.

[5]The Congregation of Savigny had not yet been incorporated into the Order of Citeaux. But they were very close to the White Monks in spirit right from the start, especially in England. The incorporation took place sixteen years later, in 1148.

[6]Cf. (1) and EP, ch. 3.

[7]Cf. (2), (7), (12), and EP, chs. 1, 3.

[8]Cf. (20) and EP, ch. 2.

[9]Cf. (10), (11) and (15) and EP, ch. 9.

[10]Cf. (5), (9) and EP, ch. 15.

[11]Cf. (9) and EP, ch. 15.

[12]Cf. *ibid.*

[13]Cf. (14) and EP, ch. 15.

[14]Cf. D. Knowles, *Monastic Order in England*, I, pp. 231ff.

[15]Cf. St. Bernard, Epistle 96 to Richard (PL 182:229; James, Letter 171, p. 241) and Epistle to David, King of Scotland: "They have chosen to become poor for the love of Christ, true followers of the apostolic life and austerity." (Letter 172, p. 243).

[16]It is found among the letters appended to the collection of the letters of St. Bernard as Epistle 477—*Sancti Bernardi Opera,* I, (Paris: Gaume Bros., 1839), col. 793-802. This is reproduced in the Migne edition: PL 182:697-704, as Epistle 489 (Paris, 1852). It is substantially the same as that in W. Dugdale, *Monasticon Anglicanum* (London: Bohn, 1846) where Thurstan's Letter is found as the seventh document among the charters of Fountains Abbey, vol. V, p. 294.

[17]Cf. D. Bethell, "The Foundation of Fountains Abbey and the State of St. Mary's, York, in 1132" in the *Journal of Ecclesiastical History,* XVII (1966) pp. 11-27.

[18]Cf. EP, ch. 3 for similar statements on the part of the monks of Molesme who left to found Citeaux. Such statements are not to be exaggerated. The state of affairs at St. Mary's, York, was generally good (cf. Thurstan's own testimony in the same paragraph; also, Bethell, *loc. cit.*). The display of passion recorded in the following paragraphs (which had its parallel at Molesme) is to be judged in the context of the rougher, less refined culture of that time.

[19]Cf. St. Benedict's *Rule for Monasteries* (hereafter RB) 61:10, trans. L. Doyle (Collegeville, MN: Liturgical Press, 1948), p. 85.

[20]Cf. RB 48:1; Doyle, p. 67.

[21]We find this same humanistic appreciation for Benedictine equilibrium expressed by St. Bernard: "The variety of our observances forestalls tedium and acedia." Epistle 78, PL 182:193C; James, Letter 80, 113.

[22]RB 6:8; Doyle, p. 21.

[23]RB 42:1; Doyle, p. 60.

[24]Cf. Mt. 6:34.

[25]Cf. RB 55; Doyle, pp. 75ff.

[26]Cf. RB 39; Doyle, pp. 57ff.

[27]RB 1:2 and 13; Doyle, pp. 6ff.

[28]Cf. EP, ch. 15: "...the monk who owns his land to live on it through his own work and that of his animals...," p. 263.

[29]Cf. Gal. 6:14.

[30]Mt. 6:12.

[31]Cf. Ps. 118:57.

[32]This again is reminiscent of the Cistercian program as outlined in chapter fifteen of the EP, p. 263.

[33]RB 4:21; Doyle, p. 15.

[34]Cf. EP, ch. 15: "...poor with the poor Christ...," p. 263.

[35]Cf. Gal. 6:17; 2 Cor. 4:10.

[36]Cf. Ex. 12:31ff.; Ezra 1:2ff.

[37]Cf. Gen. 31.

[38]Cf. Mt. 23:13.

[39]Is. 29:13.

[40]Tit. 1:16.

[41]RB 61:10; Doyle, p. 85.

[42]J. Cassian, *Conferences*, XVII: Second Conference of Abbot Joseph, ch. 8; trans. E. Gibson, *The Writings of the Nicene and Post-Nicene Fathers*, Series 2, vol. XI, p. 462.

[43]Ps. 9:10. The verse as it is found here in the text differs considerably from the Vulgate text. The Vulgate has: "Et factus est Dominus refugium pauperi, adjutor in opportunitatibus, in tribulatione." Thurstan has: "Juvat nos sanctam opportunitatem appetere, qui adjutor est in importunitatibus, in tribulatione." Perhaps he had some other text in mind or was quoting from memory in a general way.

[44]Mt. 5:20.

[45]Cf. Gal. 1:8.

[46]Mt. 5:29.

[47]Cf. Mt. 10:16.

[48]EP, ch. 3, pp. 253ff.

[49]*Ibid.*, ch. 2, Letter of Hugh, Archbishop of Lyons and Legate of the Apostolic See, to Robert, Abbot of Molesme, pp. 252ff.; ch. 7, Letter of Hugh to Robert, Bishop of Langres, pp. 255ff.; ch. 12, Letter of Hugh to Pope Paschal, pp. 259ff.

[50]*Ibid.*, ch. 15, pp. 262ff.

[51]*Ibid.*, chs. 5 and 6, pp. 254ff.

A Way to Holiness

A Way to Holiness
THE BEATITUDES IN THE ALL SAINTS' DAY
SERMONS OF THE CISTERCIAN FATHERS

It has been rightly said that the corpus of doctrine which the Gospel according to Matthew has drawn together in chapters 5, 6 and 7, and which we call the Sermon on the Mount, presents us with the basic blueprint for Christian living. Here are summed up the moral exegencies flowing from an acceptance of the Revelation and from faith in Jesus Christ as the Way, the Truth and the Life.[1]

Monastic life—and we are happily more conscious of this today, perhaps, than ever before—is basically an effort to live the Christian life with a certain fullness and intensity.[2] It does not claim extension—to be expressive of all the aspects of Christian existence. It is a deliberate choice of a specific expression, but one that is especially conducive to the greatest possible intensity, and undivided commitment. Therefore it is not surprising but rather to be expected that its way should embrace fully the essentials of the Christian way.

If the Sermon on the Mount is a distillation of the Christian way, the beatitudes with which our Lord opens this discourse are its distillation. Not surprisingly, then, the Cistercian Fathers have turned to the beatitudes to sketch out the Cistercian way to holiness.

There is of course another reason why on the Feast of All Saints the beatitudes come readily to their minds and into their sermons. These men are formed in the School of the Liturgy. It is largely through this school of the living Church that they learn and ruminate on the revealed message of the Sacred Scriptures. Their sermons are the fruit of their personal reception of this message in the midst of the community gathered in prayer, and their reflection on it. As the community completed their celebration of the long night watch or vigils on this feast, each of these abbots stepped to the lectern to proclaim to his monks the opening lines of the Sermon on the Mount, the beatitudes. Undoubtedly in the quiet hours that followed before the celebration of Prime they will have been naturally and supernaturally invited to reflect on them.[3] So that, when the community gathered after Prime the theme of their discourse was ready at hand.

FOUR FATHERS

A comparative study of the way four Cistercian Fathers—Bernard of Clairvaux, Guerric of Igny, Aelred of Rievaulx and Isaac of Stella— approach their subject brings out the unity and complementarity of the different members of the Cistercian school, even while through contrast it emphasizes their rich personal uniqueness.

Their journey is basically one, through the active life to the contemplative and on to eternal beatitude, traced out with greater or lesser detail. Common biblical themes emerge, though often employed differently. Aelred, like Bernard, speaks of serving up spiritual food to his brethren[4] and then quotes from Moses.[5] He does not however develop the idea of a New Law, like Bernard,[6] or even explicitly mention it as does Guerric.[7] He brings in Zachaeus[8] but for a different lesson. Bernard uses Zachaeus as an example of the merciful of the fifth beatitude,[9] while for Aelred the little man climbing the tree exemplifies the need to go apart from the crowd if we would hear Christ,[10] a theme much more fully developed by Isaac.[11] Isaac's treatment of the beatitudes is by far the longest, though proportionately Bernard's introduction is longer,[12] but there is a great similarity in the way they both reach out to the Sacred Text in all directions to enrich and express their thought. Nevertheless there is a notable difference between the two, for Isaac, actually belonging to the succeeding generation,[13] shows much more markedly the influence of the emerging new ways of the schools. If he can still claim kinship with Bernard and the other Cistercian Fathers when he resorts to non-Christian authors and personages,[14] he has a more marked tendency to define his terms precisely[15] and to evoke examples from the natural sciences.[16] This will be even more pronounced in the sermons preached a half-century later by Helinand of Froidmont on this same feast.[17]

Isaac joins Aelred in speaking of the beatitudes as a way or ways.[18] As Aelred tells his brethren: "This is the way, my dearest ones, by which we must return to the fatherland, and join the society of those whose feast we celebrate today."[19] Both, too, speak of "steps,"[20] as does Guerric. For the latter this is the basic analogy. The beatitudes are the eight steps of Ezekiel's vision,[21] by which one ascends to the temple and sees God.[22] For Aelred, the basic analogy is the seven days of creation, each with its morning and evening,[23] a theme to which Isaac gives passing reference;[24] just as Aelred makes passing use of Adam's fall to illustrate his doctrine[25] while it is Adam and Eve's history that Bernard employs as his basic biblical analogy. At the same time, while they use these constructs drawn from Scripture, they clearly interrelate the beatitudes themselves, showing their organic coherence, though in different and complementary ways.

But for all of them, central always and that toward which all is ordered is

Christ, the Word. No one could express this more beautifully than does Isaac of Stella in this passage:

> *Ipse mihi meditatio, ipse mihi delectatio.*
> *Ipsum propter ipsum super me quaero.*
> *Ipso ab ipso inter me pasco.*
> *Ipse mihi ager in quo laboro,*
> *Ipse mihi fructus pro quo laboro.*
> *Ipse mihi causa,*
> *Ipse mihi effectus,*
> *Ipse mihi principium,*
> *Ipse mihi finis sine fine,*
> *Ipse mihi in aeternum.*[26]

SETTING THE SCENE

In their opening remarks the Fathers commonly bring out three points: the ascent away from the crowd, Christ's sitting, and his opening his mouth. "Seeing the crowd Jesus went up into a mountain,"[27] and if one is to receive his teaching, he too must leave the crowd and go up. Isaac develops this the most and sums it up by noting that to seek and receive the Word we need a threefold solitude: of place, of spirit, of God.[28] It is not enough to be in a solitary place. The heart too must leave the crowd and adhere to heavenly things.[29] But this spiritual withdrawal is not only facilitated but almost essentially conditioned by a certain physical solitude: "My Lord Jesus, and perhaps he alone, can in a crowd not be distracted by the crowd from seeing the crowd."[30] But it is only the man "who sees it [the crowd] well, who can fully despise its attractions, easily go out from it and freely forget it."[31] Distance is needed for perspective and true spiritual freedom. But the solitude we most seek and for which physical and spiritual solitude are a preparation is the solitude to be found in God. And the beatitudes are the way to this.[32]

As he traces out this way, Jesus sits; he who descended to us from exalted majesty, meekly sits so that we need have no fear of approaching him.[33] He sits as the teacher.[34] And "he opens his mouth." This little phrase evokes delight in the Fathers. It is seen as a consummation of God's loving advances through all the centuries, when we are let in on the secrets that have been eternally hidden in God himself.[35]

POVERTY

And first *"audiamus pauperes pauperem pauperibus paupertatem commendantem*—let us poor ones hear the Poor One commend poverty to the poor."[36] The teaching here is immediately connected with the introductory remarks, it is part of the going apart, it is renunciation of the world.[37] It is the first step, for beginners,[38] "who have left all things, who have nothing, for whom every bit of personal possession is strictly proscribed"[39] by the Rule they profess. Yet the teaching of these abbots who profess the Rule of St. Benedict is marked by its balance and discretion. While the material poverty is important to them, and the more complete communal poverty of other Orders is admitted and abuses in their own Order reprimanded,[40] still "sometimes it may be useful to own things."[41] The Cistercian way of poverty is more a thing of the spirit. It is "to be found more in humility of heart than in a mere privation of everyday possessions, it consists more in renunciation of pride than in a mere contempt for property. ...the devil owns nothing in this world nor does he desire to own anything."[42]

Bernard says frankly that material want is no blessed thing, but rather something miserable.[43] What Christ is speaking of is a voluntary poverty, and not only that, but one that is "spiritual," motivated by a spiritual intent or desire, namely to please God alone and to save souls.[44] Aelred most clearly distinguishes them; there is "poverty of the flesh" (*paupertas carnis*) and "poverty of spirit" (*paupertas spiritus*). The one is simply a lack of possessions; the other is the voluntary embracing of a lowly state in mind and body for the sake of God.[45]

Bernard, who in his schema presents the beatitudes as remedies for the first sins that marred creation, contrasts this voluntary abjection with Lucifer's lunge for self-enrichment. He lost heaven; those embracing poverty for God's sake gain heaven.[46] Aelred takes this up too: "pride was the beginning of all sin; all justice begins from humility." For him as for Guerric humility is the key word, humility flowing from self-knowledge: "This is what distinguishes between day and night, darkness and light, justice and iniquity, the elect and the reprobate, the damned and the saved."[47] From this he goes on to the analogy of his schema—the first day of creation when light and darkness were divided. If in the evening of the first day we know ourselves with all our infirmities we will come through to the dawn of renewed life.[48]

MEEKNESS

Although we find a beautiful coherence among the Fathers in their teaching on the first beatitude—they all show themselves true Cistercians and sons of St. Benedict with their emphasis on humility—it is perhaps in watching the springboard they take to get from the first to the second beatitude that one sees which facet stands out most clearly in the mind of each.

Bernard shows himself a very practical pastor. Material poverty, lack, privation, which is the specific of this expression of humility and which Bernard expects to be a part of the monk's ordinary life, can grind on a man and lead to murmuring and impatience. Therefore one needs meekness so as not to succumb to such temptation.[49] Isaac too stays with the material aspects of poverty but thinks of it more on the community level. If the monks are poor they will not be drawn into contention and lawsuits over properties and revenues. He points to the good example of the Carthusians and the monks of Grandmont on this score, admitting that he cannot say the same for his own Order.[50]

Guerric, for his part, does not develop the interrelationship here but simply sees meekness leading to obedience.[51] Aelred however does dwell on humility. Self-knowledge opens the way to knowledge of God, for the humble man is open to learning. In his schema the firmament created on the second day is the Holy Scriptures by which man passes from the evening of human ignorance to the dawn of divine illumination.[52] The land then which the meek are to possess is for Aelred the land of promise where they will see God fully revealed. For Bernard, the practical moralist, it is man's own body.[53] If a man wishes to rule himself he must meekly submit to God and to those who hold his place; and here he joins Guerric's consideration of obedience. In Bernard's schema, Eve commits the second sin by not waiting meekly for God to beatify her but seeking to seize it; so she loses control of her land and the promised land.[54]

MOURNING

From this Bernard glides smoothly into the third beatitude. The monk who wants to be meek finds counter-passions strong within himself,[55] and weeping he ponders on his end, on death, judgment, hell, and his own great weakness.[56] For Aelred it is the "firmament" of Sacred Scripture that makes the monk so conscious of this personal misery and sin and fills him with true fear.[57] This seems to be the point of true inner conversion. And so I think these Fathers see it. For the evening of tears which water the land of the heart to bring forth fruit (Aelred's third day of creation) leads to the dawn of contemplation,[58] the consolation which the merciful Father and God of all consolation bestows.[59] For these Fathers, mourning and tears are not a good in themselves. They are but a means: "weeping is a way to joy, to consolation."[60] Joy, not gloom, is characteristic of Cistercian life. Eve made her mistake when she sought consolation, not by turning to God in tears, but by turning to her husband, evoking the third sin,[61] seeking companionship in sin—scandal in the strictest sense of the word.

JUSTICE

For Guerric, repentance and weeping for sin leads one to beg for justification, and the first taste of it leads one to hunger and thirst for more.[62] Bernard's thought is similar, a taste of God's consolation makes one hunger and thirst for more. And here he enunciates a very important principle: *"Quantumcumque desiderare potuerit, tantum est accepturus"*—insofar as we desire, so will we receive, but not in the imperfect manner of our desires; rather, pressed down, shaken together and flowing over.[63] Hunger and thirst implies seeking the fullness of justice. Here is where Adam failed. He was just in compassionating his wife, but as her "head" he should have disciplined her, and he should have fulfilled too his obligation toward God.

Aelred comes to this step somewhat differently. His quest is quite openly one for contemplation, and such a quest has its difficulties. It requires a real hunger and thirst to keep going. The evening of temptation and hunger comes on him. But God gives lights, the examples of the saints in patience and forbearance, and with dawn will come the Sun of Justice and satiety.[64]

For Isaac, justice is a certain apex standing for all the virtues. It is not the natural justice of philosophers, nor the justice of the Law which belongs to the Jews, but that of Christian faith. We are coming to the consummation of the active life.[65]

MERCY

But as Isaac unhesitatingly says: "It is not safe even for the just to contend with the Most Just."[66] "What is all our justice before God?"[67] "No one is so just that he does not need mercy."[68] And how are we to obtain mercy? "If you want to receive mercy be merciful to others," responds Aelred.[69] *"Sola misericordia misericordium consequetur*—Mercy alone obtains mercy."[70]

Guerric approaches mercy from a somewhat different perspective. He seems to remain more constantly in the community context. When a monk hungers and thirsts for justice he seeks it in his brother as well as in himself. And lest his zeal become immoderate and lead to vice, mercy must temper it.[71]

It is Isaac who has the longest and most practical development here, proposing the question: "How can the monk who has nothing exercise mercy?"[72] In response he notes that mercy has two expressions, to give and to forgive, and three degrees in each of these. One can give of his possessions. But the monk can no longer do this because he has embraced the second degree, he has given up all his possessions. There remains only the third degree, giving self. The Latin brings out the steps concisely: *dare de suis, sua omnia, se.*[73] He can give his time, his counsel, his example, fraternal correction, "and six hundred other species"; and he can forgive all injuries.[74]

TO SEE GOD

With all the Fathers we reach a cardinal point at the sixth beatitude. "When a man has learned to become merciful and just by diligent practice of these virtues he will then perhaps be fit to enter upon the way of contemplation."[75]

Man, so experiencing the mercy of God, one so good, necessarily experiences a great desire to see him. But he becomes painfully conscious of the blocks—his own concupiscence and past sin—and seeks to purify himself of these by prayer and confession.[76] This is where Adam and Eve failed, committing the sixth sin. Instead of confessing, they excused themselves.[77] Isaac like Bernard indicates that this active purification must come first.[78] Aelred concentrates more on what follows. The man who has turned from evil and learned to do good deserves to understand and be enlightened.[79] There are in man two wounds from original sin: perversity of will and blindness of intellect.[80] The first five beatitudes have reordered man's will. Now the mind must be purified of all phantasms coming from the senses and the imagination.[81] For Aelred it is divine illumination itself that does this. But here he is speaking of the "evening" knowledge that is in a mirror and an enigma. The dawn of full vision has not yet come.[82]

Isaac's *Fourth Sermon*, which treats of this beatitude, is an extremely beautiful tract on contemplation. As he develops the knowledge of the night, the *tenebrae in lumine*,[83] he enters into a whole tradition[84] which goes forward to the modern classic expression in John of the Cross. Like the waters drawn up into the clouds and rising above all the movement of the earth, to attain the apex of his spirit where he will see God, man must rise above all natural being and every image of it and even above shifting thoughts, to the serene silence of the luminous cloud.[85]

UNION

Beyond this there is only union, infinite peace, oneness with God by becoming truly identified with the Son.

According to the classical definition, peace is the tranquillity of order.[86] One who has followed the path of the beatitudes has come to true order. He is integrated in himself—his activity is guided by his free will, which is guided by his enlightened reason, which sees all things under the light of the wisdom of the Word of God.[87] As he sees and hears in the Word, so he judges, tempers and orders all things beneath himself,[88] and attains to a proper relation to God. He has passed from being an enemy to being a servant, then a friend, a brother of Christ, a son, heir, and finally one with the Inheritance, who is God himself.[89]

If this is what peace is, fully understood, then no wonder Isaac can so exalt it:

> *Super omnes virtutum gradus locatur,*
> *super omnis merita ponitur,*
> *omnium arcem obtinuit,*

omnium beatitudinem altissimam et maximam tribuit.
Hic est thesaurus in agro absconditus:
haec pretiosissima margarita
  studiossissime quaeranda
  carissime emenda
  avarissime possidenda.[90]

For Aelred, as for Isaac, the whole emphasis here is on being and contemplative activity. For Aelred it is entering into the vision of God; all that remains is the Sabbath rest, the seventh day.[91] It is a question of union and communion with God as a son.[92]

On the other hand, Bernard and Guerric see the man become son sharing in the Son's mediatorial role. The monk who has been reconciled fully with God, himself and his neighbors, will in gratitude have concern for the reconciliation of his brother with God and will do what he can to achieve it. Bernard resumes the whole of the beatitudes in terms of reconciliation. The first three reconcile the monk with himself, his own soul. The spirit of poverty leaves him at peace with regard to the future, meekness establishes him in peace with the present, and tears wash away the disturbances of the past. The fourth and fifth beatitudes, justice and mercy, set him at peace with his fellow men, and purity of heart opens out his relation with God. He is now ready to reach out to help others attain this.[93]

We can perhaps see Bernard's thought influenced here by his own personal experience and his pastoral zeal as an abbot. This is even more evident in Guerric, who says: "He who bears the name and office of a son of God through having become the father and servant of other men will then and only then be worthy to be a peacemaker between them and God. Thus he will fulfill the office of mediator and advocate and be worthy to make peace among the brethren themselves and even between the brethren and those who are outside our community."[94] However, I do not think their intent is to restrict this further expression of shared divine sonship to abbots alone. What Bernard goes on to say seems open to all the community: "With how much affection ought we to embrace that brother who lives among the brethren without quarrel, who is most solicitous that there be nothing in his conduct that others will have to bear with and at the same time most patiently bears with what is onerous in others; who considers the scandals of each to be his own . . . indeed, he is a son of peace, and worthy to be called a son of God."[95]

THE EIGHTH BEATITUDE

The eighth beatitude receives relatively little attention from the Fathers; indeed, Isaac does not speak of it at all. For Bernard, it is something special—*maxime martyribus convenit*—but he takes the opportunity to note that the same reward is promised to voluntary poverty (the first beatitude) because it too is truly a type of martyrdom.[96] Aelred and Guerric see the relation of the eighth to the other beatitudes, each moving from the particular doctrine he has developed in relation to the seventh. Aelred sees the saints who persevere in this way to perfection being consoled and strengthened by this final beatitude when they encounter difficulties on the way.[97] Guerric rather applies it to the Christ-mediator. He suffers persecution in his office even from those he is serving and thus is like the martyrs, attaining to the same virtue and merit.[98] Perhaps we have some autobiographical data here.

CONCLUSION

Each of these Cistercian Fathers has traced, in ways that are similar and complementary, the path of Cistercian holiness in the context of the beatitudes. We see the whole pattern fall together: poverty of spirit enables one, on leaving the world, to leave even affection for it and for oneself (1); a meek opening out that docilely receives the revelation and obediently seeks to follow its guidance (2); thereupon repentance, a sincere conversion (3); and striving after virtue (4); tempered by a mercy that neither demands too much of others nor expects too much of self, knowing one's need of mercy (5); these virtues bringing one to purity of heart and the way of contemplative vision (6); which flowers into a full union with and sharing in the life of Christ the Son (7); ready to sustain all for, with, and in him (8). As we have seen, Bernard sums it all up in the context of increasing integration or reconciliation. Man finds unity with himself, his fellow man, his God, and becomes with Christ, his God, an active agent of human solidarity and peace—the desire rises out of his very nature, a God-given built-in vocation; and Christ, the Word and the only Way as well as the Term, opening his mouth traces out the way. As Isaac so beautifully expresses it:

> *Beatitudinem loquitur ipsa beatitudo,*
> *paupertatem factus pauper,*
> *panis saturitatem,*
> *misericordiam ipsa misericordia,*
> *mundicordiam cordium munditia,*
> *pacificentiam et filiationem*
>   *verus pacificus, et natura Filius.*[99]

After this, with Aelred we ask: *Quid igitur restat nisi Sabbatum!*[100]

NOTES

[1]As Guerric of Igny happily expresses it: "A happy beginning of the New Law."—
Sermon Fifty-three: For the Feast of All Saints, the Liturgical Sermons of Guerric of Igny I,
Cistercian Fathers Series 8 (Spencer, MA: Cistercian Publications, 1970), (hereafter
referred to as Guerric, followed by the paragraph number), n. 1.

[2]Certainly, though, the early Cistercians were not unconscious of this fact. See
for example the Epistle of Thurstan of York, where he speaks of the intent of the
founders of Fountains Abbey, whom he likens to the founders of Citeaux itself: "We
ought to recall what happened in the affair of the Molesme monks, which is quite
similar" (n. 22). ". . .men who were determined to correct their way of life according
to the Rule of St. Benedict, or rather according to the truth of the Gospel" (n. 3).
"These brethren, with many tears, sought nothing but. . .that they might not be
impeded from living in evangelical peace and observing the Rule of the blessed
father Benedict" (n. 14). "All of them are seeking full observance of the Rule and of
their profession, likewise of the Gospel" (n. 19). ". . .these men who wish truly to
obey the Gospel of Christ and the Rule of St. Benedict. . ." (n. 20).

[3]The Rule of St. Benedict explicitly provides for this—RB 8:3. Bernard of Clairvaux describes for us with some color his meditations in preparation for his sermon:
First Sermon for the Feast of All Saints, (hereafter referred to as Bernard 1, with the
paragraph number), n. 3.

[4]Aelred of Rievaulx, *Third Sermon for the Feast of All Saints,* (hereafter referred to as
Aelred 3, with the paragraph number), n. 1; Bernard 1:2ff.

[5]Aelred 3:1.

[6]Bernard 1:6.

[7]Guerric 1.

[8]Lk. 19:2ff.

[9]Bernard 1:12.

[10]Aelred 3:1.

[11]Isaac of Stella, *Sermon One: For the Feast of All Saints,* n. 1ff.; trans., H. McCaffrey,
The Sermons of Isaac of Stella I, Cistercian Fathers Series 11 (Kalamazoo, MI: Cistercian
Publications, 1979), hereafter referred to as Isaac, with the Sermon and paragraph
numbers.

[12]For Bernard almost half his matter, seven out of fifteen paragraphs, is given
over to introduction; Isaac devotes most of his first sermon to introduction, but he
will have four more sermons to develop his teaching on the beatitudes themselves.

[13]Isaac became abbot in 1147, only six years before Bernard's death; Bernard had
then already been an abbot for thirty years.

[14]Although in the other commentaries on the beatitudes which we are considering here this does not occur, it is certainly to be found elsewhere among the writings
of the Cistercian Fathers: e.g. Bernard of Clairvaux: *Sermon Thirty On the Song of Songs,*
n. 10, *The Works of Bernard of Clairvaux,* vol. 3, CF 7; *On Precept and Dispensation,* n. 43, *The
Works of Bernard of Clairvaux,* vol. 1, CF 1; Guerric of Igny: *Sermon Eleven: First Sermon for
the Epiphany,* n. 2, *The Liturgical Sermons of Guerric of Igny I,* CF 8; *Sermon Twenty-four: Third
Sermon for the Feast of St. Benedict,* n. 6, *Liturgical Sermons of Guerric of Igny II,* CF 32; Aelred

of Rievaulx, *The Mirror of Charity,* Part I, n. 23; Part II, nn. 5, 24, *The Works of Aelred of Rievaulx,* vol. 3, CF 17.

15E.g., Isaac 3:1: "Virtue is a habit of the will and soul"; 3:3. "Justice is that which assures equality to all, rendering to each what is his due."

16E.g., 3:3 (where he speaks of the galaxy), 4:4 (the development of clouds), 4:6 (the five elements).

17In his three sermons for the Feast, Helinand quotes eleven pagan authors, which equals the number of Fathers he quotes, and he evokes to illustrate his teaching such characters as Hercules, Mars, Jupiter, Nero, and Julian the Apostate.

18Isaac 1:18, 2:12.

19Aelred 3:6.

20Aelred 3:3; Isaac 5:6.

21Ezek. 40:31.

22Guerric 1.

23Aelred 3:3ff. An interesting diagram of this sermon could be drafted showing the correspondence of each beatitude and its virtue and reward, with each day of creation and its evening and morning.

24Isaac 1:2.

25Aelred 3:3.

26Isaac 5:13; "He himself is my meditation; he is my delight. Him for his own sake I seek above me; from him himself I feed within me. He is the field in which I labor; he is the fruit for which I labor. He is my cause; he is my effect. He is my beginning; he is my end without end. He is for me eternity."

27Mt. 5:1.

28Isaac 5:15.

29Aelred 3:2.

30Isaac 1:3.

31Isaac 1:1.

32Isaac 5:21.

33Bernard 1:6.

34Aelred 3:2; Isaac 1:12.

35Mt. 5:2; Bernard 1:7; Aelred 3:3; Isaac 1:13.

36Isaac 1:18.

37Guerric 2.

38*Ibid.*

39Isaac 3:13.

40Isaac 2:7.

41Guerric 5.

42*Ibid.*

43Bernard 1:8.

44*Ibid.*

45Aelred 3:3.

46Bernard 1:8.

47Aelred 3:3.

48*Ibid.*

49Bernard 1:9.

[50]Isaac 2:7.

[51]Guerric 2.

[52]Aelred 3:4.

[53]Bernard 1:9. Aelred, when speaking of the third beatitude, speaks of "the land of our heart."

[54]*Ibid.*

[55]Bernard 1:9.

[56]Bernard 1:10.

[57]Aelred 3:4.

[58]*Ibid.*

[59]Bernard 1:10.

[60]Isaac 2:13.

[61]Bernard 1:10.

[62]Guerric 2.

[63]Bernard 1:11.

[64]Aelred 3:4.

[65]Isaac 3:2ff. Active life, of course, is here understood in the earlier traditional sense, namely the time to acquire the moral virtues in preparation for the contemplative life. See especially Guerric 2.

[66]Isaac 3:10.

[67]Bernard 1:11.

[68]Aelred 3:4.

[69]*Ibid.*

[70]Isaac 3:11.

[71]Guerric 2.

[72]Isaac 3:11.

[73]Isaac 3:15ff.

[74]Isaac 3:17.

[75]Guerric 2.

[76]Bernard 1:13.

[77]*Ibid.*

[78]Isaac 4:15.

[79]Aelred 3:5.

[80]Isaac 4:1.

[81]*Ibid.*

[82]Aelred 3:5.

[83]Isaac 4:5.

[84]See the introduction to *The Liturgical Sermons of Guerric of Igny I,* Cistercian Fathers Series 8.

[85]Isaac 4:4.

[86]See Thomas Aquinas, *Summa Theologiae,* II-II, 29, 1.

[87]Isaac 4:18ff.

[88]Isaac 5:16.

[89]Isaac 5:1ff.

[90]Isaac 5:6ff.: "Peace is to be found above all levels of virtue, it is placed above every merit, it stands at the apex, it gives one the highest and greatest beatitude of

all.... It is the treasure hidden in the fields; it is the most precious pearl which is sought most zealously, bought for the greatest price, and possessed most avariciously."

[91]For a fuller treatment of Aelred's concept of the Sabbath Rest see the third part of *The Mirror of Charity.*

[92]Aelred 3:5.

[93]Bernard 1:14.

[94]Guerric 2.

[95]Bernard 1:14.

[96]Bernard 1:15.

[97]Aelred 3:6.

[98]Guerric 2.

[99]Isaac 1:14: "Beatitude itself speaks of beatitude, the One made poor of poverty, Bread of satiety, Mercy itself of mercy, the Cleanness of heart, the true Peacemaker and natural born Son of peace and filiation."

[100]Aelred 3:5: "What remains except the Sabbath?"

The Four Evangelists of Citeaux

Saint Bernard of Clairvaux

Straight from the Shoulder of St. Bernard

In some respects St. Bernard's *Apologia* is his most famous or infamous work, but in other respects it is one of his least known. This is due in part to the fact that it has rarely been translated.[1] This is unfortunate, for this relatively short treatise contains a wealth of very solid monastic doctrine. It should be particularly precious to the Cistercians, for the Abbot of Clairvaux speaks very frankly and straightforwardly to the monks of his own Order.

In the first paragraph of his treatise St. Bernard adds, as if in passing, a listing of what to his mind are some of the essential practices of the Cistercian way of life: "...the diet that is lean and unlovely...the well-known cheapness and roughness of our clothes...the sweat of daily toil, our continual fasts and vigils and all the austerity of our way of life...."[2] While these are undoubtedly important to Bernard, his attitude toward them is one of great balance and of that discretion which is the hallmark of the true follower of St. Benedict. Before many paragraphs have passed he returns to each of these observances and through the use of Scriptural allusions makes very clear their relative value.

But first he quotes from Scripture some fundamental principles, such as: "The kingdom of God is within you,"[3] and "The kingdom of God is not food and drink, but righteousness and peace and joy in the Holy Spirit."[4] Then he goes on to touch on the different particulars:

> There are people who go clad in tunics and have nothing to do with furs, who nevertheless are lacking in humility. Surely humility in furs is better than pride in tunics. After all, God himself made clothes for the first man out of animal skins, John the Baptist in the desert wore a leather girdle round his waist, and Benedict himself, in his hermit days, wore animal skins instead of a tunic.
>
> We condemn rich food as though it were not better to take delicate fare in moderation than to bloat ourselves to the belching point with vegetables. Remember that Esau was censured because of lentils, not meat; Adam was condemned for eating fruit, not meat; and Jonathan was

under sentence of death for tasting honey, not meat. On the other hand, Elijah ate meat without coming to grief, Abraham set a delicious meat dish before the angels, and God himself ordered sacrifices of the flesh of animals.

Surely it is more satisfactory to take a little wine on account of weakness than to down greedy draughts of water, since Paul counsels Timothy to take a little wine. The Lord himself drank wine and was called a wine bibber because of it. He gave it to his Apostles to drink and from it was established the sacrament of his Blood. On the other hand, he would not countenance the drinking of water at a marriage feast, and it was at the waters of Meribah that he punished the people severely for their complaining. David, too, was afraid to drink the water that he desired, and those of Gideon's men who in their eagerness to drink from the stream, fell on their faces, were considered unworthy of the fight.

And finally, concerning manual work:

And what have you to boast about in your manual work? Martha worked as you do and was rebuked, whereas Mary remained at rest and was praised. Paul says quite plainly that "bodily work is of some value but spirituality is valuable in every way."[5]

After all this, Bernard is sensitive to an objection which might be raised: "It looks as though you are so concerned with the spiritual side of things that you discredit even those material observances imposed on us by the Rule." And he replies:

No, such things ought to be done, but without neglecting the others. At the same time, if it happens that one or other element must be left aside, it is better that it be the material. For, just as the soul is more important than the body, so spiritual practices are more fruitful than material ones.[6]

And further on he says:

I don't mean by this that external means can be overlooked, or that the man who does not employ them will quickly become spiritual. Spiritual things are certainly higher, but there is little hope of attaining them or of receiving them without making use of external means, as it is written: "It is not the spiritual that comes first, but the physical; and then comes the spiritual." Jacob was unfit to win Rachel's longed-for embraces until he had known Leah. So too we read in one of the psalms: "Strike up a song and play on the drum." This means "take up spiritual things, but first make use of physical things." The man in the best position is he who makes use of both, as occasion demands, and with discernment.[7]

The same balanced discretion is applied by Bernard when he approaches the Rule as a whole. He was no staunch advocate of a rigid literal interpretation. Quite the contrary:

> If you think that all those who make profession of the Rule are obliged to keep it literally (*ad litteram*) without any possibility of dispensation, then I dare say you yourself fail as much as the Cluniac. It may be that he is deficient in many points of external observance but even you cannot avoid occasional faults and you know of course that anyone who fails in a single point is guilty of everything. If, on the other hand, you admit that some things can be changed by dispensation, then it must be true that both you and the Cluniac are keeping the Rule, though each in his own way. You keep it strictly; he, perhaps, keeps it more reasonably.[8]

However, Bernard is no man for compromise or unwarranted mitigation. While true discretion is to be exercised, laxity is not to be condoned. And he very straightforwardly calls a spade a spade. What he has to say in this regard might be a salutary warning for monks as they weigh their experimental adaptations in this time of renewal:

> I would hate to think that the holy Fathers would have commended or allowed the many foolish excesses I have noticed in several monasteries. I am astonished that monks could be so lacking in moderation in matters of food and drink and in respect to clothing and bedding, carriages and buildings.... Abstemiousness is accounted miserliness; sobriety, strictness; silence, gloom. On the other hand, laxity is labeled discretion; extravagance, generosity; talkativeness, sociability; and laughter, joy. Fine clothes and costly caparisons are regarded as mere respectability, and being fussy about bedding is hygene. When we lavish these things on one another we call it love. Such love undermines true love. Such discretion disgraces real discretion. This sort of kindness is full of cruelty, for it so looks after the body that the soul is strangled.[9]

And while we are thinking of renewal we might note two other principles which are taught by St. Bernard in this same part of the *Apologia* which are most pertinent to our present-day situation. One is the personal responsibility of each and every monk. Bernard points out some of the excuses which might be adopted by individual monks to exonerate themselves from sharing the responsibility for the adaptations which are taking place in their monastery:

> It is condoned by almost everyone unquestioningly and in all innocence, though not for the same reasons. Some monks are detached in their use of such things, so they incur little or no guilt. In other cases, simplicity or

necessity or charity is the motivation. They are monks who simply do what they are told, and who are quite prepared to act otherwise if they are so bidden. Some monks try to avoid trouble with those among whom they live. They do not aim at fulfilling their own whims, but at safeguarding the peace of others. Finally, there are monks who cannot withstand the majority voice which vigorously insists that such things are all right, and with all its might resists any attempt on the part of right reason to restrict or change anything.[10]

St. Bernard indicates that such excuses do not indeed wholly exonerate the monk who "goes along with things"—he is not living up to his own personal commitment to a true monastic life.

Another note consonant with the principles of renewal which the Second Vatican Council has given is that of looking to the Founders. St. Bernard turns to them more than once in this brief treatise:

> Long ago, when the monastic Order began, who would have dreamed that monks could become so slack? Oh, how far we have moved from Anthony and his contemporaries! If, from time to time one of them paid a call to the other, they were both so avid to receive spiritual nourishment from the other that they forgot all about their meals. Often they spent the whole day with fasting stomachs, but their minds were feasted. This is the correct order of precedence, when the greater in dignity is served first. This is real discretion, when the more important part is more amply provided for. Finally, this is true love, to attend carefully to souls for love of whom Christ died.[11] . . .
>
> Should we laugh or cry at such foolishness? Is this the way Macarius lived? Is it Basil's teaching or Anthony's command? Did the Fathers of Egypt adopt such a manner of life? Finally, did the holy men whom they claim as the founders and teachers of their Order—Odo, Majolus, Odilo and Hugh—did they hold with such things or value them? All these men were saints, and because of this they were in accord with what the Apostle taught. . . .[12]

Clearly, Bernard is very much in tune with our times: a balanced adaptation of the observances, personal responsibility in this matter, drawing authentic inspiration from the monastic founders. It is these sources: the tradition of the Fathers, each one's responsibility to respond to a God-given vocation, and the need of a life well adapted to facilitate such fidelity, that inspire Bernard to give observances the relatively important place they hold in his consideration of the monastic life. It is only when the all-too-often quoted caricatures of the third part of the *Apologia* are seen in the light of this more basic doctrine that one can really begin to grasp the message which St. Bernard is trying to convey. He is using a particular literary genre to bring home with pleasure as well as with force the importance of a well adapted monastic observance. There may indeed be some excess in Bernard's satire, but it must be admitted that we are too far separated from the times and the *mores* to make a truly objective judgment.

One thing does stand out, and it is the greatness and the true humanity of the writer. For it is only a great-souled man who can see clearly the larger dimensions of life and the proportionate littleness of its oddities, who has so firm a grasp upon the great values which mean much to him, that he can laugh and invite others to laugh with him at these very human rationalizations and deviations.

If perhaps we find it difficult to appreciate the particular kind of reprimand that Bernard is offering some of his contemporary monks in this satirical fashion, I think we do find ourselves very much in accord with the even more severe remonstrances which he directs toward some of his fellow Cistercians. Here, as he denounces with an almost ferocious vehemence the spirit of the Pharisee, he again shows his firm grasp upon the reality that the observances have only relative importance. Indeed, if they are not accompanied with humility and charity, Bernard does not hesitate to denounce them as being only a miserable way to get to a miserable end. Those who practice them are worse off than open sinners:

> Even though sinners will have to suffer forever because of life's joys, at least they enjoyed plenty of good things in this world. Oh, unhappy are they who carry a cross, not like the Savior, who carried his own, but like the Cyrenian who carried another's.... Twice unhappy are they who are both proud and poor. Twice unhappy, I repeat, are those who carry Christ's Cross without following after him, who share in his sufferings with no thought of imitating his humility.[13]

He goes on in this vein in another paragraph, drawing a most pitiful picture of the man who is faithful to observance yet fails in humility and love.

This leads Bernard into the expression of another attitude which is very consonant with our times and the spirit of renewal. It is a very genuine appreciation for the vocation of others and a deep realization that one's own vocation, wonderful though it be, is but one of many with its own relative merits and not an absolute good. Bernard gives concrete expression to this deep appreciation:

> I am always delighted to see any of its [Cluny's] members. I receive them with all due honor; I converse with them respectfully, and encourage them in all humility.... This way of life is holy and good. Chastity is its adornment, discretion its crown. Organized by the Fathers and predestined by the Holy Spirit, it is evidently suited for the saving of souls.

... I have asked them to pray for me. I have attended their community meetings. I have spoken a great deal with many of them about the Bible and the salvation of souls, both publicly in Chapter and privately. I have never secretly or openly encouraged anyone to leave that Order and come to ours; in fact, I have rebuffed many monks who wanted to come, and if any came knocking, I turned them away.... From it, I earnestly ask prayers for myself and accept them with gratitude.[14]

Very closely related to this deep respect for the Cluniac monks, and serving as the theological foundation for it is another attitude of Bernard's which is very much in keeping with the spirit of our time—the principle of pluralism. As Bernard says very directly, "No one order is suitable for everybody."[15] For Bernard, the Church is that Spouse of Christ who, like the queen in Psalm 44, is arrayed with a wide variety of adornments—the various religious orders. Drawing further on biblical imagery,[16] he sees here Joseph's famous robe of many colors: "There must be within the Church the married and the celibate, monks and canons regular, cenobites and hermits. There is room for Mary and for Martha. This is the gift which Christ left to his Church, his bride, 'a robe of many colors, but woven from top to bottom.' "[17]

> It is many-colored because of the many different religious orders that are distinguished in it. It is seamless because of the undivided unity of love that cannot be torn apart, as it is written: "Who will separate us from the love of Christ?" First, hear how the robe is many-colored: "There are varities of graces, but the same Spirit; there are different works, but the same Lord." Then, after listing the various charisms, which correspond to the different hues of the many-colored robe, the Apostle adds the following, to show that it is also seamless, woven from top to bottom: "All these are the work of the one and the same Spirit, proportioned to each as he pleases. For love has been poured forth in our hearts by the Holy Spirit, who has been given to us."[18]

And he goes on to develop the idea even futher:

> Therefore, let there be no division within the Church. Let it remain whole and entire according to its inherited right. Concerning the Church it has been written: "At your right hand stands the queen in a golden robe, interlaced with variety." This is why different people receive different gifts. One man is allotted one kind, one another, irrespective of whether he be a Cistercian or a Cluniac, a regular or one of the laity. This applies to every order and to all languages, to both sexes, to every age and condition of life, everywhere and always, from the first man down to the last.[19]

For Bernard there is great variety in the Church among religious and among monks, but "all contribute to the perfection of the saints, and all press on together toward mature manhood, according to the measure of the age of Christ's fullness."[20] And in this commonness of end and purpose, in this communion in the one Christ, we find the foundation and source of the unity which must always mark the pluralism of the Church.

This leads us to what is certainly the focal point of the spiritual doctrine of Bernard here and in all his writings, a focal point for all the principles for monastic life and renewal which he gives, that center which is the source of unity and the principle of pluralism in the one Person adored and loved: Jesus Christ. For Bernard, the observances are nothing other than carrying Christ's Cross, and they have value only if in carrying that Cross one truly follows him in his obedience and humility.[21] The monk's life is one of imitating Christ in his labor, his poverty and his humility.[22] The great variety and diversity in the Church is nothing else than serving Christ in different ways. Again, it is Christ's garment or it is the garment of his spouse which he has given to her.[23] This garment is more precious and beautiful to God because it is dyed in the Precious Blood of him who trod the winepress alone, of him who was obedient unto death. It is the Blood of Christ that gives value to any and all of the services within the Church.[24] And it is all ordered, as we mentioned above, toward each individual's attaining "to the measure of the age of Christ's fullness."[25] All the glory that the Church has belongs to her as the bride of Christ.[26] And all this is to the praise of the Holy Name of Jesus Christ.[27]

Thus we see that for Bernard the ultimate norm for discerning the value of anything, be it observances, traditions, or variety within these, is its relationship to Jesus Christ. Whatever a person does has value only if in doing it he follows Christ in his humility and in his obedience. Bernard brings this out at the conclusion of his consideration of pluralism. He has his interlocutor propose this question: "If you have such an esteem and appreciation for the Benedictine way of life, why don't you become a Cluniac?" Bernard's answer is one of obedience: "My reply is this: 'Because, as the Apostle says: Everyone should remain in the vocation in which he was called.'" He then goes on to have his interlocutor ask him: "If this be the case, why did you not pick the Cluniacs in the first place?" And here Bernard gives witness to his humility: "The reason is that I am an un-spiritual man, sold under sin. I knew that my soul was so weak as to require a stronger remedy. Different remedies are prescribed for different illnesses; the more serious the illness, the more drastic the remedy."[28]

We have here very solid doctrine to guide us in the question of pluralism in vocation. We must readily acknowledge that there are different ways of living the one monastic life, of entering into the one monastic tradition. As

St. Bernard has said, the Cistercian keeps the Rule more strictly while others keep it more reasonably. But the reason why the Cistercians keep it more strictly is because they have greater need. They are less spiritual. They are more prone to sin. They need the observances of the monastic life more, to strengthen them and help them to find greater freedom to respond more totally to their call, to go on to the perfection of the saints, "to the measure of the age of Christ's fullness."[29]

In developing the theological basis for this pluralism of function and mode of living within the unity of the Church, Bernard comes up with a very valuable insight—one worthy of note. It is the fact that while following a particular vocation one can through love possess the work and merit of all vocations, and indeed possess them even more than the men and women who are actually striving to live these particular vocations. This is the amazing power of love:

> I am attached to all the orders by love. But it is in one alone that I find my work. Yet I trust that my love will so bring it about that I will share also in the fruits of those orders to which I do not belong. I will even go further. You yourself must be very careful, for it could happen that your work would be fruitless; on the other hand, it is quite impossible that my love for your work should be so. Oh, how bold is love! One man works without loving, a second man loves without working. The first man's labor is lost, the other man's love will never fail.[30]

Bernard was indeed a truly great man and also a very great writer. No matter what form his writings took, be it letters or treatises, sermons or conferences, theological tracts or biography, hymns for an office or official documents such as the prologue for the antiphonary, he showed a masterly ability to express himself in any of these forms, and there always comes through his deep spiritual insight, his grasp of doctrine and his very solid monastic orientation. I think we have here in the *Apologia* a good example of this. All too often it has been dismissed as a piece of excessive polemic by those who have heard a few phrases of it or some secondhand comment upon it. But as we have tried to indicate here, perhaps all too briefly, in this short treatise written in Bernard's younger days, there is rich monastic doctrine and spirituality. In it, perhaps, as nowhere else in his writings, he speaks "straight from the shoulder" to his brother Cistercians and in so doing gives principles which, while they are the principles of the twelfth-century Cistercian renewal, may perhaps strike us as being surprisingly at one with the principles which the Second Vatican Council has enunciated as guidelines for renewal in this twentieth century.

I believe this stands in confirmation of a statement made recently by a Benedictine scholar speaking of the achievement of Citeaux: "It is here [at

Citeaux] that we meet a real renewal in twelfth-century monasticism.... That is why I believe that the twelfth century offers the clearest analogies to the contemporary situation, and marks the only reform in Benedictine history that actually achieved for its time what is demanded of us today."[31]

NOTES

[1]It was only in 1970 that Cistercian Publications published for the first time a complete English translation.

[2]St. Bernard, *Apologia* (hereafter Apo), trans. Michael Casey, *The Works of Bernard of Clairvaux,* vol. 1, CF 1 (Spencer, MA: Cistercian Publications, 1969) p. 34.

[3]Lk. 17:21.

[4]Rom. 14:17.

[5]Apo 12, CF 1:48ff.

[6]Apo 13, CF 1:49ff.

[7]Apo 14, CF 1:51.

[8]*Ibid.,* CF 1:50ff.

[9]Apo 16, CF 1:52ff.

[10]Apo 18, CF 1:54.

[11]Apo 19, CF 1:54ff.

[12]Apo 23, CF 1:58ff.

[13]Apo 2, CF 1:35ff.

[14]Apo 4, CF 1:37ff.

[15]Apo 5, CF 1:39.

[16]Gn. 37:3.

[17]Apo 6, CF 1:40.

[18]Apo 6, CF 1:40ff.

[19]*Ibid.* Bernard applies this same doctrine to his own community in his *Second Sermon for Septuagesima:* "Among us, dearest brethren, let there be a union of souls. Let our hearts be one by loving the One, seeking the One, cleaving to the One, and entertaining the same sentiments. Thus external division shall involve no danger and give no scandal. For, although each one will have his own particular occupation, and sometimes also his own particular view regarding the administration of worldly affairs, yes, and there are even 'diversities of graces' (1 Cor. 12:4), the members of the body have not all the same function; nevertheless, the interior union and harmony of souls shall bring and bind together such multiplicity, using the glue of charity and the bond of peace (Eph. 4:3)."—*S. Bernardi Opera,* ed. Leclercq & Rochais, vol. 4 (Rome: Editiones Cistercienses, 1966) p. 352 (trans. mine).

[20]Apo 5, CF 1:40. For Bernard, pluralism does not end on earth; indeed, it finds its exemplar and fulfillment in the heavenly Jerusalem. He develops this idea at some length: "Why wonder at this variety during this time of exile, while the Church is on pilgrimage? Why wonder that its unity is also plurality? Probably even in the homeland, where unity will be supreme, there will be different forms of equality. Thus it is written: 'In my Father's house there are many rooms.' Just as there are many rooms in a single house, so there are many different orders in the one Church.

Just as on earth there are different graces, but the one Spirit, so in heaven there are different types of glory within a single house. In both cases unity consists in a singleness of love. Here below, diversity resides in the differences of orders and the various allotments of work; in heaven, diversity will take the form of an obvious and well-ordered gradation of merit. The Church understands this mingling of harmony and discord when it says: 'He led me along paths of virtue for his name's sake.' Paths is plural, virtue, singular; hence neither the diversity of works nor the unity of workmen is overlooked.

"The Church looks forward to this manifold unity, and devotedly sings glad tidings: 'The squares of Jerusalem will be paved with pure gold and all her streets will cry, *Alleluia*.' The squares and the streets may be understood to represent the different crowns and glories. In the gold with which the city is said to be adorned and in the single song of *Alleluia*, you may recognize how alike are the different types of glory, and understand how it is that many minds can be united in a single spirit of devotion. There are many paths that can be taken, for the dwelling places to which we journey are many." (Apo 8, CF 1:41ff.).

[21]Apo 2, CF 1:35ff.
[22]Apo 3, CF 1:36.
[23]Apo 5, CF 1:38ff.
[24]Apo 5, CF 1:39ff.
[25]Apo 5, CF 1:40ff.
[26]Apo 6, CF 1:40ff.
[27]*Ibid.*
[28]Apo 7, CF 1:42.
[29]Apo 5, CF 1:40.
[30]Apo 8, CF 1:43.
[31]C. Piefer, "Monastic Renewal in Historical Perspective," in *American Benedictine Review* 19 (1968) 14ff.

St. Bernard's Steps of Humility and Pride
An Introduction

The Steps of Humility is Bernard of Clairvaux's first published work.[1] And yet surely it is not the work of an amateur, as both its immediate popularity[2] and its continued popularity through the centuries clearly attest. It has been published in English translation more frequently than any of his other works, with the possible exception of his treatise *On Loving God.*[3]

The title of the treatise does not really prepare the reader for what is to be found in it.[4] This is not a new discovery. Bernard's first critics said the same. And the sensitive young abbot felt the need to defend himself in his *Retractatio.*[5]

The Retractatio

A tradition going back to manuscripts contemporary with Bernard himself places the *Retractatio*[6] at the head of the treatise.[7] It is certainly an important document, not so much because of the correctives it brings to the text as for what it tells us about the author. It assures us that he "practices what he preaches." It may be spirited, but it certainly is the expression of a truly humble man. Where he had been wrong, he readily confessed it. He had no desire to conceal it; he wanted to right the wrong. We see a man who readily accepted himself as fallible, a man genuinely and courageously self-possessed. He did not have to be right. This same spirit is evinced in his willingness to set forth a personal opinion as a personal opinion. Yet his was true humility, based on truth. Where his critics were wrong he was not ready to make any false protestations but firmly stood his ground. All the virtues are interconnected; the truly humble man is also truthful and courageous.

But the *Retractatio* tells us something else about the author, something it is well to keep in mind when reading not only this treatise but all his subsequent writings. Bernard tells us here that when he quoted Scripture he depended on his memory, and not a verbal memory, but rather a general sense of the passage.[8] This was true even in a case where the text in question was the basis of his whole line of reasoning. Thus as we read St.

Bernard we should not be surprised at times to find that his Scriptural texts are not exactly those found in our Bibles. He may have had in mind the Vulgate or the Old Latin version,[9] or, more likely, texts from these employed in the liturgy where they are sometimes adapted to the context. Or, as he admits here, he may have been speaking from the general sense of the passage. Bernard was not usually too concerned with the literal sense of the Scriptural texts he employed (though sometimes he certainly was, as we can see from this treatise). He was quite ready to leave the husk to get at the inner meat, the typological meaning.[10] And even there, for this man so typically monastic, it was the practical moral sense that most interested him—what he and his brethren could be doing to respond to the reality revealed—rather than the allegorical or anagogic meanings.[11]

The *Retractatio* also tells us something about the diffusion of Bernard's works. We do not know exactly when it was written but it could have been at the most a matter of only a few years after the initial publication.[12] Yet already "many copies had been made." For those times this was significant. Copies were made only by the painstaking labors of a copyist. One did not undertake the expenditures and troubles involved in copying a book unless there was a real demand for it. Bernard's writings, even in his lifetime, were in great demand and widely read.[13]

Bernard would learn from his experience with the *Steps of Humility*. In the future he would be more cautious in publishing.[14] Usually he would submit his work to friends for their judgment.[15] He was not always fortunate, however, in his choice of critics. We know now that some of the sharpest passages in his *Apologia* were not originally his own but were inspired by one of these chosen critics.[16] We find, too, that sometimes these critics could not resist the temptation to "leak" the work.[17]

GODFREY OF LANGRES

Like most of Bernard's works, this first one was written in response to the behest of a friend who had some title to make such a demand on the busy abbot. Besides the title of friendship, often there were other accompanying claims. In this case it was that of filiation. The *Steps of Humility* was written for Godfrey of Langres who was then abbot of Clairvaux's second foundation, Fontenay.[18]

We should know more about this man for he was perhaps the man closest to Bernard, the Abbot. For a time he was Bernard's prior, then he was sent off to head the second foundation. Soon again we find him back at Clairvaux.[19] We might well ask why. We have seen parallel instances in modern times and the reasons are various. Some men make excellent priors but poor first superiors. This may have been the case with Godfrey. But his subsequent election as Bishop of Langres in 1139 and his successful administration of that diocese for about twenty-three years would seem to indicate that he had real ability to lead and govern. The reason for the return might have been the same as that which motivated his later resignation from the bishopric: a nostalgia for Clairvaux, a basic lifelong attraction to live the simple, free life of a monk. We have parallels to this, as for example in the case of the Blessed Humbert, the founding abbot of Igny, who after ten years of service, in spite of Bernard's strong disapproval, laid down his charge and returned to the ranks at Clairvaux.[20] But perhaps the real answer lay in the needs of Bernard and Clairvaux. It was a rapidly developing community. Young and old were flocking to it, foundations were going forth from it at a disturbing rate.[21] Bernard would often be off on the business of Church and State.[22] There was need of an exceptionally capable second-in-command. Yet he would have to be very truly a second-in-command; there was no room for undue independence. Bernard, the genius, even with all his commitments, kept a close watch on things. Bernard, the spiritual father, knew his sons and kept in close personal contact with each one of them, as is evident from some of the stories that have come down to us.[23] The prior would "perform respectfully the duties enjoined on him by his abbot and do nothing against the abbot's will or direction."[24]

THE YOUNG BERNARD

Whether we are reading the treatise to get in closer touch with the exciting, unusual and extremely significant period of history during which it was written, or to get to know a fascinating personality better, or simply to deepen our own spiritual insight, we do well to consider the man who speaks to us, to have a real feel for him, so that, in a sense, we can enter into dialogue with him.[25]

Bernard of Les Fontaines was by origin a man of the upper classes. His family had its place among the nobility of the emerging French nation. He was well educated. His writings give evidence of some familiarity with the classics and an excellent training in composition. He uses every literary form, is masterfully at home in all of them. In the fullest sense of the word, he is literate.

And he had extraordinary powers of leadership. When he decided Citeaux was the right answer, he did not go alone. He led thirty relatives and friends into the marshes. He was not a naive lad, unfamiliar with the ways of the world. He pursued a married brother into a front-line army camp, he spoke frankly to uncles and brothers and friends alike. He would be well prepared and knowledgeable when he later offered advice and direction to kings and princes, bishops and clerics, knights and scholars. And he could identify with the poor.

The man who wrote the *Steps of Humility* was not humble by origin, nature or temperament. It was a virtue he knew, from experience, that had to be cultivated—and at a price. The aspirant of twenty-three (we must remember that twenty-three in those days represented a good bit more maturity than its parallel today) must also have been maturing spiritually. Otherwise it would hardly have been possible for him to have reached so rapidly that spiritual fullness which would have allowed the Abbot of Citeaux, St. Stephen Harding, to send him forth as the spiritual father of Citeaux's third daughter house.

When Bernard wrote the *Steps of Humility* he had been abbot for about ten years. He had known the rigor of a Cistercian novitiate—made more rigorous by his own zeal—a couple of years of community life as a simple monk, and then years of ever more weighty responsibility as the abbot of a rapidly growing community. He was plagued by serious ill health. He had to travel much—much for an ordinary Cistercian abbot, though not much in comparison to what the future would demand of him—seeing bishops and nobles to get the permission, backing and finances for Clairvaux's initial foundations—the first in what would be a steadily growing stream. His life had been enriched by sharing it with some wonderful friends: William of Champeaux, his bishop; William of St. Thierry, his closest friend, who convalesced with him; Guerric of Igny, who came to Clairvaux in 1123, a saintly scholar with years of learning and prayerful solitude behind him; and Bernard's own remarkable brothers and uncles. Though still young, only thirty-five, the Abbot of Clairvaux had a lot to draw on when he set about responding to the Abbot of Fontenay.

The Steps of Humility

What Bernard dictated to his secretary was not wholly new. Godfrey in making his request had in mind some conferences which he himself had heard from the lips of the Abbot when he sat at his right in the chapter house at Clairvaux. Now Godfrey found himself in the center chair and he wanted to provide equally good food for the community that had been entrusted to his care.

The Steps of Truth

Bernard is a good teacher. Before constructing his steps of humility he arouses his reader's interest by showing him the heights to which they can lead. After all, who is interested in a ladder except the man who wants to climb up to something? And that something is truth, but truth taken in a very large and full sense; not just a moral habit or a quality of the mind, but the Incarnate Word, God himself known and contemplated, and that truth which in man operates by charity.

In speaking of his goal Bernard the teacher seeks a paradigm and finds it again in steps. For him there are three steps or degrees of truth. Threefold divisions are a constant in his treatise; they occur again and again.[26]

Even before going into the three degrees of truth, Bernard pauses to speak of the three fruits to be gained by mounting these steps of humility: humility itself, love, and contemplation. These correspond to the three degrees of truth, or more accurately, as Bernard notes, the three degrees of perception of truth: the truth in oneself, the truth in one's neighbor, and the Truth in itself. Bernard asserts there is a precise order here and establishes this both by intrinsic reasons and by an appeal to authority. His authority is Christ Jesus teaching on the Mount, it is the Beatitudes.

Just as under the guidance of the Spirit the inspired writer or redactor gathered in summary form the full teaching of Christ into the three chapters of Matthew's Gospel that form the Sermon on the Mount,[27] so the essence of that whole sermon is distilled in the Beatitudes that stand at the head of it. The Cistercian Fathers clearly perceived this and used this text to trace out a Cistercian way to holiness.[28] Bernard would do this later in his First Sermon for the Feast of All Saints.[29] But here in this first treatise he already makes use of the Beatitudes as a sure guide for the ascent in truth. First the poor, meek sinner humbles himself with tears and thirsts for justice.[30] He sees himself as he truly is, with all his sin and misery. Such a heart that knows misery, knows mercy. Thus he can readily identify with his brother. Bernard demonstrates his understanding of human psychology here as he declares: "A man who does not live in harmony with his brothers . . . has no sympathy with them because their feelings do not affect him; he can never really see the truth in others. . . . A brother's miseries are truly experienced only by one who has misery in his own heart."[31]

The second degree of truth, a real understanding of others, is attained only by the merciful, and one is merciful only when he first perceives his own misery. But once he is merciful, he will obtain mercy, as is said in the fifth Beatitude: "Blessed are the merciful for they shall obtain mercy."[32] That mercy will purify him. Then as one clean of heart he will see God.[33] He will have reached the third degree of truth, he will know Truth in itself and go out of himself (*excessus*) in contemplation of it.

Bernard teaches all of this quite concisely but his illustrations greatly amplify the text. Christ is always his prime exemplar. It is when showing Christ becoming acquainted with infirmity that he might be merciful that Bernard goes off on his longest digression, exploring the knowledge of Christ. It is here that his memory fails him—modifying a Scripture text, with the result that the argumentation flowing from it is unfounded. The point is not central and Bernard had already given other bases for his opinion. In actual fact it is a question still debated by theologians today—the question of the growth of Christ the man through the acquisition of new knowledge. As the question is a bit off the point here, which Bernard himself admits in the text,[34] he does not have difficulty later when he must retract it. When it is merely a question of theological speculation Bernard has little difficulty in ceding a point.[35]

Besides the example of Christ he offers two others. The Psalmist also shows the humble man how to act, while the Pharisee shows him exactly what not to do.

But Bernard, the contemplative, the mystic, the theologian, soars aloft to find even more sublime exemplars as he reaches into the Trinity itself and directs the reader's gaze to the Father, Son and Holy Spirit. The Son, by word and example, teaches humility. The Spirit pours out his compassionate love into the hearts of the humble. And the Father beatifies them through Truth. They progress from disciples to friends to sons. The Son who is Truth works in the mind; the Spirit who is love, in the will; but the Father draws men out of themselves into ecstatic contemplation, to the third heaven, to the attainment of the third and highest degree of truth.[36]

Twelve Steps of Humility

It is the ladder of humility that gets a man up to the first step of truth. And Bernard now finally turns his attention to his ladder. It is not an unknown climb, for the way of humility and the way of pride are the very same. The way we have descended by pride we must ascend by humility.

It is a good pedagogical principle that one should go from the known to the unknown. Bernard does this, using the opportunity to give further evidence of his own humility. Instead of describing the steps of humility in themselves, he exemplifies them by their opposites, saying this is the way he knows them best—not by climbing up the ladder, but by sliding down it through pride.

His paradigm here is Benedict's twelve degrees or steps of humility as they are sketched out in the seventh chapter of the *Rule for Monasteries*, something that would have been very familiar to his monastic audience. This is the Rule that was so dear to the early Cistercians, the observance of which they saw to be the very living of the Gospel.[37] It was the desire to live this Rule more perfectly that animated the Founders of Citeaux,[38] the men who inspired and formed Bernard as a monk. Chapter seven has always been considered the heart and center of the Rule, the essence of Benedictine ascesis, the Benedictine way to perfect love.[39] It perhaps says something for the sureness of Bernard's insight into the meaning of his Cistercian vocation and the Cistercian way of life that his first treatise is concerned with the very center of the Rule. And the way he goes about it indicates something of the specific emphasis of the Cistercian spirit. For, as we have seen,

Bernard clearly sees that the whole value of the ladder, of Benedictine ascesis, lies in its ability to bring us to the way of truth with its culmination in ecstatic contemplation. The Cistercians are Benedictine contemplatives.

If the reading has sometimes been heavy, even laborious, in the first part of this treatise, especially when Bernard struggled with the problem of the knowledge of Christ, it now takes a lighter turn—though certainly not frivolous. It is undoubtedly this latter part with its delightful vignettes that has made the treatise so popular.

The order of Bernard's treatment, then, is wholly determined by that of his master, Benedict. At the end of the first part he indicates precisely how his twelve descending steps of pride correspond to Benedict's twelve ascending steps of humility. Actually this is more fully presented at the head of the whole treatise where the two ladders or rather the two directions of the same ladder are presented in summary form. Whether this is the work of Bernard or a very early redactor we do not know but it is part of the manuscript tradition.[40]

In his treatment of the twelve steps St. Bernard reverts to his much favored tripartite division and shows, as an appendix to the tenth step of pride, how the first six steps show contempt for the brethren, the next four for the superiors, and the last two for God. Conversely the first two steps of humility are in relation to God and it is only when a man has attained this humility that he will want a superior over him and enter a monastery. Thus St. Bernard argues that the last two steps of pride will be found only outside the monastery—some consolation for monks!

The reader immediately notices that Bernard's treatment of the first step of pride is as long as his treatment of the other eleven put together. This might have been forced on Bernard by external circumstances. He might have wanted to treat them all more fully, drawing abundantly on Scripture for illustrations, as he does with the first, but the pressure of time or a waiting messenger or an impatient Godfrey may have forced him to conclude his work hastily.[41] But we have no evidence that this was actually the case. His reason might have been that he thought this was where most of his hearers were or were in the greatest danger of being. Or it may have been simply that his charismatic freedom was spurred on by the abundance of relevant Scriptural passages that sprang to mind. Certainly his long excursus on the apostate Seraph has much to do with the length. It parallels in some ways his long excursus on the knowledge of Christ found in the first part. Perhaps in this balance we have a bit of subtle artistry which we do not really perceive or appreciate.

We could also note another parallel here, certainly not intended by the author. Of the two points treated in the *Retractatio*, one is found in each of these sections. When Bernard launches out into speculation he is not only less interesting and lively but also more apt to err as he ventures to set forth his own opinions.

Since the text itself offers a summary schema of the twelve steps down and up,[42] there is no need to summarize them here. After studying the schema one will want to enter simply into the reading and thoroughly enjoy the delightful illustrations with which Bernard colors his presentation. Bernard brings out clearly enough in the text how one step leads to another and how each step of pride corresponds to its relative step of humility. As we have already noted, after the tenth step he offers a brief three-part summary which is also helpful.[43]

At the conclusion of the twelfth step Bernard launches into another, perhaps more interesting excursus, struggling with an exegetical problem. John the Evangelist has written—Bernard applies the text to the habitual sinner of the twelfth step—"For such a one I would not that anyone should pray."[44] This is a hard saying, especially for the loving heart of the Abbot. He subtly undermines the text by reducing its application to expressed petition. Modern exegetes come at the problem from another approach, but Bernard has the authority of Augustine for his.[45] And it is a satisfying answer he gives, one that corresponds to lived experience. The heart does not need words, nor can words and precepts obliterate the longings of a loving heart which God cannot fail to see.

As we finish reading the steps of pride we are inclined to expect our teacher to begin now the ascent. But a bit of reflection will make us realize that not only has he related the steps of pride to the corresponding steps of humility but in so doing he has fully instructed us in the latter. Nonetheless it is with a certain amount of disappointment that we bump into a conclusion.[46] Bernard sensed this reaction and most of the brief concluding paragraph is devoted to showing how one knowing the descending steps of pride knows at the same time the ascending steps of humility. In spite of these concluding remarks there were readers who yet felt they had been deceived in their expectation (and so might we). This is evident from the fact that Bernard had to touch again on the matter in his *Retractatio*.[47]

It might be useful to offer the reader a schematic outline of the treatise here:

Preface
A. The Goal of the Steps of Humility—Truth (doctrinal presentation)
 1. The Sources
  a. Scriptural: the teaching of Christ (1)[48]
  b. Patristic: Augustine's definition of humility (2)
 2. The Goal in general—the three fruits: humility, charity, contemplation (3-5)

SOURCES

One of the first things that usually strikes one when he first reads St. Bernard is the copious use of Scripture. Texts flow from Bernard's pen without cease. When he is not actually quoting a text he is frequently using biblical words and phrases to express his own ideas.

We have already mentioned the freedom Bernard takes when using Scriptural texts. He is always more intent on content. Sometimes he does

argue his point from a biblical text, employing the type of tight argumentation which we are inclined to associate with the scholastic method. We find
some examples of this in the opening paragraph of this treatise. Although
the "last of the Fathers" spoke disparagingly of the philosophers of the
schools,[49] he knew the new methods and made use of them.[50] But it is
evident that it is the Fathers who have more fully informed his mind and
shaped his method and style. He usually employs Scripture in the more
contemplative and existential way of patristic tradition.

In this treatise his dependence on the Fathers is extensive right from the
beginning where he employs Augustine's definition of humility (2). He
weaves into his fabric themes and interpretations common to the Fathers,
such as the interpretation of Isaiah 14:13 and Ezekiel 28:12 (31, 35) or the
theme of Eve, mother of the dying (30).

The Fathers who seem to have the greatest influence on him in this
treatise are men of the West: Augustine and Gregory the Great, but Origen
is not absent. There are also evidences of Justin, Cyprian, Tertullian,
Ambrose and Anselm.[51] The works of all these Fathers, with the possible
exception of Justin, were to be found in the *armarium* at Clairvaux.[52]

There are also quotations coming from pagan authors such as Terence (6)
and Persius (40). Bernard may have remembered these from his school
days, though there is greater likelihood that they came to him through the
Fathers.

Obviously the primary source here is Benedict of Nursia, who is responsible for the whole structure of the second part and even at times provides
the very words Bernard uses.

The liturgy also provides Bernard with inspiration and content. As we
have already indicated, his Scriptural texts often come to him through the
liturgy. In paragraph twenty-two he employs a phrase that comes from the
Sanctus of the Mass or the *Te Deum*, a phrase inspired by Isaiah: "The heavens
and the earth are filled with your glory."[53] And one of his final arguments in
the treatise rests on liturgical practice, on the way the Church prays in the
prayers of the faithful on Good Friday (56).

THE STYLE OF THE TREATISE

Very much could be written about the style of St. Bernard, even if one
limited himself to the consideration of this initial treatise. I will touch on
only a few points.[54]

One thing that is very evident is the order in the treatise. It is carefully
planned and well executed. The outline offered above makes this quite
clear. Yet another facet of Bernard is equally in evidence: his freedom even
when working within a structure. Besides the three main excursuses which
we have already indicated (7-12, 31-38, 52-56), there are a number of other

instances where he has rambled down a side road. It is something of which he is frankly aware: "But to come back to our subject." (13) "I am afraid I am 'speaking in my excess' now myself and have wandered away from my subject.... Well, let us come back to the point." (17-18) "How did we get on to this matter...? I wandered off into this by-path...." (38)

Basically though, even with his vagaries, the author of this treatise is a good teacher. The use of the twelve steps and the very frequent use of the tripartite division are useful memory aids. The interrelationship of the different parts and aspects is clearly brought out.[55] Principal terms such as humility and pride are clearly defined[56] and distinctions are neatly made.[57] Argumentation, flowing in good theological fashion from Scripture texts, is clearly pursued and brought to a conclusion.[58] Even very deep theological questions such as the properties of the three divine Persons, concomitance and attribution, are handled with a simplicity and clarity that is readily intelligible to the average lay reader.[59]

However, Bernard's pedagogical style, order and clarity detract not at all from the literary value of his treatise.[60] Unfortunately much of the beauty of Bernard's Latin is not and probably can never be captured in translation. The emphasis and alliteration of *Carnalis videlicit populi sententiam de carne inquirens, nomen carnis posuit* (11) is not found in "When he was inquiring what a carnal people thought about the human body they saw before them he used the title that referred directly to the human nature...."[61] Alliteration abounds in the Latin.[62] The constant balancing of words, again often with alliteration, delights both ear and mind:

> ...*sicut prius misericordes quam mundicordes, sic prius mites quam misericordes....*
> (14) *Si non accessisset, non attraxisset;* ...*se solum decipit, quem solum excipit....*
> (17) ...*vel de virtute confidam, vel pro labore diffidam.* (22) ...*ideoque nascimur morituri, quia prius morimur nascituri.* (30)

But even in translation Bernard's skill as a writer stands out in the delightful character sketches in the second part—delightful to the reader, but one suspects that they might have caused more than one monk to squirm when they were first sketched out in the chapter house at Clairvaux. Not only are they full of humor, but paint their subject with such vividness that we can immediately see and hear the loquacious eccentric braggart:

> ...his eyes are wandering, his glance darts right and left, his ears are cocked (28) ...he simply cannot stop laughing.... He is like a well-filled bladder that has been pricked and squeezed. The air, not finding a free vent, whistles out through the little hole with squeak after squeak.... In embarrassment he buries his face in his hands, tightens his lips, clenches his teeth. It is no use. The laughter must explode, and if his hand holds it in his mouth, it bursts out through his nose. (40)

While he is at his meal, he casts his eyes around the tables and if he sees anyone eating less than himself he is mortified.... He would rather starve.... He wonders what others think about the appearance of his face and as he cannot see it he can only guess whether it is rosy or wan by looking at his hands and arms, poking at his ribs, and feeling his shoulders and loins to see how skinny or fleshy they are.... He will stay awake in bed and sleep in choir. After sleeping through the night office while the others were singing psalms, he stays on to pray alone.... He makes sure that those sitting outside know he is there, modestly hidden in his corner, clearing his throat and coughing and groaning and sighing. (42) He must have the first place in gatherings, must be the first to speak in council. He comes without being called. He interferes without being asked. He must rearrange everything, redo whatever has been done. (44)

...when they[63] are caught out...their eyes are cast down, they humble themselves to the very dust, they will wring out some tears if they can, sighs and groans interrupt their words.... They accuse themselves of things so great, so incredible, that you begin to doubt the charges you were certain of before. (46)

The force of the satire is heightened by the realism of the descriptions.

The same mastery of description is to be found at work when biblical scenes or personalities are brought in to illustrate a point.[64]

Through all this Bernard shows his depth of psychological insight. We have already noted this in the first part. We see it again in the last sentence just quoted above, and again as he speaks of the community's reaction when the proud hypocrite is unmasked: "Now everyone knows what he is, everyone condemns him, and they are all the more vexed because of the good opinion his fraud fooled them into holding for so long." (47)

B. R. V. Mills tells us that we have in Bernard a thinker, a theologian, a monk, a mystic and a moralist.[65] I think quite a few additional adjectives could be joined even to this impressive array.

THE SUBTITLES

The subtitles go back to the twelfth century and are probably contemporaneous with Bernard himself.[66] They are found in most of the ancient manuscripts, one common set with few variations; though there are some later manuscripts where they do not appear. Sometimes they are listed at the head of the whole treatise rather than inserted in the text. And in some manuscripts they are both listed and inserted in the text.[67]

Whoever inserted the titles—and he quite possibly had Bernard's approval in the matter—was more concerned with utility and clarity than with symmetry. They are far more numerous in the second part, where each step commands its own title, and also the excursus on the apostate

Angel. In the first part there are, besides the heading of the Preface, only two subtitles and these are drawn from the text itself.

CONTEMPORARY SIGNIFICANCE

Perhaps one of the clearest and most concrete indications of the perduring value of this treatise is the fact that there has been sufficient demand for it to warrant constant republication in many languages. In English alone in the last fifty years there have been Barton Mills' translation, based on his own edition, published by SPCK in 1929; G. Bosworth Burch's, with its long introductory study on Bernard's epistemology, published by Harvard in 1940 and 1942 and republished by Notre Dame in 1963, and G. Webb and A. Walker's version appearing in Mowbrays' Fleur de Lys Series in 1957.[68] In 1974 a translation by Ambrose Conway, O.C.S.O., based on the new critical edition of Dom Jean Leclercq appeared in the Cistercian Fathers Series.[69]

The reason for this popularity is within the treatise itself. As we have seen, it is rich in humor—everyone can enjoy a bit of satire. It is perhaps the work of Bernard that is easiest to read. Again, every man can find himself within it. It stoops down to the lowest sinner. But it not only stoops down—it points him up toward the most sublime heights. There is hope for all.

Its attractiveness for many most fundamentally lies in the fact that the author truly exemplifies what he teaches and with extraordinary literary skill conveys this effectively to the reader. The reader senses that Bernard has looked deeply into himself, knows himself, and approaches the reader, his fellow man, with deep understanding and true compassion. The young Bernard has already come to love all men and in the sublime vision of man which he has seen in God he has a deeper respect and a greater appreciation for the greatness of each than most men have for themselves. As Bernard meets each on the rung of misery and pride on which he is presently lodged he does not fail to assure the poor wretch that he is not alone and that he has every reason to hope for great things. Every degree of pride has its corresponding degree of humility. If Bernard's satire is at times a bit stinging, and here we perhaps perceive some of the yet unmellowed zeal of youth, there is such good humor in it that we can enjoy it, just as the Black Monks of his time so enjoyed the *Apologia*.[70]

Although he may not naturally use Bernard's terminology, every man finds within himself some of the experiences Bernard so graphically depicts. What is more, he quickly identifies his own deepest longings in Bernard's description of the goal: the freedom of truth, universal love, the experience of the Transcendent God. Bernard's straightforward assurance, his calm witness that God really cares and is personally involved in man's strivings and fulfillment, is like a cool mountain breeze wafted across a placid lake into a city of feverish activity. It is immensely refreshing and offers one life and hope; it lifts one's eyes to the mountains and draws one out beyond the hustle to serene heights where he can perceive deeper meanings and experience true hope. Bernard very effectively communicates to his reader the invitation to glory in his infirmities, for therein lies true strength and the hope of unending glory, meaning, fulfillment.

Enough has been said by way of introduction. Let the reader now proceed to the text and enjoy it to the full. For it offers him not only passing enjoyment, but, if he would have it, a way to a fuller—the fullest possible—life and happiness.

NOTES

[1]Godfrey of Langres, to whom this Treatise is addressed, in the Fourth Book of the *Life of St. Bernard (Vita Bernardi)*, speaks of "his first work concerning the steps of humility."—c. 8, PL 185:320. For a fuller treatment of this question and indeed for an excellent introduction in general, see the Introduction in *Sancti Bernardi Opera* (hereafter OB), ed. J. Leclercq, H. Rochais (Rome: Editiones Cistercienses) vol. 3 (1963) pp. 3-11. On this particular point see also J. Leclercq, "Le premier traité authentique de saint Bernard?" *Recueil d' études sur saint Bernard et ses écrits* (Rome: Edizioni di Storia e Letteratura) vol. 2 (1966) pp. 51-67, reprinted from *Revue d'histoire ecclésiastique* 48 (1953) pp. 196-210.

[2]This is evident from the diffusion of the manuscripts. See OB 3:4ff.

[3]See J. Bouton, *Bibliographie Bernardine* (Paris: Lethielleux, 1957).

[4]Mills echos the sentiment of many when he says in his Introduction: "The title of the book is somewhat misleading."—St. Bernard, *The Twelve Degrees of Humility and Pride,* tr. B. R. V. Mills (London: SPCK, 1929) p. viii.

[5]"Some have objected to the title: *The Steps of Humility,* on the ground that I have described the steps not of humility but of pride. They must not have understood or have not noticed my note at the end where I briefly explain the title."—"The Steps of Humility and Pride," (hereafter Hum) "Reconsideration," in *Treatises II, The Works of Bernard of Clairvaux,* vol. 5, CF 13 (Washington: Cistercian Publications, 1974) p. 25.

[6]The English "Retraction" does not do justice to the content of the Latin word; it is rather a reconsidering of the matter—in this case, in the light of some objections, which are answered with both a retractation and a spirited defense.

[7]See OB 3:5ff.; CF 13:25.

[8]"I quoted, as I thought, the text and then found that it was not in the Gospel at all. I had no intention of falsifying the text but I was depending on my memory of the general sense of the passage and made a slip in the words."—CF 13:25. Dom Jean Leclercq has pointed out to me that Wordsworth and White in their *Novum Testamentum latine* (Oxford, 1887-98) 1:253, indicate that at Mk. 13:32, the text Bernard quoted, *filius hominis* (Son of Man) is found in some mss., including the *Book of Armagh* (Dublin) and the Book of Kells (Dublin), so a certain "Irish" tradition may have been responsible for the text first employed by Bernard.

⁹Watkins Williams in his Preface quotes Dr. White, Dean of Christ Church: "...his considered opinion is that St. Bernard 'probably used an ordinary Vulgate text which had preserved a certain number of Old Latin readings, as so many of the Vulgate mss. did; and also that he often quoted from memory.' " Williams goes on to say, still depending on White: "A salient instance of the former would be the addition of 'quanto magis' in John 13:15." But Bernard was probably influenced by his patristic sources in this instance. There is no indication that White considered the possibility that Bernard received some of his Scripture sources through the liturgy. See *Select Treatises of S. Bernard of Clairvaux*, Cambridge Patristic Texts, ed. W. Williams and B. Mills (Cambridge: University Press, 1926) pp. viif.

¹⁰"Now, under the Spirit's guidance, let us try to draw out the spiritual fruit which lies underneath the rind of the letter."—Sermons on the Song of Songs (hereafter Cant.) 51:2, OB 2 (1958) p. 84; CF 31:40. "Such is the literal sense, the portion of the Jews. But for me, following the counsel of the Lord I will search for the treasure of spirit and life hidden in the profound depths of these inspired utterances."—Cant. 73:1-2, OB 2:234. (Trans. mine.)

¹¹"I had indeed hoped that the discussion of the mystical sense of our text would not have detained us so long. I actually thought that one sermon would suffice, and that passing quickly through that shadowy wood where allegories lurk unseen, we should arrive, after perhaps one day's journey, on the open plain of moral truth."—Cant. 16:1, OB 1:89-90, CF 1:115. For an excellent and comprehensive treatment of the way in which the Cistercian Fathers and their contemporaries used the Scriptures with their four senses see H. de Lubac, *Exégèse Médiévale: Les Quatre Sens de l'Ecriture,* 4 vols. (Paris: Aubier, 1959-1964). There are many references to St. Bernard in the indexes.

¹²The "long after" (*multo post*) of the *Retractatio* has to be understood in the context. It was much too late after publication for Bernard to introduce into the text the corrections he would have liked to make. It does not mean necessarily that many years had elapsed. After the publication of many more significant and controversial works he would not have been apt to concern himself about publishing a retractation concerning relatively minor matters in this first treatise.

¹³The diffusion of the manuscripts solidly establishes this.

¹⁴Unlike most of his works there seems to have been no successive redaction of this treatise after the first one was published. See the Introductions in OB and CF.

¹⁵E.g., in the case of his next treatise, the *Apologia*. He had sent it to Oger, a Canon Regular of Mont-Saint-Eloi, and wrote to him in this vein: "...do not, on any account, allow anyone to see or copy the aforesaid booklet until you have been through it with him [William of St. Thierry], discussed it with him, and have both made such corrections as may be necessary so that every word of it may be supported by two witnesses. I leave to you both to decide whether the preface you have put together out of my letters will stand, or whether it would not be better to compose another."—Letter 88:3, PL 182:213, tr. B. S. James, *The Letters of St. Bernard of Clairvaux* (London: Burns and Oates, 1953) n. 91 (James' numbering is different from that of the PL) pp. 136f. This is cited in Leclercq's Introduction in CF 1:7f. In his Prologue to the treatise, *On Grace and Free Will*, Bernard wrote to William of St. Thierry: "You please read it first...if you notice something obscurely stated...

do not hesitate either to emend it yourself or else to return it to me for emenda-tion...." OB 3:165, tr. Fr. Daniel O'Donovan, CF 19:51. See also two articles by Leclercq, "Les formes successives de la lettre-traité de s. Bernard contre Abélard" in *Revue bénédictine* 78 (1968) pp. 87-105 and "Les lettres de Guillaume de Saint-Thierry," *ibid.* 79 (1969) pp. 375-391. Also, CF 1:7ff.

16See CF 1:24f.

17So Bernard had to write to Oger: "That other booklet I lent you, I had meant you only to read, but you tell me that you have had it copied...I did not intend that you should send it to the abbot...."—Letter 88:3, 1c.

18Fontenay was founded in 1119. See L. Janauschek, *Originum Cisterciensium* (Vienna: Hoelder, 1877) p. 8, where all the details are given as well as a brief biographical sketch of Godfrey.

19There is some discussion as to when he returned to Clairvaux. Leclercq (OB 3:3), citing Vacandard (*Vie de saint Bernard, Abbé de Clairvaux* [Paris: Lecoffre, 1895] 1:166, note 4), sets his return sometime before 1126. Janauschek (1c) and Mills (*op. cit.* vii), citing *Gallia Christiana* (4:374) has him return around 1135.

20See J. Morson and H. Costello, Introduction in Guerric of Igny, *Liturgical Sermons I*, CF 8:xvi.

21In the years Godfrey would have been prior, if we accept Leclercq's date, Clairvaux would have acquired 25 new daughter houses. In all it was to acquire 65 during Bernard's term of office. See the chart in the back of Janauschek.

22It was during Godfrey's tenure that Bernard had to struggle among other things with the papal schism which was settled just prior to Godfrey's election as bishop, an election, incidentally, which was first given to Bernard, who declined the office.

23See J. Leclercq, "St. Bernard of Clairvaux and the Contemplative Community" in *Contemplative Community: An Interdisciplinary Symposium*, CF 21 (1972) pp. 108-149.

24RB 65:16.

25Perhaps the best biography of Bernard is still that of Vacandard (cited above in note 19) but one should not overlook the *Vita Prima* (PL 185:225-416, partial tr., G. Webb and A. Walker, *Saint Bernard of Clairvaux* [London: Mowbrays, 1960]). The most recent authoritative study of Bernard is that of Leclercq, *St. Bernard and the Cistercian Spirit*, CS 16.

26E.g. way, truth, life (1) [the numbers in parentheses refer to the paragraphs in the treatise] humility, charity, contemplation (3-5) truth, mercy, illumination (13-19) humility of the Son, love of the Spirit, light of the Father (20-21). Even the 12 steps are divided into three: despising one's brethren, one's superiors, one's God. See below note 36.

27Mt. 5-7.

28See above, "A Way to Holiness."

29OB 5:327-341.

30"Blessed are the poor in spirit, for theirs is the kingdom of heaven.
  "Blessed are those who mourn, for they shall be comforted.
  "Blessed are the meek, for they shall inherit the earth.
  "Blessed are those who hunger and thirst for righteousness, for they shall be
      satisfied."—Mt. 5:3-6.

31Hum 6, CF 13:35.

32Mt. 5:7.

33"Blessed are the pure in heart, for they shall see God."—Mt. 5:8.

34Hum 13, CF 13:41.

35This is evident in many passages in his sermons, e.g. "Whether I am right in assigning it to such a source, I leave it to you to judge. It is also for you to consider and decide whether I have correctly attributed the same kind of humility to the Savior.... Another question awaiting your determination is whether I am right in supposing...."—Cant. 42:8, OB 2:38, CF 7:216; "Nevertheless, if you still insist.... I shall not quarrel with your conviction...."—Cant. 50:2, OB 2:79, CF 31:31; "The Fathers seem to have held divergent views on the problem.... But I am of the opinion that knowledge of these matters would not contribute greatly to your spiritual progress."—Cant. 5:7, OB 1:24, CF 4:29.

36What has been said here might be summed up in schematic fashion something like this:

Person	operates in	to make	producing in them	corresponding Beatitude
Son	intellect	disciples	humility: knowledge of self of neighbor	1-4
Holy Spirit	will	friends	love, mercy, compassion	5
Father	rapture	sons	contemplation of God, Truth	6

37Thurstan of York, in his Epistle concerning the founders of Fountains, speaks of this as "...thirteen men who were determined to correct their way of life according to the Rule of St. Benedict, or rather, according to the truth of the Gospel." And he goes on to put these words into the mouth of the leader, Robert of Fountains: "We must undertake with all our strength to observe by God's grace the true and age-old service of our blessed Father Benedict, or rather, the more ancient Gospel of Christ...." And Thurstan goes on to comment: "We ought to recall what happened in the affair of the Molesme monks which is quite similar. The Cistercians went forth to establish and found a most perfect way of life.... They faithfully undertook a renewal of the Holy Rule and a total living of it.... Indeed, it is clearer than light that in their wonderful way of life the truth of the whole Gospel shines forth."—par. 3, 4, 22; see above pp. 24-25, 30.

38This is evident throughout the *Exordium Parvum:* e.g., "These men while still living in Molesme and inspired by divine grace often spoke, complained and lamented among themselves over the transgression of the Rule of St. Benedict, the Father of Monks.... That was the reason why they came into this solitude, namely, to fulfill their vows through the observance of the Holy Rule."—c. 3, *Nomasticon Cisterciense,* ed. H. Séjalon (Solesmes: St. Pierre, 1892) p. 55, tr. R. Larkin in L. Lekai, *The White Monks* (Okauchee: Cistercians, 1953) p. 253.

[39]See my article "Toward Discerning the Spirit of the Founders of the Order of Citeaux," above, pp. 3-14, especially pp. 6-8.

[40]There is no basis for asserting that they are actually Bernard's work, yet they are contemporary with him. See OB 3:9f.

[41]We have an example of this occurring in the case of the *Apologia* where Bernard says: "I am prevented from going on by the burdens of my office, and by your imminent departure, dear brother Oger. You will not agree to stay any longer, and you refuse to go without this latest little book."—*Apologia* 30, OB 3:106f., CF 1:67.

[42]OB 3:13f.; CF 13:26f.

[43]Hum 49, CF 13:75f.

[44]1 Jn. 5:16.

[45]See *City of God*, 21:24.

[46]I am aware that Leclercq has indicated this treatise as one where Bernard achieved a beautiful ending (J. Leclercq, "L'Art de la composition dans les traités de s. Bernard," *Recueil*, vol. 3 [1969] p. 117. This article is reprinted from *Revue bénédictine* 76 [1966] pp. 87-115). I am not disagreeing with this. My "bump" is something more psychological. The treatise, even in its ending is a beautiful masterpiece of literature.

[47]"Some have objected to the title: 'The Steps of Humility,' on the grounds that I have described the steps not of humility but of pride. They must not have understood or have not noticed my note at the end where I briefly explain the title."—CF 13:25.

[48]The numbers in parentheses refer to the paragraphs in the text.

[49]E.g., *Third Sermon for Pentecost*, 5 (however it is interesting to note that even in this very sermon Bernard examines his matter through what philosophers would call the four causes, and does it in an excellent philosophical form), OB 5:173; *Sermon for the Fourth Sunday after Pentecost*, 3, OB 5:203; Cant. 22:10, OB 1:136, CF 7:23.

[50]In fact we can find in the second paragraph of this treatise a perfect syllogism with its major, minor (*Sed*) and conclusion (*ergo*). See OB 3:18.

[51]The notes in OB should be consulted.

[52]See A. Wilmart, "L'Ancienne bibliothèque de Clairvaux," *Collectanea OCR* 11 (1949), pp. 101-127, 301-319.

[53]Is. 6:3.

[54]A fuller treatment of this matter can be found in J. Leclercq, "L'Art de la composition dans les traités de s. Bernard," *Recueil*, vol. 3 (1969) pp. 105-162, reprinted from *Revue bénédictine* 76 (1966) pp. 87-115.

[55]See above, note 36.

[56]"Humility is a virtue by which a man has a low opinion of himself because he knows himself well." (2) "For what else is pride but, as a saint [Augustine] has defined it, the love of one's own excellence?" (14).

[57]E.g., in relation to the two kinds of excess, par. 16-17.

[58]E.g., in par. 1. See Leclercq, "L'Art...," p. 114.

[59]See par. 20-22.

[60]Leclercq concludes his consideration of the treatise by saying: "One finds in this treatise of Bernard *junior* a doctrinal synthesis which will lose none of its value in the

face of his more mature works. But also in regard to composition this first work is already a masterpiece."—"L'Art...," p. 117.

[61]CF 13:39.

[62]E.g., *Hauris virus peritura, et perituros paritura.* (30)...*ut scire sciatur quod scit.* (41)...*miserabilius mirisque clamoribus miram misericordiam meruit....*(54) *Sapere enim malum, sapere non est, sed desipere.* (30).

[63]Bernard switches back and forth from the singular to the plural in his illustrations.

[64]E.g., Dinah (29), Eve (30).

[65]*Op. cit.*, pp. xvff.

[66]See Leclercq, "Pour l'histoire des traités de s. Bernard," *Recueil* 2:116ff. The article is a reprint from *Analecta SOC* 15 (1959) pp. 56-78.

[67]See OB 3:5ff.

[68]See the *Bibliographie Bernardine*, cited above in note 3.

[69]CF 13.

[70]See CF 1:21 and note 51 there. Surviving mss. of the *Apologia* seem to indicate it was perhaps even more widely circulated among the Black Monks than among the White (or Grey, as they were then called). This should not be too surprising, since Bernard's reprimands of the Black, though stinging, were delightfully satirical; his reproofs of his own brothers were more straight from the shoulder.

Three Stages of Spiritual Growth
According to St. Bernard

When modern persons hear of the stages of spiritual growth they are apt to think first of the three stages popularized by St. John of the Cross and subsequent writers: purgative, illuminative, unitive; and then perhaps of the seven mansions of St. Teresa. The monk of the West will perhaps more readily think of the twelve steps of St. Benedict's ladder of humility. Among the writings of the Cistercian Fathers we find many divisions, but the threefold division which goes back to the earliest traditions of the Church[1] is the more common.[2] St. Bernard, too, speaks of three stages[3] but also of seven effusions[4] and twelve degrees,[5] and other progressions[6] as well.

I would like to consider here, however, the three stages of the spiritual life as they are developed by St. Bernard with much imagery and intricacy in the first twelve sermons on the Song of Songs, as I believe the doctrine here is very characteristic of Bernard and brings out much of the spiritual richness of his entire corpus of spiritual doctrine.

THE THREE BOOKS OF SCRIPTURE

St. Bernard begins by assigning three Books of Scripture to three stages in spiritual growth. First, there is the *Book of Ecclesiastes*, which enlightens the mind and enables the reader to discover the vanity of worldly glory, to come to truth, to fear God and seek the observance of his commandments rather than human interests and earthly desires. Such fear is the beginning of true wisdom.[7] The *Book of Proverbs* goes farther. "Using the hoe of discipline, it grubs out whatever is corrupt in our morals and whatever is superfluous in the indulgence of the flesh."[8] It leads to good observance, to putting into practice the commandments of the Lord, and this is the consummation of wisdom, for "the only true and perfect wisdom consists in avoiding evil and doing good."[9] Having arrived at this state, we are ready to take in hand the *Song of Songs*, which is the book on holy contemplation. "Being the fruit of the preceding labors it should be entrusted only to sober minds and chastened ears."[10] The labors of a life of virtue having attained their end, we are now ready for the rest and repose of contemplation.

THE THREE KISSES

Inspired by the opening words of the Song of Songs,[11] St. Bernard then describes the three stages under the imagery of the kiss. He notes how apt is the image of a kiss, for it is the natural sign of peace and reconciliation, of oneness.[12] He develops in a rich theology the supreme analogate of his image, bringing out that the Kiss is the Holy Spirit, who unites the Father and the Son.[13] He is most properly the Kiss which unites the "mouths" of the Father and the Son. Again, under another aspect Bernard sees the Kiss to be Jesus Christ, the Mediator of God and man, who unites the "mouths" of the divinity and the humanity.[14]

Since, therefore, the Kiss of the mouth is the Spirit of God, what we aspire to is not the Kiss itself but rather the kiss of the Kiss: "Let him kiss me with the Kiss of his mouth." What we aspire to is union with Christ the Lord, with God, in the Holy Spirit. But we may not leap immediately to this intimate union. We must rather progress toward it through the three stages. These Bernard develops in his third and fourth sermons.

First there is the kiss of the feet. This is the beginning of the spiritual life: conversion and repentance:

> Let not the soul seek at once to reach the lips of his supreme Bridegroom but rather like me throw himself at once at the feet of his most dread Lord, trembling and with downcast eyes, like the publican not daring to lift his gaze to heaven.[15]

When we have persevered in our repentance, the divine hand reaches down to us, cleanses us and lifts us up. This is the second step: we, grateful to our benefactor, kiss his hand, and with this hand we do the works of justice.[16]

Even in these first two stages, St. Bernard points out, we have a certain "experience" of God, of the divine benevolence. Inspired by this, our confidence increases and we dare to ask for more, knowing that "everyone who asks receives." So we seek "the kiss of infinite condescension and indescribable sweetness."[17] Thus St. Bernard briefly traces out the three stages:

> You have seen the way we must follow, the order of procedure. First we cast ourselves at his feet, we "kneel before the Lord, our maker," deploring the evil we have done. Then we reach out for the hand that will lift us up, that will steady our trembling knees. And finally, when we shall have obtained these favors through many prayers and tears, we humbly dare to raise our eyes to his mouth, so divinely beautiful, not merely to gaze upon it, but—I say with fear and trembling—to receive his kiss; for

"Christ the Lord is a Spirit before our face." And he who is joined to him in a holy kiss becomes, at his good pleasure, one spirit with him.[18]

Lest anyone object to his anthropomorphism, Bernard, in his fourth sermon, enters upon a rather long excursus to defend God's complete simplicity and spirituality: "There is no doubt, 'God is a Spirit,' his simple substance cannot be considered to have bodily members."[19] However, pointing to Scripture for justification, Bernard goes on to affirm: "My contention is that God has a mouth by which 'he teaches knowledge,' he has a hand 'with which he provides for all living creatures' and he has feet for which 'the earth is his footstool.'" But God does not have these members by nature; rather, "they represent certain modes of our encounter with him."[20]

If we consider him in himself, "His home is inaccessible light . . . he has no need of bodily instruments . . . . Not merely does he know all things without a body's intervention but he also makes himself known to 'the pure of heart,' without the need for recourse to it" (a body).[21] It is only for the sake of us imaginative men that the Scriptures, and Bernard who is so completely inspired by them, have recourse to anthropomorphical analogy.

Having defended the absolute spirituality of God and justified the anthropomorphism of his imagery, St. Bernard goes on to develop this imagery further, tracing out more fully the dispositions proper to each stage of the spiritual life. First of all, for the feet: "These feet I consider to be justice and mercy." In particular he relates the feet with the sacred humanity:

> That the Lord has assumed the foot of mercy together with the flesh to which he is united is evident from the Epistle to the Hebrews. There we read that Christ was tempted in all things as we are, though he is without sin, that he might become merciful. As regards the second foot, which I take to mean justice, does not the Incarnate Word himself plainly imply that it too was assumed with and belongs to the humanity, when he declares that the Father has given him power to do judgment because he is the Son of God?[22]

These feet "walk through living souls, constantly illuminating them, and searching the hearts and the reins of the faithful."[23] And they make their impress. Their imprint upon the soul is hope and fear. This is the response of the soul, the kiss of the feet;[24] these are the dispositions most proper to the Christian starting out on the ways of the spiritual life. The beginner must ponder upon the divine judgment and justice, repent of his sins and be sorry for them. But lest the knowledge of his sins and the fear of God lead to despair, he must also look to the other foot, the foot of mercy, and lift up his heart in hope. In its turn this hope must be moderated by fear lest he settle in some false sense of security.

In bringing out this balance which is to be found even in the beginning of the spiritual life, Bernard appeals to his own experience:

> Even to me, miserable as I am, it has been given sometimes to sit at the feet of the Lord Jesus and to embrace with all devotion now one foot, now the other, insofar as his gracious mercy deigned to permit. But whenever, under the sting of my conscience, I lost sight of the divine mercy and clung a little too long to the foot of justice, immediately I became oppressed with an indescribable terror and a miserable confusion, and, enveloped in the most horrible darkness, I could only cry tremblingly: "From out of the depths, who knows the power of your anger and who for fear of you can endure your wrath?" Yet if, leaving the foot of justice, I should chance to lay hold of that of mercy, I straightaway grew more tepid at prayer, more slothful at work, more ready for laughter, more imprudent in speech. In short, my whole being, body and soul, showed evidence of greater inconstancy. Therefore, taught by experience, no longer judgment alone or mercy alone but both "mercy and judgment, I will sing to you, O Lord."[25]

When the divine goodness sees the monk at his feet repenting his sins and placing all his hope in the divine mercy, he reaches down with his hands to lift him up. St. Bernard speaks very briefly of these hands:

> I will speak not of one hand but of two, and will give to each its proper name. Let the one be called liberality, the other fortitude. With the former God gives abundantly, with the latter he protects what he has bestowed.[26]

And just as briefly he speaks of the monk's response, the kiss of the hands: "If we are not to be reputed ingrates we shall kiss both, acknowledging and proclaiming him not only as Author of all good, but as the Preserver of the same."[27] The hands of the divine liberality are operative in the soul of the Christian, strengthening it by renewing its vigor,[28] enabling it to perform all manner of good works. But the soul remains solely dependent upon its divine benefactor and therefore it is of the greatest importance to the soul that the Lord repent not his gift but give with it also the grace of perseverance.[29] The soul, steadfast now in good works, must readily recognize that this is the doing of the hands of God and not its own:

> Surely, in receiving the gifts you must not forget to kiss the hand of the giver; that is, you must readily recognize that this is the doing of the hands of God and not your own. Surely in receiving the gifts you will not

forget to kiss the hands of the giver, that is, you must give glory not to yourself but to his name.[30]

Thus the attitudes which mark the second stage are steadfast perseverance in virtuous action and humble praise and thanksgiving to the Lord.

Naturally, as one begins to appreciate more and more the overflowing goodness of God, there is the desire for an ever greater union with him. And thus the soul begins to say: "Let him kiss me with the kiss of his mouth." This is another aspect of the second stage, one of longing and desire, which leaves one unsatisfied and indeed even in suffering and pain. St. Bernard in describing it appeals to the experience of his listeners and indeed what he has to say will not be unfamiliar to many of us:

> Many of you, as I remember in the manifestations of conscience which you make to me privately, are wont to complain of this aridity and languor of soul, this heaviness and dullness of mind whereby you are rendered incapable of penetrating the profound and hidden things of God and can experience little or none of the sweetness of the spirit. What is that, my brethren, but a longing to be kissed?[31]

As the soul goes on in this stage, reflecting more and more on its experience of the divine goodness, it perceives that goodness more and more. This revelation of the divine, St. Bernard compares to the two breasts of the spouse and gives them the names of long-suffering and benignity. Looking back we realize how patient the Lord was with us as we went on our way as sinners, as he waited for us finally to come to embrace his feet in repentance and hope. And then we recall his wonderful goodness in readily accepting us and lifting us up and helping us when we did finally return to him.[32] As the soul realizes more and more this divine goodness, it experiences an ever growing desire for the final and full embrace of union with One so good, so lovable, and so loving.

And thus Bernard finally comes to the kiss of the Kiss of the mouth. It comes in the midst of much longing as something rather sudden and unexpected and sometimes even unrecognized. Here Bernard draws a comparison with Jesus joining the disciples on the way to Emmaus.[33]

As we have seen above, the Kiss of the mouth is the Spirit himself. The lips that we raise to God to be kissed are the intellect and the will: "his intelligence for understanding and his will for wisdom."[34] And as we receive the kiss of God, they are filled. For Bernard, the kiss of the Kiss of the mouth is nothing other than the indwelling of the Holy Spirit: "The kiss of the Kiss is that of which we read, 'for we have not received the spirit of this world but the Spirit that is of God, that we may know the things that are given us from God.' "[35]

Here Bernard makes an important distinction between two different modes of receiving the Kiss of the mouth, receiving the Spirit of God, receiving the divinity: "I say that he who receives the plenitude receives the Kiss of the mouth and he who receives of the plenitude receives the kiss of the Kiss." Christ, who could say: "I and the Father are One," is related with the Father as an equal, embraces him as an equal and "instead of soliciting a kiss from a lower level, as an equal he presses mouth to mouth; thus by a singular prerogative he receives the Kiss of the mouth."[36] Christ's kiss, then, is the plenitude and ours is a participation of it. We receive "the kiss of the Kiss." Yet, indeed, it is a very precious thing to participate in the divine Sonship. And here Bernard appeals once again to the witness of his monks' own personal experience:

> My brethren, is there among you one who sometimes in the depths of his heart hears the Spirit of the Son crying, "Abba, Father"? If such there be, let him feel assured of the love of the Father, for he has the testimony of his own conscience that he is led by the same Spirit as the Son. O soul who are such, whoever you are, have courage, have confidence, and fear nothing. In the Spirit of Christ you can recognize yourself as a child of the Father.[37]

THE EFFECT OF THIS KISS, OF THIS INDWELLING OF THE SPIRIT

The effects are manifold. "For the grace of the kiss communicates at once both the light of knowledge and the warmth of love.... We not only know God but also love the Father who without doubt is not fully known until he is perfectly loved."[38] Moreover, this union is fecund. It bears fruit, it produces spiritual richness, not only for the recipient but also for others and most especially for his brethren in the community. To use Bernard's image, as new life stirs within the soul, the breasts swell with spiritual milk. The monk is now able to bring sweetness into the lives of others through what Bernard calls "the two maternal affections, compassion and congratulation"; the ability to enter into and share the sorrows and the joys of our brethren, to console and to encourage.[39] Even the deep personal inner union of the soul with the Spirit is not meant for the soul alone but is to bear fruit for the brethren.

THREE OINTMENTS

Having discoursed at length through a whole series of sermons on the stages of the spiritual life under the imagery of the sign of love—the kiss—Bernard, inspired by his text, which goes on to speak of the breasts as "smelling sweet of the best ointments," recapitulates his doctrine briefly in speaking of three ointments.[40] They are the ointments of contrition, devotion, and piety.

The first is a pungent odor, made from our sins, crushed in the mortar of conscience and melted down and fused by a heart burning with sorrow and repentance. It is an ointment proper to the first stage, the ointment one uses to anoint the feet of the Lord, the ointment of Magdalen's tears. Yet it is not so mean and contemptible an ointment that it could not fill the whole house with a sweet fragrance. It is a fragrance that gives delight to all the courts of heaven—the conversion of a sinner.[41]

The second ointment is not made of anything of our own. It comes rather from the goodness and bounty of God and most especially the goodness of God, which is revealed to us in the Redemption of Christ Jesus. St. Bernard takes the opportunity here[42] to bring out again how contrition must be tempered by hope, to show how greatly God has loved us by the self-emptying of Christ and how this is for us a total cause for hope. Our minds have been deceived, but he, the Son, the Truth, comes to us. Our wills were agitated by passion, but he sends to us the Spirit of peace and love. Our memories have been forgetful of the divine goodness, but the Father, with his eternity and power, drives all forgetfulness away. This ointment of devotion, derived as it is from the redemptive goodness of Christ, is most properly poured out on our Head, who is Christ, in gratitude and love. It is the ointment proper to the second stage of spiritual growth:

> When these spices (the divine benefits bestowed on the human race) have been placed in the mortar of the breast and crushed and pounded under the pestle of frequent meditation and all fused together by the heat of holy desires and finally mingled with the oil of gladness, the result will be, without any doubt, an ointment far more precious and excellent than the first.[43]

But there remains a third ointment which far excels both of these. This Bernard calls the unguent of piety. It is closely associated with that sweetness of the breasts which we spoke of above, that ability to have the compassion of a mother because one has been filled with the love and understanding of the Spirit. And therefore it is proper to the third stage of the spiritual life, to a fullness when one can go out to others: "It is extracted from the necessities of the poor, the anxieties of the oppressed, the sorrows of the sad, the sins of the guilty—in a word, from all the miseries of the miserable, even of those who are enemies."[44]

St. Bernard brings forth from the Scriptures a whole litany of persons who exemplify this spiritual fullness: Paul, Job, Joseph, Samuel, Moses, David. But then with his accustomed affectiveness and true personalism he addresses himself immediately to his audience:

> You also, my brother, if you willingly share with us your brethren the gifts you have received from above, if you show yourself everywhere among us obliging, affectionate, grateful, obedient and humble, you also

shall receive the testimony of all that you too are redolent with the best of ointments. Yes, every one among you, my brethren, who not only supports with patience the corporal and spiritual infirmities of his brother, but, insofar as he is permitted and has power, assists him by kind services, comforts him by his words and directs him by his counsels, or, if the Rule will not allow for this, consoles the weak one at least by his fervent and incessant prayer—every such brother, I say, exhales a good odor in his community and smells sweet with the best ointments.[45]

THE CONTEMPLATIVE AND THE CHURCH

St. Bernard then transcends the bounds of his community. The other ointments were poured, one upon the feet, the other upon the head of Christ. But this ointment is meant to be poured out upon the whole body, and for Bernard, this is the whole Church.[46]

But some see a contradiction here in the life of the contemplative monk. Bernard speaks of it. Recalling something of his own personal experience:

Sometimes (if I may here digress a little) when prostrate and in tears at the feet of my Jesus, offering him, at the thought of my sins, the "sacrifice of my afflicted spirit," or when standing at his head (a grace more rare with me) and exulting in the memory of his benefits, I also have heard people complain and ask, "To what purpose is this waste?" They complained, I mean, that I was living for myself alone, when I might, as they supposed, be assisting many. "For this," they said, "could have been sold for much and given to the poor."[47]

St. Bernard's response to this challenge is a humble one. First of all he notes with the Scriptures: "What does it profit a man if he gains the whole world and suffers the loss of his own soul?" Then he takes refuge in an affirmation of his own weakness. What he is doing is a good work. For this he appeals to the testimony of the Lord. Let him continue in this good until he gets strength to do better.[48] And he goes on to call upon his brethren to reverence those who have undertaken the arduous toils of the active ministry and not to sit in judgment upon them even though they may occasionally fail in different ways: "He who labors for the good of people performs a more excellent, a more manly work. And if this cannot be done without some degree of iniquity, that is, without departure from strict regularity of life and conversation, you must bear in mind that 'charity covers a multitude of sins.' "[49]

Bernard then gives all who serve with full breasts and sweet smelling ointments, that is, with compassion and effective mercy, cause for humble consideration: "But which of us can spend even a single hour so justly and perfectly as not sometimes to grow unfruitful in speech or remiss in action?"[50] His answer is that of a most worthy son of the Church: "Yet, there is one who can make such a boast with all truth and justice. I mean the Church."[51] And then he goes on to bring out his deep understanding of what it means to be within the Church:

> In her universality the means are never lacking. . . . For what she lacks in one of her members she possesses in another according to the measure of the gift of Christ and the distribution of the Holy Spirit, "who bestows on each one according as he wills.". . . But although none of us, my brethren, would be so presumptuous as to dare to call his own soul the spouse of Christ, nevertheless, as we are members of the Church which rightly glories in this title and in the reality corresponding to the title, we at least may each claim a participation in that high prerogative. What we all possess collectively in a complete and perfect manner without doubt we also possess individually by participation.[52]

Finally, Bernard ends with a word of humble gratitude:

> Thanks to you, Lord Jesus, who have vouchsafed to number us among the members of your Church, not only that we might be your faithful servants, but also that as your spouses we might be united to you in the sweet and chaste and everlasting embrace of love and be admitted to contemplate the glory of your unveiled face. . . . [53]

Bernard, with all his uniqueness and unique eminence remained ever a community man, a true cenobite. For him even the greatest contemplative gifts, the deepest personal intimacy with God, found its context within and was even in some sense ordered to community, not only the local community of love but the greater community which is the Church. No Apostle ever lived and labored more for the whole Body of Christ, nor understood more deeply, nor expressed more beautifully what it meant to be a contemplative in the Church.

RECAPITULATION

Let us try then to recapitulate briefly the three stages that are traced out by St. Bernard in these first twelve sermons on the Song of Songs.

The first stage, that of conversion, which is guided by the wisdom of the *Book of Ecclesiastes*, is imaged in the kiss of the feet and the pungent odor of the ointment of contrition. It responds to the divine justice and mercy with fear and repentance and a lively hope.

The second stage, that of the active life (in the earlier sense of the term—the development of the virtues), which is guided by the wisdom of the *Book of Proverbs*, is imaged in the kiss of the hands and the ointment of devotion. It experiences the divine liberality and strength through reflecting upon God's long-suffering and benignity, above all in the redemptive goodness of Jesus Christ. It responds with perseverance in good works, humble gratitude and an intense longing for an ever deeper union, an ever fuller union with such goodness.

Finally, the third stage, that of the contemplative life, which is illuminated by the wisdom of the *Song of Songs*, is imaged by the kiss of the mouth and the ointment of pity and compassion. It delights in the experience of the indwelling Spirit with his infusions of understanding and love which overflow to all about us in encouragement, compassion and effective mercy, stretching out in concern to the whole Body of Christ.

NOTES

[1]It actually has roots in St. Paul who, although he more frequently contrasts simply the spiritual and the carnal (e.g. Rom. 7:14; 15:27; 1 Cor. 3:1; 9:11), introduces in 1 Thess. 5:23 the threefold: spirit, soul, body (*pneuma, psyche, soma—spiritus, anima, corpus*) which is taken up by Origen and others to speak of the spiritual, animal and carnal. (E.g., *In Epist. ad Romanos*, 1, 18; PG 14:866A; *De Principiis*, III, 4, 3; PG 11:323B). Origen employed other trilogies such as: faith, intelligence, wisdom (*pistis, gnosis, sophia—Contra Celsum*, PG 11:1309C). He had a profound influence on the later developments and this is true among the Cistercians (cf. e.g., J.-M. Déchanet's introduction to William of St. Thierry's *Exposition on the Song of Songs* in *The Works of William of St. Thierry*, vol. 2, CF 6 [Spencer, MA: Cistercian Publications, 1969]).

[2]E.g., St. Aelred, the three Sabbaths, *Mirror of Charity*, III, c. 1ff., trans. G. Webb and A. Walker (London: Mowbrays, 1962), pp. 62ff.; William of St. Thierry, three states of soul: animal, rational, and spiritual (*Exposition on the Song of Songs*, Preface, no. 13, CF 6:11) and again in his *Letter to the Brethren of Mont Dieu*, where he adds the equivalents of: beginners, progressors, and perfect (*The Golden Epistle*, 41; trans. T. Berkeley, *The Works of William of St. Thierry*, vol. 4, CF 12 [Spencer, MA: Cistercian Publications, 1971], p. 25).

In the same *Letter* he traces out spiritual growth in three degrees of likeness to God (for in this lies the perfection of man, the likeness to God): the natural likeness of spirituality, the voluntary likeness of goodness, and the likeness not named likeness but unity, immovably one with God in will (no. 260ff., CF 12:95). In his *Sixth Homily on the Blessed Virgin Mary*, Amedeus of Lausanne used the three meanings of Scripture: historical, moral, and mystical, as an analogue for the stages of spiritual growth, *Huit Homelies Mariales*, ed. J. Deshusses, Sources Chrétiennes, no. 72 (Paris: Cerf, 1960), VI, 137ff., p. 168; trans. Marie Bernard Said and Grace Periga, in *Magnificat, Homilies in Praise of the Blessed Virgin Mary by Bernard of Clairvaux and Amedeus of Lausanne*, CF 18 (Kalamazoo, MI: Cistercian Publications, 1979) p. 133. And finally we might indicate Isaac of Stella's threefold division in his *Letter on the Mass*: sacrifice of penance (marked by compunction), sacrifice of justice (marked by devotion), and sacrifice of understanding (marked by contemplation). (*Epist. de officio missae*, PL 194:1892).

[3]E.g., carnal, rational, and spiritual love (*Sermons on the Song of Songs* [hereafter Cant.] 20:9; trans. K. Walsh, *The Works of Bernard of Clairvaux*, vol. 2, CF 4:154f.); three apartments (Cant. 23:5; CF 7:20); threefold growth in charity: giving all for love, spontaneous love to all our neighbors, doing good to those who hate us (Cant. 27:10-11; CF 7:83f.); three degrees of truth: the labor of humility, the affection of compassion, the ecstasy of contemplation (*The Steps of Humility*, 4; CF 13:32f.).

[4]E.g., the sevenfold infusion of the Holy Spirit found in Sermon 18 on the *Song of Songs*. Bernard compares spiritual growth to the healing of a sick man: excision—compunction; ointment—devotion; joyous hope as one gains control over passions and sin; poultice—penance: watching, fasting, prayers; nourishment—meat: good works and doing the will of God; drink—prayer; rest—contemplation; dreams—God vaguely felt and apprehended in a passing way by an obscure and transient vision, the fullness of love. CF 4:137ff.

[5]E.g., the twelve steps of humility following St. Benedict (*The Steps of Humility*, CF 13:56ff.).

[6]E.g., the four stages of organic growth: the vine of faith, the branches of virtues, the grapes of good works, the wine of devotion (Cant. 30:6; CF 7:116); the four degrees of love (*On Loving God*, trans. Robert Walton, CF 13:115ff.).

[7]Cant. 1:2; CF 4:2.

[8]*Ibid.*

[9]*Ibid.*

[10]*Ibid.*

[11]"Let him kiss me with the Kiss of his mouth."

[12]Cant. 4:2, CF 4:22.

[13]Cant. 8:4, CF 4:47.

[14]Cant. 2:3, CF 4:9f.

[15]Cant. 3:2, CF 4:13f.

[16]*Ibid.*, no. 4, p. 19.

[17]*Ibid.*, no. 5.

[18]*Ibid.*, pp. 19f.

[19]Cant. 4:4, p. 23. The whole of Sermon 5 is also an excursus on the spirituality of God.

[20]*Ibid.*

[21]*Ibid.*, no. 5, p. 24.

[22]Cant. 6:6, pp. 35ff.

[23]*Ibid.*, no. 7.

[24]*Ibid.*, no. 8.

[25]*Ibid.*, no. 9, p. 37.

[26]Cant. 7:1, p. 38.

[27]*Ibid.*

[28]Cf. Cant. 4:4, p. 23.

[29]Cant. 3:3, p. 18.

[30]*Ibid.* no. 4, p. 19.

[31]Cant. 9:3, p. 55.

[32]*Ibid.* no. 5, p. 57.

[33]*Ibid.* no. 4, p. 56.

[34]Cant. 8:5, p. 48.
[35]*Ibid.,* no. 6, p. 49.
[36]*Ibid.,* no. 8, pp. 51f.
[37]*Ibid.,* no. 9:52.
[38]*Ibid.,* nos. 5 and 8, pp. 48 and 57.
[39]Cant. 10:1-2, pp. 61f.
[40]*Ibid.,* no. 4, p. 63.
[41]*Ibid.,* no. 5-6, pp. 63f.
[42]*Ibid.,* no. 7-8, pp. 65f.; Cant. 11:2, pp. 70f.
[43]Cant. 10:7, p. 65.
[44]Cant. 12:1, p. 77.
[45]*Ibid.,* no. 5, p. 81.
[46]*Ibid.,* no. 6, pp. 81f.
[47]*Ibid.,* no. 8, pp. 83f.
[48]*Ibid.,* p. 84.
[49]*Ibid.,* no. 9, pp. 84f.
[50]*Ibid.,* no. 11, p. 86.
[51]*Ibid.*
[52]*Ibid.*
[53]*Ibid.*

St. Bernard on Composing Liturgical Offices

Today with the universal adoption of liturgical pluralism, many find themselves called upon to utilize their talents in creating new offices. For such work undoubtedly many technical skills are needed. It will, therefore, usually be the work of a team. But experience shows that if a group is to be truly productive it must ordinarily crystallize around a single creative and ordering spirit which is usually incarnate in an individual—not necessarily the organizational leader of the group but the actual focal point of its activity.

All such creative genius must in some way be subjected to a discernment which will validate the authenticity of its insights. In creating a renewed liturgical expression Christians want among other things, and this certainly not the least, to be totally faithful to the Christian spirit and heritage.

St. Bernard once found himself in the position of a liturgical composer when he was called upon by the Abbot and monks of Montiéramey[1] to compose for them an office for the Feast of St. Victor.[2] In his reply to them, a relatively short letter, Bernard expressed some of the norms which should guide one in preparing a liturgical office. Without pretending that this letter presents an exhaustive answer or all embracing criteria, it yet can be very profitable to reflect on it.

Above all one is struck by Bernard's great reverence for the liturgical texts, a respect which flows from his reverence for the God in whose honor they are employed, for his saints, for the Church in whose name they are offered, and for her members, his brothers and sisters who must celebrate the office. Such reverence leads to great diffidence in the composer. "Fools rush in where angels fear to tread."

St. Bernard's Letter to Abbot Guy and the Monks of Montiéramey

To Guy, the Venerable Abbot of Montiéramey,
  and the holy Brothers who are with him,
From Bernard, their servant,
  that they might serve the Lord in holiness.

You ask me, my dearest Abbot Guy, and at the same time all your Brothers who are with you, that I write for you an office which you can solemnly recite or sing on the Feast of St. Victor, whose sacred relics are preserved in your midst. When I delay, you insist; when I make excuses, you urge me on, ignoring my embarrassment, even though it is fully justified. You enlist others to join in your request, as if anything could incline me to your will more cogently than your own desires. But indeed in considering this matter you ought to think not of your affection for me but rather of my place in the Church. In a matter of such importance it is not a friend that you are looking for but one who is learned and worthy, whose authority is greater, whose life is holier, whose style is more developed and whose work shows forth and is in keeping with true holiness.

Should the writings of one who is so insignificant among the people of God be read in the Churches? How little is my genius and eloquence that one should single me out to ask for texts of celebration and praise for him whom the heavens already hold to be praiseworthy and glorified. To want to add something to the heavenly praises is to detract from them. Not that men should fail to praise one who has been glorified by the angels, but in their celebrations anything savoring of novelty or frivolity would be out of place. There is room here only for the authentic and the traditional which edifies the Church and bears the stamp of her dignity. If something new is to be heard, because the situation requires it, I believe, as I have said, those things are to be used which will please the hearts of the hearers and be useful to them because of the dignity both of the expression and of the author. Furthermore, the texts must be clear, shining forth with unclouded truth, proclaiming justice, urging humility, teaching equity. They should bring forth truth in our minds, virtues in our action, crucify our vices, inflame devotion, and discipline our senses. The chant if it is employed should be quite solemn, nothing sensuous or rustic. Its sweetness should not be frivolous. It should please the ear only that it might move the heart, taking away sorrow and mitigating wrath. It should not detract from the sense of the words, but rather make it more fruitful. It is not a little blow to spiritual profit when more attention is paid to feats of voice than to the meaning of words.

This then is what ought to be heard in the Church and the kind of man the author ought to be. Am I such a man, and have I ever composed such things? And nevertheless, you come pounding on the door of my poverty, arousing me. If not because of your friendship, certainly because of your importunity, I have risen, according to the word of the Lord, to give you what you have demanded.[3] I have given you not what you really wanted, but what has come to my hand; what I could manage, and not what you wished. Basing myself on the facts found in the ancient life of the Saint which you sent me, I have dictated two sermons, using my own mode of expression. I have tried not to be tiresomely long. Then in regard to the singing I have composed a hymn in which I have sacrificed the meter in order that the meaning might stand out better. I have arranged twelve responsories and twenty-seven antiphons,[4] putting each in its proper place. There is also a responsory for the first vespers and, according to your custom, two short responsories for the feast, one for lauds and the other for vespers. For all this I demand my pay. I will not be without my reward. What? Whether you are pleased with it or not, that matters little, for I have given you what I have, therefore, give me my pay: your prayers.

NOTES

[1]The Abbey of Saint Peter, sometimes referred to as Montier-Ramey.

[2]A translation of this Office with an introduction can be found in CF 1:163-179. Jean Leclercq has studied it in "Saint Bernard Ecrivain d'après l'Office de Saint Victor" in *Revue Bénédictine* 74 (1964) 155-169; *Recueil d'Etudes sur Saint Bernard et ses Ecrits II* (Rome: Edizioni di Storia e Letteratura, 1966) pp. 150ff.

[3]Lk. 11:8.

[4]"Twenty-seven" is the reading in Mabillon, but the more common reading of "Thirty-seven" would seem to be the correct one. There are also manuscripts which read "Thirty-four." See Leclercq, *op. cit.*, p. 156.

The Influence of Bernard of Clairvaux on Thomas Aquinas

We commemorated in 1974 a goodly number of centenaries. Most were perhaps conscious of the seventh centenary of the death of St. Thomas Aquinas[1] and St. Bonaventure[2] and of the Council of Lyons. Cistercians thought of the eighth centenary of the passing of Peter II of Tarentaise,[3] one of the three canonized Cistercian saints. And there was another anniversary marked that year: the eight-hundredth anniversary of the canonization of Bernard of Clairvaux on January 18, 1174.[4]

The coincidence of anniversaries invited me to think of Bernard and Thomas together. But that was not the only incentive. When Thomas was stricken en route to the Council at Lyons he asked to be taken to the Cistercian Abbey of Fossanova and consciously chose it as his last abode in this world. His biographer tells us that as he arrived there he grasped the doorpost and quoted the psalm, "This is my resting place forever and ever; here I will dwell, for I have chosen it."[5] Thomas never spoke but *formaliter.* Here was a conscious, deliberate choice.

As he lay dying in the midst of the Cistercians, at their behest he gave a brief commentary on the Cistercians' favorite book of the Scriptures, the Song of Songs.[6] That which Bernard did all his life long, Thomas did in the end.[7]

A younger Thomas had cogently argued that there were three kinds of religious life: active, contemplative and apostolic (sometimes called mixed).[8] The latter, the apostolic, which passes on the fruits of contemplation, is the superior. Bernard would readily agree with this philosophy. For him, those who could only contemplate were weak souls, and he readily counted himself among them:

> There have been times, if I may digress a little, when as I sat down sadly at the feet of Jesus, offering my distressed spirit in sacrifice, recalling my sins, or again, at the rare moments when I stood by his head, filled with happiness at the memory of his favors, I could hear people saying: "Why this waste?"... But let those who accuse me of indolence listen to the Lord

who takes my part with the query: "Why are you upsetting this woman?" By this he means: "You are looking at the surface of things and therefore you judge superficially. This is not a man, as you think, who can handle great enterprises, but a woman. Why then try to impose on him a burden that to my mind he cannot endure? The work he performs for me is good, let him be satisfied with this good until he finds strength to do better." ... My brothers, ... let us admit that our powers are unequal to the task, that our soft, effeminate shoulders cannot be happy in supporting burdens made for men ... the man who helps many acts with more virile purpose, fulfilling a higher duty.[9]

But in the end Thomas saw that all his magnificent writings, which have passed on to us the fruit of his contemplation, were in final evaluation just so much straw.[10]

When one is truly introduced into the "inner chamber," then the best one can do is to be silent. And if a pastoral duty or fraternal charity demand that one speak and share, one might best comment on the divine love song.

How much the influence of St. Bernard on the life of Thomas had to do with all this it would be difficult indeed to establish. Ultimately they both had the same Master, the Holy Spirit. Yet we do know from his works that Thomas read Bernard with admiration and drew inspiration from him.

Through the centuries many have studied the conformity or the lack thereof to be found in the doctrine of Bernard and Thomas. In 1675 Bernard de Sayne published an extensive work: *Sapientium sanctorumque Doctorum Bernardi Melliflui ac Thomae Angelici doctrinae conformitas.*[11] Many monographs touching on particular points of doctrine have also been published.[12]

We find monastic authors making such blanket statements as "The doctrine of St. Thomas faithfully recapitulates the whole of the monastic middle ages,"[13] and "St. Thomas shows himself to be perfectly knowledgeable and a complete disciple of the traditional [monastic] teaching."[14]

In spirit these claims are certainly true, but many distinctions might be called for. Jean Leclercq—and no one knows Bernard better than this man who joyfully calls him his "friend"[15]—notes rightly that it is not fair simply to compare the doctrine of the two Saints. Over a century separates them and the theological insight of the Church ever grows and evolves.[16] However, I think we would all agree with Hayen that the doctrine of St. Bernard was a necessary part of the progress which made the theology of St. Thomas possible.[17]

Frankly, though, I do not think that comparative studies of doctrine or even of words and expressions can prove very much concerning the influence of Bernard or the dependence of Thomas. Wherever similarities occur they can usually be readily attributed to a common source. Take, for example, the two Saints' treatment of the nine choirs of angels.[18] Here they are in complete agreement. And yet there is little doubt that this is because they depend on a common source—Dionysius the Pseudo-Areopagite.[19] It might be significant that on an important question which received its definitive answer with Thomas, namely, that charity is an accidental quality, a virtue infused into the soul, and not the Holy Spirit himself,[20] Bernard differed from his friend, Peter Lombard,[21] in precisely the same way Thomas did later.[22] However, I do not feel that even here too much can be proved; and I am of the opinion that Bernard himself was influenced in this by his friend, William of St. Thierry.[23] The idea, certainly, was common enough.

In order to ascertain a clearer idea of the influence of Bernard on Thomas, I think we ought rather to survey the use Thomas makes of Bernard in his writings. Explicit references to Bernard are scattered throughout his works and actual quotations are many. In addition, editors do not hesitate in their notes to identify Bernard often enough among the "some," "others," "as the saints say," "it is accordingly said," etc.[24] In some cases, as for example in Thomas' *Opusculum, De dilectione Dei et proximi,* there is only one explicit quote, the opening line of the section, *De decem gradibus amoris.*[25] Yet this text sets the tone of the whole and Bernard's ideas can be seen surfacing constantly as Thomas develops the section. In other cases, as for example the *De humanitate Jesu Christi Domini nostri,* there are references to Bernard in almost every article, and quotations abound.[26] At the same time it is true that in not a few of his works, especially the philosophical ones, but also in such significant texts as the *Catena aurea,* Bernard's name does not appear.[27]

In this relatively short paper it would be impossible to survey all of Thomas' works. Therefore I would like first to look at his most significant work, the *Summa theologiae,* to see what it indicates, and then, as a control, to look at the *De veritate* to see if it confirms the conclusions drawn from the *Summa.*[28]

First, some statistics. I have been able to find in the *Summa* twenty explicit references to St. Bernard's writings.[29] In three of the instances, however, Thomas attributes the text quoted to other Fathers: Jerome, Gregory the Great, and Augustine[30]—Bernard certainly is in good company! There is another instance where Thomas attributes a text to Bernard which in fact belongs to William of St. Thierry.[31] Of the twenty citations there are three in the First Part, none in *Prima secundae,* ten in *Secunda secundae,* one in *Tertia Pars,* and six in the Supplement. Two of these citations are in the body of an article (in one of the two cases Thomas cites Bernard only to disagree with him), two are in *Sed contra's,* three in responses to arguments and thirteen in arguments at the beginning of an article.

These twenty citations are drawn from seven different works of St.

Bernard: three are from his collection of *Sermons for the Liturgical Year*, three from his *Sermons on the Song of Songs*, and fourteen from five of his eight *Treatises*: one each from *De gradibus humilitatis et superbiae*, *De diligendo Deo*, *De gratia et libero arbitrio*, three from *De praecepto et dispensatione* and seven from *De consideratione*.[32]

Now, what can be drawn from this? First of all I think it is significant what sources Thomas uses. More than two-thirds of his citations are taken from *Treatises*. Now in the critical edition of the Works of St. Bernard which has just been completed, the *Treatises* make up only one of the nine volumes, the *Sermons* comprise five volumes.[33] Thomas' interest clearly lies with what was Bernard's most formal theological work.[34] In addition, he turns most frequently to Bernard's most mature work, the *De consideratione*.[35]

Secondly, we note that Bernard is most frequently cited in the *Argumenta*. This indicates for one thing that Bernard was being frequently cited among the scholastics, that his writings were circulating and being read even outside the monastic circles.[36]

But it also indicates that Thomas in large part did not agree fully with the use the scholastics were generally making of Bernard as an authority. With his usual conservative and harmonizing genius he usually distinguishes, giving some plausible explanation to the words of Bernard, though frankly this sometimes seems to depart from what one would expect Bernard to have meant according to his own context.[37] In other cases, however, Thomas is substantially in agreement with Bernard.[38]

St. Thomas himself, as we have indicated, calls upon Bernard's authority only once in the body of an article,[39] in the *Sed contra* twice,[40] and three times in responding to arguments.[41]

Can we conclude anything from this? I think so. I believe there is indicated here that Thomas did not take Bernard too seriously as a theological source. Thomas' theological thinking was not significantly or extensively formed by his reading of the Abbot of Clairvaux. Bernard's extensive treatment of the Christian mysteries in his many *Sermons* is hardly represented; his critique of Abelard, his refutations of heresies in his Sermons on the *Song of Songs* are not mentioned. We know from his other works that Thomas not only knew of the existence of these writings but had at least some acquaintance with them. Yet he chose not to use them.

Let us turn now to the *De veritate*. What do we find here? The pattern is very similar. There are in all seventeen citations, if we include one drawn from the excerpts of Bernard's *Sermons* compiled by his former secretary and successor in office, Geoffrey of Auxerre.[42] None of these are found in the body of an article or in a response to an argument. Nine are found in arguments.[43] The remaining eight are in *Sed contra's*.[44] But in the *De veritate*

Thomas often responds also to the *Sed contra* to distinguish the teaching of the authority cited. He does this in three of our eight cases.[45]

The same pattern emerges here as in the *Summa*. Perhaps, too, we find here a candid expression of St. Thomas' general attitude toward Bernard as a theological authority. In question thirteen, article four, argument one, a text of Bernard's is brought forth in defense of the position that the sacraments are merely signs and not causes of grace. We know St. Thomas had very definite convictions on this point. The citation that is adduced here will be brought up by Thomas again in the *Summa*. It is the occasion where he brings Bernard into the body of his article only to disagree with him.[46] Here in the *De veritate* a younger Thomas seems to lose some of his ordinary "cool" and responds quite bluntly: "Bernard does not deal adequately with the nature of the sacraments of the New Law." I think Thomas might be somewhat annoyed here, not so much because a saint whom he reveres is being brought forth as an authority against a cherished position—that is not infrequent in the arguments—but because the citation is taken from a *Sermon*.[47] I think Thomas' response supports the conclusion that he does not really look to the *Sermons* of Bernard as theological sources offering authoritative teaching.

There is, however, one significant citation in *De veritate* which should not go unnoticed. It occurs in the first *Sed contra* of article two of question twenty-four. Here Thomas cites Bernard along with Damascene[48] as an authority for affirming that man is the image of God by virtue of his free will. Thomas does not say which work of Bernard's this comes from, but it does in fact come from a Sermon, Bernard's *First Sermon for the Feast of the Annunciation*.[49] Considering the importance that this basic insight plays in Thomas' later ordering of the *Summa*, this is worthy of note. There Thomas cites only Damascene;[50] here, in the earlier work[51] he acknowledges another source which later he may have forgotten or thought less of.

There is among the writings of St. Thomas that have come down to us one very positive expression of his admiration for St. Bernard—in fact it is grandiloquence—and that is the Sermon he prepared for the feast of St. Bernard.[52] Thomas says of the Abbot of Clairvaux:

> His mouth was a precious vessel, a golden mouth, a mouth adorned with gems.... It inebriated the whole world with a delicious wine.... Bernard was pure gold, such was his holiness; his noble deeds and his many virtues made him a cluster of gems. There were nine gems in this cluster, those of which Ezekiel spoke in his twenty-eighth chapter.... These stones which adorned Bernard signified the nine orders of angels, because he possessed the virtues and fulfilled the works of all the angelic orders....[53]

It is fitting that Thomas should have used the analogy of the nine choirs of angels. Not only is this a place where his doctrine does perfectly coincide with Bernard's, but in a very real sense, Bernard can be called the "Doctor of the Angels," so extensive is his treatment of them.[54] To appreciate fully what Thomas is saying of Bernard here we have to look at his summation of the virtues and offices of the angels in articles five and six of question one hundred and eight in the First Part of the *Summa*. Here Thomas speaks of the various orders of angels as:

—being full of strength and fortitude to receive divine movements and to accomplish all the divine work proper to them;

—being more richly endowed with divine communications, channeling them to others and leading them to higher things;

—strong and righteous in government, giving way to no servile acts nor to the influence of others;

—desirous for a participation in the true lordship of God;

—burning with charity in a continuous upward movement, unalteringly moving into God and being united with him while overflowing into subordinates and purifying them;

—having inextinguishable light, perfectly enlightening others and entering into the divine secrets;

—receiving a fullness of divine light and seeing in God the beautiful order of all things deriving from him and able to share this knowledge abundantly with others;

—and being steadily raised above earthly things, readily receiving God within themselves, then seeing immediately in God the reasons for the divine actions.

One could hardly give a richer or more exalted description of the contemplative. And this, Thomas, speaking *formaliter,* ascribed to Bernard in his concise tribute. Yet, note, there is included in this wonderful array of endowments no power of induction or deduction or theological reasoning. It is all a question of seeing, receiving, passing on, leading, enlightening, but never arguing, proving or disproving.

When the dying Thomas was asked by his hosts to "comment on the Song of Songs as Bernard did at Clairvaux," he replied, "Give me the spirit of St. Bernard and I will take up his commentary."[55] Would it be pushing our thesis too hard to see here a recognition on the part of Thomas that he and the holy Abbot of Clairvaux had received different charismata in service of the brethren? Thomas was to serve as a theologian, a teacher, a man who would relentlessly apply reason to faith and seek to demonstrate its reasonableness and orderliness. As long as it was his God-given work to construct his monumental *Summa,* he had to tend to that work. And in that task he would turn to Bernard only insofar as he was a contributing theologian or theological authority. But the day would come, and did come, when the love and admiration he had for Bernard and his contemplative way could be given full expression. It may be read as a historical accident that Thomas found himself at length in a Cistercian monastery, a filiation of Clairvaux, but Thomas knew too much about Divine causality to write it off as such: "...here I will dwell, for I have chosen it."

In the end perhaps he would agree with Châtillon: "It is evident that Thomas admired Bernard more as a saint than as a scholar, his persuasiveness more than his theology."[56] And this, in the end, is what he imitated, what truly influenced him.

What I am saying implicitly here is that when we do come to consider the question of influence, we cannot stop at doctrines and texts. Maritain called St. Thomas "the most existential of philosophers"[57] and Déchanet has said the same of Bernard.[58] The thinking of these men was never detached from what they were; indeed it profoundly influenced and enriched it. Bernard undoubtedly came into the life of Thomas as a formative influence quite early—if not before, certainly during his time at Monte Cassino. (We might recall here in passing that one of Thomas' last written words was a response to another Bernard, the Abbot of Monte Cassino.)[59] The deeper spiritual quality of Thomas' life because of this influence—certainly only one among many, but nonetheless one, and one of some significance—added quality to all his reasoning by a greater inflowing of divine light and a fuller functioning of the infused gifts and virtues. This dimension of the philosophic life, even when philosophy is understood in its modern scientific sense, is something that the Christian philosopher should best be able to understand and appreciate.

At this point, before finally concluding, perhaps succumbing to the temptation of wanting to seem to pass from the ranks of the weak "mere contemplatives" to the fruitful apostolics, I would like to add a practical word or two.

In our time there is widespread and well justified concern about our senior citizens. Their numbers are fast growing. Their vitality and longevity, thanks to the wonders of modern medicine, are on the increase. The challenge to make the remaining years meaningful for them stands squarely before each one of us as a personal concern and a shared social concern. Perhaps the example of St. Thomas gives us all, and in a very special way the philosophers, a key—the best key. The last years of life can be the richest, the fullest years—making all the wonderful things that went before (and who can begin to appreciate the writings of Aquinas sufficiently?) seem as straw. We can become Christian philosophers in the earlier sense of the expression—to be theologians—men and women who move from conceptualization and thought to love, to the love that is knowledge, to experience.

But do we need to wait until we are too old to do anything else before having some such experience and perhaps bringing some of its fruits into our own lives and the lives of others? God has created us free. As we have seen, both Thomas and Bernard affirm that in this freedom, most properly, we are created in his image. And no one respects our freedom as does the one who created it. In the final book of Revelation, Truth says: "Behold, I stand at the door and knock. And *if* a man open, I will come in and sup with him." *If* we open. We are free. He never pushes the door in. If we open, then Truth will share himself with us. And this Truth is Light—the Light of the world—and how it will illuminate our philosophizing!

NOTES

[1]† March 7, 1274.

[2]† July 15, 1274.

[3]† September 14, 1174.

[4]PL 185:619-628.

[5]Ps. 131:14. This is recounted by Bartholomew of Capua. See James A. Weisheipl, *Friar Thomas D'Aquino: His Life, Thought and Work* (Garden City: Doubleday, 1974) p. 326.

[6]*Ibid.*, pp. 326f.

[7]Already in the 1120s Bernard is recorded to be familiarly commenting on the Song of Songs with his friends; in 1135 he began his formal series of conferences which ended only with his death. Cf. PL 185:259; also *Sancti Bernardi Opera*, ed. J. Leclercq, C. H. Talbot, H. M. Rochais, 9 vols. (Rome: Editiones Cistercienses, 1957-), 1:xv.

[8]It is interesting to note that the Council Commission preparing the decree on religious life for the Second Vatican Council consciously set aside this threefold division so long employed in Church documents. It had been found in the first two schemata, but in the third there is a long explanatory note, affirming that there is in fact no such thing as a purely active life for religious; all religious are called to contemplation. For some this is the whole of their way of life; for others there is the call to pass on the fruits of their contemplation to others. *Relatio super schema emendatum propositionum de religiosis quod nunc inscribitur de accommodata renovatione vitae religiosae* (Vatican: Typis Polyglottis, 1964) p. 17.

[9]Serm. 12:8f., *On the Song of Songs*, *Opera* 1:65f., trans. K. Walsh, *Works of Bernard of Clairvaux*, vol. 2, CF 4, pp. 84f.

[10]After the mystical experience at Mass on December 6, 1273, Thomas left off all writing and gave himself up to a life of prayer and contemplation. When his beloved Reginald urged him back to work, Thomas replied: "... All that I have written seems like straw to me." A few months later, replying again to the insistent friend, Thomas again asserted, "All that I have written seems like straw to me," adding, "...compared to what has now been revealed to me."—Weisheipl, *op cit.*, pp. 321f.

11Mt. Hannon: Harvard, 1675. It was republished in 1706.

12To point out a couple of the earlier ones, there are the monographs of C. Briger, *Perenne Solstitum, Currus igneus,* and *Opera in hoc mundo non de hoc mundo,* and *Opera in hoc mundo de hoc mundo* (Crembsius: Praexl, 1731-1732) and later in the same century Honnat Göhl, *Schola humilitatis et charitatis ex S. Bernardi et D. Thomas opusculis collecta* (Augustae Vindelicorum: Rösl, 1793). Recently we have Hayen, *S. Thomas d'Aquin et la vie de l'Eglise* (Louvain, 1952) and E. Boissard, "La Doctrine des anges chez s. Bernard," in *Saint Bernard Théologien, Analecta S.O.C.* 9 (1953): 114-135.

13A. Louf in "Bulletin de Spiritualité Monastique," *Collectanea O.C.R.* 27 (1963): 90.

14C. Dumont, *ibid.,* p. 417.

15Leclercq has devoted some thirty years of study to Bernard in preparing the critical edition of his works, and has published three books and innumerable articles on him.

16J. Leclercq, "S. Bernard et la théologie monastique du XII siècle," in *St. Bernard Théologien,* p. 7.

17*Op. cit.,* pp. 5-22.

18*Summa Theologiae,* I, q. 108, aa. 5-6 for Thomas, and *On the Song of Songs.* Sermon 19, and *De consideratione,* V, iv-v, 7-12 for Bernard.

19*De coelesti hierarchia,* cc. 7ff., PG 3:205ff. They are both also indebted to Gregory the Great, Hom. 34, *In Evangelium,* PL 77:1249ff.

20*Summa Theologiae,* II-II, q. 23, a. 2.

21*Sententiarum,* I, d. 17, c. 1; QR 1:106.

22*De diligendo Deo,* 35; *Opera* 3:149. See "Two Treatises on Love," below, pp. 146-160.

23*Ibid.* See William of St. Thierry, *De natura et dignitate amoris,* 15, ed. M.-M. Davy, *Deux traités de l'amour de Dieu* (Paris: Vrin, 1953) p. 88.

24E.g., the Leonine editors of Thomas' *De veritate* point to Bernard in this way seven times: q. 8, a. 9 corp.; q. 22, a. 5 ad 7; q. 24, a. 1 ad 10, a. 4 corp.; q. 26, a. 6 arg. 8; q. 27, a. 4 corp.; and q. 29, a. 1 sed contra 2.

25"Ut dicit Bernardus, 'Magna res est amor,' sed sunt in eo gradus." *Sancti Thomae Aquinatis opera omnia,* ed. P. Fiaccadori (New York: Musurgia, 1950) 17:254.

26*Opera,* 17:185-234. In the first article alone there are eleven quotations from Bernard amounting to seventy-five lines of text in the Fiaccadori edition.

27His absence from the latter work is readily understandable. For there St. Thomas is largely using the Fathers of the Church, East and West, and Bernard was too close to Thomas to be considered, as yet, "the last of the Fathers." Also, Thomas was primarily using here those who wrote specific commentaries on the Gospels—something Bernard never did.

28For my purposes here I do not think it is necessary to distinguish the work of the editor of the Supplement from that of St. Thomas in the rest of the Summa; in fact it is helpful to have this broader sampling.

29I, q. 11, a. 4 sed contra; q. 51, a. 1 arg. 1; q. 83, a. 2 arg. 2; II-II, q. 14, a. 2 arg. 4; q. 24, a. 6 arg. 3; q. 25, a. 11 arg. 3; q. 27, a. 6 sed contra; q. 73, a. 4 corp.; q. 99, a. 3 ad 3; q. 162, a. 4 arg. 4; q. 180, a. 3 arg. 3, ad 1; a.v 4 arg. 2; III, q. 62, a. 1 corp; Supple. q. 4, a. 2 ad 3; q. 8, a. 4 arg. 5; q. 11, a. 1 arg. 1; q. 96, a. 6 arg. 3, ad 12; q. 98, a. 2 arg. 1.

30II-II, q. 24, a. 6 arg. 3 (Gregory); q. 25, a. 11 arg. 3 (Augustine); q. 99, a. 3 ad 3 (Jerome).

[31]II-II, q. 24, a. 12 arg. 2. The reference is to William's *De natura et dignitate amoris*, 6 (PL 184:390). Thomas cannot be blamed for this. Shortly after Bernard's death the two treatises on love written by his intimate friend: *De contemplando Deo* and *De natura et dignitate amoris*, passed under the name of Bernard (as was the case of others of his writings). They formed a trilogy with Bernard's own *De diligendo Deo* and were often considered one threefold work on love. The doctrine is very similar, but they have their differences, too. See my article, cited above, note 22.

[32]There might be some argument here. There is one text which seems to me to come from *De consideratione*, but some editors attribute it to *De gratia et libero arbitrio*. Thomas himself attributes it to the *Sermons on the Song of Songs*, which does not seem to be the case.

[33]*Opera* cited above in note 7. The Treatises are vol. 3 (1963). The first two volumes are the *Sermons on the Song of Songs*; vols. 4 and 5 are the *Sermons for the Liturgical Year*, and vol. 6, a double volume, has Bernard's *Occasional Sermons*. There is also a volume of *Sentences* and *Parables*, which are also sermon material (vol. 7) and two volumes of *Letters* (vols. 8-9).

[34]This is not to say there is not some very real theological writing in Bernard's other works. His critique of Peter Abelard is in a *Letter*, and his refutation of Gilbert of Porrée is found in *Sermon 80 on the Song of Songs*. But there is much positive theological teaching also.

[35]The *De consideratione* was written in 1147/8-1152/3, the last of his *Treatises*. Only some of the *Sermons on the Song of Songs* were produced after this.

[36]See Jean Châtillon, "L'influence de s. Bernard sur la pensée scholastique au XII et au XIII siècle," in *Saint Bernard Théologien*, pp. 268-288. In the course of his extensive research in preparation of the critical edition, Leclercq found not less than 111 mss. of Bernard's *Sermons on the Song of Songs*, dating from the twelfth and early thirteenth centuries. (*Opera*, 1:ix), 69 of *De gradibus humilitatis et superbiae* (*Opera*, 3:5), 60 of *De diligendo Deo* (*Opera*, 3:112), 57 of *De gratia et libero arbitrio* (*Opera*, 3:158) and more than 70 of *De consideratione* (*Opera*, 3:381). This, of course, being eight centuries later, represents only a fraction of those that must have been in existence at the time of St. Thomas. Bernard was the number one "best seller" of the twelfth century, and this carried over into the thirteenth.

[37]E. g., Thomas' response to argument one of article one, q. 51, *Prima Pars*, concerning the angel's need for a body. See E. Boissard, art. cit. (note 12).

[38]This is most evident in Suppl. q. 96, a. 6 where the text used in arg. 3 is used by Thomas in his response to arg. 12.

[39]The citation is not that significant. It is in a moral question in *Secunda secundae*: "Detrahere vel detrahentem audire quid horum damnabilius sit, non facile dixerim."—II-II, q. 73, a. 4, from *De Consideratione* II, xiii, 22.

[40]One instance is in the case of charity: whether God is to be loved for his own sake (II-II, q. 27, a. 6); the other is in relation to the unity of the Trinity (I, q. 11, a. 4).

[41]In one of these instances it is under the name of Jerome (II-II, q. 99, 2. 3 ad 3); none of the contributions are substantive.

[42]*Declamationes de colloquio Simonis cum Jesu ex S. Bernardi sermonibus collectae*, PL 184:437-476.

43Q. 13, a. 3 arg 5; q. 21, a. 6 arg. 12; q. 22, a. 6 arg. 6; q. 24, a. 1 arg. 11; a. 4 arg. 8; a. 8 arg. 5; a. 10 arg. 15; q. 27, a. 4 arg. 1; q. 28, a. 1 arg. 9.

44Q. 10, a. 11 sc 3; q. 18, a. 1 sc 2; q. 22, a. 5 sc 2, 4; q. 24, a. 2, sc 1; q. 28, a. 3 sc 2; q. 28, a. 8 sc 6, 8.

45Q. 22, a. 5 sc 2 and 4, q. 28, a. 8 sc 6.

46III, q. 62, a. 1.

47*In cena Domini* 2, *Opera* 5:69.

48*De fide orthodoxo* 2:12, PG 94:920B.

49Par. 7, *Opera* 5:19.

50*Summa,* II-II, Prol.

51The *De veritate* was written 1256-1259, the *Prima secundae* about ten years later.

52*Sermones D. Thomae de Aquino Doctoris Angelici* (Rome: J. Accaltum, 1571), fol. 134. Weisheipl does say: "Research on Thomas' sermons has not progressed enough to assert which sermons published under his name are authentic. These sermons cannot be determined from the catalogues, but only from the MSS, a work now undertaken by Bertrand Guyot, O.P., for the Leonine Commission."—*op. cit.,* p. 403. But the *Sermon for the Feast of St. Bernard* is listed by P. Mandonnet and J. Destrez, *Bibliographie thomiste* (Ke Saulchoir, 1921), p. xvii, and M. Grabmann, *Die Werke des hl. Thomas von Aquin,* 3 ed. (Munster, 1949) seems to accept it without question.

53This excerpt can be found in PL 185:629.

54His most formal doctrine on the angels is to be found in *De consideratione,* V, iv-v, 7-11, and *On the Song of Songs,* Serm. 19.

55See A. Forest, "S. Bernard et S. Thomas," in *Saint Bernard Théologien,* p. 310.

56Jean Châtillon, *op. cit.,* p. 284: "Visiblement il (St. Thomas) admire en lui (Saint Bernard) plus le saint plus que le docteur, et son éloquence plus que sa théologie."

57*Sort de l'homme,* p. 72

58J.-M. Déchanet, "Aux sources de la pensée philosophique de s. Bernard," in *Saint Bernard Théologien,* p. 57.

59This was written in early 1274 after he had had his extraordinary mystical experience and had left off work on the *Summa.*

William of St. Thierry

Abbot William of St. Thierry

In 1971 we had the joy of marking the 1000th anniversary of the coming of the Benedictines to St. Thierry, a joy that was greatly increased by the fact that Benedictines were once again living in full their traditional life of liturgy and *lectio*, labor and love on the Mount of Hor. By a very happy inspiration, the good nuns, with their friends in the city of Reims, decided to mark the centenary by calling upon collaborators from many lands to help prepare an exhaustive study of the "Land of St. Thierry," one that would not only recount facts and figures, but would seek to bring to life for us today the great monks of the past and the vibrant spirituality that made St. Thierry the home of saintly men.

It was my privilege to be invited from the distant shores of America and from William of St. Thierry's adopted Order, the Cistercians, to join in this task. Quite naturally my main interest was in the second part of the undertaking. The history of St. Thierry was divided into three parts. The first considered the sources and the earlier history of the abbey; the third, its later history; but the second centered upon the person who was called to rule the abbey in its greatest hour and to extend its influence widely in the monastic renewal of the twelfth century: Abbot William. Nine scholars from almost as many countries accepted assignments to study this man and his work, the influences on him and the influence he brought to bear on others. In large measure this great spiritual master has been too hidden, much by his own choice, in the shadows of his great friend, Bernard of Clairvaux. Now he is beginning to emerge.

To indicate this, let me recount briefly the work that has been done just in the last few years. Five doctoral studies have been completed. What is especially striking about them is the wide variety of approaches taken by the authors; the study of William is truly interdisciplinary. At the Catholic University of America, the Jesuit, Father Louis Savary, wrote on the *Psychological Themes in the Golden Epistle,* and his study has been published in Munich. Father Stanislaus Ceglar, a Salesian from Yugoslavia, reexamined the chronology of William's life and came up with some challenging new dates which he has published along with his study of William's treatise, *On the Nature and Dignity of Love,* and some other minor works, considered from the point of view of language and literature. He has also established William's authorship of the *Reply to Cardinal Matthew of Albano,* emanating from the Chapter of Benedictine Abbots held at Reims in 1132. At the same university, John Anderson did a study and translation of William's *Enigma of Faith,* collating the standard manuscript Charlville 114, with a later one recently discovered by Father Jean Leclercq in the State Library at Upsala, Sweden.

Thomas Tomasic, a philosopher, presented a brilliant thesis at John Carroll University (Cleveland) on the modes of intersubjectivity in the thought of William of St. Thierry. In the same year, Dr. E. Rozanne Elder, the Director of the Institute for Cistercian Studies, defended her theological study of William's Christology before the faculty of the University of Toronto.

Each year, at the Cistercian Studies Conference sponsored by the Institute for Cistercian Studies at Western Michigan University (Kalamazoo) a section is dedicated to William, and many interesting papers have been presented. The Institute and Cistercian Publications, out of which it has developed, have sponsored several International Cistercian Studies Symposia at which William has been well represented. The most significant was that at Oxford University (England) in August-September, 1973, where three papers on William were presented. Cistercian Publications has been publishing the papers from these Conferences and Symposia in its Cistercian Studies Series. In this same Series an English translation of Déchanet's pivotal work, *William of Saint Thierry: the Man and His Work,* has also appeared. Cistercian Publications has also been publishing the writings of William in new English translation with introductions, notes and indexes. Six volumes have already appeared, including: *On Contemplating God, Prayer, Meditations, Exposition on the Song of Songs, Mirror of Faith, Enigma of Faith, Commentary on the Epistle to the Romans,* and the *Golden Epistle.*

A translation of William's treatise *On the Nature of the Body and the Soul* appears in a volume of collected works on Cistercian anthropology. Professor John Cummings is preparing an edition of William's treatise, *On the Nature and Dignity of Love,* as a basis for a translation. Professor David Bell published a translation of the *Ancient Life (Vita Antiqua)* of William in *Cistercian Studies.* Thanks to the availability of these new translations, William is being widely read and studied in America today.

My concern here is primarily with William as abbot of St. Thierry. But let us delineate our subject even further. St. Thierry was a Benedictine abbey, and Benedict of Nursia had laid down a rather detailed description of the physiognomy of the Benedictine abbot:

An abbot...is believed to hold the place of Christ in the monastery...his commands and his teachings should be a leaven of divine justice kneaded into the minds of his disciples...he ought to govern his disciples with a twofold teaching...showing them all that is good and holy by his deeds even more than by his words, expounding the Lord's commandments in word to the intellectual among his disciples, but demonstrating the divine precepts by his action for those of harder hearts and ruder minds. ... Let him make no distinction of persons...show equal love to all and impose the same discipline on all according to their deserts .... In his teaching the abbot should always follow the Apostle's formula: "Reprove, entreat, rebuke.".... Let him not shut his eyes to the faults of offenders. ... He should always remember who he is and what he is called...and understand what a difficult amd arduous task he has undertaken, ruling souls and adapting himself to a variety of characters.... Let him not neglect or undervalue the welfare of souls committed to him in a greater concern for fleeting, earthly, perishable things. (Chapter 2) His duty is to perfect his brethren rather than to preside over them. He must therefore be learned in the divine Law, that he may have a treasure of knowledge from which to bring forth new things and old. He must be chaste, sober and merciful. Let him exalt mercy above judgment .... In his commands let him be prudent and considerate...discreet and moderate...and temper all things so that the strong may have something to strive after, and the weak may not fall back in dismay. And especially let him keep this Rule in all its details. (Chapter 64)[1]

It is an ideal which William tried to live up to, albeit somewhat reluctantly, and as best we can judge he was quite successful. Our sources for making this judgment are fortunately many.

First of all, we have William's own writings which either date from the period of his abbatial service or directly or indirectly reflect his thoughts and attitude during that time. William was a very pure soul, candid and very open, and quite ready to share his struggles as well as his more beautiful experiences. This undoubtedly is one of the reasons why he is so popular today. There is good reason to believe that his very rich and personal presentations which we have in his various treatises are in substance chapter talks which he earlier gave to his brethren at St. Thierry. I think this can be said of both his treatises *On Contemplating God* and *On the Nature and Dignity of Love*. His treatise *On the Nature of the Body and the Soul*, as well as his *Commentary on the Epistle to the Romans* are frankly composed of borrowings from others, as are the *Commentaries on the Song of Songs* drawn from St. Gregory and St. Ambrose. What is significant in these is the choice of texts, the ordering and the conclusions drawn. I believe that these, too, substantially served as bases for chapter talks. The *Meditations*, while finally actually edited for publication at Igny, were in part drafted at St. Thierry and are revealing of William's inner life during the time of his abbacy. In addition we have the *Brief Commentary on the Song of Songs*, a number of his letters, the *Vita Antiqua*, the *Chronicle of Igny*, the records of the Chapter of Reims, his *Reply to Cardinal Matthew*, written for the Chapter, and some letters written to him, most notably those from his friend, Bernard of Clairvaux. Few men of that now distant century are so completely revealed to us, even though we lack certainty about such fundamental facts as the year of his birth and of his death. Maybe this lack of chronology is a providential indication that William, like his teaching, belongs to all times and is always relevant in the deepest sense of the word.

I think it can be asserted that William, even as a Benedictine abbot, shared much in common with his great Cistercian contemporaries. This similarity in teaching and life, as well as the formative role his writings have had on successive generations of Cistercians, rightly place him among the "Four Evangelists of Citeaux." At the same time the influence which the Abbot of St. Thierry had both directly and indirectly through his friend at Clairvaux, on the renewal of Black Benedictinism in the twelfth century cannot be minimized.

William of St. Thierry's final and uncompleted work was a labor of love, a biography of his beloved and revered friend and master, Bernard of Clairvaux. In the first book of the *Vita Prima*, William candidly and enthusiastically expresses his admiration—one could almost say "adoration"—for Bernard. But as he pens his portrait of the abbot, the ideal abbot, I think we can say he is describing for us in substance an ideal which he truly made his own and quite successfully brought into being in his own life at St. Thierry. In a word, he has let us see the Abbot of St. Thierry in the Abbot of Clairvaux:

> His great desire was for the salvation of all mankind and this has been the greatest passion of his heart.... All the time there is a conflict in his heart between his great desire for souls and the desire to remain hidden from the attention of the world, for sometimes in his humility and low esteem of himself he confesses that he is not worthy to produce any fruitful increase for the Church, while at other times his desire knows no bounds and burns so strongly within him that it seems nothing can satisfy it but the salvation of all mankind, and so it was that his love for God and his creatures gave rise to an unfailing trust and faith in God, although this too was held in check by his humility.... It became increasingly obvious that the Spirit spoke in and through him, giving added force to his words and deepening his understanding of the Scriptures. For his hearers his words took on more authority and became more a delight to hear. And towards the brethren who were spiritually needy

and weak and those doing penance for the pardon of their sins, his dealings grew in wisdom and understanding.... His brethren became for him a great joy, and with them he shared his delight in the fruitful results of his entry into the monastic life.... One could follow his perfect example of how life should be led in complete and loving conformity with the Rule as he organized his monastery and took part in all its many activities. He was indeed building a dwelling place for God on earth.... He learned to consider the weak and feeble by sympathizing in their weaknesses...for others he was full of tenderness and care, but paid no attention to his own well-being. He was a model of obedience in all things.... Both by day and by night he prayed in a standing position...he scarcely ever excused himself from taking part in the common exercises of the community either during the day or the night, and only occasionally was he forced to forego the fulfillment of the obligations and tasks belonging to the office of abbot.... Never did he leave unfinished because of his infirmity any task which he could finish with the help of the grace the Lord gave him.... By his word and his example he attracted countless men from the world and its ways, not only to a new life but even to perfection.[2]

The wise, beautiful, simple but sublime teaching of this blessed abbot still attracts, encourages and leads countless people, both in the cloister and outside, to the true fulfillment of man, a deep, loving union with God in Christ.

NOTES

[1]*St. Benedict's Rule for Monasteries*, tr. Leonard J. Doyle (Collegeville, MN: The Liturgical Press, 1968).

[2]*S. Bernardi Vita Prima,* Liber I, cc. vii-viii, PL 185:245-252, tr. Geoffrey Webb and Adrian Walker, *Saint Bernard of Clairvaux,* (Westminster, MD: Newman Press, 1960) ch. xii-xv, pp. 53-67.

Abbot William
Spiritual Father of St. Thierry

In their study of the fourteen hundred years of the history of the Abbey of St. Thierry, scholars seem to agree that the hour of glory for the monastery on Mount Hor coincides with the fourteen years that William of Liège sat in the abbot's chair.[1] If we were to ask William what he considered to be his greatest achievement during those years, his response would be a personal one, a subjective one. All his writings prepare us for this. He would say that the most important thing he did during those years was to become a contemplative, a man, a monk who "truly sought God."[2] If we pressed him further, and asked what he thought was his greatest achievement precisely as *abbot*, I think he would reply, "To have opened the contemplative life to my monks."

As historians we might have answered the question for William differently, perhaps giving an answer which we would think to be more objective. Most would probably point to his leadership at the Benedictine reform chapters as his greatest achievement, or the whole of his activity in fostering monastic renewal.

But if we reflect a little more, we would perhaps see the validity of William's answer (or my guess as to what would be his answer). For, behind all that William accomplished at home and abroad was his own personal monastic *conversatio* with its depth and quality of contemplative understanding and life.

St. Thierry reached a moment of great significance in the first half of the twelfth century because it was blessed at that time with a great abbot, an abbot after the heart of St. Benedict. William sketched his image of the ideal abbot and abbey in his *Life of Saint Bernard*.[3] It clearly reflects the ideal depicted in Benedict of Nursia's *Rule for Monasteries*.[4] It undoubtedly proclaimed the ideal toward which the dedicated and energetic abbot of St. Thierry guided his own life and that of his abbey. If St. Thierry reached a pinnacle of greatness at that period it was because its holy abbot was striving to help it become all that it should be as a Benedictine abbey. He was truly moving with the grace of his vocation. He was heeding the Master's words: "Your heavenly Father knows all your needs. Set your hearts on his kingdom first, and on his righteousness, and all these other things will be given you as well."[5]

A LITERARY HERITAGE

It is possible to marshal a certain number of historical facts concerning the life of William of St. Thierry and his abbatial rule. Very capable historians have been doing this for us. And these facts do give us some indications as to the kind of man, monk and abbot William was.[6] Yet the image they portray for us would remain fairly hollow if we could not gain access to his thought, and above all, to his spirituality. We are indeed fortunate, especially when we consider the paucity of manuscripts in the tradition, that we do have in our hands today so many of William's spiritual writings.

I would see this as a special disposition of a very benign Providence who knew not only the great need of our times but also how exceptionally well the very personal, open, and existential writings of the Abbot of St. Thierry would respond to our needs. Without hesitation the seeker of the late twentieth century could turn to these writings and find in them a very relevant and helpful guide and spiritual master. We, too, can turn to them in our quest to learn how William so efficaciously fulfilled his primary task as abbot—to teach his monks.[7] And also how he himself strove to live. For, what Gregory the Great said of St. Benedict is no doubt equally true of William: "Anyone who wishes to know more about his life and character can discover in his Rule (his writings) exactly what he was like as an abbot, for his life could not have differed from his teaching."[8]

There are differences among the scholars in dating the various writings of William.[9] Yet there is fairly common agreement as to which of them come from or reflect his years as abbot of St. Thierry. Unfortunately we do not have any of Abbot William's chapter talks, nor do we have any letters or diaries or journals that reveal to us the content of these talks or the nature of his spiritual direction as abbot. But I am convinced that his early treatises do reflect his conferences to his community,[10] and his writings reveal something of how he viewed his role as abbot.

SPIRITUAL ITINERARY

We can, I believe, trace William's own spiritual itinerary through his writings. Around the year 1119 he paid his first visit to Clairvaux.[11] It was for him a profound experience which had a lasting effect on his life, as we can easily see by the way he wrote of it some thirty years later.[12] It was in a way a conversion experience and came on the eve of another great change in his life, his election as abbot of St. Thierry. Coming into contact with a man who so uniquely embodied the contemplative ideal of the Christian tradition, William's thoughts and aspirations turned in that direction. These found expression in his earliest extant treatise, *On Contemplating God.*[13] At the heart of this contemplative experience is love, and so this, too, had to be explored, the task of his second work, *On the Nature and Dignity of Love.*[14] Both of these came from the first years of William's abbatiate, as did probably the *Prayer*[15] and some of the *Meditations*[16] or the notes on which they were based.[17]

These early years as abbot were blessed with illness, something not uncommon in the careers of zealous young abbots. I say blessed, and singularly so in William's case, because it gave him not only the opportunity to reflect and pray, but in his particular case, to lie side by side with Bernard of Clairvaux, cementing a friendship and enlivening a mystical ideal.[18] The fruit of this is first perceived in the *Brief Commentary on the Song of Songs.*[19] But before the seeds sown at that time would fully blossom they would be fertilized by other sources.

In the meantime, William's total zeal for righteousness would make demands on him and not allow his talent as a theologian, undoubtedly developed earlier in the schools, to lie completely fallow. A trace of possible heresy concerning the Eucharist came to his attention and evoked, to our benefit, his treatise *On the Sacrament of the Altar.*[20] This treatise, along with the related *Letter to Rupert*[21] and the dedication to St. Bernard[22] affords us a number of important insights into the Abbot of St. Thierry as a spiritual father. The loving care and concern and affection he showed toward Rupert even as he corrected Rupert's errors, demonstrates a remarkable combination of zeal for truth and reverence for persons. The prologue addressed to Bernard is an eloquent witness to the humility of the teacher at St. Thierry.

It was the theologian in William that made him grapple also with the question of predestination and grace and free will;[23] it was the fullness of Christianity, his firm grasp on the incarnational principle—that spirituality subsists only in a man of body and soul—that called forth his study *On the Nature of the Body and the Soul.*[24] This work is a creative compilation, as are, of course, his commentaries on the Song of Songs drawn from Gregory the Great[25] and Ambrose of Milan.[26] While all of these may well have been set down on parchment at Signy, they most probably represent work which was undertaken while William was still abbot[27] and which informed and enriched the teaching he offered his monks.

William's own *Exposition on the Song of Songs*[28] undoubtedly belongs to the leisure found at Signy, when all this previous study of the Fathers blossomed forth in his own creation. However, this work, like all the others of later date, does throw oblique light back on the earlier days. Allowing always for the maturing that came from leisure, prayer, sharing, and controversy, the synthesis of the *Golden Epistle*[29] and the ideal of the *Vita*

Prima cannot be untrue to what William sought to teach the monks of St. Thierry by word and example in all the years he served them as their spiritual father.

To Seek His Face

My concern here is to indicate something of the way William traced out for his men as their spiritual father—how he fostered that spiritual life which was at the heart of St. Thierry's greatness in its golden hour. William was very conscious of a divine call to serve his monks as spiritual father. Again and again in his writings he speaks of his willing reluctance to put aside his own leisure and enjoyment of the delights of contemplation in order to serve his sons and lead them into those same delights.[30]

The path he sought to trace out for his followers and along which he strode is illumined by the face of God. This expression, drawn especially from the Psalms,[31] is central and constant in his spiritual writings.[32] Its meaning and significance are perhaps most fully and concisely developed in the third of William's *Meditations*, those soliloquies which he considered apt "for forming novices' minds to prayer."[33] By God's grace William finds himself drawn in this safe and sure way of life and points it out to his readers:

> I seek your face, by your own gift I seek your countenance.... I know indeed and I am sure that those who walk in the light of your countenance do not fall but walk in safety, and by your face their every judgment is directed. They are the living people, for their life is lived according to that which they read and see in your face, as in an exemplar.[34]

What precisely does William mean when he speaks of seeking the face of God? What is he looking for, to what way is he pointing? He himself in the same *Meditations* asks this question: "By your almightiest goodness, Lord, I pray you, by your most tender patience toward us, yield something to my quest, and tell my soul what she desires when she seeks your face."[35] And in response we hear that the Triune God, through the Holy Spirit, "reveals himself to any friend of God on whom he would bestow especial honor," so that he sees God "as the Father sees the Son, or the Son the Father...but not in every way the same."[36]

There is a trace of the apophatic in William's teaching: "...Reason cannot see God except in what he is not.... What, indeed, can reason grasp, however hard it may try, of which it dare say, 'This is my God'? It can discover what he is only by inferring from what it knows him not to be.[37]... That knowledge is best known in this life by unknowing; the highest knowledge that a man can here and now attain consists in knowing in what way he does not know."[38]

Yet, essentially, William's way is a way of light, filled with illuminating grace. As William immediately went on to say in this same *Meditation*:

And yet, O Lord, though you have made the darkness of our ignorance and human blindness the secret place that hides your face from us, nevertheless, your pavilion is round about you, and some of your saints undoubtedly were full of light. They glowed and they gave light, because they lived so close to your light and your fire. By word and example they kindled and enlightened others, and they declared to us the solemn joy of this supreme knowledge of you, for which we look hereafter, when we shall see you as you are, and face to face. Meanwhile, through them the lightnings of your truth have illumined the world, and flashes have shown forth that rejoice those whose eyes are sound; although they trouble and perturb those who love darkness rather than light.[39]

William not only wanted to have "sound eyes," he wanted to be and was one of those saints "full of light" who "kindled and enlightened others."

William speaks beautifully, with much feeling, about the human face of God, the face of Christ Jesus.[40] He was certainly one with St. Bernard in his tender devotion to the Passion of Christ,[41] and in his own way a precursor of that devotion to the Sacred Heart[42] which later Cistercians would be led to develop.[43] Meditation on the Passion was important in William's teaching, especially for the beginner in his efforts to control his many thoughts— a kind of plague of flies that erupts into one's eyes and almost drives one out of his house.[44] In his very practical advice on this matter William tells how one is to call to mind and summon to his aid those thoughts that he has drawn out of the Savior's wells.[45]

Yet, like the other Cistercian Fathers,[46] William is quick to quote St. Paul: "Even if we did once know Christ in the flesh, that is not how we know him now."[47] If we, "attracted to the human form of him who is one Person with the Son of God, develop a sort of carnal devotion, we do not err."[48] For, as William "confidently asserts" in speaking to the Lord:

It was not the least of the chief reasons for your incarnation that your babes in the Church, who still need your milk rather than solid food, who are not strong enough spiritually to think of you in your own way, might find in you a form not unfamiliar to themselves. In the offering of their prayers they might set this form before themselves, without any hindrance to faith, while they are still unable to gaze into the brightness of the majesty of your divinity.[49] Yet, in so doing, we do retard and hinder spiritual prayer.[50]

William himself, however, wanted to "enter wholly into Jesus' very heart," for it was "the holy of holies, the ark of the covenant, the golden urn, the soul of our humanity that holds within itself the manna of the Godhead...."[51] He wanted to see the very face of God. For to see God is faith's proper desire.[52] But how is this to come about?

First of all, one must go beyond, or leave off all images, thoughts and concepts.

Of what avail are mental images? Can reason, or rational understanding effect anything? No. For, although reason sends us to you, O God, it cannot of itself attain to you. Neither does that understanding which, as a product of reason, has lower matter for its sphere of exercise, go any farther than does reason itself; it is powerless to attain you.[53]

One must turn to the other eye of spiritual vision: "There are two eyes of the spiritual vision forever straining to see the Light which is God, and their names are love and reason."[54]

The "soul's sense is love; by love it perceives whatever it perceives."[55] "Love leaves behind what God is not, and rejoices to lose itself in what he is."[56] When the lover reaches out in this way, a certain change takes place in him by which he is transmuted into the Object loved; he does not become the same nature as that Object, but by his affection he is conformed to what he loves.[57] For William this is the work of the Holy Spirit. The common Will and mutual Love of the Father and the Son is given to us to make us like God—seeing the Father as the Son sees him, and seeing the Son as the Father sees the Son—and to unite us to him.[58] Thus the image of God is restored in us.[59]

O Charity, Charity, you have brought us to this that because we love God and the Son of God, we are called and we are gods and the sons of God.[60]

And yet we are never to say: "It is enough!"[61] "It does not yet appear what we shall be."[62] Whatever awareness we have here of seeing God, whatever faith here teaches us about him, is a riddle, darker at times, indeed, at others clearer.[63] This connatural knowledge or understanding which comes from above controls the believing mind when and as far as the Holy Spirit wills. He serves to soothe the lover, for there is clearly nothing in it of that which is not God, and although it is not wholly what God is, it is not different from the Reality.[64]

Thus William portrays the deepest, fullest and richest meaning of Christian life in a very simple and direct way. He invites his disciples to begin with meditation on the human life of Christ, and through his blessed Passion to come into contact with the divine love which it preeminently reveals. Love calls forth love and the love called forth transforms the lover into the likeness of the Beloved, a likeness which changes communion into union with the Triune. So simply then does William trace out the way and express the call to transforming union.

Yet this love affair does not develop in a vacuum. And William is well aware of this. The monastic way of life is there to create a climate most favorable to fostering its growth. The "labor of obedience"[65] is an essential element. William has the Lord address these words to him:

> I will go before you, and you must follow as you see me go before. I endured and labored and you must labor too. I suffered many things; it behooves you, too, to suffer some. Obedience is the way to charity, and you will get there if you keep to it.[66]

Especially does he exhort the beginner to walk in this way. The neophyte does not yet have the knowledge and experience he needs and so he must submit his judgment to one who knows the way if he wishes not to be lost. But if he is to be severe with himself in being gently and obediently humble toward the fathers and brothers who guide him, they are to moderate his severity and be properly indulgent, lest he lose heart.[67]

Furthermore, he is to be supported by the exercises of the common life. Lofty though his spiritual doctrine be, summoning his disciples to the very heights, William was a true Benedictine, fully appreciating the importance of a well moderated daily observance. The signature of the Abbot of St. Thierry on the Acts of the Chapter of Soissons,[68] not to speak of the key role attributed to him in the *Reply to Cardinal Matthew*,[69] is ample evidence of this. In his well developed treatise on love he speaks explicitly of the role of the various monastic practices, great and small, in the way of obedient love:

> The beginner in obedience must embrace cleanness of heart, purity of body, and silence, or well controlled speech. His eyes must not wander. He must not look proud. His ears must not be itching to hear. If he is temperate in food and sleep, he will not hinder the efficacy of a diet of good works. His hands should be held in check and his gait should be quiet. Lewdness of heart should not burst out in a loud laugh, but a sweet smile should show its grace. He must be conscientious in reading and meditation—and these should be spiritual and not prompted by mere curiosity. He must show subjection to his superiors; he must reverence the brethren and cherish the younger ones. He must not wish to be in a position of authority, but must love to be commanded. He must wish to be useful to everyone. He must not let severity overwhelm him, nor mildness make him soft. Let him have cheerfulness in his face and sweetness in his heart towards all, and kindness in all his acts. For this is

the time and place for sloughing off sensuality, for rooting out vice, and breaking self-will...let him who loves the more run the faster.[70]

As the beginner progresses, the role of the observances as factors fostering formation and development will become less significant. They will become more the expressions of fraternal love and harmony.

Nor need past sins cause the monk to lose heart as he pursues this exalted way of love. William candidly admits his own, and gives good and simple example as to how they should be handled:

> Let them be gathered in a single bundle to be burned. . . . I do not specify or make a list of them, nor am I able to, but howsoever much and in whatever way I have in truth sinned before you, O Truth, I own myself to be the sinner that you know I am. Let nobody make light of my misdeeds to me, nor yet exaggerate; let no one make them out as either less or more, not even I myself. Before you, O God, I stand trial...I am committing myself with complete trust into your hands.[71]

But even though one hold steadfastly to the labor of obedience and the exercises of the common life and be free from the burdens of past sin, he does not always progress steadily on the way of love. "For, so long as 'the body that is subject to corruption weighs down the soul, and the earthly habitation presses down the mind that muses upon many things,' the soul is bound to experience vicissitudes, however much it loves."[72] For, as William says to the Lord:

> As I see it, love is a natural thing, but to love you belongs to grace; the feeling of love is a manifestation of grace, and of that the Apostle says: "To each one is given the manifestation of the Spirit to profit withal.". . . In the soul of your poor servant, therefore, Lord, your love is always present; but it is hidden like the fire in the ashes till the Holy Spirit, who blows where he wills, is pleased to manifest it profitably the way and to the extent he wishes.[73]

Thus as one makes his way along this path of transforming love, seeking the face of God, obedience and docility in the Holy Spirit are essential. God's ways are not always those men would spontaneously choose.

William certainly experienced this. He had to cope constantly with a frustrated desire for greater contemplative leisure as the "truth of love" summoned him to the service of his sons and brothers.[74] He sums up his balanced understanding of the matter in *Meditation Eleven*:

> Let us review our affections and actions. Let our affections be set on the center of truth, and then outward actions will correspond thereto. Every affection is indeed owed to God. When he is adhered to faithfully,

wherever the circle of activity revolves, it cannot err.... Affection is sufficient if circumstances do not demand action or the possibility of acting is lacking. For, when the demands of love require action, true charity owes it to God or to a neighbor, as the case may be; if necessity does not require it, the love of truth makes it our duty to hold ourselves at leisure for itself. And as we always owe our entire affection to God, so also when we are at leisure, we owe our whole activity to him.... But anyone whom need summons to action must not be so eager to perform that he fails to take stock of his own ability. The center of truth must be consulted as to whether he has the ability to do it. If he has not, and yet presumes to act, he is not cleaving to the center.... Let him from whom action is urgently demanded, if indeed he can perform it, fix his attention on the truth, and not refuse to do the act of service. If the truth, when consulted, tells him he is unequal to the task and no fit person for it, then let him fix his soul in stillness on the stability of truth....[75]

It must be admitted though, that although William taught and lived a doctrine that preserved the true Christian balance and relationship between the holy leisure of Rachel and Mary and the fruitful activity of Lia and Martha, yet he places relatively little emphasis on community life. This is no doubt influenced by his own eremitical leanings.[76] This is very evident in his interpretation of the *vae soli*—"Woe to him who is alone"—of Ecclesiastes.[77] Contrary to the other Cistercian Fathers, William applies it to man without God, rather than to man without brethren.[78] Again, Christ's words in John 17:21, "I will that, as you and I are one, so may they be one in us," are habitually applied by William to the unity of the human spirit with God without any explicit reference to the unity of Christians among themselves.[79]

Yet, in his ex-professio treatise on Love, the Abbot does not fail to develop this essential dimension of Christian charity. To cite just one very beautiful expression of this:

Likewise the holy souls of whom we speak, if made superiors, acquit themselves of their office with all solicitude, and are like fathers to their sons. But if they are made subject to others, then they obey with humility and are like sons to their fathers. If they are obliged to live with others, they do so with charity. If they live in community, they make themselves servants of all. They are lovingly inclined towards everyone, and live in peaceful agreement about all that is good. They come together with joy, and go out of their way to show charity towards one another. To those who are below them in any way, they show a tender affection in their deeds. On their elders they bestow love to the point of subjection. To those above them their obedience goes as far as slavery. They do not seek their own interests, but those of the brethren. Whenever possible they make the common good their own, in spite of detriment to themselves. For they have received that pledge which is the Holy Spirit's gift, and they know that bodily service will soon pass into the adoption of those who will be revealed as the sons of God. Therefore they find it easy to bend both body and will to whatsoever thing the greatest of commandments orders.[80]

And later in the same treatise he becomes almost lyrical as he describes the effect on the community life of a full living out of the way of love.

These brethren find that the least touch (of Divine Wisdom) carries such an incitement to charity that their monastery becomes a very paradise of spiritual delight. Their transfigured faces and bodies, their holy life and behavior, their mutual service and devotion, so bind each brother to his brothers that their hearts and souls cannot but be one. The future glory, which will be perfect in the life to come, stands revealed in them already.[81]

Thus we see that for Abbot William the search for the face of God was to be lived out in and supported by a monastic milieu created by obedience, monastic observance, conversion, docility to the Holy Spirit, contemplation and active service in a community of brothers.

CONCLUSION

In these pages I have relied almost exclusively on the writings that date to William's abbatial service. Many texts from his later writings could be brought forward to underline the doctrine found here. But I wanted to present only that which William indisputably offered his men while he was spiritual father of St. Thierry. During the ensuing years, his doctrine was deepened and enriched until it was set forth in a somewhat different framework in that masterful synthesis which has rightly been called the *Golden Epistle.*[82] Yet in this earlier teaching I do not think there is any essential of that later synthesis lacking. And certainly there is, as I hope my brief presentation has indicated, a teaching that is more than sufficient to inspire and lead a community of monks to the fullest experience of Christian life and mysticism. It was this as it was taught and lived out that drew attention to St. Thierry in the early twelfth century and produced that radiance which inspires historians unhesitatingly to speak of the abbatiate of Abbot William as being at the heart of the Golden Age of St. Thierry.

NOTES

[1]There is some uncertainty as to the actual date of William's election as abbot of St. Thierry. Father Ceglar, whom we follow here, offers a closely reasoned argument for a shift from the commonly held date of 1119 to 1121. Stanislaus Ceglar, *William of St. Thierry: The Chronology of His Life with a Study of His Treatise* On the Nature and Dignity of Love, *His Authorship of the* Brevis Commentatio, *the* In Lacu, *and the* Reply to Cardinal Matthew (Ann Arbor, MI: University Microfilms, 1971) ch. IV; William's Tenure as Abbot of Saint Thierry, pp. 131-166.

[2]*St. Benedict's Rule for Monasteries,* tr. Leonard J. Doyle (Collegeville, MN: The Liturgical Press, 1968), 58:7.

[3]*S. Bernardi Vita prima, Liber I,* PL 185:225-268. See especially Cc. VII-VIII, cc. 245-252. Tr. Geoffrey Webb and Adrian Walker, *St. Bernard of Clairvaux* (Westminster, MD: Newman Press, 1960) ch. XII-XV, pp. 53-67.

[4]RB, ch. II and LXIV.

[5]Mt. 6:33 cited by RB 2:35. With the little documentary evidence that we do have it is difficult to evaluate the degree of success William had as a spiritual father in his own community. There are some arguments in favor of its being very limited but these are far from being conclusive.

[6]Besides Ceglar, *op. cit.,* see A. Adam, *Guillaume de Saint-Thierry, sa vie et ses oeuvres* (Bourges, 1923), J. M. Déchanet, *William of Saint Thierry, the Man and His Work,* tr. Richard Strachan, CS 10 (Spencer, MA: Cistercian Publications, 1972).

[7]RB 2:11ff.

[8]*Dialogorum Libria IV,* bk. II, 35, PL 66:200; tr. Odo John Zimmerman, *Dialogues,* Fathers of the Church 39 (New York: Fathers of the Church, 1959) p. 107.

[9]Besides Ceglar, *op. cit.,* see A. Wilmart, "La Serie et la Date des Ouvrages de Guillaume de Saint-Thierry," *Revue Mabillon* 14 (1924) 157-167; J. M. Déchanet, *Aux sources de la spiritualité de Guillaume de Saint Thierry* (Bruges: Beyaert, 1940); F. Vandenbrouche, *La Morale Monastique du XI au XVI siècle, Analecta Mediaevalia Namurcencia* 20 (Louvain-Lille, 1966) pp. 135-143.

[10]See J. Hourlier, "Introduction," *On Contemplating God, Prayer, Meditations,* tr. Sister Penelope (Lawson), *The Works of William of Saint Thierry,* vol. 1, CF 3 (Spencer, MA: Cisterican Publications, 1971) p. 12.

[11]The date of this visit has been set as early as 1116, but Ceglar argues convincingly for placing it in late 1119 or before Autumn, 1120; *op. cit.,* ch. II: William's First Meeting with St. Bernard, pp. 28-60. Ceglar also argues that William was at the time an abbot-emeritus of Crepyen-Hainaut and prior of St. Thierry, but others argue against this.

[12]"It was about this time I myself began to be a frequent visitor to him and his monastery, and when I first went to see him with a certain other abbot, I found him in that little hut of his. . . . Going into the hovel which had become a palace by his presence in it, and thinking what a wonderful person dwelt in such a despicable place, I was filled with such awe of the hut itself that I felt as if I were approaching the very altar of God. And the sweetness of his character so attracted me to him and filled me with such a desire to share his life amid such poverty and simplicity, that if the chance had been given me I should have asked nothing more than to be allowed

to remain with him always, looking after him and ministering to his needs." *Vita Prima*, ch. VII, n. 33, PL 185:246; tr. Webb and Walker, ch. XIII, p. 56.

¹³*De Contemplando Deo* (hereafter Contemp), PL 184:365-380. Critical ed. Jacques Hourlier, *De la Contemplation de Dieu, l'oraison de Dom Guillaume,* SC 61 (Paris: Cerf, 1961). Tr. Sister Penelope. See above, note 10.

¹⁴*De Natura et Dignitate Amoris* (hereafter Nat Am) PL 184:379-408. Tr. Geoffrey Webb and Adrian Walker, *On the Nature and Dignity of Love,* Fleur de Lys Series, 10 (London: Mowbrays, 1956).

¹⁵*Oratio Domni Willelmi* (hereafter Orat). Tr. Sister Penelope, see note 13 above.

¹⁶*Meditativae Orationes* (hereafter Med) PL 180:205-248, ed. M. M. Davy, *Meditationae Orationes,* Bibliothèque des Textes Philosophiques. (Paris: J. Vrin, 1934); Robert Thomas, *Oraisons meditées,* Pain de Cîteaux, 21-22 (Chambarand, 1964); J. M. Déchanet, "Meditativa Oratio No. XIII. Une page encore inédité de Guillaume de Saint Thierry." *Collectanea O.C.R.* (1940) 2-12, reprinted in *Aux Sources* (see above n. 9). Tr. Sister Penelope, see above n. 13.

¹⁷See above n. 9. In regard to the particular Med see J. Hourlier, "Introduction," CF 3:83-86; Ceglar, *op. cit.,* pp. 191-192.

¹⁸*Vita Prima*, ch. XII, n. 59-60, PL 185:259-60. This section is not found in the English tr.

¹⁹*In Cantici canticorum priora duo capita brevis commentatio* (hereafter Brev com) PL 184:407-436. Ceglar argues strongly for the conclusion: "It can be taken for certain that *BC* is a more or less faithful literary record of the spiritual conversations of the two friends, as described by William in the *Vita Bernardi,* XII, 59." *Op. cit.,* ch. IX, pp. 350-379.

²⁰*De Sacramenti altaris liber* (hereafter Sacr altar), PL 180:345-366.

²¹PL 180:341-344.

²²PL 180:343-346.

²³Med 1, PL 180:205-208; CF 3:89-94; *Expositio in Epistolam ad Romanos,* PL 180:547-694.

²⁴*De natura corporis et animae,* PL 180:695-726; tr. Benjamin Clark, "The Nature of the Body and the Soul," in *Three Treatises on Man. A Cistercian Anthropology,* ed. Bernard McGinn, CF 24 (Kalamazoo, MI: Cistercian Publications, 1976) pp. 106-155.

²⁵*Excerpta ex libris s. Gregorii Papae super Cantica canticorum,* PL 180:441-474.

²⁶*Commentarium in Cantica canticorum e scriptis sancti Ambrosi.* PL 15:1851-1962.

²⁷See Déchanet, *William of Saint Thierry,* CS 10:35; also "Introduction" in *Exposition on the Song of Songs,* tr. Columba Hart, *The Works of William of Saint Thierry,* vol. 2, CF 6 (Spencer, MA: Cistercian Publications, 1970) p. viii, and n. 7.

²⁸*Expositio altera super Cantica canticorum,* PL 180:473-546. Critical ed., J. M. Déchanet, *Exposé sur le Cantique des cantiques,* SC 82 (Paris: Cerf, 1962). Tr., see previous note.

²⁹*Epistola ad Fratres de Monte Dei* (hereafter Ep frat), PL 184:307-364. Critical ed. J. M. Déchanet, *Lettre aux Frères du Mont-Dieu* (Lettre d'or) SC 223 (Paris: Cerf, 1975). Tr. Theodore Berkeley, *The Golden Epistle. A Letter to the Brethren at Mont Dieu. The Works of William of Saint Thierry,* vol. 4, CF 12 (Spencer, MA: Cistercian Publications, 1971).

³⁰See Contemp 1, Med 11:8ff., Nat am 8, Cant. 51. See also CF 3:36, n. 4 and CF 6:41, n. 10.

³¹Pss. 15:1; 16:2; 23:6; 26:8; 30:21; 88:16.

[32]Just to cite some of the places in his early writings: Contemp 2, 3, 8, 12; Nat am 27, 37; Brev com 2, 3, 23; Orat; Med 2:9; 3:1-10; 4:10-11; 5:8; 6:2; 7:1-8; 8:1-7; 9:1; 6, 9, 12; 10:7, 9; 11:1; 12:5, 8. See CF 3:134, n. 1 and CF 628f., n. 17.

[33]Ep frat, Prefatory Letter, 9.

[34]Med 3:3.

[35]Med 3:6.

[36]*Ibid.*

[37]Nat am 25.

[38]Med 7:7.

[39]Med 7:8.

[40]Med 8:2.

[41]See e.g., Med 8:2-3; 10:1-9.

[42]Contemp 3; Med 6:10-12, 8:4.

[43]St. Lutgarde of Aywieres (1182-1246). Thomas Contipratanus, *Life of St. Lutgarde* in *Acta Sanctorum,* ed. J. Cornandet (Paris: Palme, 1867) Junii IV, pp. 187-210. For a modern biography see Thomas Merton, *What Are These Wounds?* (Milwaukee: Bruce, 1950).

[44]Med 9:2.

[45]*Ibid.*

[46]See e.g., Bernard of Clairvaux, *Sermones super Cantica Canticorum, S. Bernardi Opera,* ed. J. Leclercq, H. Rochais (Rome: Editiones Cistercienses, 1957-) Sermon 20:7, vol. 1, p. 119; tr. Edward John Mullaney, *On the Song of Songs. The Works of Bernard of Clairvaux,* vol. 1, CF 4 (Spencer, MA: Cistercian Publications, 1971) p. 153; Guerric of Igny, *Sermons,* 2 vols., ed. John Morson and Hilary Costello, SC 166, 202 (Paris: Cerf, 1970, 1973); tr. Monks of Mount St. Bernard Abbey, *Liturgical Sermons,* 2 vols., CF 8, 32 (Spencer, MA: Cistercian Publications, 1970, 1971) Serm. 3 for Easter, 2; Serm. 2 for Pentecost, 5; Serm. 2 for the Nativity of the Blessed Virgin Mary, 1.

[47]2 Cor. 5:16 in Med. 10:5. William again uses this text in Ep frat 175, see CF 12:69, n. 9.

[48]Orat, CF 3:74.

[49]Med 10:4.

[50]Orat. See CF 3:74, n. 15.

[51]Contemp 3.

[52]Med 3:9.

[53]Med 3:10.

[54]Nat am 25.

[55]Med 3:8. In regard to the expression "sense of the soul" see CF 3:106, n. 31.

[56]Nat am 25.

[57]Med 3:8.

[58]Med 3:6, 6:7-8; Contemp 11. We have in these early texts, concisely but adequately expressed, the essence of William's creative teaching on the Trinitarian aspect of the Christian's sanctification. For a good general presentation of this see Odo Brooke, "William of St. Thierry" in *The Month* 214 (1968) 377-384. "The great contribution of William of St. Thierry is to have evolved a theology of the Trinity which is essentially mystical, and a mystical theology which is essentially Trinitarian" p. 351. This is more completely and scientifically presented in that portion of

Brooke's doctoral thesis published in *Recherches de Théologie ancienne et médiévale:* "The Trinitarian Aspect of the Ascent of the Soul to God in the Theology of William of St. Thierry," RTAM 26 (1959) 85-127.

[59]Med 3:8, 6:8. The theme of the restoration of the image of God in man is common in William as in the Cistercian Fathers generally; see, e.g., Orat; Med 1:3, 3:8, 4:6, 6:8, 9:6, 12:14; Contemp 7, 11; Nat am 5, 6, 40; Sacr altar 1. William's approach to this theme is somewhat different from that of Bernard and the others; see CF 3:90, n. 13.

[60]Med 3:9.

[61]Contemp 6; Nat am 14.

[62]1 Jn. 3:2.

[63]Med 3:9.

[64]Med 3:11.

[65]RB Prol. 2.

[66]Med 13:4.

[67]Nat am 9.

[68]The text can be found in Ursmer Berlière, *Documents inédits pour servi à l'histoire ecclésiastique de la Belgique,* 2 vols. (Maredsous, 1894) pp. 92-93.

[69]Ceglar offers convincing arguments both from internal and external evidence to "show that William was the one who composed it." *Op. cit.,* ch. XI, The Authorship of the *Reply to Cardinal Matthew,* pp. 103-110. This text also bears witness to other qualities of the author. Nat am 10f. See also his beautiful description of the "School of Love" in the same treatise, par. 30.

[70]Nat am 10f. See also his beautiful description of the "School of Love" in the same treatise, par. 30.

[71]Med 12:4f.

[72]Med 12:17.

[73]Med 12:17f.

[74]Contemp 1. See CF 3:36, n. 4.

[75]Med 11:13.

[76]Med 2:2, 4:9.

[77]Eccles. 4:10.

[78]See CF 3:95, n. 3.

[79]Contemp 7, 11; Med 8:5. Cf. Cassian, *Conferences,* 10:7.

[80]Nat am 28.

[81]Nat am 51.

[82]See above, n. 29.

The Correspondence of William of St. Thierry

Any of us who have done work in the field of Cistercian studies have grateful thoughts of Leopold Janauschek and his successors, Jean de la Croix Bouton and Eugene Manning, for the excellent and most useful tool they have put at our disposal: the *Bibliographia Bernardina*.[1] We have also gratefully employed Dom Anselm Hoste's *Bibliotheca Aelrediana*.[2] It is not surprising then, as plans were shaped for a publishing venture to commemorate the millennium of the Benedictines at St. Thierry, one that would center on the monastery's most notable abbot, William of Liège, that the program would include a similar bibliographical tool for the study of William.[3]

It was in the course of the preparation of that bibliography that I came to interest myself in the correspondence of William of St. Thierry.

For a number of his contemporaries, such as his closest friend, Bernard of Clairvaux, and his somewhat alienated confrère in Black, Peter the Venerable, we have rather substantial collections of letters.[4] This is due in part to the zeal of the authors themselves, as well as devoted secretaries.[5] In William's case we are not so fortunate. Undoubtedly during his fourteen years as abbot,[6] not to speak of the years before and after that service, many epistles went out bearing his name and seal. And yet there remains to us a very meager collection indeed, and most of this is found within the corpus of the Bernardine writings.

THE BERNARDINE CORRESPONDENCE

It has often been asserted that William was, as it were, lost in the shadow of his great friend. But that must be seen, at least in part, as a protecting shadow. For much of William's literary heritage—and it is largely from this that we know him—has come down to us, thanks to the patronage of St. Bernard. Several of his treatises were ascribed to the Abbot of Clairvaux,[7] and most of what we know of his correspondence comes from Bernard's letters to William. Let us then look first at William's correspondence with Bernard.

The earliest surviving letter is one that was not included in Bernard's own collection. Indeed, it is not certain that it was addressed to our William. But Dom Jean Leclercq, who first published this letter in *Revue Bénédictine* in 1951[8] and later in volume one of his *Recueil d' études sur saint Bernard et ses écrits,*[9] holds that it is more probably addressed to William of St. Thierry.[10] And Fr. Stanislaus Ceglar seems to take it for granted.[11] Ceglar, who brings to his study of the chronology of William all the sagacity and pertinacity of a Sherlock Holmes, dates the letter in the first days of 1121, before William became abbot of St. Thierry, and places the discussion it refers to, during Advent or more probably during the octave of Christmas, 1120.[12] In the letter Bernard goes over an explanation of the Gospel of the Circumcision and Purification which he recently shared with "Brother G." (Guillelmo, William), to whom he addresses the letter, and *domino episcopo*[13] whom both Leclercq and Ceglar conjecture to be William of Champeaux.[14] Bernard does not want William to write out the explanation before they can confer on it again—or, if he has already written it out, not to let anyone read it before Bernard sees it.[15] We may have here a hint of how the *Brevis Commentatio*[16] would later originate.[17] It betrays an eagerness on the part of William to write down and share what he received in his treasured conversations with Bernard. Bernard's concern here was that they were so intent on the moral sense that in some cases they erroneously departed from the truth of the letter.[18] It tells us something of Bernard's use of Scripture in his meditations and teaching, a concern frequently expressed in his writings, most notably in the retractation he prefixed to his treatise, *On the Steps of Humility and Pride.*[19]

The concluding lines express Bernard's respect and care for William, as he expresses his regret that William slipped away without the escort that had been promised him.[20]

In a note appended to William's incomplete life of St. Bernard, Abbot Burchard of Balerne notes that Bernard had written "many letters" to William.[21] The same statement is found in the *Vita Antiqua Willelmi* edited by Poncelet in 1908.[22] In the next letter we have—if it is the next letter—Leclercq dates it vaguely "around 1125"[23]—Bernard himself admits that William has written him many letters. He actually says "I have not yet once answered your many letters to me,"[24] so perhaps Leclercq's dating is late and this letter should be placed before even the preceding one and thus dated 1120. Ceglar has placed William's meeting with Bernard in the spring of this year or perhaps some months earlier.[25] Considering the tremendous impression that Bernard made on William at that first visit,[26] a spate of letters could well have followed.

Yet this letter, unlike the preceding, is addressed to the "Lord Abbot William,"[27] and so perhaps Bernard's statement has to be taken in a more

relative sense and this letter dated somewhat later. William probably
assumed his office as abbot of St. Thierry around Easter, 1121,[28] although
there has been some conjecture about his being abbot elsewhere prior to his
coming to St. Thierry.[29]

From Bernard's letter we catch a glimpse of the content of William's
latest. He complains, and Bernard quotes him here, "My affection for you is
greater than yours is for me."[30] Under a postscript he avers that Bernard's
messengers pass by his gate without ever stopping in with some token of
Bernard's love.[31] To this petulant lover Bernard gives a long involved
response, concluding: "I love you as much as I can according to the power
which is given to me."[32] Bernard goes on to say, "that little preface which
you ask to be sent you I have not got by me at the moment. I have not yet
had it copied, because I did not think it worth while."[33] Bruno Scott James
identifies this preface as the letter which in some editions precedes this
Apologia, Bernard's Epistle 84 bis.[34] If this is so it would justify dating this
letter "around 1125," but there is little more here than conjecture.

The next letter,[35] one of the most crucial letters William received from
Bernard, can be dated quite accurately. It was written on September 9,
"almost certainly" in 1124. Ceglar admits it "could have been a year or two
earlier, although this is very unlikely."[36] Bernard had received a letter the
day before from William with the greeting: "To his friend, all that a friend
could wish," and he makes the greeting his own in reply.[37] As we can see
from Bernard's response, William had written about a certain fugitive Black
Monk, inquired for the nth time about Bernard's health and, most impor-
tantly, laid before Bernard his desire to resign and join him at Clairvaux.
Bernard's reply is full of love and pastoral concern—love and concern in
regard to the poor fugitive whom he had sent off and who had taken refuge
with William. He was to be scolded and sent on home, but not without a
letter to his abbot on his behalf; love and concern in regard to William. If
they followed their hearts, William would be immediately welcomed at
Clairvaux. But, says Bernard:

> It is safer for me and more advantageous for you if I advise you as I think
> God wishes. Therefore I say, hold on to what you have, remain where
> you are, and try to benefit those over whom you rule. Do not try to
> escape the responsibility of your office while you are still able to dis-
> charge it for the benefit of your subjects. Woe to you if you rule them and
> do not benefit them, but far greater woe to you if you refuse to benefit
> them because you shrink from the burden of ruling them.[38]

The deep affection that bound these two men was validly based on divine
love and faith. William took Bernard's words to heart and continued to rule
for another eleven years. Thanks to this decision, we have further corres-

pondence between the two monks, some of which was to have far-reaching effects.

APOLOGIA

Not long after this exchange of letters, perhaps a few months or half a year, William wrote one such letter. The content is known from Bernard's reply, Epistle 84 bis, sometimes placed as a preface to the *Apologia*.[39] William laid a heavy charge upon his friend. Relations between the Cluniacs—and remember that William was abbot in a house which, while not directly subject to Cluny, yet followed Cluniac observances—and the Cistercians were rapidly deteriorating. For a number of reasons Cluniac venom was centering on William's friend Bernard. And so William urged him to act to remove this scandal from God's kingdom, convince those who complain that the Cistercians are slandering the Order of Cluny, that the malicious tale which they believe and spread abroad is not true and at the same time condemn the Cluniac excesses in food, clothing and other areas.[40] It is unfortunate we do not have this letter, for Bernard says: "I have read and reread your beautiful letter—with ever more enjoyment, since it does not pall with repetition."[41] William was a good writer.

In his reply Bernard gave what was to be in fact the outline of the *Apologia*: "Perhaps I could say first that the Order (of Cluny) itself is quite praiseworthy, and that those who censure it should themselves be censured, and then go on to condemn the excesses present in it."[42] Bernard's responsiveness to William—one might say, his dependence on him—is striking: "Tell me frankly if this is what you want, or whether you think a different approach is called for. Do not hesitate to tell me what you want, and I will do it."[43] This is all the more striking because Bernard was as yet a young abbot and controversy was not yet his common experience. His previous writings had been largely the spiritual teachings of a father abbot. He went on to frankly express his feelings to William: "At the same time you should be aware that I find this sort of writing rather distasteful. It means a great loss of devotion and an interruption of prayer...."[44]

In the Bernardine corpus we find another letter, Epistle 452, addressed "to a certain abbot," which is undoubtedly a variant on this particular letter, almost identical with it except for some amplification in the first paragraph.[45]

When Bernard's *Apologia* was finally published it was addressed to William: "To the Reverend Father William..."[46] and Bernard lets it be known that it is written at William's request.[47] Bernard's Epistle 88 to Oger makes clear the role William also had in editing the text for publication.[48]

There is another letter of Bernard's to an unnamed recipient, Epistle 446,[49] which Ceglar judges was "almost certainly to William."[50] In fact, by means of rather ingenious reasoning he is able to date it as precisely as the first week of Advent, 1125.[51] That it is to William he argues from the inscription *Quidquid sibi*—not unlike that used by Bernard in other letters to William[52]—and the circumstances. Bernard has just recovered from a grave illness and is replying to a friend who had been at his bedside in this crisis—William describes such a circumstance in his *Vita Bernardi*[53]—and after leaving wrote of his continued concern.[54] Bernard spoke of his gradual recovery and his desire to see his friend.[55]

One thing stands out very clearly in this correspondence: Bernard had a very high regard for William as a guide and editor, especially in the area of theology. We have already noted William's role in the preparation of the *Apologia*. In 1128 Bernard addressed his theological treatise, *On Grace and Free Will* to William and in the prologue asked him to evaluate the work and correct it, if need be, or return it to himself for correction.[56] Finally, in the famous or infamous Abelard controversy, William played a key role.

However, before this last exchange an event occurred which has left some epistolary traces. By 1135, William felt he had reached the point where he had done all he could be expected to do for the monks of St. Thierry, and he quietly slipped off to the Cistercian abbey of Signy. He evidently did this without Bernard's approval, and when Bernard next wrote he spoke of William's new-found leisure. Perhaps William's sense of guilt caused him to read something into Bernard's words, for he wrote back defensively, expressing the fear that their old friendship was not surviving William's somewhat impetuous move. All this we gather from Bernard's reply "To his friend Wi" which was first published by Hüfner in 1886;[57] and which is Epistle 506 in the new Leclercq-Rochais edition. The ascription is not absolutely clear, but Ceglar holds the letter was "almost certainly addressed to William" and dates it at the end of 1135 or early 1136.[58] After assuring Wi of the abiding nature of their friendship and just what he meant by his remark about leisure—that holy leisure zealous for good and fruitful for eternity, of which he himself was envious, though unworthy— Bernard speaks of some sermons that had been requested: "The sermons you ask for are not yet ready, but they will be gotten ready and you shall have them."[59] Ceglar conjectures these are the first sermons on the Song of Songs,[60] which may well be the case, as William was to be engaged with this book for some years to come. This would tie in with the date of the letter, for Bernard first started his famous series in 1135.[61]

There is another letter, Bernard's Epistle 422, addressed "to a certain Abbot"[62] who, Ceglar says, "quite probably" is William.[63] The letter must date then from some time before 1135. It tells us little new. Bernard excuses again the brevity and aridity of his letters which displease the recipient. This short note is to send on a candidate who was from the recipient's own area.

THE ABELARD CONTROVERSY

Perhaps the least needs to be said of the correspondence between the two friends concerning the Abelard affair, for it has been widely studied and by masters in the field.[64] Recently Leclercq has published an edition of William's letter,[65] the first extant letter of William to Bernard that we have if we discount the dedication of his treatise *On the Sacrament of the Altar,* or *On the Body and Blood of the Lord,* which William addressed to Bernard in 1128.[66] William lays aside the loving labors of his holy leisure to rouse Bernard and Geoffrey of Lèves.[67] He sends along a list of the errors he has found in Abelard's writings,[68] and goes on to prepare his own response.[69] In his response Bernard gives a summary commendation of William's work and calls for a meeting as soon as possible, but after Easter, to discuss the whole affair; for, says Bernard, "I am not in the habit of trusting much in my judgment, especially in such grave matters," and "I know little or nothing at all of these things."[70] Ceglar dates both letters in Lent of 1140, depending on a well worked out and precise chronology of the whole course of events leading up to the Council of Sens.[71]

AN ABELARDIAN DISCIPLE

Perhaps encouraged by the effective role he was able to play through Bernard—there are those who think that Bernard depended wholly on William for his knowledge of Abelard's theological errors—not long after, William again addressed a letter to Bernard, a call to action, this time in the face of the errors of William of Conches. It was probably in 1141 that William wrote this long letter which was also recently edited by Dom Jean Leclercq.[72] William of Conches was a disciple of Abelard, coming from the school of Chartres.[73] He published a *Philosophia*[74] which, as William put it, revived and aggravated Abelard's theories on the Trinity and on the Holy Spirit as the world-soul.[75] William's letter displays a certain antagonism. Although there was no personal acquaintance between them, so far as we know, a certain flippancy in the way Conches spoke of God rubbed William the wrong way. Yet his refutation remains a well reasoned thing and it exemplifies William's own attitude toward the writings of the Fathers and his views of the relation between the intellect and faith. We have no record of action taken by St. Bernard, but Conches soon retired from Chartres to take up a post at the Norman court. In his later works he exercised greater care and sought a formal cause for the cosmos in some created force called "nature."[76]

RUPERT OF DEUTZ

Besides these exchanges with Bernard, we have only two other samples of William's correspondence. Possibly around 1126,[77] though there is no sure way of dating the letter, he wrote to a Black monk named Rupert, the abbot of Deutz.[78] This is a lengthy letter[79] involved in a careful theological critique of Rupert's treatise *De Officiis*.[80] In main it seeks to show the error of Rupert's contention that the Body of Christ present in the Eucharist lacked "animal life." But what stands out in the letter is its warmth and affection, the truth of its charity and the charity of its truth. Rupert, his *frater in Christo charissimus*, could not question William's attestation that he in no way doubted the integrity of his faith but wrote only out of loving solicitude for him.

This letter to Rupert has always been closely associated with William's treatise *On the Body and Blood of the Lord*,[81] which, as we have noted above, was addressed to Bernard. In his brief prologue,[82] William returns Bernard's confidence in him as editor, calling upon Bernard to now correct his work. The reason he gives is significant: "so it can be the work of both of them—*et meum opus et vestrum sit*."[83] But, he notes, the ideas and even the very words he uses are, by preference, those of the Fathers.[84]

THE GOLDEN EPISTLE

The final letter we have to consider, the last extant from William's pen, has, rightly indeed, been dubbed by Mabillon *The Golden Epistle*.[85] The treatise, which sums up the whole of William's spirituality, is well known. It is more the prefatory letter addressed to Prior Haymon and an unknown H. that interests us here. It is found in two forms, both probably authentic,[86] the fruit of an evolution, as is the treatise itself.[87] The letter is especially precious for what it tells us of its author. First of all, it contains an authentic list of his writings, some of which, including even the accompanying treatise, were long accredited to others.[88] Again, it exemplifies William's monastic ideals, his pastoral and paternal solicitude, his special love and concern for the young. And finally, it betrays a certain humble sensitivity: "I prefer that if my writings be found of no use they should be delivered to the avenging flames by my friends, acting not as judges but as counselors, rather than suffer the malicious assaults of detractors."[89]

A SPURIOUS LETTER (?)

Before concluding we might note a curious case of "even Homer nods" twice. In his classic work on William, Déchanet speaks of a spurious letter of William to Bernard cited in Manrique's *Annales Cistercienses*.[90] However, when we consult the cited text we find that Manrique is speaking of a letter not from William to Bernard but from Bernard to William.[91] However, when we consult Manrique's citation we find the text, indeed, but that the letter is from Bernard to Abbot Geoffrey of St. Medard.[92] So it is not a spurious letter; there is just a little confusion as to who is writing to whom.

CONCLUSION

Our study of the correspondence of William of St. Thierry has not unearthed anything really new; it has made no startling discoveries. In fact, we have relatively little. Bringing it all together in the context of his life may be of some service. It fills in a little more some of the lines and shadows of a very attractive personality. Certainly it portrays a warmth and integralness in the humanity of this twelfth-century monk and his closest friend that belies some of the harshness that stereotypes have projected. If these two monks are typical of the kind of spiritual fathers who formed the Cistercians of the mid-twelfth century—and we have every reason to believe they are—we can readily understand why it was indeed a golden age. As we see the interplay of these two great personalities in this fragmentary correspondence, we are fascinated; we would like to see much more. Many questions come to our minds. Who was indeed the master of whom—or has love so made them equal that such a question is without meaning? Can we hope to find yet other letters? I doubt it. But I do not think we have yet begun to mine fully the richness of these few we have. May their publication in the new Latin editions and in English translation facilitate such a rewarding undertaking!

NOTES

[1] L. Janauschek, *Bibliographia Bernardina*, Xenia Bernardina, Pars Quarta (Vienna, 1891, reprint Hildesheim: Olms, 1959); Jean-de-la-Croix Bouton, *Bibliographie Bernardini*, 1891-1957, Commission d'Histoire de l'Ordre de Cîteaux, 5 (Paris: Lethielleux, 1958); E. Manning, *Bibliographie Bernardine* (1957-1970), *Documentation Cistercienne* 6 (Rochefort, 1972).

[2] Anselm Hoste, *Bibliotheca Aelrediana*, Instrumenta Patristica II (The Hague, Nijhoff, 1962).

[3] See M. B. Pennington, "St. Thierry: The Commemoration of a Benedictine Millennium," *Cîteaux* 23 (1972) 118-122.

[4] St. Bernard, *Opera omnia*, ed. J. Mabillon, PL 182:67-716, ed. J. Leclercq and H. Rochais, *S. Bernardi opera*, 9 vols. (Rome: Editiones Cistercienses, 1957-1970). Peter the Venerable, *Opera omnia*, PL 189:61-486; ed. G. Constable, *The Letters of Peter the Venerable*, 2 vols. (Cambridge: Harvard U. Press, 1967).

[5] See J. Leclercq, "Lettres de s. Bernard: histoire ou litterature?" *Studi Medievali* 12 (1971) 1-74; "Recherches sur la collection des épîtres de saint Bernard," *Cahiers de civilisation médiévale* 14 (1971) 205-217.

[6] According to the catalog of abbots of St. Thierry as cited by Mabillon, PL 182:207, note 255. See S. Ceglar, *William of St. Thierry. The Chronology of His Life with a Study of His Treatise* On the Nature of Love, *His Authorship of the* Brevis Commentatio, *the* In Lacu, *and the* Reply to Cardinal Matthew, (Ann Arbor: University Microfilms, 1971) ch. IV: The Beginning and the End of William's Tenure as Abbot of St. Thierry, pp. 131-158.

[7]William's treatises, *On Contemplating God, On the Nature and Dignity of Love* and the *Golden Epistle*, are to be found in the fifth tome of Mabillon's edition of *S. Bernardi opera omnia* (PL 184:307-408) because they had been ascribed to Bernard.

[8]Leclercq, "St. Bernard et ses Secretaires," *Revue Bénédictine* 61 (1951) 208-229.

[9]J. Leclercq, *Recueil d' études sur saint Bernard et ses érits,* vol. 1 (Rome: Ed. di Storia e Letteratura, 1962) pp. 10-11.

[10]*Ibid.,* p. 9.

[11]Ceglar, *op. cit.,* p. 156.

[12]*Ibid.*

[13]"Fratri G. frater B. de Claraualle dictus abbas, salutem. Explanationes illam quam nuper una cum domino episcopo tecumque conferendo super historiam evangelicam texuimus. . ."—Leclercq, *Recueil* 1:10-11.

[14]*Ibid.,* p. 10, n. 1; Ceglar, *op. cit.,* p. 156. Bernard had frequent contacts during the first years of his abbatiate with William of Champeaux, the bishop of Chalons. The bishop died on January 21, 1121. This fact is used in proposing a date for the letter.

[15]"I do not want you to write out that explanation until you first confer with me again about it. But if perchance you have already written it out, do not give it to anyone to read before me."—Leclercq, *Recueil* 1:11.

[16]*Brevis commentatio in Cantici canticorum priora duo capita,* PL 184:407-436.

[17]See Mabillon, PL 185:259, Leclercq, *Etudes sur saint Bernard, Analecta S.O.C.* 9 (1953) 106-107, 216; Ceglar, *op. cit.,* ch. IX: William's Part in the *Brevis Commentatio,* pp. 350-379.

[18]". . .deprehendi nos dum moralibus adinueniendis sensibus nimis intenti essemus, nonnullis in locis a veritate litterae per errorem exorbitassi."—Leclercq, *Recueil* 1:11.

[19]OB 3:15; trans. Ambrose Conway, CF 13:5.

[20]"De caetera noueris multum nos contristatos quod ita a nobis absque conductu qui nobis promissus fuerat discessistis. . . ." Leclercq, *Recueil* 1:11.

[21]". . .plures epistolas idem sanctus (Bernard) scripsit ad illum (William)." PL 185:266.

[22]*Vita Willelmi. Vie ancienne de Guillaume de Saint-Thierry,* ed. A. Poncelet, *Mélanges Godefroid Kurth,* 2 vols. (Liège, 1908) 1:90.

[23]OB 7:30, n. 1.

[24]Ep. 85:2, *ibid.,* p. 221.

[25]Ceglar, *op. cit.,* ch. II; William's First Meeting with St. Bernard, pp. 28-54.

[26]"It was about this time that I (William) myself began to be a frequent visitor to him (Bernard) and his monastery. . . . Going into the hovel which had become a palace by his presence in it, and thinking what a wonderful person dwelt in such a despicable place, I was filled with such awe of the hut itself that I felt as if I were approaching the very altar of God. And the sweetness of his character so attracted me to him and filled me with desire to share his life amid such poverty and simplicity, that if the chance had then been given to me I should have asked nothing more than to be allowed to remain with him always, looking after him and ministering to his needs." *S. Bernardi vita prima* I, vii, 33, PL 185:246: trans. G. Webb and A. Walker, *St. Bernard of Clairvaux* (Westminster, MD: Newman, 1960) p. 56.

[27]"Domno abbati Guillelmo, frater Bernardus, charitatem de corde puro, et con-

scientia bona, et fide nonficta." PL 182:206, Leclercq omits this salutation in his ed. OB 7:220.

28Ceglar, *op. cit.,* p. 135.

29See *Gallia christiana* 9:187, Lecuy, "Guillaume de St. Thierry," in Michaud, *Biographie Universelle ancienne et moderne,* 45 vols. (Paris: Delograve) 18:170; A. Adam, *Guillaume de Saint-Thierry, sa vie et ses oeuvres* (Bourge, 1923) p. 34.

30Ep. 85:1, OB 7:221; trans. B. S. James, *The Letters of St. Bernard of Clairvaux* (Chicago: Regnery, 1953) (hereafter referred to as *Letters*) Letter 87, p. 125.

31*Ibid., Letters,* p. 126.

32Ep. 85:4, OB 7:222; *Letters,* p. 127.

33*Ibid.*

34*Letters,* p. 127, n. 1; PL 182:895-898.

35Ep. 86, OB 7:223-224.

36Ceglar, *op. cit.,* p. 114.

37"To his friend all that a friend could wish, from Brother Bernard of Clairvaux. It was you who gave me this formula of greeting when you wrote, 'To his friend all that a friend could wish.' " OB 7:223, *Letters,* Letter 88, p. 127.

38OB 7:224, *Letters,* p. 128.

39OB 7:219, trans. CF I:5-6; see Mabillon, PL 182:895-898.

40This is evident from the text of St. Bernard's letter:

> I am quite prepared to undertake the task you have enjoined on me for the removal of scandal from God's kingdom,...and I understand that you want me to convince those who complain that we are slandering the Order of Cluny, that the malicious tale which they believe and spread abroad is not true. However, it seems contradictory to me, having done just this, to turn around and condemn their excesses in food and clothing and the other areas you mention. *Ibid.*

41*Ibid.*

42*Ibid.*

43*Ibid.*

44*Ibid.*

45PL 182:643.

46OB 3:81, trans. Michael Casey, CF 1:33.

47"Prior to this, if you had asked me to do some writing, I would not have agreed, or if I had agreed, it would have been reluctantly.... Now that the situation has become really serious, my former diffidence has vanished. Spurred on by the need for action, mine is the painful position of having no alternative but to comply...." *Ibid.*

48"Do not hesitate, I beg you, to find an opportunity of going to see him [William], and do not on any account allow anyone to see or copy the aforesaid booklet [The *Apologia*] until you have been through it with him, discussed it with him, and have both made such corrections as may be necessary, so that every word may be supported by two witnesses. I leave to the judgment of you both whether it shall be published, or shown to only a few, or to no one at all. I also leave to you both to decide whether the preface you have put together out of my other letters will stand

or whether it would not be better to compose another." Ep. 88, OB 7:234, *Letters,*
Letter 91, pp. 136-137.

49PL 182:639-640; *Letters,* Letter 464, p. 519.

50Ceglar, *op. cit.,* p. 32.

51*Ibid.,* p. 118.

52Ep. 85: "Quidquid vel tibi vel amicis tuis recte vis, qui dedit velle, det et perfi-
cere." (OB 7:223; *Letters,* Letter 87, p. 127) which spells out the full meaning of the
greeting; Ep. 422 (PL 182:629-630, *Letters,* Letter 453, p. 515). However, the argument is not too strong, for Ep. 422 is to an anonymous abbot who, Ceglar holds, is
"quite probably" William (p. 32) for the same reason, and at the same time he grants
the Ep. 450 (PL 182:642; *Letters,* Letter 460, p. 520) which has a similar salutation
(*idem quod sibi*) is not addressed to William.

53PL 185:258-259; Webb and Walker, *St. Bernard of Clairvaux,* pp. 74-75.

54See Ceglar, *op. cit.,* pp. 105-106.

55"On the First Sunday of Advent I was able for the first time to approach the altar
of God for the reception of the Sacrament without anyone helping me; and I have
written this letter with my own hand. From these two signs you will be able to
gather how much better I am, by the goodness of God, in both body and mind. I
would be glad to see you, if it could be arranged conveniently and without any
bother." Ep. 466, PL 182:640; *Letters,* p. 519.

56"You please read it first.... Then, should you judge it useful to be read publicly,
if you notice something obscurely stated which, in an obscure subject, might yet
have been more clearly expressed, without departing from due brevity, do not
hesitate either to amend it yourself or else to return it to me for emendation...."
OB 3:165, trans. Daniel O'Donovan, CF 19:3.

57G. Hüfner, *Vorstudien ze einer Darstellung des Lebes und Wirkens des heiligen Bernhard von
Clairvaux* (Munster, 1886) p. 213; trans. *Letters,* Letter 89, pp. 128-129.

58Ceglar, *op. cit.,* pp. 148-151.

59*Letters,* p. 129.

60Ceglar, *op. cit.,* p. 150.

61See Leclercq, *Saint Bernard Mystique* (Paris, 1948) Appendix II—"La date de premier sermon sur les Cantiques des cantiques," pp. 480-483.

62PL 182:629-630; *Letters,* Letter 453, p. 515.

63Ceglar, *op. cit.,* p. 32.

64J. Leclercq, "Les formes successives de la lettre-traité de saint Bernard contra
Abelard," *Revue Bénédictine* 78 (1968) 97-105; "Les lettres de Guillaume de saint-
Thierry à saint Bernard," *Revue Bénédictine* 79 (1969) 375-391; Edward Little, *The
"Heresies" of Peter Abelard,* unpublished doctoral thesis, University of Montreal, 1969;
"Bernard and Abelard at the Council of Sens, 1140" in *Bernard of Clairvaux: Studies
presented to Dom John Leclercq,* CS 23 (Washington: Cistercian Publications, 1972)
pp. 55-71; "The Sources of the *Capitula* of Sens (1140)" in *Studies in Medieval Cistercian
History II,* CS 24, (Kalamazoo: Cistercian Publications, 1975) 96-100.

65Cited in the previous note.

66PL 180:343-346.

67"There is also *Against Peter Abelard,* and it was this which prevented me from
completing the preceding work (*Exposition on the Song of Songs*) for I did not think I was

justified in enjoying such delightful leisure within doors while outside he, with naked sword, as they say, was ravaging the confines of our faith." *The Golden Epistle*, Pref. 10, ed. R. Thomas, *Lettre aux frères du Mont-Dieu*, Pain de Cîteaux 33 (Chambarand, 1968) p. 28, trans. T. Berkeley, CF 12:6.

⁶⁸Leclercq, "Les Lettres de Guillaume...," pp. 377-378. PL 182:552.

⁶⁹*Adversus Petrum Abelardum*, PL 180:283-332.

⁷⁰Ep. 327, PL 182:553; *Letters*, Letter 236, p. 315.

⁷¹Ceglar, *op. cit.*, pp. 172-187.

⁷²Leclercq, "Les Lettres de Guillaume...," pp. 382-391; there is an earlier edition in PL 180:333-340.

⁷³See P. Delhaye, "William of Conches" in *New Catholic Encyclopedia*, 14 vols. (NY: McGraw-Hill, 1967) 14:923-924.

⁷⁴PL 90:1127-78, 172:39-102.

⁷⁵Leclercq, "Les lettres de Guillaume...," pp. 382-383; PL 180-333.

⁷⁶Delhaye, *loc. cit.*

⁷⁷J. M. Déchanet, *Oeuvres choisies de Guillaume de Saint Thierry* (Paris: Aubier, 1944) p. 47; *William of St. Thierry: The Man and His Work*, CS 10 (Spencer: Cistercian Publications, 1972) p. 33, n. 87.

⁷⁸Rupert (1129), a monk of St. Laurence of Liège, where he received his education, became abbot of Deutz (Tuy) in 1120. He was well known for his literary style and knowledge of Scripture, leaving extensive writings (PL 167-170). His principal work, *De divinis officiis*, which William criticizes, was completed in 1111. While he lived he was a figure of continual controversy, challenged by such notables as William of Champeaux and Anselm of Laon, but after his death he received little attention until the Reformation, when his imprecise language on the Eucharist caused him to be accused of teaching "impanation." See P. Séjourné, "Rupert de Deutz" *Dictionnarie de théologie catholique*, 15 vols. (Paris: Letouzey, 1930-1946) 14:169-205; B. S. Smith, "Rupert of Deutz" *New Catholic Encyclopedia* 12:723.

⁷⁹PL 180:341-344.

⁸⁰PL 170:9-332.

⁸¹PL 180:345-366.

⁸²PL 180:343-346.

⁸³PL 180:345-346.

⁸⁴*Ibid*.

⁸⁵PL 183:307-364. A better edition is that of R. Thomas, Pain de Cîteaux 33-34 (Chambarand, 1968). Trans. Theodore Berkeley, CF 12.

⁸⁶J. M. Déchanet, "Les manuscrits de la Lettre aux Frères du Mont-Dieu de Guillaume de Saint-Thierry et le problème de la 'preface' dans Charlville 114," *Scriptorium* 8 (1954) 236-271, especially 264-268.

⁸⁷See J. M. Déchanet, "Les divers étates des texte de la 'Lettre aux Frères du Mont-Dieu' dans Charlville 114." *Scriptorium* 11 (1957) 63-86.

⁸⁸See note 7 above; also D. Massuet, PL 184:299-308. William's *Meditations* were also attributed to St. Bernard by various editors and his *Commentary on the Song of Songs drawn from St. Ambrose* to Anthony de Mouchi (Déchanet, *Oeuvres choisies*, pp. 41-42). See also A. Wilmart, "La série et la date des ouvrages de Guillaume de Saint-Thierry," *Revue Mabillon* 14 (1924) 157-167; "Les écrits spirituelle des deux Guiges, la

Lettre aux Frères du Mont-Dieu," in *Revue d'Ascétique et de Mystique*, 5 (1924) 127-158.

[89]Pain de Cîteaux 33:30-32; CF 12:7.

[90]CS 10:17, n. 53.

[91]A. Manrique, *Annales Cisterciences*, 4 vols. (Lyons, 1642; reprinted Westmead: Gregg, 1970) 1:130.

[92]PL 182:174; OB 7:162.

William's Letter Against Abelard

To: The Reverend Lords and Fathers in Christ,
      Geoffrey, Bishop of Chartres and
      Bernard, Abbot of Clairvaux
      Life and Good Days!

1. God knows how embarrassed I am before you, finding myself, I, who am a nobody among men, compelled to speak to you, Lords and Fathers, about a matter of common and grave concern, even while you and others remain silent. For when I see the faith upon which we ground our common hope, that faith which Christ consecrated for us with his own Blood, for which the Apostles and Martyrs fought even unto death, which the holy Doctors defended with strenuous labors and great sweat, and passed on whole and uncorrupted to our most miserable times, when I see that faith very seriously and dangerously corrupted, and no one resisting, and no one speaking out in response, my very "inners" waste away, and a burning heart and a sorrowing spirit compel me to speak out for it. For, if it were necessary and opportune, I would wish even to die for it.

I am not speaking of minor matters, but of faith in the Holy Trinity, of the Person of the Mediator, of the Holy Spirit, of the grace of God, of the sacrament of our common redemption. For Peter Abelard again teaches novelties, and writes of them, and his books go across the seas and over the Alps. His new propositions of faith and his new dogmas are spread throughout provinces and kingdoms; they are widely preached and freely defended, even to the point that they are said to have authority in the Roman Curia. I tell you, it is dangerous for you to keep silent—dangerous both for you and for the Church of God. For a "nothing" we allow that faith to be corrupted for which we have denied our very selves to ourselves. We fear offending neither God nor man, lest we be offensive. I tell you, until now this innovator has been but giving birth to this evil, but unless he be overtaken, he will come forth as a leader[1] and there will hardly be found anyone to speak against him. Listen to why I say this:

2. By chance I recently happened to read a certain book by this man, entitled *The Theology of Peter Abelard* (*Theologia Petri Abelardi*). I must confess, this title aroused my curiosity. However, there are actually two books which contain almost the same thing, except what is said more fully in the one is found more briefly stated in the other. When I found something that greatly agitated me in these books, I noted it down, and I also noted why it agitated me, and with the books themselves I send this to you. Whether I

was rightly agitated, it is for you to judge. For, since I was very greatly disturbed by the novel words which were not common in the expression of faith and the new ideas with their unheard of meanings, and since I had no one to whom I could refer, I chose to turn to you among all others, and to call on you to respond to the cause of God and the whole Latin Church. For that man fears you, and he avoids you. Close your eyes, then, and whom will he fear? And one who has already said what he has said, what will he not say when he fears no one? Indeed, almost all the teachers of ecclesiastical doctrine have perished from the Church. This domestic enemy rushes, as it were, into an empty Church. He seizes for himself alone the teaching role in it, and he introduces into the Divine Scriptures, just as he used to in dialectics, his own ideas and his perennial novelties. He stands as the censor of the Faith, not its disciple; he corrects it rather than follows it.

3. Therefore, here are the articles gathered from his works which I thought should be brought to your attention:

1) He defines faith as the estimation of things which are not seen.

2) He says that in God the names of Father, and Son, and Holy Spirit are improper; rather this is a description of the fullness of the Supreme Goodness.

3) The Father is the fullness of power, the Son a certain power, the Holy Spirit no power.

4) Concerning the Holy Spirit, he says that he is not from the substance of the Father and Son as the Son is from the substance of the Father.

5) The Holy Spirit is the soul of the world.

6) By free will, without the help of grace, we can will and act well.

7) Therefore Christ did not assume flesh and suffer to free us from the yoke[2] of the devil.

8) Christ, God and Man, is not the Third Person in the Trinity.[3]

9) In the Sacrament of the Altar, the form of the previous substance remains, perduring in the air.

10) He says that diabolical suggestions are expressed in men by physical means.

11) We do not contact the guilt of original sin from Adam, only the penalty.

12) There is no sin except in the consent to sin and contempt of God.

13) No sin is committed through concupiscence, pleasure, and ignorance; what comes from these is not sinful but natural.

4. These few articles, gathered from his writings, I thought should be initially presented to you to arouse you and to explain ourselves lest we seem to be upset for no good reason. While others are falling in with these ideas, I, nevertheless, by the help of him in whose hands we and our words

rest, have disagreed more and more with them. I think it of little account if I should have displeased you by my letter, as long as I fail not in faith. If I have been able in any way to show you that I am justly disturbed, let you also be disturbed and not fear to be a foot or a hand or even an eye in the service of the head. I have loved him and I want to love him, God is my witness, but in a matter such as this, no one will ever hold the place of intimate or friend to me. This evil is not to be handled by a secret warning of correction. By his own doing, it has become so public. Moreover, I hear there are still other works of his. To name them: *Sic et Non, Scita te ipsum,* and other such. I fear their dogma is as monstrous as their names. But as the saying has it, they hate the light. When they were sought, they were not to be found. But now we have covered this matter.

NOTES

[1]William here uses colorful words: *incantator,* a sorcerer, to cast spells on the *regulum,* the petty king.

[2]Charlville 67, Mabillon (*S. Bernardi Opera,* Ep. 326, [Paris, 1680] 1:302) and Leclercq (*Rev. Ben.* 79:378) have "yoke," *ingo;* but Migne (PL 182:532) has "right" or "power," *iure.*

[3]The argument here is not whether Christ is second or third Person but whether he is one of the three Persons. Medievals frequently spoke of him as the Third Person although we today tend to think of him as the Second Person of the Trinity. Where the three persons are absolutely one and equal it makes little difference who we say is second or third as long as we affirm the equally divine personhood of all three.

Two Treatises on Love

Whenever one speaks of William of St. Thierry one immediately thinks of Bernard of Clairvaux. And I believe Bernard would be happy if whenever one spoke of Bernard of Clairvaux, William would come to mind. At least Bernard's letters give us a strong basis for saying this.[1] The lives of these two twelfth-century monks, alike and unlike in so many ways, were intimately intertwined.[2] At their very first meeting[3] they seem to have discovered "another self" in each other, and no matter what popular notions about monks and friendship may prevail,[4] these two totally dedicated and saintly monks did not hesitate to take even extraordinary measures to foster and enjoy their friendship.[5]

Until quite recently, Bernard was assumed to be wholly the master—William the admiring disciple.[6] However, in recent years, as William has come more into his own, this is being questioned more and more. Dom Jean Leclercq has clearly established William's influence on Bernard's *Apologia*[7] and his *Adversus Abaelardum*.[8] In the one case it is perhaps more extrinsic; in the other William clearly acts as Bernard's theologian.[9] But the matter is not so clear when we come to their spiritual doctrine. All sorts of conjectures have been made in the light of the *Brevis commentatio*.[10] My aim in this brief paper is not so ambitious as to try to solve this extremely complicated question, but rather to make a very modest contribution to its study by comparing, under certain aspects, the rather brief and relatively early treatises on love which each of these monks has left us.[11]

Even though we cannot date either piece with certitude, the chronology is fairly well established. William's treatise seems quite certainly the earlier. Most would date it around 1120.[12] It may be conjectured that it is substantially composed of chapter talks given to his community in his early days as abbot of St. Thierry. We might add to this conjecture by suggesting the following development:

William, as a significant member of the community of St. Nicaise, accompanied his abbot on a trip south.[13] On their way back they broke their journey to see the young abbot of Clairvaux whose reputation was rapidly growing even then. That Bernard made a profound impression on William at that first encounter cannot be doubted. Some thirty years later, William would still speak of it with awe:

> It was about this time that I myself began to be a frequent visitor to him and his monastery. . . . Going into the hovel which had become a palace by his presence and thinking what a wonderful person dwelt in such a despicable place, I was filled with such awe of the hut itself that I felt as if I were approaching the very altar of God. And the sweetness of his character so attracted me to him and filled me with desire to share his life amid such poverty and simplicity, that if the opportunity had been given to me then, I should have asked nothing more than to be allowed to remain with him always, looking after him and ministering to his needs. . . . But it is not really true to say that he was alone, for God was with him, and the holy angels came to console and watch over him. . . . Although unworthy of so great a privilege, I remained with him for a few days, and as I looked about me I thought I was gazing on a new heaven and a new earth, for it seemed as though there were tracks freshly made by men of our own day in the path that had first been trodden by our fathers, the Egyptian monks of long ago.[14]

Undoubtedly William returned home inspired to seek a more truly contemplative life. But the way was not to be easy for him, for he was very soon elected abbot of the not insignificant abbey of St. Thierry. Something of his struggle—one that would grow and be reflected in all his writings until it was resolved by his resignation in 1135—is expressed in his earliest extant work, a soliloquy, *On Contemplating God*.[15] In this William poured out his longing for that contemplative experience which he saw irradiating the life and countenance of his recently acquired friend. He perceived that such an experience was to be obtained essentially through desire and found in love. This naturally led to his investigation of the *Nature and Dignity of Love*.[16]

Bernard's treatise, *On Loving God*,[17] certainly was written later. The inclusion of the *Letter to the Carthusians*[18] and the fact that Cardinal Haimeric, to whom the treatise is addressed, became chancellor only in 1126, makes that year the earliest possible date for the treatise's composition. The death of the Cardinal determines the other extreme: 1141.[19] But chronological succession does not settle the question of dependency nor even throw much light on it. William probably visited Clairvaux more than once before he wrote his treatise.[20] We could well imagine the neophyte abbot on his visits carefully listening to his renowned friend's talks to his community and taking mental, if not actual, notes which he would make use of when he returned home and spoke to his own community.

We may find some evidence of this if we compare sections 18-24 of his treatise[21] with Bernard's Tenth Occasional Sermon.[22] These *Sermones de diversis* are probably in good part some of the ordinary chapter talks that Bernard gave his community. From its position toward the beginning of the series, it can be surmised that *Sermon Ten* was preached and/or written early in Bernard's career, at a date perhaps not too far removed from the time William spoke in the same vein to his own community. There is a certain amount of conjecture here, but if we read the two passages we will see that they are undoubtedly related:[23]

Sermon Ten

If you consider the matter carefully you can see that love is a multifold thing and perhaps is fivefold like the five senses of the body....

Then, if you care to examine the matter more carefully you will perhaps see that, indeed, the first form of love, love of one's own relatives, is like the sense of touch. This sense perceives only what is closest to it and is joined to the body, and so also is that love given to those closest to our own flesh. And this also enters into the likeness: this sense alone is found in everybody, because this love is natural to all flesh....

We can see how much social love is like the sense of taste, both because of the greater sweetness it brings into one's life and because this is the particular sense of which human life stands more in need. I cannot see how one can be said to live, at least in this common life,

The Nature and Dignity of Love

There are, as we have said, five bodily senses, and by means of these the soul gives sense-life to the body.

Likewise there are five spiritual senses, by means of which charity gives life to the soul....

The love of near relatives is compared to the sense of touch, for this disposition is inherent in all men and we think of it as common and somehow tangible. It wells up in everyone in the most natural way, and there is no way of stopping it. The sense of touch is wholly corporeal, and it comes about by the contact of any two bodies. Contact will engender touch in any body which is alive.

Social love is compared to the sense of taste. This is brotherly love, the love of the holy Catholic Church.... Taste is admittedly a corporeal function, but its purpose is to bring about the savoring of food within the body, which savoring is for the soul's appreciation. So we may say if he does not love those among whom he lives.

General love, by which all men are loved, is like the sense of smell in this that this sense perceives more distant things and while it is not wholly divorced from bodily pleasure, it nevertheless experiences it less insofar as it is more extended.

Hearing for its part perceives things much more remote, and among men no one is so far removed from the lover as the one who does not love. While in the other senses the flesh has some share in the pleasure, and they seem to belong more to the flesh, hearing is almost wholly that this sense is mainly a bodily thing, but quite evidently it also belongs in some measure to the soul. This is equally true of social love, which comes as the result of people living together and of sharing the same profession or studies or such like things. It provides a common bond and grows through mutual help and exchange. It would seem to belong to the soul in its relationship with the body (being based on physical cohabitation and common material interests), but it is in large part spiritual. For just as flavor is in tasting, so does brotherly love yield that love....

To the sense of smell we can compare natural love, by which we mean that love which causes us to love every man in virtue of our sharing in the same nature, and to ask for nothing in return .... Natural love then belongs more to the spirit than to the soul which vivifies the body, for it considers only the human connaturality of the loved one, and has no respect for consanguinity, society, or any other kind of obligation. Spiritual love we compare to the sense of hearing. By spiritual love we understand the love of our enemies. Hearing, instead of producing its effect within the body, works after an exterior fashion. That is to say, it knocks on the ear and calls on the soul to come out and hear. Likewise the love of our outside the realm of the flesh. And hearing rightly seems to apply to that love which arises from obedience, for that quite evidently belongs to hearing....

Finally, sight is like divine love. It is more excellent than the others and of a rather unique nature. It is more perceptive and discerns things at greater distances. Certainly smell and hearing do seem to perceive distant objects but they are believed to do this through air which they take in. But this is not the case with sight which rather seems to go out and approach objects. So it is in the matter of love. In a certain sense we take to ourselves our neighbor whom we love as ourselves, and also our enemies whom we love, so that they might be as we are, friends of God. But if we love God, as he deserves, with all our strength, all our soul and all our heart, it is more of a question of going out to him, and with all speed seeking to approach him who is inexpressibly above us. Indeed it is true and manifest that sight excels all the other bodily senses, and hearing has greater dignity than the other three. The sense of smell seems more eminent, if not more useful than taste and touch; and taste excels touch. This is manifest from the position of the various members of the body. The eyes have the highest place, the ears just a bit lower. The nostrils are lower

enemies is not stirred in our hearts by any power of nature, nor by any spontaneous affection, but by obedience alone, which hearing signifies.

Divine love is compared to sight, for sight is the highest of all the affections.... The power of seeing is located in the highest part of the body, and because of this it has all the other instruments of sense beneath it. Those which belong rather to the soul are nearer to it than those which belong more to the body. The least of the senses, and the lowest, is touch, which is most proper to the hand although it is common to the whole body. The mind, which is the head of the soul, must be the seat of the love of God, so that from this position it may illumine, govern, and guard all the loves below itself, giving them of its own warmth and light. The more spiritual loves will be nearer to it than the more carnal ones, when we have learned to love God with all our heart and soul and strength, and when we really love our neighbor as ourselves.

than the ears, the lips below the nose, and the hands and the other parts of the body which pertain to touch are clearly below the mouth. In this way the relative dignity of the various senses of the soul can be considered; but since you can already easily see this, because of the lack of time I will move on. I will leave that to your diligence to reflect on....

The whole of these two texts should actually be read and compared but the excerpts given here clearly demonstrate the similarity of thought and construction. William's treatment is more developed and many Scripture texts are brought forth. Did he respond to Bernard's concluding invitation and diligently consider the matter, developing it in his own presentation? Or was Bernard excerpting the essence of William's text? It does not seem likely that he would have invited his hearers to develop the theme on their own if he and they already had at hand a text written by William. Unless they are drawing from some common source, I think we would have to affirm some interdependency. And I would be inclined to say it is William who is developing Bernard as he has been invited to do.

Let us consider another factor. A summary of Bernard's treatise is to be found in an earlier letter, which Bernard did not hesitate to add to his treatise (even though it includes some relatively unrelated material[24]). This indicates that the ideas were long in his mind. This letter was not an important piece of writing and therefore did not call for a particular literary endeavor to be creative. When Bernard wrote to the Carthusians in 1125 he probably used ideas that were already in his mind, ideas he could well have discussed with his fellow abbot as they recuperated together. William tells us explicitly that they discoursed on the *Song of Songs*,[25] and Bernard does connect the consummation of his degrees of love with the *Song*.[26]

It is significant that the passage in the two treatises that most closely relates them is in the case of Bernard to be found in the earlier letter. It is in the central passage on the essential nature of charity. Compare the two:

On Loving God	The Nature and Dignity of Love
God is love. Therefore it is rightly said, charity is God, and the gift of God. Thus charity	Charity is God, and "God is charity." A short praise for charity, but it sums up everything.

gives charity; substantial charity produces the quality of charity. Where it signifies the giver it takes the name of substance; where it means the gift, it is called a quality.

Whatever can be said of God can also be said of charity. Considered according to the nature of gift and giver, the name of the substance of charity is in the giver, the name of the quality of charity is in the gift.[27]

Again, unless a common source can be affirmed, the dependency of one upon the other is clear. But, again, it is not easy to affirm in which direction the dependency lies.

The most obvious general similarity between the two treatises is that they both trace out four stages in the development of love. But the categories they employ are in fact quite different. William is more allegorical. He compares man's growth in love with his natural growth, passing from infancy (*voluntas*—choice), through youth (*amor*—love) and manhood (*caritas* —charity) to old age (*sapientia*—wisdom).[28] These stages provide the whole context of his treatise.

Not so for Bernard. The stages or degrees of love are introduced only after a long treatment of the motive, measure and profit of love.[29] His presentation of the degrees and indeed the whole treatise is more philosophical than William's. Maybe he means to warn us that this is to be the case by his allusion in the Prologue to his being considered a philosopher.[30] It is not that William despises philosophy or a philosophical approach. He draws on philosophy in developing his treatise.[31] In his earlier work he points to the "true and divine philosophy" that is found in the teaching of the Lord Jesus to his disciples.[32] Bernard actually does not depart from William in this. If he does begin his treatise with rather precise synthetic distinctions as he develops his initial thought, he quickly moves into the patristic style to which he is more accustomed. His tender love for our Lord is very much in evidence. And the same is true of his friend. William's long *excursus* on Christ during his treatment of "old age" is truly a work of beauty, the fruit of a deep, personal and tender love.[33]

The way the two monks develop their theme is quite different—the *way*, but there is actually not much difference in their approach.[34] What of the content?

As we have already seen, in the expression of the essence of charity, of love, they are at one. Can their respective four stages be identified? It is difficult to equate them. William's whole ladder is set a bit below Bernard's. His first step is naked will, image of God, free, moving toward the initial choice that leads it on to the second step of love. Here he joins Bernard's first step, carnal love, and touches the underpart of his second, where the soul begins to love God for the benefits it has received. William's third step of charity is founded on Bernard's second and most fully on his third, where God is loved because of his own goodness. Wisdom, the savor of God, William's "old age," is already found in Bernard's third degree of love, but as it reaches out beyond, it parallels Bernard's fourth—love of self and all else only for God's sake. While all the elements are there, William's treatment seems to lack the richness and depth found in Bernard. William honestly says:

> This is the wisdom which the Apostle "speaks among the perfect," and which we also speak who have heard but not seen. . . . And if we had actually seen it, we would be able to say more than we do, describing it more fully.[35]

Here I believe is a fundamental difference. Both are essentially existential writers in the best sense of that word, writing out of their own lived experience. But William has been but recently drawn into the contemplative way. His description of the way is much fuller than Bernard's, more helpful to the young, no doubt. But when he gets to the heights his treatment is more speculative, more a thing of hearsay and desire.[36] But Bernard writes more from personal experience. William just touches on rapture in passing;[37] Bernard writes on it at length.[38] William adapts the first great commandment to his four stages;[39] Bernard declares it can only be fulfilled in the resurrection of the body.[40] William does not fail to speak of the eschaton;[41] but it does not form a significant part of the fabric of his fourth degree as it does for Bernard.[42]

I would say in conclusion that while there are touch points between Bernard and William in these two treatises, there is a very great independence. In many incidents where similar themes are touched on, they are handled in very different ways.[43] William's explicit use of liturgical texts[44] and pagan authors[45] finds no echo in Bernard, while Bernard's very traditional presentation of the three kinds of fear, which is developed at length, is not mirrored in William's text even though occasions offered themselves for its introduction.[46]

Where a textual relationship is present I do not think that a study of these texts alone establishes in which direction the dependence lay. Bernard could have read his friend's treatise and used ideas from it in speaking to his community (*Sermon Ten*) and in writing to the Carthusians. Just as readily, as we conjectured above, William could have heard *Sermon Ten* while visiting Clairvaux and Bernard could have shared his thoughts with him on the nature of charity, and then William could have used these ideas in talks at home and in his treatise. The more general argument coming from William's idolization of Bernard and Bernard's leadership qualities I do not think proves William the disciple in every case. William, too, was a leader.[47] Moreover, we have evidence of the dependence of Bernard on William as a theologian.[48] Indeed, this fact might argue strongly for Bernard's dependence on William in the case of the clear distinction concerning the essence of charity as an accidental quality. This was a still disputed question at this period. And Bernard's contemporary and friend, the Master of the Sentences, Peter Lombard, held the opposing position[49] and had to be refuted by Aquinas.[50] Again, though, the argument is far from being apodictic.

As I said at the beginning, this is meant to be but a very modest contribution to the much more extensive study that must take place before we can hope to have anything like a satisfying understanding—if we can ever have it—of the ways and degree in which these two great monks influenced each other's thought.[51] While a comparison of the two treatises does show a commonness of spirit between the friends and some kind of interdependence, it does not establish a dependence on the part of William, at least at the time of this writing—a significant fact, given the adulation he heaped upon Bernard. This conclusion may depend more on my lack of perception than on the actual facts. I suspect William had Bernard in mind when he wrote: "The wise have a way of speaking to one another by means of their mutual love, and this they communicate to each other by means of a glance...a language strange to the stranger."[52]

NOTES

[1]See Bernard's Letters to William of St. Thierry: Ep. 85 and 86; PL 182:206-210; tr. Bruno Scott James, *The Letters of St. Bernard of Clairvaux*, Letters 87 and 88, pp. 124-128, where we read such passages as: "I love you as much as I can according to the power that has been given to me." "It was you who gave me this formula of greeting when you wrote: 'To his friend all that a friend could wish.' Receive back what is your own, and in doing so realize that my soul is not far from one with whom I share a common language." James includes as Letter 89 (pp. 128-129) one that might have been addressed to William at the time he went to Signy against Bernard's will. Here we read Bernard writing of William: "I do not ask for my friend back, because I have never lost him. I cling to him, and there is no one who can take him from me."

[2]I hesitate to say "Cistercians" since over half the time William and Bernard were friends, William was a Black Monk, as he was for the greater part of his monastic life. Yet William is spoken of as one of the "Four Evangelists of Citeaux."

[3]We cannot say for certain exactly when William first visited Bernard. Jean-Marie Déchanet, *William of St. Thierry: The Man and His Work*, CS 10, tr. Richard Strachen (Spencer, MA: Cistercian Publications, 1972) p. 24, says: "Toward the end of the year 1118, when he was still a monk at St. Nicaise...". But Stanislaus Ceglar, who explores the question extensively (*William of St. Thierry: The Chronology of His Life with a*

Study of His Treatise On the Nature of Love, *His Authorship of the* Brevis Commentatio, *the* In Lacu, *and the* Reply to Cardinal Matthew [Ann Arbor, MI: University Microfilms, 1971] pp. 33-40) gives the opinions of all the authors and himself concludes: "If, then, one puts the probable approximate time of our William's first visit to Clairvaux in the early spring of 1120, one could hardly be more than five months wrong."—p. 40.

⁴For a thorough study of the attitude of the early Cistercians on friendship see M. Adele Fiske, *Friends and Friendship in the Monastic Tradition,* CIDOC Cuaderno 51 (Cuernavaca: CIDOC, 1970).

⁵In his life of Bernard, William candidly admits that after their first encounter he became a frequent visitor: "It was about this time that I myself began to be a frequent visitor to him and his monastery." (*Vita Bern,* I, 7, 32-4; PL 185:246). And Bernard himself took an active part in developing the friendship. William writes: "I was unwell at St. Thierry, drained of strength and quite worn out by an illness that dragged on and on. When the man of God heard the news he sent his brother Gerard, of blessed memory, to bid me come to Clairvaux. . . . Bernard's illness itself worked for my good, while I lay ill beside him. Flat on our backs, the two of us, we spent the livelong day talking. . . ." (*Vita Bern,* I, 12, 59; PL 185:259).

⁶See note 14 below.

⁷See Jean Leclercq's Introduction to the *Apologia* in *Sancti Bernardi Opera,* 9 vols. (Rome: Editiones Cistercienses, 1957-1973 [hereafter OB]), 3:63-7.

⁸Jean Leclercq, "Les lettres de Guillaume de Saint-Thierry à saint Bernard," *Revue Bénédictine* 79 (1969) 375-82. Leclercq concludes: ". . .il ressort que la dépendance de Bernard à l'égard de Guillaume est, non seulement manifeste, mais très étroite, beaucoup plus qu'on aurait pu s'y attendre de la part de saint Bernard."

⁹See Edward Little, "Bernard and Abelard at the Council of Sens, 1140," in *Bernard of Clairvaux: Studies presented to Dom Jean Leclercq* (Washington, D.C.: Cisterican Publications, 1973) pp. 35-51; especially the Appendix where Little lists the Nineteen Propositions of Bernard and the Thirteen Propositions of William, stating: "Bernard's nineteen propositions are a re-working of a list of thirteen, which William of St. Thierry had included in a letter he had written to Bernard and to Bishop Geoffrey of Chartres. Bernard took some of William's propositions unchanged (William's no. 3, 5); he altered some (William's no. 4, 6, 7, 8, 10, 11, 13); he omitted some (William's no. 1, 2, 9, 12); he added some of his own . . ." (pp. 50-51). See also Jean Leclercq, "Les formes successives de la lettre-traité de saint Bernard contre Abelard," *Revue Bénédictine* 78 (1968) 86-105.

¹⁰Ceglar studies the question at length (*William of St. Thierry,* Chap. IX: "William's Part in the *Brevis Commentatio,*" pp. 350-379) and concludes: "It can be taken for certain that *BC* is a more or less faithful literary record of the spiritual conversations of the two friends, as described by William in the *Vita Bernardi,* xii, 59" (p. 352). See also, J. Hourlier, "Guillaume de St.-Thierry et la *Brevis commentatio in Cantica,*" ASOC 12 (1956) 105-114; Jean Leclercq, "Le commentaire bref du Cantique attribué à St. Bernard," in *Etudes sur St. Bernard et le texte de ses écrits,* ASOC 9 (1953) 105-124.

¹¹Dom Hourlier has already done a comparative study of these two treatises: "St. Bernard and Guillaume de St. Thierry dans le *Liber de Amore,*" in St. Bernard Théologien: *Actes du Congrès de Dijon,* 15-19 September 1953, ASOC 9 (1953) 223-233. It is

hoped the additional ideas presented here will complement that study and bring the whole question a step forward.

¹²Déchanet in *William of St. Thierry* (p. 11) says: "Written between 1119 and 1122..." and in his chronological listing in *Oeuvres choisies du Guillaume de St. Thierry* (Paris: Aubier, 1944) says "Vers 1120" (p. 39). Ceglar says Hourlier accepts this (Ceglar, *William of St. Thierry*, p. 377) but this is not clear in the text of Hourlier (*La contemplation de Dieu*, SCh 61 [Paris: Cerf, 1959] pp. 15-17). Ceglar himself studies the question and concludes: "...Déchanet's dating...is certainly wrong" (p. 377). "In short, there are no cogent reasons to date *CD* and *NDA* [the treatise we are considering] before the mid-twenties of the XII century (1124-26)" (p. 378). A. Wilmart ("La serie et la date des ouvrages de Guillaume de St. Thierry," *Revue Mabillon* 14 [1924] 156-167) and R. Thomas (*Notes sur Guillaume de St. Thierry*, 4 vols., Pain de Cîteaux, 1-4 [Chambarand, 1959], 1:33) hold for around 1120.

¹³Admittedly, it is not clear from the text that the abbot in question is his own abbot: "...when I first went to see him with a certain other abbot...."—*St. Bernard of Clairvaux*, tr. Geoffrey Webb and Adrian Walker (Westminster, Maryland: Newman Press, 1960) p. 56.

¹⁴*Ibid.*, pp. 56-58.

¹⁵The critical edition of this was published by Hourlier, SCh 61 (See note 12 above). An English translation is available in the Cistercian Fathers Series: Sister Penelope [Lawson] *CSMV, The Works of William of St. Thierry*, Vol. 1: *On Contemplating God, Prayer, Meditations*, CF 3 (Spencer, MA: Cistercian Publications, 1971) pp. 36-64.

¹⁶Perhaps the best edition of *Nat am* is that of Robert Thomas, Pain de Cîteaux 24 (Chambarand, 1965). Webb and Walker published a translation in 1956, *On the Nature and Dignity of Love* (London: Mowbrays, 1956) based on the Migne edition (PL 184:379-408) and on that of M. M. Davy (*Deux traités de l'amour de Dieu: De la contemplation de Dieu, De la nature et la dignité de l'amour* [Paris: Vrin, 1953]) who employed only a very limited number of manuscripts in the preparation of her edition.

¹⁷OB 3:119-154: *On Loving God*, tr. Robert Walton, O.S.B., CF 13 (Washington, D.C.: Cistercian Publications, 1974).

¹⁸OB 3:148-154; CF 13:125-132.

¹⁹See Leclercq's Introduction, OB 3:111-112.

²⁰See note 5 above.

²¹Davy, *Deux traités*, pp. 96-100; Webb and Walker, *On the nature*, pp. 30-33.

²²OB 6-2:121-124. There is so far no published translation of these *Sermones de diversis*, but one is in preparation for the Cistercian Fathers Series.

²³

Sermo 10

Porro dilectionem quidem multiplicem, si diligenter advertas, et fortasse secundum quinque corporis sensus quinquepertitam poteris invenire.

Denique, si curiosius considerare delectat, non immerito fortasse

Nat am

Per quinque sensus corporis, mediante vita, corpus anime conjungitur: per quinque sensus spirituales, mediante caritate, anima Deo consociatur.

Tactui comparatur amor parentum: quia affectus iste promptus videbitur primus, id est parentum amor, tactui convenire, quod hic sensus sola proxima et corpori iuncta percipiat, quemadmum amor ille nullis exhibetur nisi proximis carnis nostrae. Sed nec illud quidem discrepat a ratione similitudinis, quod hic solus e sensibus per corpus diffunditur universum, quoniam et amor ille naturalis est omni carni, adeo ut ipsa quoque animalia bruta et diligant fetus suos, et diligantur ab eis.

Amor quoque socialis videre licet quam proprie dicatur gustui convenire, ob maiorem profecto dulcedinem, et quoniam solus hic sensus est, quo magis eget humana vita. Nec video qua ratione vivere dicendus sit, saltem hac communi vita, qui non eos diligit inter quos vivit.

Amor autem generalis, quo videlicet omnes homines diliguntur, odoratus habet similitudinem, in eo utique quod hic sensus iam remotiora percipiat, et quod non ex toto carnalis delectationis expers, eo tamen tenuiorem eam habeat, quo diffusiorem.

Auditus autem multo magis re-

omnibus, et quodammodo grossus et palpabilis, sic se omnibus naturali occursu prebet et ingerit, ut effugere eum non possis, etiam si velis. Tactus enim sensus et totus corporalis qui ex quorumlibet corporum conjunctione conficitur....

Secundo, gustui comparatur amor socialis, amor fratrum, amor sancte et catholice Ecclesie.... Gustus etiam lecet corporaliter exerceatur saporem tamen introrsum generat, quo anima afficitur. Propter quod corporalis quidem sensus hic maxime, sed tamen ex parte aliqua etiam animales esse comprobatur. Sic et amor socialis, qui ex corporali cohabitatione in unum, ex similitudine professionum, ex parilitate studiorum, aliisque hujusmodi causis, confederatur mutuisque officiis enutritur, maxime animalis esse videtur. Sed tamen ex magna parte etiam spiritualis est, qui secut sapor est in gustu, sic affectus fraterne caritatis flagrat in affectu....

Tertio, odori comparatur amor naturalis, qui naturaliter exipsius nature similitudine et consortio absque omni spe recompensationis omnem hominem diligit.... Sic et amor naturalis magis spiritualis esse videtur quam animalis; qui, preter solum connaturalis humanitatis respectum, non consanguinitas, non societas, nec aliqua omnino in eo necessitudo hujusmodi consideratur.

Quarto, auditui comparatur amor

motiora capit, nec inter homines ab amante quisquam remotior est quam non amans. Denique cum in ceteris sensibus nonnulla carnis ipsius oblectatio sit, et ad carnem magis pertinere videantur, auditus paene totus exit a carne, et ei dilectioni non immerito convenire videtur, cuius tota causa obedientia est, quam pertinere ad auditum satis evidens est, cum ceterarum, ut diximus, dilectionum nonnulla a carne sumatur occasio.

Porro visus quidem in eo sibi vindicat amoris divini similitudinem, quod ceteris omnibus excellentior et singularis cujusdam naturae, perspicacior quoque ceteris invenitur, et discernit multo remotiora. Denique odoratus quidem et auditus videntur utique remota sentire; sed ad se magis quem sentiant aerem creduntur attrahere. Visus autem non ita, sed magis ipse exire videtur et ad remota procedere. Sic et in dilectionibus est. Quodammodo enim attrahimus proximos, quos tamquam nosipsos diligimus: Attrahimus et inimicos, quos ad hoc diligimus, ut sint et ipsi sicut nos, id est ut sint amici. Deum vero si, ut dignum est, tota virtute, tota anima, toto corde diligimus, ipsi magis in eum pergimus, et tota festinatione in eum, qui ineffabiliter supra nos est, properamus. Iam vero et id manifestum est, quoniam in corporis sensibus visus quidem ceteris omnibus, auditus vero reliquis tribus dignior est; odoratus quoque et gustum, et tactum, etsi non utilitate, dignitate tamen superare videtur, et gustus tactui superexcellere, quod manifestat etiam dispositio ipsa membrorum. Oculis siquidem

spiritualis, amor inimicorum. Auditus enim nichil interius, id est intra corpus operatur, sed exterius quodammodo, id est ad aures pulsans, animam evocat ut exeat et audiat. Sic et amorem inimicorum in corde nulla vis nature, nullius alicujus necessitudinis suscitat affectus sed sola obedientia, que per auditum significatur.

Quinto, visui comparatur amor divinus. Visus enim principalis est sensus: sicut inter omnes affectiones principatum obtinet amor divinus.... Visus in eminenti corporis arce et insigni capitis loco positus etiam secundum pisius corporis formam infra se habet et ordine, et dignitate, et virtutis potentia omni ceterorum sensum instrumenta, ipsosque sensus, quos, ut ita dicam, animaliores, propinquiores, quos vero corporaliores, remotiores. Infimus enim omnium et ceteris ignobilior tactus, licet communis videatur esse totius corporis, tamen proprie manuum est. Sic mens que caput est anime, et principale ipsius mentis, sedes esse debet amoris Dei, ut sub se habeat et regat et illustret ceteros amores, nec sit in eis quod se abscondat a calore et lumine ejus; quos spiritualiores, habens propinquiores, quos animaliores vel carnaliores, remotiores: cum dilexerimus Dominum Deum nostrum et ex toto corde nostro, et ex tota anima nostra et ex omnibus viribus nostris et post proximum nostrum sicut nos ipsos.—Nat am 18-24; Davy, *Deux traités,* pp. 96-100; Webb and Walker, *On the nature,* pp. 29-32.

in summitate locatis, aures inferi-
ores esse quis nesciat? Sic et auri-
bus nares, et naribus fauces, ipsis
quoque faucibus manus pariter et
reliquas corporis partes, ad quas
pertinet tactus, subesse manifestum
est. Secundum hunc ergo modum,
et in sensibus animae considerare
licet alterum altero digniorem,
quod, quia facile iam potestis adver-
tere, brevitatis causa praetereo.
Illud quoque vestrae nihilominus
diligentiae considerandum relinquo
. . . . —OB 6-1:122-123.

[24]Most notably the development of the stages of fear, par. 36, OB 3:150-151; CF
13:127-129.

[25]"It was then, so far as the length of my illness allowed, that he expounded the
Song of Songs to me; though only in its moral sense, without launching upon the
mysteries with which the book abounds. This is what I hoped for, what I had asked
him to do."—*Vita Bern*, I, 12, 59; PL 185:259.

[26]Par. 31-33; OB 3:145-147; CF 13:122-125.

[27]

Dil

Deus caritas est. Dicitur ergo
recte caritas, et Deus, et Dei donum.
Itaque caritas dat caritatem, sub-
stantiva accidentalem. Ubi dantem
significat, nomen substantiae est;
ubi donum, qualitatis. Par. 35; OB
3:149; CF 13:127.

Nat am

Caritas autem Deus est; Deus,
inquit, caritas est. Brevis laus, sed
concludens omnia. Quidquid de Deo
dici potest dici et de caritate; sic
tamen ut, considerata secundum
naturas doni et dantis, in dante
nomen sit substantie, in dato qualitatis. . . . Par. 15; Davy, *Deux traités*,
p. 88; Webb and Walker, *On the
nature*, p. 24.

[28]Par. 4; Davy, *Deux traités*, p. 74; Webb and Walker, *On the nature*, p. 14.

[29]Par. 23; OB 3:138; CF 13:115.

[30]Prologue; OB 3:119; CF 13:91: ". . . lest silence make me pass for a philosopher."

[31]Par. 49; Davy, *Deux traités*, p. 128; Webb and Walker, *On the nature*, p. 54.

[32]Contemp 12; SCh 61:110; CF 3:60.

[33]Par. 40-46; Davy, *Deux traités*, pp. 118-126; Webb and Walker, *On the nature*,
pp. 46-51.

[34]This in part explains how this treatise of William could have come to be united to
that of Bernard and commonly offered together with it as being the work of
Bernard.

[35]Par. 47; Davy, *Deux traités*, p. 126; Webb and Walker, *On the nature*, p. 525.

[36]William's later and more mature work stands in marked contrast to the present work in this regard: *Exposition on the Song of Songs*, J.-M. Déchanet, etc., *Exposé sur le Cantique des cantiques*, SCh 82 (Paris: Cerf, 1962); Sr. Columba Hart, tr. *The Works of William of St. Thierry*, vol. 2, CF 6 (Spencer, MA: Cistercian Publications, 1969).

[37]Par. 8; Davy, *Deux traités*, p. 80; Webb and Walker, *On the nature*, p. 17.

[38]Par. 27; OB 3:142; CF 13:119-120.

[39]Par. 33; Davy, *Deux traités*, p. 110; Webb and Walker, *On the nature*, p. 42.

[40]Par. 29; OB 3:143f.; CF 13:121.

[41]Par. 52f.; Davy, *Deux traités*, pp. 134-136; Webb and Walker, *On the nature*, pp. 58-60.

[42]Par. 30-33; OB 3:144-147; CF 13:121-125. Bernard's strong, clear affirmation for the resurrection of the body stands out here.

[43]Besides those just noted, we might also note their respective treatment of fear.

[44]E.g., in proving his point concerning the mediation of Christ, he brings in the text used by the Church in concluding all prayers: "Through Jesus Christ our Lord." Par. 36, Davy, *Deux traités*, p. 114; Webb and Walker, *On the nature*, p. 44.

[45]E.g., Terence in par. 21 (Davy, p. 98; Webb and Walker, p. 31), Horace in par. 39 (Davy, p. 108; Webb and Walker, p. 39), Juvenal in par. 32 (Davy, p. 110; Webb and Walker, p. 41).

[46]See par. 7, Davy, *Deux traités*, p. 78; Webb and Walker, *On the nature*, p. 16; par. 41-42, Davy, pp. 120-122; Webb and Walker, pp. 49-50.

[47]Besides being the abbot of a prominent abbey, William exercised a leadership role in the reform of the Black Monks; see Ceglar, *William of St. Thierry*, pp. 400-404, V. Berliere, ed., *Documents inedits pour servir à l'histoire ecclésiastique de la Belgique*, 2 vols. (Maredsous, 1894) 1:91-110.

[48]See above, notes 8 and 9. R. Javelet, *Image et ressemblance au douzième siècle*, 2 vols. (Paris, 1967) notes the influence of William on Bernard in regard to his doctrine on grace and free choice (1:196-197).

[49]*Sententiarum*, Lib. I, distc. xvii, cap. 1; OR 1:106.

[50]*Summa theologica*, 2-2, q. 23, a. 2 c.

[51]Certainly William's *Exposition on the Song of Songs* would have to be carefully compared with Bernard's *Sermons on the Song of Songs*; e.g., Cant 4 with SC 79:1.

[52]Nat am 51; Davy, *Deux traités*, p. 132; Webb and Walker, *On the nature*, p. 56.

The Cell
The Teaching of William of St. Thierry

Any student of Cistercian architecture or anyone who has had the joy of visiting one of the awesome twelfth-century abbeys that still grace the European countryside would be familiar with the spacious dormitories that characterized the east and west ranges of Cistercian monasteries.[1] The open dormitory, with long rows of simple cots and straw pallets, was seen as a literal and proper interpretation of Benedict of Nursia's *Rule for Monasteries*.[2] It was part of being 'poor with the poor Christ.'[3]

It was in periods of decline, when numbers and fervor diminished, that monks staked out for themselves portions of the spacious dormitory area and constructed for themselves private rooms and even suites of rooms.[4] With each successive reform or renewal the dormitory was restored, though modern sensitivity allowed for partitions of various sorts. In general, though, the dormitories were reserved for sleeping and a curtain rather than a door closed off the individual cubicle.[5] In no way then were they to be cells in the classical monastic sense.

The Second Vatican Council called for a radical renewal in every segment of the Roman Catholic Church and in every detail of its life. The Cistercians were not to be exempted. The principles of this renewal were not only the Holy Gospels and the sacred traditions, but also the signs of the times.[6] As the General Chapter of the Cistercians of the Strict Observance courageously examined, in the light of these principles, the way of life prevailing in the monasteries now scattered around the globe, some traditions as old as the Order were set aside. For the first time, not because of decline, but for the sake of renewal, the Cistercians decided to enter upon the almost irreversible experiment of transforming their dormitories into private or individual cells.[7]

Following another newly incorporated principle, namely, pluralism, each monastery was left free to decide whether it would embark on the experiment or not, and how it would employ the newly constructed cells. There were many variations in practice, but the vast majority of the communities decided to move ahead with the experiment. For some, this meant building new wings; others were in the process of construction and incorporated the new design. Many renovated existing dormitories as best they could, some with rather flimsy partitions, others with very solid and virtually sound-proof rooms, replete with their own heating and cooling systems and bathroom facilities.

Many plans were beset with the problem of the fewness and placement of the windows and support columns in the existing dormitories, giving rise to rooms of many sizes and shapes. The furnishings of the new rooms also expressed a very wide spectrum of ideas and values.

As the monks and nuns moved into the new cells—and in some cases, rushed into them—for the most part they did not foresee what a great impact this change was going to have upon their lives. In most monasteries, the adoption of cells paralleled the abandonment of the sign language and many of the rules of silence. In this regard it was indeed a great experiment. It may take decades to fully evaluate the impact of the private cells on Cistercian life, but a decade has been sufficient for the impact of altered patterns of communication and silence to be keenly felt, reviewed, and repeatedly revised. The struggle between contemplation and community goes on, more acutely than ever, happily for most communities a vitalizing challenge calling to an ever deeper commitment to both of these values.[8]

The individual monks and nuns, moving from the context of the common dormitory, scriptorium, and reading cloister to the full or partial use of a private cell, have felt the need of guiding principles that were not a part of their earlier formation. Novice masters and mistresses forming today's candidates for the use of the cell have little personal experience on which to draw. Communities sense the need of 'guidelines,' sometimes confessing that they have come to the realization a bit late, for they could have benefited by more guidance in the actual construction of the cells.

It is in this area that Providence has provided for the Cistercians in a unique and beneficent way. Given the history of the Order, one could hardly have expected that the Cistercian Fathers would have explicitly addressed themselves in a precise and positive way as regards both the construction and the use of private cells. Yet, the guiding hand of the Lord did bring it about that one of the four 'Evangelists of Citeaux' and the one most experientially qualified, did give some precise and insightful instruc-tions on the cell.

William of St. Thierry, Bernard of Clairvaux's most intimate friend, lived most of his life in a private cell.[9] Monastically, he grew up in a Benedictine abbey and then for a long time served another as abbot. In both of these abbeys he probably had the use of a private cell. Even after his entrance into the ranks of the Cistercians, by special provision of the General Chapter, at the behest of St. Bernard, he was to enjoy the use of a cell. Finally, he had the opportunity for an extended period to witness at close quarters the use of the cell by a fervent community of Carthusians. By historical necessity, his teaching on the cell is directly addressed to these monks, the Brothers of Mont Dieu, but it is a teaching that is clearly flavored by his Cistercian outlook, and in its spirit and practice is fully applicable to today's Cistercians as they begin to dwell in cells.

I would like to summarize here some of the most immediate and principal lineaments of William's teaching on the cell. In fact, almost the whole of his *Letter to the Brethren of Mont Dieu*, better known as the *Golden Epistle,*[10] addresses itself to life in the cell. We will begin by looking at his teaching on the construction of the cell itself.

The monks to whom William writes find themselves in a position similar to that of many Cistercian communities today. Already some of the cells are constructed, and there is question as to whether they really do accord with the true spirit of the Order and the monastic life. William is gentle and less than direct in pointing out the excesses.

Immediately we perceive William's Cistercian optic. At least four times he urges that the monks build their own cells.[11] This was certainly the Cistercian way. Blessed with large numbers of lay brothers, many skilled in the various crafts, as a rule, they built their own abbeys, and did a perduring and magnificent job of it.[12] But manual labor did not play the same role in Carthusian life—as William elsewhere acknowledges.[13] Yet the principle William evokes for urging the monks to do their own construction is a valid one. The builder necessarily leaves his own impress on his work. If the cell is to be truly monastic it should be the product of a monastic heart. Outside architects cannot be expected to achieve the inner harmony with monastic values that the construction should reflect. Secular workers will not only leave an alien imprint but also an atmosphere filled with worldly vibrations that may take a long time to eradicate. Let us listen to William:

> Is it right that the place where God dwells with men should be made by men of the world? Let it be themselves, they to whom is shown in the heights of their spirit the model of the true beauty of God's house, let it be themselves who do their own building. Let it be themselves, they who are bidden by their preoccupation with interior things to scorn and disregard all outward things, let it be themselves who do their own building. No skill on the part of hired craftsmen will be so successful as their own lack of worldly concern to produce an expression of poverty, the beauty of holy simplicity, and the traditional sobriety of the Fathers.[14]

In this text we also hear an enunciation of the basic qualities that should mark the cell of the monk: poverty, the beauty of holy simplicity, and traditional sobriety.

In speaking of the spirit and actuality of poverty that should mark monastic construction, William gives forceful expression to concerns that respond directly to some of our modern sensitivities: the common steward-ship of the goods of the earth and the rights of the poor to an equal share in what we have been given to use. In building our cells we are using "money that does not belong to us,"[15] the funds that "came from the alms of the poor."[16] To build "costly...imposing cells...which display a religious respectability" is to miss the mark; it is to compassionate weaknesses rather than to foster and confirm strength. William exhorts to that "holy rustic-ity" commended by "Solomon" (Sir. 7:16)[17] and points to the example of the Fathers. It is enough for the monk "to weave a cell out of pliant boughs, plaster it with mud, cover it with anything that comes to hand" (we think here of St. Benedict's prescription that the monks are to use the material that can be found most cheaply in the locality)[18] and so come by a dwelling-place "eminently suited to him."[19] The Fathers worked with their own hands and fed the poor with the fruits of their toil. While they themselves went hungry, they contributed food from the wastes of the desert to feed the prisons and the hospitals of the cities and succored those who were laboring under any form of distress. Yet all this time they lived by the work of their own hands and dwelt in buildings their own hands had erected.[20]

The emphasis on manual labor here is very Cistercian, as is the response to the needs of the poor. But this quality of poverty—a humble and simple fabric—has also an inner meaning for the monk. William elaborates an important and basic principle:

> What is within us is benefited in no slight degree by what is around us, when it is arranged to accord with our needs and in its own way to correspond with the ideals we have set before us.[21]

Then he immediately begins to apply it to the matter at hand: "Poorer surroundings check ill-ordered desires,...they awaken the conscience to love of poverty."[22] On the other hand—and this William asks his readers to take on faith, hoping they will not learn by experience—"imposing exte-riors are quick to slacken a manlike determination and tend to make the masculine spirit effeminate."[23] Modern sensitivity to sexist typology might react to this mode of expression. It is an evocation of William's whole use of the *anima—animus,* the animal and the rational man.[24] But what he is saying is simply true, that soft living leads to softness in the spiritual struggle. Influenced no doubt by St. Benedict's imagery as well as by Scriptural types, William sees the monk as a *pilgrim,* as a soldier on campaign, who must live in something as detached from this world as a tent so that he is ready to leave his earthly dwelling at a moment's notice for his fatherland, his own city.[25] More positively, he affirms that "a spirit that is intent on interior things is better served by an absence of decoration and trimmings in the things around it.... The interior life is effectively brought into harmony when all externals are proclaimed to be of little value."[26]

William is sensitive to those who would argue: 'Well, one gets used to these things being around. After a time they have little impact.' His response, drawn undoubtedly from long pastoral experience, is:

> ...although there may be some who use such things as if they were not using them (1 Cor. 7:31), yet attachments of this kind are rooted out and vanquished more effectively by contempt than by use.[27]

Moreover, there is the question of witness. The monks' poverty and simplicity "show that they have their minds elsewhere most of the time ...that their preoccupations are of another order."[28]

What then is to be done with cells that are already constructed and offend against these monastic values of poverty, simplicity, and sobriety? Herein William displays not only his moderation, but also his creative ability to see good coming out of every situation. The "elegant cells" are to remain standing. To demolish them would be wasteful and contrary to true poverty. The brethren are certainly not to construct others like them. Rather they are to embrace poverty and simplicity in the new construction, and the senior monks who have grown in sensitivity to these values are to move out of their elegant cells into the new and poorer ones. Thus they will give an example to the newcomers and succeeding generations, showing that when they possessed elegant cells they scorned them.[29]

The "elegant cells" are to be used in infirmaries. "Infirmaries" here has a special meaning, although William probably would not object to the better cells actually being used to care for those physically unwell. Here he is harking back to an earlier passage of the *Epistle* where he noted that beginners, those in the 'animal state', are as yet sick and need to regain their health. For these, then, the cell is an infirmary where they submit to the healing treatment of obedience.[30] Let the 'elegant cells' be assigned to newcomers "until they regain their health; that is, begin to desire, not infirmaries for sick men but the tents of those who are on campaign in the camps of the Lord."[31]

So much for the physical fabric of the cell.

When William begins to treat of the spiritual nature of the cell, he draws upon an etymology which may give us some difficulty, but his meaning is clear. William tells us that the word 'cell' *cella*, comes from the same root as the word for heaven, *celum: celare*, to hide. What takes place in the cell and in heaven is hidden from the eyes of men and is similar in nature. The cell is the monk's heaven, the place of encounter with God. There, leisure devoted to God, the enjoyment of God, is the occupation, the preoccupation.[32] Any other occupation undertaken there is actually idleness,[33] a giving way to acedia. When the monk's leisure is devoted to God with fidelity and fervor, then heaven and the cell are close together. Even the angels regard the cell as heaven. The monk at death moves quickly and easily from one to the other.[34]

> The cell is a holy place, holy ground; the place in which the Lord and his servant often talk together as a man does with his friend; in which the faithful soul frequently has intercourse with the Word of God; the bride is in the company of the Bridegroom, the heavenly is united to the earthly, the divine to the human.[35]

William draws a daring parallel and then goes one step farther: As a church is a place holy to God, so the cell is the sanctuary of God's servant.[36] Holy things are practiced in both places, but William dares to affirm, more continuously and in a more heavenly manner, in the cell:

> In a church *at certain times* the sacraments of Christian religion are dispensed visibly and *in figure,* while in cells as in heaven *the reality which underlies* all the sacraments of faith is *constantly* celebrated with as much truth, in the same order, although not yet with the same untarnished magnificence or the same security that marks eternity.[37]

Given the sublimity of the cell, or "the dignity of the cell," as William calls it,[38] who can be worthy to dwell in a cell? It "would seem to be only for the perfect."[39] Yet William, responding to the work of the Spirit as he has perceived it in souls, is not so demanding:

> In fact, cells are to be peopled with two kinds of men, either with the simple who in their hearts and their good will seem to possess the fervor and the ability to arrive at religious prudence; or with the prudent who are proved to be eager for religious and holy simplicity.[40]

Simplicity and prudence—"simple as doves and wise as serpents," to quote William's Master—are the two qualities essential for a successful and holy life in a cell. There is room for growth, but one must have a grounding in at least one of these dispositions.

William reaches for another Scriptural analogy further on in his letter— that of Psalm 83: "How lovely are your tents, Lord of Hosts! In them the sparrow finds a home for itself and the turtledove a nest in which to lay its young."[41] The turtledove and the sparrow: the "spiritual men on the low ground—the simple—and beginners in the heights—the prudent—make a like progress."[42]

William is certainly aware that there is an inner cell in everyone: the conscience where God dwells with the spirit of the person. And this cell has a preeminent dignity. This is "where renewal takes place and one puts on the new self which is created in God's image, justified and sanctified through the truth."[43]

> It is there that the Spirit is fashioned, there that a good understanding is acquired by all those who seek for it, there that, in accord with the rule that the Apostle gives, "in all things we are taught to show ourselves as God's ministers, with great patience, in affliction, need, difficulty, hard work, vigils, in the prison of the cell, fasting, chastity, knowledge, forebearance, graciousness, relying on the Holy Spirit, in unfeigned charity, in the word of truth, in the power of God."[44]

Our concern in this paper is with the outer cell, the house where the soul dwells with the body. This outer cell is a sacrament of the inner: "The door of the outward enclosure is a sign of the guarded door within you, so that as the bodily senses are prevented from wandering abroad by the outward enclosure, so the inner senses are kept always within their own domain."[45]

The outer cell, the concrete physical structure, redolent of poverty, simplicity, and sobriety, is, for William, not just a privileged environment,[46] a place of most sacred encounter, a sacrament. It is in some ways an active agent in engendering and educating "the son of grace, the fruit of its womb."[47] It "cherishes, nourishes and enfolds," it "leads to the fullness of perfection" and "makes worthy of converse with God."[48] Negatively—and here William uses very graphic language—the cell quickly expels as an abortion the man who does not belong to it, is not its true son; it "vomits him forth like useless and harmful food."[49] If this unworthy one resists, he is apt to become more a prisoner than a son of the cell. His plight becomes so pitiable that William likens him to a living person trapped in a sepulchre.[50]

Active though the cell may be in nurturing, it does not do the whole thing itself. The cell is a "workshop of piety,"[51] and the monk must be a diligent worker. Much of the *Golden Epistle* is dedicated to describing the work to be undertaken and to guiding the monk in it. William sums up the work in a general way in this sentence:

> Learn in it, according to the laws of the common observance, to take charge of yourself, to plan your life, to set your behavior in order. Judge yourself, be your own accuser and often also condemn yourself and do not leave yourself unpunished.[52]

The greatest enemy of the monk in this workshop, the one that can most effectively draw him away from his task, is curiosity. Curiosity seizes upon the affections and the intellect. One is filled with harmful, distracting, or idle thoughts and robbed of devotion. The monk turns aside from "the King's highroad of common observance," and grabs for novelties, disgusted with the ordinary.[53]

Every day fresh occupations are taken up, fresh activities and fresh work are devised, different reading matter is found, not to edify the spirit but to allay the boredom of a day that passes too slowly.[54]

The result of all this is that the monk rejects all the tradition, all that he has been accustomed to and trained in. Then even the attraction of the new wears off. "Nothing remains but hatred of the cell and a speedy departure."[55]

If the great adversary of the cell-dweller is the ill-regulated movements of curiosity, his great ally is his spiritual father:

In order that your solitude may not appall you and that you may dwell more safely in your cell, three guardians have been assigned to you: God, your conscience, and your spiritual father. To God you owe devotion and the entire gift of self; to your conscience, the respect which will make you ashamed to sin in its presence; to your spiritual father, the obedience of charity and recourse in everything.

If you will take my advice, you will choose for yourself a man whose life is such that it will serve as a model to impress upon your heart, one whom you will so revere that whenever you think of him you will rise up because of the respect you feel for him, and put yourself in order. Think of him as if he were present and let the charity you feel for one another act in you to correct all that needs to be corrected, while your solitude suffers no infringement of its secret. Let him be present to you whenever you wish and let him come sometimes when you would have preferred him to stay away. The thought of his holy severity will make it seem as if he were rebuking you; the thought of his kindness and goodness will bring you consolation; the purity and sanctity of his life will set you a good example. For you will be driven to correct even your thoughts, as if they were open to his gaze and visited by his rebuke, when you consider that he is watching.[56]

This spiritual presence of the father can be a powerful help to the disciple, not only on the psychological level. It can make present effectively in a sacramental way the prayer and mediation of the father and his own sacramental power to make God the Father present in the life of his disciple.

There is also the support that comes from the brethren, for the monks for whom William writes, and for the Cistercians today, although they live in cells, yet live in community. There is a 'holy intercourse' that goes on between well-regulated cell-dwellers, says William. They hold converse with each other even in their silence. They enjoy one another even while remaining apart—in fact, "more while remaining apart." They are an occasion of progress for one another, and even though they do not see one another, they find matter for imitation in each other.[57]

William calls for a deep, profound, and beautiful unity among the brethren, even though they live less in common, more apart. It is not a unity based on uniformity. His principles and guidelines are broad and leave the way open to very different expressions. He wholeheartedly endorses pluralism:

> As one star differs from another in brightness, so cell differs from cell in its way of life.[58]

There are beginners, those making progress, and the more perfect, and even within these stages of growth there will be plurality of responses and activities.

Pluralism is not the same as diversity. Diversity is persons doing different things in different ways. Pluralism is persons doing the same thing in different ways. Cistercians, whether in common dormitories or private cells, if they are true Cistercians, will be doing the same thing. At heart there will be a deep unity. It is important that the community, even as it enjoys very diverse expressions, does have some incarnate expressions of this deep unity so that it can be commonly experienced in the midst of the differing practices. Otherwise the community may begin to sense that it is drifting away from unity and pluralism into diversity. One of the ways this might effectively be done in regard to the cells and their use would be a communal study and affirmation of the values, principles, and guidelines that come from our Cistercian heritage through this *Epistle* of William of St. Thierry. The more a community is in touch with and experiences its unity, the more joyfully and freely can it affirm in its midst a plurality of expression.

William of St. Thierry's treatment of the cell, presented here all too briefly, is sufficiently complete and flexible to provide a solid grounding for a practical set of guidelines for any Cistercian community. These guidelines challenge us to respond to values, to be incarnationally realistic, and to keep clearly before our eyes the transcendent meaning and goals of the Cistercian monastic life.

NOTES

[1]Excellent photographs of these and floor plans can be found in M. Anseleme Dimier et al, *L'Art Cistercien*, 2 vols. (La Pierre-qui-vire: Zodiaque, 1962-71).

[2]St. Benedict, *Rule for Monasteries* (hereafter RB), c. 22.

[3]*Exordium parvum*, c. 15; English trans., Robert E. Larkin in Louis Lekai, *The White Monks* (Okauchee, WI: Cistercian Fathers, 1953) p. 263.

[4]See e.g., Lekai, *op. cit.*, p. 63; also *The Cistercians* (Kent State University Press, 1977) pp. 73, 113, and especially 373f. One can see examples of this perduring in some of the monasteries in France and Austria.

⁵See e.g., *Regulations of the Order of Cistercians of the Strict Observance* (Dublin: Gill, 1926) n. 295.

⁶*Perfectae Caritatis,* 2; trans. Walter M. Abbot, ed. *The Documents of Vatican II* (New York: Guild Press, 1966) p. 468.

⁷Minutes of the Sessions of the Sixtieth General Chapter, May 20-June 5, 1967, p. 115. See also the discussion on pp. 76-79.

⁸For an extensive Cistercian study of this, see M. Basil Pennington, ed. *Contemplative Community. An Interdisciplinary Symposium,* Cistercian Studies Series 21 (Washington, DC: Cistercian Publications, 1972).

⁹The best available biography of William is that of Jean Marie Déchanet, *William of St. Thierry. The Man and His Work,* Cistercian Studies Series 10 (Spencer, MA: Cistercian Publications, 1972).

¹⁰Jean Déchanet, ed. *Lettre aux Frères du Mont-Dieu,* Sources chrétiennes 223 (Paris: Cerf, 1975), English trans. Theodore Berkeley, *The Golden Epistle,* The Works of William of St. Thierry, vol. 4, Cistercian Fathers Series 12 (Spencer, MA: Cistercian Publications, 1971). Paragraph numbers without further indication refer to this text.

¹¹Par. 148ff.

¹²For a solidly-based historical novel on the building of Le Thoronet by twelfth century Cistercians see Fernand Pouillon, *The Stones of the Abbey* (New York: Harcourt, Brace & World, 1970).

¹³Par. 86.

¹⁴Par. 150.

¹⁵Par. 147.

¹⁶Par. 148. In his *Exposition on the Song of Songs,* William speaks much more strongly on this question of poverty, with a direct reference to cells. J. M. Déchanet, ed., *L'Exposé sur le Cantique,* Sources chrétiennes 82 (Paris: Cerf, 1962); English trans. Sr. Columba Hart, *Exposition on the Song of Songs,* The Works of William of St. Thierry, vol. 2, Cistercian Fathers Series 6 (Spencer, MA: Cistercian Publications, 1970) n. 194.

¹⁷Par. 147.

¹⁸RB 55:7.

¹⁹Par. 151.

²⁰Par. 158.

²¹Par. 153.

²²*Ibid.*

²³Par. 152.

²⁴Par. 147.

²⁵Par. 151.

²⁶Par. 154.

²⁷Par. 152.

²⁸Par. 154.

²⁹Par. 155.

³⁰Par. 47ff.

³¹Par. 155.

³²Par. 31.

³³Par. 81.

[34]Par. 32.

[35]Par. 35.

[36]*Ibid.*

[37]Par. 36. Italics mine.

[38]Par. 141.

[39]*Ibid.*

[40]Par. 143.

[41]Par. 187.

[42]Par. 193.

[43]Par. 213.

[44]Par. 214.

[45]Par. 105.

[46]Par. 106. The cell is a shelter—not a hideout—where one can abide in greater safety.

[47]Par. 34.

[48]*Ibid.*

[49]Par. 37.

[50]*Ibid.*

[51]*Ibid.*

[52]Par. 107.

[53]Par. 64ff.

[54]Par. 67.

[55]*Ibid.*

[56]Par. 101ff.

[57]Par. 193.

[58]Par. 41.

English Language Bibliography

Translations of His Works

ON CONTEMPLATING GOD

Lawson, Sr. Penelope, CSMV, with introduction by Dom Jacques Hourlier, OSB, in *The Works of William of St. Thierry*, vol. 1, Cistercian Fathers Series 3 (Spencer, MA: Cistercian Publications, 1970) pp. 36-64.
Webb, Geoffrey and Walker, Adrian, Fleur de Lys Series (London: Mowbrays, 1955).

ON THE NATURE AND DIGNITY OF LOVE

Davis, Fr. Thomas X., OCSO, with introduction by David N. Bell, in *The Works of William of St. Thierry*, vol. 10, Cistercian Fathers Series 30 (Kalamazoo, MI: Cistercian Publications, 1981).
Webb, Geoffrey and Walker, Adrian, Fleur de Lys Series (London: Mowbrays, 1956).

ON THE NATURE OF THE BODY AND SOUL

Clark, Benjamin, OCSO, with an introduction by Bernard McGinn, in *Three Treatises on Man: A Cistercian Anthropology*, Cistercian Fathers Series 24 (Kalamazoo, MI: Cistercian Publications, 1977) pp. 104-180.

EXPOSITION ON THE EPISTLE TO THE ROMANS

Hasbrouck, Fr. John Baptist, OCSO, with introduction by John D. Anderson, in *The Works of William of St. Thierry*, vol. 9, Cistercian Fathers Series 27 (Kalamazoo, MI: Cistercian Publications, 1980).

MEDITATIONS

(Lawson, Sr. Penelope, CSMV) A Religious of CSMV, *The Meditations of William of St. Thierry* (New York: Harper Bros. and London: Mowbrays, 1954).

Including *Meditation Thirteen*: Lawson, Sr. Penelope, CSMV, with introductions by Dom Jacques Hourlier, OSB and Dom Jean Marie Déchanet, OSB (for Meditation Thirteen) in *The Works of William of St. Thierry*, vol. 1, Cistercian Fathers Series 3 (Spencer, MA: Cistercian Publications, 1970) pp. 77-190.

PRAYER

Lawson, Sr. Penelope, CSMV, with introduction by Dom Jacques Hourlier, OSB, in *The Works of William of St. Thierry*, vol. 1, Cistercian Fathers Series 3 (Spencer, MA: Cistercian Publications, 1970) pp. 67-76.

EXPOSITION ON THE SONG OF SONGS

Hart, Sr. Columba, OSB, with introduction by Dom Jean Marie Déchanet, OSB, *The Works of William of St. Thierry*, vol. 2, Cistercian Fathers Series 6 (Spencer, MA: Cistercian Publications, 1970).

THE MIRROR OF FAITH

Davis, Fr. Thomas X., OCSO, with introduction by E. Rozanne Elder in *The Works of William of St. Thierry*, vol. 5, Cistercian Fathers Series 15 (Kalamazoo, MI: Cistercian Publications, 1979).
Webb, Geoffrey and Walker, Adrian, with introduction, Fleur de Lys Series (London: Mowbrays, 1959). Partial text.

THE ENIGMA OF FAITH

Anderson, John D., with introduction, *The Works of William of St. Thierry*, vol. 3, Cistercian Fathers Series 9 (Washington, DC: Cistercian Publications, 1974).

THE GOLDEN EPISTLE: THE LETTER TO THE BROTHERS OF MONT-DIEU

Berkeley, Theodore, OCSO, with introduction by Dom Jean Marie Déchanet, OSB, *The Works of William of St. Thierry*, vol. 4, Cistercian Fathers Series 12 (Spencer, MA: Cistercian Publications, 1971).
Shewring, William, ed. by J. McCann, OSB with introduction (London: Sheed and Ward, 1930 and 1973).

THE LIFE OF ST. BERNARD

Webb, Geoffrey and Walker, Adrian, *St. Bernard of Clairvaux* (London: Mowbrays, 1960). Partial text.

Studies

Anderson, John D., "The Use of Greek Sources by William of St. Thierry, especially in the *Enigma fidei*" in *One Yet Two: Monastic Tradition East and West,* ed. M. Basil Pennington, OCSO (Kalamazoo, MI: Cistercian Publications, 1976) pp. 242-253.

"William of St. Thierry's *Exposition on the Epistle to the Romans*" in *Cistercian Ideals and Reality,* Cistercian Studies Series 60, ed. John R. Sommerfeldt (Kalamazoo, MI: Cistercian Publications, 1978) pp. 136-151.

Bell, David N., "The Vita Antiqua of William of St. Thierry" in *Cistercian Studies* 9 (1976) 246-255.

Benton, John F., "Fraud, Fiction and Borrowing in the Correspondence of Abelard and Heloise," English revision of a communication presented at the Colloque International Pierre Abélard-Pierre le Vénérable, Abbaye de Cluny, July 4, 1972, unpublished.

Bouyer, Louis, C. Orat., *The Cistercian Heritage,* translated by E. Livingston (Westminster, MD: Newman, 1958).

Bredero, Adrian Hendrik, "The Canonization of Saint Bernard and the Rewriting of His Life" in *Cistercian Ideals and Reality,* Cistercian Studies Series 60, ed. by John R. Sommerfeldt (Kalamazoo, MI: Cistercian Publications, 1978) pp. 80-105.

Brooke, Odo, OSB, "Faith and Mystical Experience in William of St. Thierry" in *Downside Review* 82 (1964) 93-102.

"The Speculative Development of the Trinitarian Theology of William of St. Thierry in the Aenigma Fidei" in *Recherches de théologie ancienne et médiévale* 27 (1960) 193-211, 28 (1961) 26-58.

"The Theology of William of St. Thierry: a Methodological Problem" in *Cistercian Studies* 6 (1971) 261-268.

"Toward a Theology of Connatural Knowledge" in *Cîteaux* 68 (1967) 275-290.

"The Trinitarian Aspect of the Ascent of the Soul to God in the Theology of William of St. Thierry" in *Recherches de théologie ancienne et médiévale* 26 (1959) 85-127.

The Trinity in Guillaume de St. Thierry Against the Anthropological Background of his Doctrine of the Ascent of the Soul to God (Rome, 1957). Unpublished doctoral thesis.

"William of St. Thierry" in *The Month* 28 (1962) 342-352; reprinted in *Spirituality Through the Centuries: Ascetics and Mystics of the Western Church,* ed. James Walsh, SJ (New York: Kenedy, 1964) pp. 121-131.

"William of St. Thierry's Doctrine of Ascent to God by Faith" in *Recherches de théologie ancienne et médiévale* 30 (1963) 181-204, 33 (1966) 282-318.

Ceglar, Stanislaus, SVD, "The Chapter of Soissons (Autumn, 1132) and the Authorship of the *Reply of the Benedictine Abbots to Cardinal Matthew*" in *Studies in Medieval Cistercian History II,* ed. John R. Sommerfeldt, Cistercian Studies Series 24 (Kalamazoo, MI: Cistercian Publications, 1976).

William of St. Thierry: The Chronology of His Life with a Study of His Treatises On the Nature of Love, *His Authorship of the* Brevis Commentatio, *the* In Lacu, *and the* Reply to Cardinal Matthew (Ann Arbor, MI: University Microfilms, 1971) (No. 71-25, 239).

"William of St. Thierry and His Leading Role at the First Chapters of the Benedictine Abbots (Reims 1131, Soissons 1132)," paper delivered at the Colloque International d'Histoire Monastique, Reims-St. Thierry, October 11-15, 1976, not yet published.

Cheneviere, Etienne, OCSO, "William of St. Thierry: the Man of Faith" translated by Robert Kevin Anderson, OCSO. Unpublished.

Chydenius, Johan, "The Symbolism of Love in Medieval Thought" in Societas Scientiarum Fennica: *Commentationes Humanarum Litterarum* 44 (1970) 1-68.

Constable, Giles, "Twelfth Century Spirituality and the Late Middle Ages" in *Medieval and Renaissance Studies,* ed. O. B. Hardison, Jr. (Chapel Hill: University of North Carolina Press, 1971) pp. 27-60.

D'Arcy, Martin, *The Mind and Heart of Love* (New York: World Publishing Co., 1957).

Déchanet, Jean Marie, OSB, Introduction to the *Exposition on the Song of Songs* in *The Works of William of St. Thierry,* vol. 2, Cistercian Fathers Series 6 (Spencer, MA: Cistercian Publications, 1970) pp. vii-xlviii.

Introduction to the *Golden Epistle* in *The Works of William of St. Thierry,* vol. 4, Cistercian Fathers Series 12 (Spencer, MA: Cistercian Publications, 1971) pp. ix-xxxiii.

Introduction to *Meditation Thirteen* in *The Works of William of St. Thierry,* vol. 1, Cistercian Fathers Series 3 (Spencer, MA: Cistercian Publications, 1970) pp. 181-185.

"William and St. Bernard" unpublished mss.

William of St. Thierry: the Man and his Works, translated by Richard Strachan, Cistercian Studies Series 10 (Spencer, MA: Cistercian Publications, 1972).

Elder, E. Rozanne, "And Yet I Have Loved Him: The Judgment of William of St. Thierry on Peter Abelard" (Western Michigan University, 1964) unpublished Masters' thesis.

"The Image of the Invisible God: The Evolving Christology of William of St. Thierry" (University of Toronto, 1972) unpublished doctoral thesis.

"The Way of Ascent: the Meaning of Love in the Thought of William of St. Thierry" in *Studies in Medieval Culture,* vol. 1, ed. John R. Sommerfeldt (Kalamazoo, MI: Western Michigan University, 1964) pp. 39-47.

"William of St. Thierry and the Greek Fathers: Evidence from

Christology" in *One Yet Two: Monastic Tradition East and West*, Cistercian Studies Series 29, ed. M. Basil Pennington, OCSO (Kalamazoo, MI: Cistercian Publications, 1976) pp. 254-266.

"William of St. Thierry: The Monastic Vocation as an Initiation of Christ," in *Cîteaux* 26 (1975) 9-30.

"William of St. Thierry: Rational and Affective Spirituality" in *The Spirituality of Western Christendom*, Cistercian Studies Series 30, ed. by E. Rozanne Elder (Kalamazoo, MI: Cistercian Publications, 1976) pp. 85-105.

"William of St. Thierry's Reading of Abelard's Christology" in *Cistercian Ideals and Reality*, Cistercian Studies Series 60, ed. John R. Sommerfeldt (Kalamazoo, MI: Cistercian Publications, 1978) pp. 106-124.

Fiske, Adele M., RSCJ, *Friends and Friendship in the Monastic Tradition*, CIDOC Cuaderno 51 (Cuernavaca: CIDOC, 1970).

"Paradisus homo amicus" in *Speculum* 40 (1965) 436-459.

"William of St. Thierry and Friendship" in *Cîteaux* 12 (1961) 5-27.

Gilson, Etienne, *The Mystical Theology of St. Bernard*, translated by A. H. C. Downes (London: Sheed and Ward, 1939; New York: Sheed and Ward, 1955).

Haring, N. M., "The Case of Gilbert de la Porrée, Bishop of Poitiers (1142-1154)" in *Medieval Studies* 13 (1951) 1-40.

Hourlier, Jacques, OSB, Introduction to the *Meditations* in *The Works of William of St. Thierry*, vol. 1, Cistercian Fathers Series 3 (Spencer, MA: Cistercian Publications, 1969) pp. 77-88.

Introduction to *On Contemplating God, ibid.*, pp. 3-35.

Introduction to *Prayer, ibid.*, pp. 67-70.

Klibansky, J., "Peter Abailard and Bernard of Clairvaux" in *Medieval and Renaissance Studies* 5 (1961) 1-27.

Leclercq Jean, OSB, Introduction to *An Apologia to Abbot William* in *The Works of Bernard of Clairvaux*, vol. 1, Cistercian Fathers Series 1 (Spencer, MA: Cistercian Publications, 1970) pp. 3-30.

The Love of Learning and the Desire of God (New York: Fordham University Press, 1961; Mentor Omega Books, 1962; revised, 1976).

Leclercq, Jean, OSB; Vandebrouche, Francois, OSB; Bouyer, Louis, C. Orat., *The Spirituality of the Middle Ages* (London: Burns and Oates, 1968).

Little, Edward, "Bernard and Abelard at the Council of Sens, 1140" in *Bernard of Clairvaux: Studies presented to Dom Jean Leclercq*, Cistercian Studies Series 23, ed. M. Basil Pennington, OCSO (Washington, DC: Cistercian Publications, 1972) pp. 55-71.

The "Heresies" of Peter Abelard (University of Montreal, 1969) unpublished doctoral thesis.

"The Sources of the *Capitula* of Sens (1140)" in *Studies in Medieval Cistercian History II*, Cistercian Studies Series 24, ed. John R. Sommerfeldt (Kalamazoo, MI: Cistercian Publications, 1976) pp. 87-91.

Lohr, Benedict, "William of St. Thierry" in *New Catholic Encyclopedia* (New York: McGraw-Hill, 1967) 14:938-939.

Luscombe, D. E., *The School of Peter Abelard,* Cambridge Studies in Medieval Life and Thought, Second Series, vol. 14 (Cambridge University Press, 1969).

McGinn, Bernard, *The Golden Chain: A Study in the Theological Anthropology of Isaac of Stella,* Cistercian Studies Series 15 (Spencer, MA: Cistercian Publications, 1972).

Editor with introduction, *Three Treatises on Man: A Cistercian Anthropology,* Cistercian Fathers Series 24 (Kalamazoo, MI: Cistercian Publications, 1977).

Mohler, James A., SJ, *Dimensions of Love, East and West* (Garden City, NY: Doubleday, 1975).

Monti, D. V., "The Way Within: Grace in the Mystical Theology of William of St. Thierry" in *Cîteaux* 26 (1975) 31-47.

Moore, John C., *Love in Twelfth Century France* (Philadelphia: University of Pennsylvania, 1972).

Moritz, Theresa, "The Metaphor of Marriage in the Spiritual Writings of William of St. Thierry" in *Cistercian Studies* 11 (1976) 290-308.

Morrison, Stanley Saint Clair, "The Bernardine Biographers: Notes on Some Twelfth-Century Authors in France" in *The Irish Ecclesiastical Record* 73 (1950) 344-351, 505-515; 74 (1951) 40-53.

Morson, John, "A Newly Found Bernardine Manuscript" in *Collectanea O.C.R.* 16 (1954) 30-34.

"Texts in a Bernardine Manuscript at Mount Saint Bernard Abbey" in *Collectanea O.C.R.* 16 (1954) 214-221.

Murruy, Victor, *Abelard and St. Bernard: A Study in Twelfth Century "Modernism"* (Manchester University Press, 1967).

O'Brien, Elmer, SJ, *Varieties of Mystic Experience: An Anthropology and Interpretation* (New York: Holt, Rinehart and Winston, 1964).

Pennington, M. Basil, OCSO, "Abbot William, Spiritual Father of St. Thierry" in *Cistercian Studies* 13 (1978) pp. 152-166.

"Association for Cistercian Studies" in *Cîteaux* 24 (1973) 53-61.

"Cistercian-Orthodox Symposium" in *Diakonia* 9 (1974) 376-382; *Studia Monastica* 17 (1975) 145-155.

Editor with introduction, *The Cistercian Spirit: A Symposium in Memory of Thomas Merton,* Cistercian Studies Series 3 (Spencer, MA: Cistercian Publications and Shannon, Ireland: Irish University Press, 1969).

"Cistercian Studies in the USA, 1974" in *Cistercian Studies* 9 (1974) 399-400.

"Conference on Cistercian Studies" in *Cîteaux* 22 (1971) 181-184.

"Il Conferencia de *Cistercian Studies*" in *Cistercium* 24 (1972) 231-238.

"The Correspondence of William of St. Thierry" in *Studia Monastica* 18 (1976) 352-365, reprinted in *Simplicity and Ordinariness*, Cistercian Studies Series 61, ed. by John R. Sommerfeldt (Kalamazoo, MI: Cistercian Publications, 1980), pp. 188-213.

"Fourth Cistercian Studies Conference" in *Cîteaux* 25 (1974) 319-323.

"Getting Acquainted with the Cistercian Fathers" in *Monastic Exchange* 6 (1974) no. 3, pp. 63-78.

"Kalamazoo '73" in *Monastic Exchange* 5 (1973) no. 3, pp. 13-15.

Editor with introduction and summations, *One Yet Two: Monastic Tradition East and West,* Cistercian Studies Series 29 (Kalamazoo, MI: Cistercian Publications, 1976).

"St. Thierry: The Commemoration of a Benedictine Millennium" in *Cîteaux* 23 (1972) 118-122.

"Second Cistercian Studies Conference" in *Cîteaux* 23 (1972) 209-217.

"Sixth Annual Cistercian Studies Conference" in *Cîteaux* 27 (1976) 290-295.

"Tercer Simposio Cisterciense: La Comunidad contemplativa" in *Cistercium* 24 (1972) 129ff.

"Third Cistercian Studies Conference" in *Cîteaux* 24 (1973) 180-187.

"Tomando contacto con nuestros Padres" in *Cistercium* 27 (1975) 35-59.

"Two Treatises on Love" in *Bernard of Clairvaux: Studies in Honor of the Eighth Centenary of his Canonization 1174-1974,* Cistercian Studies Series 28, ed. by M. Basil Pennington, OCSO (Kalamazoo, MI: Cistercian Publications, 1977) pp. 137-154, reprinted in *Studia Monastica* 22 (1980) 273-285.

Reynolds, L. D., *The Medieval Tradition of Seneca's Letters* (London: Oxford University Press, 1965).

Ryan, Patrick, OCSO, "The Influence of Seneca on William of St. Thierry" in *Cîteaux* 25 (1974) 24-32.

"The Witness of William of St. Thierry to the Spirit and Aims of the Early Cistercians" in *Cistercian Spirit: a Symposium in Memory of Thomas Merton,* Cistercian Studies Series 3, ed. by M. Basil Pennington, OCSO (Spencer, MA: Cistercian Publications, 1969), pp. 224-253.

Savary, Louis M., SJ, *Psychological Themes in the Golden Epistle of William of St. Thierry to the Carthusians of Mont-Dieu,* Analecta Cartusiana 8 (Salzburg: Hogg, 1973).

Saward, Sr. Anne, OCSO, "Man as the Image of God in the Works of William of St. Thierry" in *Cistercian Studies* 8 (1973) 309-336; reprinted in

One Yet Two: Monastic Tradition East and West, Cistercian Studies Series 29, ed. by M. Basil Pennington, OCSO (Kalamazoo, MI: Cistercian Publications, 1976), pp. 267-303.

"Notes on William of St. Thierry's Use of Gregory of Nyssa's Treatise on the Making of Man" in *Cistercian Studies* 9 (1974) 394-398.

Saward, John, "The Fool for Christ's Sake: In Monasticism East and West" in *Christian* 2 (1975) 266-286; reprinted in *One Yet Two: Monastic Tradition East and West,* Cistercian Studies Series 29, ed. by M. Basil Pennington, OCSO (Kalamazoo, MI: Cistercian Publications, 1976).

Sitwell, Gerard, OSB, *Spiritual Writers of the Middle Ages,* Twentieth Century Encyclopedia of Catholicism, vol. 40 (New York: Hawthorn, 1961; second edition, 1964).

Talbot, Charles, "Verses Attributed to William of St. Thierry" in *Scriptorium* 8 (1954) 117-119.

Thomas, Robert, OCSO, "William of St. Thierry: Our Life in the Trinity" in *Monastic Studies* 3 (1965) 139-163.

Tomasic, Thomas Michael, "Faith, Hope and Love as the Existential Disclosure of the Person in the Thought of William of St. Thierry" paper read at the Conference on Medieval Studies, Western Michigan University, May 21, 1970.

"The Three Theological Virtues as Modes of Intersubjectivity in the Thought of William of St. Thierry" in *Recherches de théologie ancienne et médiévale* 38 (1971) 89-120.

"William of St. Thierry Against Peter Abelard: A Dispute on the Meaning of Being a Person" in *Analecta S.O.C.* 28 (1972) 3-76.

"William of St. Thierry: An Archetypal Distinction Between 'self' and *persona*" in *Simplicity and Ordinariness,* Cistercian Studies Series 61, ed. by John R. Sommerfeldt (Kalamazoo, MI: Cistercian Publications, 1980), pp. 170-187.

"William of St. Thierry and St. Gregory of Nyssa: An Expedition of Structures" paper written for the Orthodox-Cistercian Symposium, Oxford University, August 26-September 1, 1973.

William of St. Thierry: Toward a Philosophy of Intersubjectivity (Fordham University, 1972) unpublished doctoral thesis.

Van den Eynde, Damian, OFM, "William of St. Thierry and the Author of the *Summa Sententiarum:* Literary and Doctrinal Relations" in *Franciscan Studies* 10 (1950) 241-256.

Vogt, Carolyn J., "William of St. Thierry's Golden Epistle: Mystical Ascent Through Incarnation" in *Cistercian Studies* 8 (1973) 337-354.

Waddell, Chrysogonus, OCSO, "Humility and the Sacraments of Faith in William of St. Thierry's *Speculum fidei*" in *Liturgy* 7 (1973) no. 3, pp. 17-24, and in *Cistercian Ideals and Reality,* Cistercian Studies Series 60, ed. John R.

Sommerfeldt (Kalamazoo, MI: Cistercian Publications, 1978) pp. 125-135.

Webb, Geoffrey, "Cistercian Memoria" in *New Blackfriars* 48 (1966) 209-213.

    An introduction to the Cistercian de Anima, Aquinas Papers 36 (London: Aquin Press, 1962).

    "Love and Heresy" in *New Blackfriars* 48 (1966) 426-430.

    "The Transformation Theme," *ibid.*, 38-42.

    "William of St. Thierry: The Five Senses of Love" in *New Blackfriars* 46 (1964) 464-468.

    "William of St. Thierry: God in Man" in *New Blackfriars* 47 (1965) 522-525.

Williams, John R., "The Cathedral School of Reims in the Time of Master Alberic, 1118-1136" in *Traditio* 20 (1964) pp. 93-114.

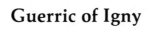

Guerric of Igny

Guerric of Igny and His Sermons
For the Feast of The Assumption

Guerric of Igny, although one of the "four evangelists" of Citeaux, is not well known. This is understandable, for we have little historical data on him.[1] And the corpus of writings that has come down to us from him is not great—only fifty-four sermons.[2] But if we take the trouble to read his sermons there does come through, not so many historical facts, but a very wonderful person, a real abbot, a man to whom we feel we can readily open our hearts.

DISCIPLE AND MASTER

We do not know even in what decade Guerric was born. Some conjecture the 1080's, others the 1070's.[3] He comes from Tournai; he was involved in the school there; he lived, at least for a while, a sort of retired or semi-eremitical life. He had some good connections, like Hugh, abbot of Marchienne, and Oger, superior of the canons of Tournai. He entered Clairvaux around 1123, a man possibly already in his forties or fifties. There is reason to believe he went there merely to see the famous young abbot, and was conquered by him.[4] He stayed.

For the next decade all we hear of Guerric is a couple of sentences of praise found in the letters of his abbot.[5] Whether he ever held any office at Clairvaux we do not know. Bernard was well impressed with him though, and when Humbert, the reluctant abbot of Igny, insisted upon resigning his office, Bernard was instrumental in having Guerric elected to the leadership of this daughter house.[6]

Guerric was in his fifties or sixties when he was elected. He was not up to all the demands of the common life[7] but he was a good abbot. He loved his monks, was open and frank with them, and laid before them good, solid, and practical doctrine. He himself said he had only one desire in preaching his sermons—to give his monks Jesus Christ (10:5).[8]

Guerric is the disciple of Bernard, there can be no doubt about this. He entered Clairvaux because he was lured there by Bernard's reputation if not by his personal charm. Bernard was the abbot who watched over his novitiate, at a time when Bernard was still more at home and able to make his personal impress more deeply upon the members of his growing community.[9]

Guerric's Latin style may not come up to the lyricism of his master, yet it is not without its moments when the kinship is very evident.[10] There is much more evidence of relationship in the doctrine; they are very definitely two men of the same school of thought. Because not so stylized,[11] because nearer to and reflecting more closely the everyday life of community and the personal charm and character of the abbot, the sermons of Guerric might well have greater appeal for the average modern reader.[12]

Like all the Cistercian abbots, Guerric would have been called upon to preach to the whole community at least fifteen times in the year. In actual fact, the collection of his sermons that have come down to us corresponds well to the listing of the Feasts of Sermons found in the earliest legislation of the Order.[13] At these high points of the Liturgical Year the monks would have gathered in the chapter after Prime, the brothers in the cloister by the door or the open bays, to hear their father abbot share with them the fruit of his contemplation. Guerric's sermons were truly liturgical sermons, for almost without exception they open with a text drawn from the liturgy of the day. The first sermon for the Assumption is something of an exception in that the text is drawn, not from the Office of the Assumption as we know it, but from a common Office of Virgins.[14] Perhaps for some reason on this first feast of the Assumption on which Guerric preached, the community had used the common Office, but this can only be a 'perhaps,' difficult to explain and with no other foundation than the choice of the text in the sermon. For the opening of his second sermon Guerric explicitly chose as text the fourth responsory from the Night Office of the feast itself.

AN EXISTENTIAL THEOLOGIAN

The Assumption sermons have a special charm because of their theme. The speaker undoubtedly loves this glorified Woman, and to hear a lover speak of his beloved is always a beautiful experience. Yet their theological content should not be underestimated. True, when we think of the Assumption we tend to think more readily of Amadeus of Lausanne whose sermon was quoted in the papal bull defining this dogma.[15] And indeed Guerric does not give any forceful expression to the dogma itself. That he did believe in the corporal glorification of Mary is evident from a statement found right at the beginning of the first sermon, but this is stated only indirectly.[16] Guerric is more concerned with personal relationships than with dogmatic statements. And when he does dwell on dogmatic realities he does not hesitate to give them a very personal form of expression.

For example, in his development of the text of the fourth responsory of Vigils[17] he employs a delightful dialogue. Here in this second sermon for the Feast we might well be getting a good glimpse of how he meditated on the mystery through the liturgical texts while he chanted succeeding psalms.[18] There is a lightsome playfulness in the dialogue that tells us of a joyful, youthful spirit, much alive—even at four in the morning! And remember, he was probably already in his sixties. But his personal expression can also be very practical, down to earth, with both feet well planted in the burden of daily living. The opening lines of the third Assumption sermon come from the mouth of a man and a monk whose limbs have known that tired, aching feeling that lingers on through a day of rest after days of laborious toil.

However, right along with the lightsomeness or realism there is theological depth. The mysteries of faith and the practical things of the day are not divorced. For Guerric, the content of faith is to leaven the daily doings, to be their wellspring of life and energy: "The fruit of this work will be that (eternal) rest; rest from work, recompense for work, of which even the remembrance in faith restores a man's strength at his work" (49:1).

Mary, Mother of Men

Perhaps Guerric's most significant and particular theological contribution is his development of the theology of Mary's spiritual maternity. Nowhere has this mystery of Mary been more beautifully treated. Undoubtedly, in this, as in other elements,[19] he reflects the Patristic tradition, but he states it with a new clarity and charm.

First, Guerric freely expresses the basis of spiritual maternity. Mary bore Christ and therefore all his members. "One was born, but we were all reborn, since in that seed which holds the power of rebirth we were all already then in him. Just as from the beginning we were in Adam by the seed of carnal generation, so even before the beginning we were there present in Christ much more by the seed of spiritual generation" (47:2). Mary, as mother, formed Christ; therefore she is the mother of all in whom Christ is formed. And finally, Mary is the mother of the Life by which everyone lives; in bringing forth that Life she brings forth all who live by the Life. She steps in where Eve failed—to engender true life in all who are reborn to life. In this she is one with the Church, the type (form) of the Church, as Mother (47:2).

Then Guerric goes on to trace Mary's nurturing role as Mother: she "shows herself a mother by her care and loving attention" (49:3).[20] She is compassionate, she is tender, inexhaustibly so. He recalls Paul's boast of bearing his Galatians in the Gospel with care and tenderness,[21] and draws the comparison:

In short, if the servant of Christ by his care and heartfelt tenderness bears his little children again and again until Christ be formed in them, how much more is this true of the very Mother of Christ? Paul begot his children by preaching the word of truth, through which they were born again; but Mary, in a manner far more holy and like to God, by giving birth to the Word Himself. I do indeed praise the ministry of preaching in Paul, but far more do I admire and venerate that mystery of generation in Mary (47:3).

We really dwell in her help, live in her protection, under the shadow of her wing: and afterwards we will share in her glory, which Guerric speaks of as being cherished not in the bosom of Abraham but in the bosom of Mary (47:4).

Finally, he finds eloquent witness to Mary's spiritual maternity in the quasi-spontaneous response of the man of faith: "Is it not true that her children seem to recognize her as their mother by a kind of instinctive devotion which faith gives them as second nature, so that first and fore-most in all their needs and dangers they run to call upon her Name just as children run to their mother's breast?" (47:4).

In another sermon, the third sermon for Christmas, Guerric develops another beautiful aspect of this mystery—our participation in Mary's spir-itual maternity. Basing himself upon our Lord's words: "Whoever does the will of my Father in heaven, he is my brother and sister and mother,"[22] he brings out how we do mother Christ in ourselves and in others (8:5).

In connection with this portrait of Mary's spiritual maternity Guerric takes pains to stress her perfect and perpetual virginity: "He is the only-begotten of his Mother. She has no other children...but rather the seal of perpetual virginity in the mother, like the mystery of Catholic unity in the offspring, remains inviolate. She is the only virgin-mother..."(47:2). Her perfect sinlessness is also noted along with the ornaments of all virtues (47:6).

A Contemplative Worker

In the third sermon we see most clearly in Guerric a combination of qualities that are especially desirous in a Cistercian abbot; a true, deep appreciation for the contemplative life which will inspire his community to fidelity in seeking their ideal, blended with that practical appreciation of the demands of everyday life which is necessary for the good administration of the abbey. It is this "down-to-earthness" in this contemplative which attracts us.

Speaking to monks who, having worked hard the preceding days under a burning August sun, and having had scant sleep the night before,[23] are looking forward to the repose of this Feast, he knows that the sublime passage of the wise man can indeed have more than one meaning for them: "In all things I have sought rest." Yes, weary bones and aching muscles are seeking rest, but for true contemplative monks there is a greater, deeper longing, not so easily satisfied, for another rest. And it is indeed this desire for the eternal rest that has goaded them on in their wearying labors.

In this and in the following sermon Guerric approaches in his own fashion the perennial question of Mary and Martha (49:2; 50:1, 3). The contemplative life and active concern—how are they to be blended? His answer is as simple as it is profound—an ardent desire for rest. But the rest in which the monk rests is Christ and Christ rests in him:

> Happy is he who in all his labors and in all his ways seeks blessed rest, always hastening, as the apostle exhorts, to enter into that rest. For desire of it he afflicts his body, but already prepares and disposes his spirit for that rest, being at peace with all men as far as it lies with him. Giving the preference, where his will is concerned, to the rest and the leisure of Mary, to the extent that necessity demands, he accepts the toil and the busyness of Martha, yet does this with as much peace and quiet of spirit as he can, and always brings himself back from that manifold distraction to the one thing necessary. A man of this sort is at rest even when he is working, just as, on the contrary, the godless man has to work even when he is resting (49:2).

Guerric concludes this sermon with a plea to his brethren that they might seek this quiet all together, creating in their community a climate of monastic prayer. For him this by no means meant any shirking of necessary work. Rather, such quiet would leave them "ready for every work" (49:6). There should be read, in conjunction with this sermon on monastic *quies,* what we might call Guerric's "theology of silence" found in his fifth sermon for Christmas (10:4).

In the fourth sermon Guerric returns again to the question of the relationship that exists between action and contemplation. Martha is the exemplar of active concern, and Mary, her sister, typifies the contemplative life. Guerric finds both in Mary, the Mother of the Lord. No one has ever been more concerned about the temporal needs of Christ than she as she ministered to his physical care. But this in no wise impeded her contemplative fruitfulness. In fact Guerric goes so far as to say, *"Since* she was not careless or remiss in Martha's work, she has not been without Mary's fruit" (50:3).[24] For Guerric there is no doubt—Mary's is the best part. Contemplation surpasses activity, but it is in some sense the reward of activity.

The Lover of Mary

Undoubtedly, what is most evident in this sermon as in the other three is Guerric's great love for Mary. In the last paragraph he gives eloquent voice to it when he quotes Mary, "All generations will call me blessed," and adds emphatically, "This is too little" (50:5).

Mary is ever for him a most loving and tender Mother—to him, but first of all to his Lord—the one most faithful and loyal to Christ (50:1). He is not put off by those occasions when Christ seemed to put her aside. Guerric's interpretation of these situations is thought-provoking and worthy of reflection. At Cana[25] Christ had to show that miraculous power came to him not from his Mother but from another source. His response to the men who broke in on his discourse with news of his Mother's arrival[26] was to bring home that spiritual things must come before those of the flesh (50:1). The same was true of the response to Mary herself in the temple.[27]

> It could not be that he spurned his mother, he who was so careful to lay down the law that parents should be honored. It could not be that on earth he showed disgust for his mother when he had desired her beauty from heaven. Rather he was setting charity in order in us, both by his words and by his example, teaching us to put before our affection for carnal attachments not only the love of God but also the love of those who do God's will (50:2).

Where Jesus might seem to some to ignore his Mother, Guerric rather sees him honor her all the more, giving her a double claim to the title of Mother—his Mother in the flesh and his Mother in the spirit. And this led to that absolutely unique glory that is hers, to see God, the King of all glory, in the diadem of the flesh with which she crowned him, to recognize God and adore him in her own body and see her own body glorified in God (50:3).

That all generations call Mary blessed is not enough. It is necessary that all the spiritual kingdom also declare her blessed. Yet this is still not enough; only one thing is sufficient: the Fruit of her womb (50:5; 48:6).

*   *   *

I have chosen to try to draw some lines of a portrait of Guerric of Igny through his sermons for the Feast of the Assumption because I believe the rich variety found in these four sermons brings out different facets of this precious gem which quietly glitters in the patrimony of Citeaux. The first sermon shows us the existential theologian, and gives us what I believe is Guerric's most significant theological contribution, his development of the doctrine of Mary's spiritual maternity. The second sermon exposes to us the light-hearted, fanciful and poetic son and disciple of Bernard of Clairvaux.[28] The third and fourth sermons are of the practical, down-to-earth, contemplative monk—the Cistercian who embraces the ascesis of the hard labor of the poor to dispose himself for the spiritual freedom of the truly rich; the monk who finds his exemplar in and shares in the predestination of Mary, the Mother of the Lord.

NOTES

[1]For a discussion of the sources see J. Morson and H. Costello, "Who Was Guerric of Igny?" in *The Downside Review*, 83 (1965), pp. 57f.

[2]There are fifty-five sermons in the collection found in the edition of Mabillon in PL 185:11ff., but the fifth sermon of the Purification of the Blessed Virgin found there is evidently not authentically Guerric's, and it is not found in the critical edition published in the Sources Chrétiennes. The *Liber Amoris* which has also been attributed to Guerric is probably not to be taken as his; see J. Morson and H. Costello, "*Liber Amoris*: Was it written by Guerric of Igny?" in *Cîteaux* 16 (1965) pp. 114ff.

[3]See Morson and Costello, "Who was Guerric..." pp. 59f. Also *ibid.*, "Guerric d'Igny" in *Dictionnaire de Spiritualité*, VI, col. 1114.

[4]See *Vita Hugonis*, in *Thesaurus novus anecdotorum*, ed. E. Martène and U. Durand, vol. 3 (Paris, 1717), col. 1723.

[5]"Our dear Guerric, concerning whose life of penance you wish to be assured, to judge by his fruit is walking worthily, you may be sure, before God, and bringing forth worthy fruits of penance." Letter 89:3, trans. B. James, *The Letters of St. Bernard of Clairvaux* (London: Burns & Oates, 1953), Letter 82:3, p. 138. "If you wish to know about Brother Guerric, or rather because you do, I can assure you that he so runs not as one uncertain of the course, and so fights not as one beating the air. But he knows that the effect comes from God's mercy, not from man's will, or man's alacrity, so he begs you to pray God for him that he who gives the power to fight and run may also give the power to conquer and achieve the goal." Letter 90:2; James trans., Letter 93:2, p. 139.

[6]*Vita Hugonis, op. cit.*, col. 1723. Bernard's influence should not be exaggerated. Guerric himself testifies that the community freely chose him: "I am no healer and in my house there is no bread. That is why I told you at the beginning: 'Make me not ruler of the peoples.' ...I told you this but you took no notice of me. You made me your ruler." Sermon for the Rogation Days, n. 1. In this paper for the translation of the sermons of Guerric we will use the one prepared by the monks of Mount St. Bernard Abbey found in volumes 8 and 32 of the Cistercian Fathers Series: *The Liturgical Sermons of Guerric of Igny*, 2 vols. (Cistercian Publications: Spencer, MA, 1970, 1971).

[7]Guerric goes on to say in the same Rogation Sermon: "Lack of health prevents me being one among them. I have not the depth of soul enough for ministering the word, nor strength of body for setting a good example."

[8]"Christ it is whom I desire to give you in my sermons, however poor they may be."—Fifth Sermon for Christmas. The numbers in parentheses in the text refer to the sermons as they are found in the critical edition and in the Cistercian Fathers Series, the first number being that of the sermon and the number following the colon indicating the section number.

[9]Later, especially with the advent of the schism caused by the anti-pope in 1130,

Bernard would be away much more than he was at home. See the *Vita S. Bernardi*, bk.
2, PL 185:267ff.; trans. G. Webb and A. Walker, *St. Bernard of Clairvaux* (Westminster,
MD: Newman, 1960), ch. 19ff., pp. 76ff. Guerric would have been in the chapter of
Clairvaux when Bernard began his series of sermons on the Song of Songs to the
extent that these were preached in chapter. See J. Leclercq, *Recueil d'Etudes sur Saint
Bernard et ses Ecrits* (Rome: Edizioni di Storia e Letteratura, 1962), part 2, ch. 3,
pp. 193ff.

    ¹⁰There is a very evident relation and dependence to be found in Guerric's Second
Sermon for the Feast of the Assumption when it is compared with Bernard's Ninth
Sermon on the Song of Songs. The *Liber Amoris* probably also depends on the same
source and this led to its being attributed to Guerric. See Morson and Costello,
"Liber Amoris..." pp. 119ff.

    ¹¹Bernard's Sermons were undoubtedly subjected to a good bit of editing for
publication as is evident from the manuscripts, actually to such an extent that it is
questioned to what extent they were ever actually preached in the chapter at
Clairvaux. See Leclercq, *Recueil,* part 2, ch. 3ff., pp. 193ff.

    ¹²It seems quite reasonable to expect that Guerric's sermons did undergo some
editing as they were written down; however there is no evidence of a great amount
of this or successive editing as in the case of Bernard or Aelred. Rather their whole
flavor is closer to what one might expect to hear from an abbot in chapter. They are
filled with many homey details (see e.g. the frank discussion of dissension in
chapter—8:4) and practical everyday advice for living the Cistercian life.

    ¹³In the earliest Customary of the Order they are listed as: Christmas, Epiphany,
Easter, Ascension, Pentecost, all the solemnities of Mary, the Birthday of John the
Baptist, the Feast of the Apostles Peter and Paul, the Solemnity of St. Benedict, All
Saints, the Dedication of the Church, the First Sunday of Advent and Palm Sunday.
See *Consuetudiens Ordinis Cisterciensis*, Part 1. *Officia Ecclesiastica*, ch. 67, in *Nomasticon
Cisterciense*, ed. nova (Solesmes, 1892), p. 141.

    ¹⁴The tenth responsory: "Come, my chosen one, and I will set up my throne in
you."

    ¹⁵"For she was full of grace and blessed among women. She alone merited to
conceive the true God of true God, whom as a virgin she brought forth, to whom as
a virgin she gave milk, fondling Him in her lap, and in all things she waited upon Him
with loving care."—Apostolic Constitution, *Munificentissimus Deus*, Nov. 1, 1950,
A.A.S., 42 (1950), pp. 763f.; trans. Daughters of St. Paul, *Papal Teachings: Our Lady*
(Boston: St. Paul Editions, 1961), p. 312. The second Vatican Council cited another
Cistercian Father, Isaac of Stella, in connection with its dogmatic teaching on Mary,
Constitution on the Church, *Lumen Gentium*, n. 64. This was done in relation to
Mary's role as exemplar for the virgin Church; and for this they might have equally
cited Guerric's First Sermon for the Feast of the Assumption. See 47:2.

    ¹⁶"*To her bodily eyes* he is seen in the form of a glorified man, but to her inward eyes
in the form of the glorifying Word."—47:1, italics mine.

    ¹⁷"Daughters of Jerusalem, tell the Beloved that I languish with love."—48:1ff.

    ¹⁸The structure of the Cistercian office was substantially that outlined by St.
Benedict in his *Rule for Monasteries*, ch. 8ff. On a feast day the fourth responsory of the
night office was followed by the chanting of six psalms.

¹⁹E. g., the New Eve; 18:1, 47:1, 51:1.

²⁰Guerric expresses this beautifully in his Second Sermon for the Nativity of the Blessed Virgin: "Although they have been born by the Word of Truth, nevertheless she brings them forth every day by desire and loyal care until they reach the stature of the perfect man, the maturity of her Son, whom she bore once and for all" (52:3).

²¹Gal. 4:19.

²²Mt. 12:50. This idea of our sharing in Mary's motherhood of Christ is a traditional theme. It is found in Origen, *Commentary on selected passages in Genesis* (PG 12:124); St. Augustine, Sermon 192, for the Feast of Christmas, n. 2 (PL 38:1012; trans. M. Muldowney, *Sermons on the Liturgical Seasons* [New York: Fathers of the Church, 1959], pp. 32f.); *Holy Virginity*, n. 5 (PL 40:399; trans, J. McQuade, *Treatises on Marriage and Other Subjects* [New York: Fathers of the Church, 1955] p. 148); Bede the Venerable, *On Luke* (11:28), bk. 4 (CCL 120, p. 237); also *On Luke* (2:6-7), bk. 1 (CCL 120, p. 48); *On Luke* (7:11-12), bk. 2 (CCL 120, pp. 157f.); *On Luke* (8:21), bk. 3 (CCL 120, p. 179); *On Mark* (3:34-35) bk. 1 (CCL 120, p. 479).

²³Since the early Cistercians went by solar time, their hours of sleep were relatively short during the summer. In addition there was the practice to rise earlier on the great feasts in order to have more time to sing the office of vigils solemnly.

²⁴Italics mine. Guerric goes on to add the text from Isaiah: "Inasmuch as her soul toiled, she shall see and be filled" (53:11). Bernard, too, often spoke of the necessity of active responsibilities supplanting or preceding the repose of contemplation; see e.g., his Sermons on the Song of Songs, Sermons 47, 50, 51, 57, 58.

²⁵Jn. 2:1ff.

²⁶Mt. 12:47.

²⁷See Lk. 2:49.

²⁸I have not said as much about the Second Sermon as about the others. It is more a thing to be enjoyed. But it is not without content and gives the strongest witness of Guerric's dependence on Bernard as well as reflecting his deep tender love for Mary.

Together Unto God
Contemplative Community in the Sermons of Guerric of Igny

Bernard Lonergan has said:

> The common meanings constitutive of communities are not the work of isolated individuals nor even of single generations. Common meanings have histories; they originate in single minds; they become common only through successful and widespread communication; they are translated to successive generations only through training and education. Slowly and gradually they are clarified, expressed, formulated, defined, only to be enriched and deepened and transformed....[1]

This is the task that lies before us today: to clarify, to express, to formulate, to define the common meanings of the Cistercian contemplative community so that today's Cistercians may in their own living of these meanings enrich, deepen and transform them. In an effort to make some contribution in this direction I would like to turn to the writings of a significant early Cistercian, Guerric, second abbot of Igny.

Guerric of Igny is sufficiently well known. For those who would want a succinct account of his life I would refer them to the excellent Introduction in the recently published English translation of his Sermons.[2] Here I would like to note only a few significant facts.

First of all, Guerric was a mature man when he entered Clairvaux.[3] He arrived with a solid formation, both intellectual and spiritual.[4] Thus he was well prepared to absorb and profit by whatever additional formation he was to receive at Clairvaux. At the same time, this added formation would always be colored by his previous life experience. "Everything that is received is received according to the mood of the receiver."[5] In this he was typical of the principal Cistercian Fathers. All of them were relatively mature men when they entered upon the Cistercian way of life.[6] This accounts in part for the rich variety to be found among them. It also makes us aware that what Guerric has to teach us about the contemplative community does not depend exclusively on Cistercian sources.

The second fact that I would like to note assures us that what he does teach is authentically Cistercian. Guerric benefited by more than ten years of tutelage under Abbot Bernard of Clairvaux.[7] And so well satisfied was the master with his disciple's living knowledge of the Cistercian way of life that he did not hesitate to promote him as abbot of Clairvaux's thirteenth daughterhouse.[8] Bernard was confident that what Guerric would teach his monks would be true to the Cistercian charism, and so we, too, can be confident that this is the case.

Finally, I would like to note that in the *Sermons* of Guerric we probably have the truest reflection of actual chapter talks of a Cistercian Father. Undoubtedly, his *Sermons* were edited for publication.[9] Nevertheless he wanted them presented as talks he gave to his monks and primarily for their benefit: "But what have we to do with outsiders? This sermon is really addressed to you. . . ."[10] In the course of his *Sermons* he often spoke of his own community[11] and shared insights that he had drawn from their experience.[12] Thus from a study of Guerric's *Sermons* we can extract perhaps the most actual and concrete image of the early Cistercian contemplative community.

COMMUNITY

Guerric's understanding of the communion that is to exist among members of a community is deeply theological. He spoke often of the Church, specifically of the Body of Christ, an organic cohesion that was to be intimately coordinated.[13] This Christian community can express itself in many varied forms. The community Guerric was especially concerned with was the Church of the Desert.[14] It was a Church, a community made up of chosen individuals[15] called to follow in a "holy way"[16]—a way of life patterned on the Apostles.[17]

This community lived a well-ordered life marked with various observances which were so many "excercises of wisdom": the divine office, private prayer, *lectio divina,* appointed daily labor, silence.[18] Manual labor played a very special role in its life.[19] Everything was shared;[20] the members were to be "poor with the poor Christ."[21]

Guerric has a well-developed theology of poverty.[22] Poverty is a blessed thing.[23] But not absolutely essential.[24] Far more important is the spirit of poverty[25] which consists in humility of heart and the renunciation of pride.[26] Christ from his birth gave an example of this.[27] The poverty of Igny was very real.[28] Yet there was no Manichaean fear of possessions: "Sometimes it may be useful to own things."[29] Even when little is possessed, "The world is full of riches for the man of faith."[30] He uses them to help him to know and love God. Guerric even goes so far as to equate material things with the Sacred Scriptures: "Creation points to the Creator in the same way as do the Scriptures."[31] Guerric's community will gratefully share in

the goods of this world[32] but it will seek to use them wisely[33] and will be
very conscious of the social obligations that flow from such possessions:
"Let us watch ourselves, brethren, lest we begin to be judged for the death
of our impoverished brethren if we hold back unnecessarily or use for
ourselves what could go to support their lives."[34]

Finally, the community which shares this same program of life with its
labors and its poverty, is to be a stable community. The members are to
"take root."[35] While Guerric, explicitly following St. Benedict,[36] lays
emphasis on stability, he is nonetheless not categoric:

> For myself, I would not think it a wise plan to suffer certain loss for a
> hope that is uncertain, even if the progress of some individuals bids me
> refrain from too hasty a judgment. Most certainly there is a great
> difference between those who become discontented out of love of wis-
> dom and those . . . made restless by some light and frivolous matter. . . . [37]

COMMUNAL DISCERNMENT

Perhaps Guerric's most precious contribution in regard to community
life is his teaching, brief but concise, on communal discernment. I would like
to quote the passage at length. Here Guerric employs the biblical image of
the two harlots who come before Solomon for judgment:

> Hence the disputes of the carnal with the spiritual, even in Chapter
> meetings where the true Solomon presides invisibly as judge. "My son,"
> the carnal say, "is alive and yours is dead. I have the Spirit of God, you
> have not; the love of God is alive in me, it is dead in you." They strive to
> make their own the authority of religion, the true substance of which is
> possessed by the spiritual, so that by depriving them of authority they
> may introduce customs to suit their own wanton desires. And in fact the
> mother wishes the child to be given alive and whole to her rival: she does
> not begrudge glory to her as long as she possesses virtue. But the other
> says: "Let it be neither mine nor yours, but let it be divided," because she
> desires to keep for herself the honor of holiness and leave to others the
> toil. But the judge makes no mistake, although he sometimes pretends
> not to notice. Solomon's sword finds the mother and allots to her un-
> divided both the affection of charity and the effect of power, both fervor
> in working and favor in commanding.[38]

Evidently at Igny as at early Citeaux and, even before, at Molesme, the
monks of the community sought together to determine the way they were
to go. In this communal discernment not all were motivated by the Holy
Spirit. There were human spirits and contention. "But the judge makes no
mistake." In the end those who are truly concerned with the welfare of the
community, the true mothers of the community's life, will prevail, not by

contention, but by the witness of their love and the power of the Lord.[39]

ROLES IN COMMUNITY

In Guerric's community there is a superior, there is no question about it. But his role is one of humble service. He is to be a man who estimates himself humbly or rather truthfully, he is to be subject to all even while his office requires him to rule.[40] Guerric's image of the abbot is undoubtedly influenced by St. Benedict's *Rule for Monasteries*.[41] He is to be skilled in the art of healing—of healing minds and hearts. He is to be a teacher. If he is not gifted with learning and eloquence, and Guerric prays for these,[42] he should at least teach by the example of his life, living the common life in the midst of his brethren.[43]

It is a faith community, where the monks are to regard each other as brothers, sons of one Father. One with Christ, his Spirit animates them to say with him: "Whoever does the will of my Father who is in heaven, he is my brother."[44] A brother to be loved with affection.[45] Guerric's ideal is no mere exercise of "charity," but a real striving after a community of love. Each member is to seek as much to be loved as to love.[46]

The brethren are to help and support each other in their quest for Christian holiness. They should be able to find in one another the example of every virtue.[47] Their lives as well as their words are to express God's message. Guerric certainly had a deep faith in his brothers as channels of the Word of God and was conscious of the responsibility this entailed.[48]

But the community is not to be simply turned in upon itself. It has a role to play in the larger society, basically a role of witness, a witness that must be free from hypocrisy,[49] a witness that is a sign of hope.[50] But for Guerric the social role does not necessarily end there. The contemplative life flows over into a mission of peace, a mediatorial role which may be exercised before God for all men and among men not only inside the monastery but even possibly in relation to those outside.[51]

CONCLUSION

It is evident that Guerric has not left us a complete or theoretical treatise on community. We have only his pastoral *Sermons* and here he speaks of community in relation to a particular community, and a particular kind of community to which he is ministering.[52] He does touch upon many of the elements essential to any community and to Christian communities: stable sharing of life and love, ministering leadership, effective fraternal concern. But the particular community he always has in mind is one with a specific goal. It is a gathering of men who have come together to strive to recapture the fullness of life.[53] And for Guerric this is to be found, in this life, in contemplation.[54]

Contemplation

STAGES OF SPIRITUAL GROWTH

In a very real sense, to treat fully of Guerric's thoughts on contemplation it would be necessary to transmit the whole of his teaching because, for him, everything is ordered to this or flows from it.[55] Several times in the course of his *Sermons* he traces out the stages of spiritual growth beginning with the lowest, man still in sin, and reaching up to the contemplative experience. Perhaps the best and most complete is to be found in the *All Saints Day Sermon* where he uses the eight beatitudes as his paradigm.[56] Other examples using various Scriptural images are to be found in Sermons 11:7 (the myrrh, incense, and gold of the Magi[57]), 13:2ff. (justice, knowledge and wisdom with a reference to the man gradually cured of blindness[58]), 23:6 (the upper and lower springs of Achsah[59]), 35:5 (Elisha restoring the child to life[60]), 45:3 (the valleys and shadows of Song), 4:5f. and 52:4 (the knowledge, fear, hope, and love of Wisdom personified[61]).

UNIVERSAL CALL TO CONTEMPLATION

Guerric expected his monks to be contemplatives. For this they were "transplanted" to the monastery.[62] All are invited to it.[63]

Some of his monks already had a deep experience of God,[64] an experience which they have shared with Guerric.[65] The others were urged on toward it.[66] Indeed, Guerric believed that all the members of his community had some experience of the mighty working of the Lord within themselves.[67]

There are passages in Guerric's Sermons which might lead one to conclude that he thought the contemplative experience was something rarely given.[68] But if the context is fully read, one quickly perceives that the rareness is due, not to any lack of willingness to give on the part of God or an exclusive call to a few, but to man's lack of efficacious desire.[69] "For if you constantly attend through faith to the presence of the Lord, veiled though he be, eventually you will even contemplate his glory with face unveiled, albeit in a mirror and an image."[70] And this is "quite often granted" to his devout friends.[71]

PREPARATION FOR CONTEMPLATION

Gift though this be, man has his preparatory role. "Happy the man who in order to receive [this experience of Truth] more worthily and more often prepares a fitting place for it in the interior of his heart."[72] This place is prepared by a quietness of soul,[73] a watchful faith[74] and ardent desire.[75] But one cannot enjoy interior quiet if he does not first confess his sins,[76] mortify himself,[77] practice the virtues,[78] especially humility[79] and fear of the Lord,[80] and above all abide in silence.[81] But even while one is still busily engaged in this task of preparing for the Lord, he sometimes comes and manifests himself to his laboring servant.[82]

A Cistercian, Guerric is faithful to the Cistercian school in giving an important place to Christ the man in his spiritual doctrine: "Christ it is whom I desire to give you in my sermons.[83] For unless he who is the Life, the Truth, and the Way anticipates his own advent to us, our way cannot be corrected...."[84] If anyone is in the doldrums of *acedia*, his solution is to "make his way to Bethlehem and there let him look upon that Word of God.... What so edifies behavior, strengthens hope, inflames charity?"[85]

But if the contemplative is to begin his quest for the experience of God in the Sacred Humanity, it is not to end there. The Truth which is Christ, whom Mary gives us clothed with flesh, grace gives us unclothed in the inpouring of the Spirit.[86] It is not easy for mortal man to see the face of supreme Truth, yet we do experience something of its naked self when the Spirit makes his entry into us.[87] Guerric sets before us the example of St. Paul: "...the gentle breeze of the Holy Spirit blew upon him, by force of which he was taken up to the interior passages."[88] Contemplatives have always been attracted to solitude as a place where they can listen to the Holy Spirit,[89] but this must not preclude seeking guidance from the Scriptures and a spiritual director.[90]

THE CONTEMPLATIVE EXPERIENCE

But what is this contemplative experience for which one must so prepare, which is the crowning point of man's striving on earth?

Here Guerric shows himself very evidently a disciple of Bernard of Clairvaux. For him the contemplative experience is an "intimate visitation"[91] of the Word which plunges the contemplative into "a sweet and happy state of absorbed admiration...."[92] God is experienced as both wonderful and lovable,[93] inspiring admiration and bringing consolation.[94] "However, this comes about in various ways, according to the capacity of the soul which receives it, or according to the judgment of the mercy which distributes it."[95] And in every case, for the monk still on the way it is always an all too quickly passing experience.[96]

This experience is not limited to the times of formal prayer: "Often Jesus whom you sought as at the tomb, at the memorials of the altars, and did not find, unexpectedly came to meet you in the way while you were working."[97] These visits of the Word first of all bring enlightenment[98] and understanding of the Scriptures,[99] which move one to praise and love.[100] They bring comfort.[101] The Spirit who comes with the Word and is poured out in the heart raises the monk above the shadows of earthly things.[102]

The matter does not end there. There is a social or ecclesial dimension:

Tested and proven in this way both in the active [taken in the earlier meaning of striving for virtue, disposing oneself for contemplation] and the contemplative life, he who bears the name and office of a son of God through his having become the father and servant of other men will then and only then be worthy to be a peacemaker between them and God. Thus he will fulfill the office of mediator and advocate, and be worthy to make peace among the brethren themselves and even among those who are outside the community.[103]

The man who is faithful in this will even attain to the virtue and merit of the martyr.[104]

Contemplative Community

We have seen briefly and in summary fashion Guerric's teaching on community and contemplation. How does he bring them together?

For Guerric his men have gathered together in community precisely to seek with earnestness the experience of God, the return to paradise: "You have come together to wrestle with the angel who guards the way to the tree of life."[105] The contemplative experience of God, intimate union with him, remains his gift, not something man can do more than prepare for, ardently desire and seek. It is therefore in the realm of preparation that one seeks to find advantage in entering into a community. Yet here a paradoxical question arises. As we have seen, preparation essentially lies in a quietness of soul and faithful attentiveness to the Word of God. The striving for self-mastery, for virtue, is to make this quietness possible. Silence, interior and exterior, is essential. Yet one enters a community where he commits himself to a Christian response to his brethren, to a life of sharing with them. How do these two dimensions, rather than crossing purposes, actually become one?

Guerric's most explicit answer is perhaps expressed in this passage:

> By the wonderful favor of God's loving care, in this solitude of ours we have the peace of solitude and yet we do not lack the consolation and comfort of holy companionship. It is possible for each of us to sit alone and be silent, because we have no one to disturb us with interruptions, and yet it cannot be said of us: "Woe to him who is alone, since he has nobody to console him or if he should fall has none to lift him up." We are surrounded by companions, yet we are not in a crowd. We live as it were in a city, yet we have to contend with no tumult, so that the voice of one crying in the wilderness can be heard by us, provided only that we have interior silence to correspond to the exterior silence that surrounds us.[106]

In a world where there is rush and noise and striving for alien values, men enter a contemplative community to find a "climate of monastic prayer,"[107] a climate that is produced by the common efforts of a community of like-minded men: "Let us all together then so make a point of being quiet that in our quiet we may always be occupied with meditation on eternal quiet...."[108] A stable commitment to abide in such a community helps one to be faithful to his quest.[109] Moreover, the brothers are channels of God's word to each other: "I reckon as God's own word, my brethren, whatever the Holy Spirit in his mercy sees fit to speak within you—every single word which avails to build up faith, stirring up love."[110] From this it follows that monks must "start to use words that are as it were God's own, so that no bad word, even in private conversation, should cross one's lips."[111] This constant personal, loving, and fraternal ministry of the Word is one of the things the monk seeks in community, where living in community ministers to his contemplative call.

The hard work necessary for the support of the community, its fidelity to Christian poverty, the other community services, the general strictness of life, all have their own very beneficial role in helping the individual member, through self-mortification and the practice of the virtues, to attain to that inner quiet which can expectantly await the coming of the Word.[112] Yet this is so only insofar as the monk enters into these with the proper disposition of soul. Guerric expresses this well in his *Third Sermon for the Feast of the Assumption:*

> Happy is he who in all his labors and in all his ways seeks blessed rest, always hastening, as the Apostle exhorts, to enter into that rest. For desire of it he afflicts his body, but already prepares and disposes his spirit for that rest, being at peace with all men as far as it lies within him. Giving preference, where his will is concerned, to the rest and the leisure of Mary, to the extent that necessity demands he accepts the toil and the busyness of Martha, yet does this with as much peace and quiet of spirit as he can, and always brings himself back from that manifold distraction to the one thing necessary.
>
> A man of this sort is at rest even when he is working....[113]

Guerric says surprisingly little about community prayer. It was so much a part of the life, it is perhaps taken for granted. He has little patience for the man "who prefers little prayers to the holy labors which he has promised to perform" or "a man, whose brother holds something against him, offering at the altar" or one who "thinks the voluntary offerings of his lips are pleasing to God—those psalms and the prayers one offers secretly—if they prevent one from saying the number of psalms laid down in the Rule."[114] He undoubtedly has the Office in mind when he says to his monks:

> So too there are not lacking clouds which will raise up our spirits to higher things provided our hearts are not too lazy and tied to earth, and

so we will be with the Lord if only for half an hour. Unless I am mistaken you know from experience what I say. For when the clouds sent out a sound, that is to say, when the voices of prophets or apostles sounded in the Church, your minds and hearts have been borne aloft as on a cloud to sublime things and on occasion carried beyond even these, so that they have merited to behold, in however small a degree, the glory of God.[115]

This is indeed the goal of community prayer.

Perhaps Guerric describes some of the characteristics he would find in the members of the contemplative community when he speaks of Simeon and Anna:

... not wedded but joined together, by a bond not of matrimony but of a more sacred mystery, peers in their faith, equal in chastity, alike in their devotion, partners in the proclaiming of grace, both advanced in age, both perfect in sanctity. Even before the Gospel they dedicated in both sexes the first-fruits of the Gospel's purity and devotion.

These two have adorned your bridal chamber, Sion, with the varied beauty of their virtues, to receive Christ the King—not the walls of your temple but the inmost recesses of your heart, the hidden places of your bedchambers.[116]

Conclusion

Guerric's teaching on contemplative life and community life in no way veers from the tradition. What synthesis he offers can hardly be called revolutionary. Yet it is worth pondering. He has a very real understanding of the correlative role of community in man's search for the fullness of the Christian experience, and a true appreciation of it. Yet he does not *ex professo* explore it, nor does he even touch on all its facets. The contribution he makes through his relatively few surviving *Sermons* must be said to be valuable but limited. Arguments against the eremitical life could possibly be drawn from the *Sermons,* but appreciation and affirmation of the values of one way of life does not necessarily preclude the values of another.

Guerric's synthesis responds well to values we see as capital today. He shows a deep respect for the individual even as he expresses the real value and role of communal life and sharing. In his talks the nature of the community and why the men he is addressing have come together are always in evidence. He believed it was of value to keep the end, the goal, always in view: "...look forward to the end to which it [the way] leads you. If you were to see how everything is to be attained, then you would say without hesitation: 'Broad indeed is your command.' ...The man who dwells sufficiently on this end I think will not only make the way easier for himself but also grow wings so that he no longer walks but flies."[117]

Communities are groups of people linked together by shared beliefs and experiences. With Guerric there is no doubt what are the beliefs that are shared. He also relies heavily on lived experience; he frequently appeals to it. True contemplative community will exist only when the members have, in sufficient numbers, experienced in their own lives the complementary values and the healthy tensions that arise out of truly seeking the experience of God in a community.

Guerric's rather challenging idea of each member having a share in mothering Christ in the community[118] can well be pondered in these days of emphasis on co-responsibility. Co-responsibility does not end with debate, politics, or votes. Though all of these can have their legitimate place in the community as in any social body, the more theological approach of the Abbot of Igny is far more conducive to the attainment of the ends of the contemplative community: humble openness, lived witness to the values held sacred, confident that in the end they will prevail by the power of the Spirit.[119]

Guerric has no illusions about the men who make up the contemplative community; they are men of flesh as well as of spirit: "We live on two levels, partly according to the flesh, partly according to the spirit."[120] The highest tribute Thomas Merton could pay to the Zen monks was tersely expressed: "They keep working at it." Guerric would ultimately ask nothing more.

NOTES

[1]B. Lonergan, "Existenz and Aggiornamento," *Focus* 2 (1965) 9.

[2]J. Morson and H. Costello, "Introduction," in *Guerric of Igny, Liturgical Sermons* 1, Cistercian Fathers Series, 8 (Spencer, MA: Cistercian Publications, 1970) pp. vii-xviii.

[3]It is difficult to assign dates for the birth of Guerric and his entrance into Clairvaux. Morson and Costello see reason for saying he was born between 1070 and 1080, though he could have been born sometime in the following decade (*ibid.,* ix). He probably entered the monastery in 1124 or 1125 (*ibid.,* xiii). Thus he would have been in his forties or at least in his late thirties when he entered.

[4]*Ibid.,* xiff.

[5]*Omne quod recipitur secundum modum recipientis recipitur.* A principle enunciated by Thomas Aquinas, e.g., *Summa Theologiae,* 1, q. 75, a. 5.

[6]Bernard of Clairvaux's twenty-three years and Aelred of Rievaulx's twenty-four years at entrance might seem quite young to us, but for those times this was a relatively mature age. G. Raciti would hold that Isaac of Stella was around thirty-five when he entered ("Isaac de l'Etoile et son siècle," *Cîteaux* 12 [1961] 303ff.). William of St. Thierry was at least fifty when he entered Signy.

[7]Morson and Costello, p. xv.

[8]There is some controversy as to the extent of Bernard's influence in the election of Guerric as abbot of Igny. See *ibid.,* xvii, also Ser. 36:1. (References to the Sermons

of Guerric are according to the English edition cited in note 1, from which all the English translations used here have been taken. The number after the colon refers to the paragraph.)

[9]Morson and Costello, p. xixff.

[10]Ser. 38:2.

[11]E.g., Ser. 8:5, 24:6.

[12]E.g., Ser. 28:5, "You have shared your experience with me and have told me how a quiet and disciplined spirit is strengthened, grows fat and flourishes in silence...."

[13]E.g., Ser. 1:1, 4:3, 7:1, 11:4, 23:3ff., 34:1, 47.

[14]Ser. 4:1.

[15]Ser. 38:2.

[16]Ser. 5:4.

[17]Ser. 44:3: "But you, brethren, who share the same property and the same house, who share also the same heart and soul, you ought especially, I think, to glory in them (the Apostles), since like olive branches you have imbibed from their root not only the sap of faith but also a pattern of life and the model of our order."

[18]Ser. 22:5.

[19]Ser. 49:1.

[20]Ser. 44:3.

[21]*Super Exordium Cisterciensis Coenobii*, c. xv: "Instituta monachorum Cisterciensium de Molismo venientium" in *Nomasticon Cisterciense*, ed. H. Séjalon (Solesmes: S. Petri, 1892) p. 63.

[22]See the study of A. Louf, "Une théologie de la pauvreté monastique chez le bienheureux Guerric d'Igny," *Collectanea OCR* 20 (1958), 207-222, 362-373.

[23]Ser. 38:3, 53:5.

[24]Ser. 43:4: "I know that many people have lived temperately and modestly in an abundance of worldly possessions and glory, while many too have behaved evilly whose garments were rougher and whose food more sparing."

[25]Ser. 53:5.

[26]*Ibid.*

[27]Ser. 10:4f.

[28]Ser. 11:5.

[29]Ser. 53:5.

[30]Ser. 53:3.

[31]*Ibid.*

[32]*Ibid.*

[33]Ser. 20:2.

[34]Ser. 18:6.

[35]Ser. 22:2.

[36]*Ibid.*

[37]*Ibid.*

[38]Ser. 8:5.

[39]For an excellent study on discernment see J. C. Futrell, "Ignatian Discernment," *Studies in the Spirituality of Jesuits* 2 (1970) 47-88, and a fuller study in *Making an Apostolic Community of Love* (St. Louis: Institute of Jesuit Sources, 1970). A summary of Fr. Futrell's teaching can be found in M. B. Pennington, "Communal Discernment,"

Monastic Exchange 2 (1970) 26-32, and a practical application to the Cistercians in *Rule and Life*, ed. M. B. Pennington, Cistercian Studies Series, vol. 12 (Spencer, MA: Cistercian Publications, 1971), pp. xix-xxiv.

[40]Ser. 36:1.

[41]Cf. c. 2 of St. Benedict's *Rule for Monasteries* with Guerric's *Sermon for the Rogation Days*, par. 1.

[42]Ser. 39:4.

[43]Ser. 36.1.

[44]Mt. 12:50.

[45]Ser. 50:2.

[46]Ser. 24:4f.: "For it is the power and nature of true love that even when it does not feel affection it nevertheless contrives to make itself loved in return. Truth readily commends itself to everyone's good will even without any other support, unless it meets with the opposition of an evil and wicked mind, ever ready to put a wrong interpretation on everything. For the commending of this holy love some have their own special gift from God, who makes their faces bright with oil, floods them with a gentle and pleasing graciousness, makes their every word and action agreeable in the sight of all. At the same time many who perhaps love not less but even more do not easily acquire that grace. But the obligation is the same for everyone. Taking thought for what is good not only in God's sight but also in men's, you must neglect neither a clean conscience through love of a good name, nor esteem of men through too much trust in a clean conscience. How can you possibly flatter yourself about this clean conscience unless you are without complaint among your brethren? Unless you show that you really are a brother among brothers in all your dealings with them?"

[47]Ser. 45:4: "No mean repast this for the faithful soul. . .where it can take from them examples of all the virtues, one from one, another from another. This one is more solidly grounded in humility, that one has a more all-embracing charity. Another is more stalwart in patience, another quicker to obey. This one is more sparing and frugal, that one does more service by his work. This one is more devout in prayer, that one applies himself to reading more studiously. This one is more prudent in administration, that one is holier in repose."

[48]Ser. 14:4.

[49]Ser. 14:3.

[50]Ser. 38:2. After a visit to a Cisterican monastery, Fr. de Lubac penned at the top of a letter from his translator: "*Saint Joseph* (the monastery's title) *c'est un signe d'espoir.*"

[51]Ser. 52:2.

[52]It might be well to call to mind a point made by Thomas Merton, namely that the monastic community is not the ideal Christian community; it is rather an abnormal celibate community, and, he adds, a state of penitential mourning. See T. Merton, "Christian Solitude," *The Current* (1967) 17.

[53]Ser. 41:2.

[54]See below, "Stages of Spiritual Growth."

[55]J. M. Déchanet in his Introduction to the *Golden Epistle* of William of St. Thierry rightly says: ". . .for William, as indeed for all the writers of his period, asceticism only exists for the sake of the mysticism which controls and crowns it."—William of

St. Thierry, *The Golden Epistle, The Works of William of St. Thierry,* vol. 4, CF 12 (Spencer, MA: Cistercian Publications, 1971) p. x.

[56]Ser. 53:2.

[57]Mt. 2:11.

[58]Mk. 8:22-25.

[59]Jos. 15:19.

[60]2 Kgs. 4:32-35.

[61]Sir. 24:44.

[62]Ser. 22:7.

[63]Ser. 38:4: "'Everyone who thirsts,' he says, 'come to the waters.' Just that. He is no respecter of persons. He takes no cognizance of their rank, nor does he inquire into their merits; he only wants those who thirst to come to him."

[64]Ser. 2:3f., 35:4, 38:4.

[65]Ser. 28:5.

[66]Ser. 2:3f., 23:6, 35:4, 49:1.

[67]Ser. 53:5.

[68]Ser. 19:6.

[69]Ser. 13:6.

[70]Ser. 19:6.

[71]Ser. 7:3.

[72]Ser. 17:2. See also Ser. 50:4.

[73]Ser. 17:3, 32:6, 49:4.

[74]Ser. 19:6, 35:3, 44:5.

[75]Ser. 3:3ff., 11:7, 17:2f.

[76]Ser. 3:4, 20:3.

[77]Ser. 43:3.

[78]Ser. 4:3, 17:3.

[79]Ser. 49:5: "Who but the humble man can be quiet?"

[80]Ser. 19:6.

[81]Thus we see that asceticism is not something negative but extremely positive, perfecting man's openness and responsiveness to God. Based on the experience of the brethren (Ser. 28:5) Guerric has a well developed positive theology of silence:

> Truly it is a trustworthy word and deserving of every welcome, your almighty Word, Lord, which in such deep silence made its way down from the Father's royal throne into the mangers of animals and meanwhile speaks to us better by its silence. Let him who has ears to hear, hear what this loving and mysterious silence of the eternal Word speaks to us. For, unless hearing deceives me, among the other things which he speaks, he speaks peace for the holy people upon whom reverence for him and his example impose a religious silence. And most rightly was it imposed. For what recommends the discipline of silence with such weight and such authority, what checks the evil of restless tongues and the storms of words, as the Word of God silent in the midst of men? There is no word on my tongue, the almighty Word seems to confess while he is subject to his mother. What madness then will prompt us to say: "With our tongues we can do great things; our lips are good friends to us; we own no master." If I were allowed I would gladly be dumb and be brought low, and be silent even from good things,

that I might be able the more attentively and diligently to apply my ear to the secret utterances and sacred meanings of this divine silence, learning in silence in the school of the Word if only for as long as the Word himself was silent under the instruction of his mother. O brethren, if we listen devoutly and diligently to this Word which the Lord has made and shown to us today, how much and how easily we can be taught by it.

There must be a real correspondence between interior and exterior silence. See Ser. 4:2.

[82]Ser. 35:4: " . . . often Jesus whom you sought as at the tomb, at the memorials of the altars, and did not find, unexpectedly came to meet you in the way while you were working."

[83]Ser. 10:5.

[84]Ser. 4:2. See also Ser. 16:3.

[85]Ser. 10:2. See also Ser. 32:5.

[86]Ser. 17:2. See also Ser. 32:1.

[87]Ser. 17:2. See also Ser. 7:3.

[88]Ser. 45:5. See also Ser. 3:3 and 17:6, where Simeon is also proposed as an example.

[89]Ser. 4:1.

[90]Ser. 4:3.

[91]Ser. 2:3.

[92]Ser. 2:4.

[93]Ibid.

[94]Ibid.

[95]Ser. 17:2. See also Ser. 46:5.

[96]Ser. 7:3, 12:7.

[97]Ser. 35:4.

[98]Ser. 3:4.

[99]Ser. 4:1.

[100]Ser. 4:1, 17:2.

[101]Ser. 7:3.

[102]Ser. 46:7.

[103]Ser. 53:2.

[104]Ibid.

[105]Ser. 41:2.

[106]Ser. 4:2.

[107]Ser. 4:1. This was the title Thomas Merton gave to the last book he prepared for publication before his tragic death: *The Climate of Monastic Prayer* (Spencer, MA: Cistercian Publications, 1969).

[108]Ser. 49:6. See also Ser. 32:6.

[109]Ser. 22:4. See also Ser. 4:1 and 5:5. William of St. Thierry says in his *Golden Epistle:* "It is impossible for a man faithfully to fix his soul upon one thing who has not first perseveringly attached his body to one place."—par. 94.

[110]Ser. 15:4.

[111]Ibid.

[112]Ser. 20:6, 50:4.

[113]Ser. 49:2.
[114]Ser. 5:2.
[115]Ser. 2:3.
[116]Ser. 16:5.
[117]Ser. 5:5.
[118]Ser. 8:5.
[119]*Ibid.*
[120]Ser. 20:1.

The Spiritual Father as Seen by a Spiritual Father, Blessed Guerric of Igny

We have in Guerric of Igny a privileged witness to the spirit and teaching of the early Cistercians. He was a favored disciple of St. Bernard and spent over twelve years with him at Clairvaux. For ten years he was the Father Immediate of Bernard's most intimate friend, William of St. Thierry.

Moreover, Guerric was a theologian of significant stature. Judging as best we can from the dates we know of him—he entered Clairvaux, c. 1125; became abbot of Igny, 1138; and died, 1157—he evidently became the Master of the School of Tournai at a relatively young age, perhaps even in his twenties or at the most, thirties. By that time Tournai's international attraction as the seat of Odo of Cambrai (a disciple of Anselm of Bec) had waned. Yet Odo was probably still living as bishop of Cambrai when Guerric succeeded to his magisterial chair.

In addition there is the fact that Guerric's witness comes down to us in a particularly living and pure form. Besides the one very enticing sermon on the Song of Songs—which gives us a faint hope that it might be part of a whole commentary which will some day come to light—there are fifty-three feast-day sermons. Both the testimony of the *Exordium Magnum*[1]—for whatever it is worth—and the state of the manuscripts[2] argues to a collection that has not suffered much from editing and therefore is quite close to what Guerric would actually have shared with his spiritual sons in the chapter house of Igny.

THE SPIRITUAL FATHER-MOTHER

In one of the early sermons of this precious corpus, Guerric gives us a very important key to a significant dimension of his concept of the role of the spiritual father. It is in the third sermon for the feast of Christmas. Considerations of the feast lead easily enough to the thought of maternity, and a gospel text invites the development of spiritual considerations:

Whoever does his will, he is mother and brother and sister. Lord Solomon, you call me mother. I profess myself to be a handmaid. I am Christ's handmaid; be it done to me according to your word. And indeed I will show myself a mother by love and anxious care to the best of my ability; but I will always be mindful of my condition. [5] Brethren, the name of mother is not restricted to prelates, although they are charged in a special way with maternal solicitude and devotion. . . .[3]

Thus we perceive that Guerric's very rich doctrine of spiritual maternity, finding its archetype in Mary, the Mother of God, and not neglecting the Church nor the universal call of the faithful,[4] is an integral part of his understanding of the service of spiritual paternity. In this he clearly shows himself to be a disciple of St. Bernard, "our Master, that exegete of the Holy Spirit,"[5] who did not hesitate to liken himself to a mother in the service of his spiritual sons.[6]

GUERRIC'S OWN CALL

The first place though that I wish to consider in this study of Guerric's understanding of the role of the spiritual father is the Rogation Day sermon where he speaks candidly of his own election as abbot of Igny:

I am no physician and in my house there is no bread. That is why I said from the start: "Do not make me your leader." It is not right for me to rule who cannot be of service. And how can he be of service who is not a physician and in whose house there is no bread? He has neither the art to heal souls nor the learning to feed them. I told you this but you would not listen. You made me your superior. There was only one course open to me. If I could not escape the burden, I had to look for the remedy. I listened to the advice of the wise man: "Have they made you ruler? Be among them as one of them." But I cannot even do this. Lack of wisdom forbids my being put over others, lack of health prevents my being one among them. I have not the depth of soul for ministering the word, nor the strength of body for giving a good example. I am not fit to be a ruler over you nor am I fit enough to be among you as one of you. What is left to me then but to choose the last and safest place and be the servant of you all? And this I can do by thinking humbly, or rather truly, about myself. There is nothing to prevent me, in fact truth itself strongly urges me to be subject in spirit to you all, even though I am compelled by my offices to rule over you.

[2] It is you yourself, Lord God, who warn me to be subject yet command me to rule. So, confident you will grant my plea, I beg you to make me humble and helpful in the ministry you have confided to me: humble in realizing the truth about myself, helpful by speaking the truth

about you. Breathe the one truth into my heart, let the other be ever on my lips. You have told us: "Open your mouth, and I will fill it." Put into my mouth the appropriate word that pleases the ear, so that this entire family of yours may be filled with blessings.... We know that to merit the ability to teach, it is not enough to show continuous zeal and perseverance in prayer, enough to make us seem shameless. I myself can rely on neither. All I can do is put before you the merits of those I must feed. They deserve what I do not.[7]

The question has often enough been discussed as to how Guerric came to be elected abbot of Igny.[8] He was a monk of Clairvaux at the time, and so the conjecture has been made even from earliest times that he was chosen by the community at the behest of St. Bernard, the Father Immediate, who would have presided at the election. There may have been some influence exerted by the persuasive Bernard, but Guerric here insists on the freedom of the community in choosing him. Among the authors considering this question I rarely find any reference to a very significant document. The Acts of Milon indicate that Guerric of Clairvaux was with the bishop of Tournai in Ypres in May of 1138.[9] As Igny was virtually half-way between Clairvaux and Ypres, given the traveling habits of monks, there is basis for a strong argument that Guerric was at Igny in 1138 and, as his sermon seems to indicate, precisely at the time of the abbatial election. The community had an opportunity to get to know this favored son of St. Bernard, so full of learning, spiritual wisdom, and charm. But the question is somewhat apart from our present consideration. What interests us here is the qualities that Guerric would have in a man whom he would consider apt to undertake the office of superior and spiritual father.

And they are very much those set forth by the Master whose Rule he professed. He must be a physician who knows how to heal, a wise man who can teach, but above all a humble man who sees his ministry as service and who knows he himself has received all that he has to give. He is to be in their midst as a living example. Knowing himself, he thinks humbly of himself; his spirit is such that he sees himself as subject to those to whom he provides the ministry, by God's choice, of ruling. The depth of soul he has to minister the Word he has received from his Friend, the true Master. Even though he has striven to live a blameless life of continuous zeal and perseverance in prayer, he knows that what he has received has been given him, more because of the merits of his sons. It is a familial scene filled with warmth. He is to seek to serve, to rule, in a helpful way and even try to please the ears of his monks.

The "job description" then that Guerric offers in these few lines is a quite complete one, though other passages in his writings will add color and warmth to it.

The only place where Guerric speaks explicitly of spiritual paternity is significantly in the passage which expresses concisely the heart of his whole teaching. If the Sermon on the Mount is the summary of Gospel spirituality, the Beatitudes stand at the head of this sermon as an epigrammatic summation of all that it has to say. The Cistercian Fathers have found in the Beatitudes the paradigm to set forth the Cistercian way to holiness.[10] And it is here that Guerric offers a contextual teaching on the spiritual father. Let us listen to this significant passage:

> The first virtue in this ascent, proper to beginners, is renunciation of the world, which makes us poor in spirit. The second is meekness, which enables us to submit ourselves in obedience and to accustom ourselves to such submission. Next comes mourning to make us weep for our sins and to beg God for virtue. It is here we first taste justice, and so learn to hunger and thirst more keenly after justice in ourselves as well as in others, and we begin to be roused to zeal against sinful men. Then, lest the zeal should grow immoderate and lead to vice, mercy follows to temper it. When a man has learned to become merciful and just by diligent practice of these virtues he will then perhaps be fit to enter upon the way of contemplation and to give himself to the task of obtaining that purity of heart which will enable him to see God. Tested and proved in this way in both the active and contemplative life, he who bears the name and office of a son of God through his having become a father and servant of other men will then and only then be worthy to be a peacemaker between them and God. Then he will fulfill the office of mediator and advocate, and be worthy to make peace among the brethren themselves and even among the brethren and those who are outside the community. For thus it is written in praise of our holy Fathers: "They were men bringing peace in their houses." If a man is faithful and constant in this office, he will often attain that virtue and merit which belongs to the martyr, for he suffers persecution for justice' sake, and this even on occasion at the hands of those for whom he is fighting, so that he can say, "The sons of my mother have fought against me," and, "with them that hated peace I was peaceful; when I spoke to them they fought against me without cause." How much glory, and how rich a reward will finally crown such perfection in heaven. . . . [11]

Here spiritual paternity is seen as a stage in the normal development of the spiritual life. One must begin with renunciation. Guerric is addressing himself here to monks, and therefore he is placing this in the context of renunciation of the world that is involved in the conversion to monastic life. But he would be concerned that it be in fact a true interior renunciation of that world to which Christ's disciples do not belong,[12] of the world of possessiveness and material aggrandizement which fetter the spirit. I do not think Guerric's teaching should be so interpreted as to limit spiritual paternity to the monk, although his teaching is given within a monastic context. Therefore, while again he speaks of obedience as it stands at the heart of monastic life, essentially he would be pointing to obedience as a school of submission to the will of the Father in imitation of Christ, an obedience one could live out in other vocations in relation to one's spiritual father. What Guerric is saying is that one must first be a son before one can be a father. He does say this more explicitly in the text.

Poverty of spirit, submission, compunction, a quest for virtue—the basic exercises of the active life, as this term was then understood and is so used by Guerric in this passage—leads to a zeal for justice, in the fullest sense of that word: God and man, each and all receiving his full due. But it is a question of virtue, which stands ever in the middle, and so must be moderated. The crusader is not apt to be a father figure. Mercy, compassion is essential, yet it comes in as a modifier of justice. A false mercy that does not make due demands and call forth to a living out of all justice is lacking in the virility of true spiritual paternity.

"Diligent practice" of mercy and justice brings one to that fullness of virtue which opens out to contemplation. For Guerric it is the latter that is the means to purity of heart—the end of the monastic life according to St. John Cassian—and the clear perception of God in prayer and in all and through all.

Having come to a certain fullness of Christian being and life through virtue and contemplation, one has the capacity now to engender life in others. In this fathering he shows himself like the Father of all and thus reveals himself to be truly his son.

Guerric then goes on to indicate something of the nature of this paternity. Immediately he links it with service: "father and servant"; and the service can be summed up in one word, "peacemaker." First of all, peacemaker with God. The spiritual father is son, closely united and formed to the likeness of the Son, and his is to make peace like the Son between the Father and his sons. His first role is that of prayer; he is "mediator and advocate." Recently when I discussed the nature of spiritual paternity with one of the great spiritual fathers on Mount Athos, he asserted strongly that the first duty of the spiritual father was to stand before the Lord in the night interceding for his sons and daughters and to visit them mystically with Christ. The father is then to lead his sons to peace among themselves and with those outside the monastery—Guerric is here speaking most specifically in the context of the abbot-father—but it is impossible for them to be at peace with each other and their fellow-men if they are not first at peace with God. Indeed, that tranquillity of order which is true peace presupposes growth in all the virtues.

Guerric is ever realistic and speaks from years of experience. He knows that fathering a group of men at all different levels of growth has its pain and sorrow. The father will suffer in his fathering, so acutely that it is a veritable martyrdom. In his quest to establish justice he will suffer from those he is actually serving in this quest. But like his Father St. Benedict he holds out to the spiritual father the encouragement of hope, the promise of the reward.

In this brief passage then we find the way to spiritual paternity, its essential expression, and its ultimate reward.

ACCORDING TO THE TEACHING AND EXAMPLE OF BENEDICT

We might at this point look at Guerric's sermons for the Feast of St. Benedict. The role Abbot Benedict fulfilled in regard to all monks, each particular abbot is to fulfill in regard to his own sons.

Actually Guerric speaks relatively little of St. Benedict in the course of these four sermons. They are filled with very solid Benedictine teaching. Great emphasis is laid on stability, perseverance in "the school of Christian Philosophy," in the exercises of wisdom: divine office, private prayer, *lectio divina*, silence, and fear of the Lord.[13] There is practical teaching on such matters as meditation, distractions,[14] and dryness.[15] In addition there is some very rich and beautiful teaching on fraternal love and community life.[16] Guerric might well have been speaking of himself when he says of the monk: "Blessed indeed is the tree whose leaves are for healing and whose fruit is for life, that is, whose words bring grace to the listener and whose actions bring life to himself performing them."[17]

Of this very rich teaching I want to highlight one element which I think is too significant to pass over without some special mention. It is one aspect of what Guerric has to say here on fraternal love. If he is in fact talking about relations between the brothers, nonetheless it pertains *a fortiori* to the relation of the spiritual father to his sons.

Guerric places his teaching in the fundamental context of the two great commandments enriched by the fullness of Christ's teaching.

> To be deserving of God's friendship: this is the supreme virtue, the best gift of grace, the choicest fruit of life because it is the surest pledge of happiness.... And if after and because of this, the sum total and cause of all grace, you should merit that further grace, so that, beloved of God, you become beloved of men as well, what a consolation that would be amid the miseries of this life, what peace, what joy, what delight.[18]

And so to be loved by the brothers is something to be merited, and not only is it to be merited, but, with proper motivation, it is something that one must strive for. "... That striving...is neglected at their peril.... For it is the power and nature of true love that even when it does not feel affection it nevertheless contrives to make itself loved in return."[19] Some have a greater facility for doing this: "For the commending of this holy love some have their own special gift from God, who makes their faces bright with oil, floods them with a gentle and pleasing graciousness, makes their every word and action agreeable in the sight of all."[20] Others are not so blessed. "But the obligation is the same for everyone."[21] Guerric touches on many aspects of this important area. The monk, right from the start, is to be concerned about winning this love and seeking to learn how to make use of it. Guerric expresses a "sincere hope" that each of his monks will attain it. He concludes the consideration with this weighty paragraph:

> Taking thought for what is good not only in God's sight but also in men's, you must neglect neither a clear conscience through love of a good name nor the esteem of men through too much trust in a clear conscience. How can you possibly flatter yourself about this clear conscience unless you are without complaint among your brethren? Unless you show you are a brother among brothers in all your dealings with them? Do you think it is enough not to scandalize them? The fact is that you do scandalize if you do not edify, that is, if you do not glorify God everywhere according to your own proper role in the community, with your own conscience and your brethren bearing witness to your goodness.[22]

As I said, it seems to me this teaching can and should be applied in an eminent way to that monk who is called upon to fill the role of spiritual father among his brethren.

In these sermons Guerric also speaks of God's spiritual paternity, undoubtedly an example for the abbot: "He [God] brings forth when he generates good will; he plants when he brings to life; he waters when he floods the mind with grace; he tills when he imposes discipline on conduct."[23] One of the spiritual father's most fundamental tasks, and sometimes the most difficult, is to engender good will; only then can he hope to call his sons forth to new life. He may by his prayer obtain showers of grace for his sons, but without that good will he will never be able to impose any sort of life-giving discipline.

In the few paragraphs where he speaks directly of St. Benedict, Guerric presents him as a leader and teacher who guides his monks with charity and discretion along the simple life-giving way of the Gospel. Benedict lived as he taught, a man of faith who knew both fear and hope, a man of meekness and gentleness who yet could burn with zeal,[24] a model for any abbot.

GUERRIC'S OWN EXAMPLE

Guerric's sermons give many glimpses of his own exercise of spiritual paternity. Many passages make it clear that he is the recipient of the confidences of his monks, that they open their hearts to him and reveal the inner secret workings of nature and grace.[25] He insists upon the importance of their doing this and receiving guidance: "If you are wise you will not be your own teacher and guide in the way along which you have never walked, but you will incline your ear to masters and acquiesce in their reproofs and advice. . . ."[26] He is well aware of their constant "falling and rising"[27] and adapts his teaching to their frailty: "I speak in human terms because of the infirmity of your flesh, or rather because of the narrowness of your mind."[28] He encourages and promises.[29] He traces out in many varied ways the stages of spiritual growth.[30] He jealously watches over his sons "with the jealousy of God," and warns them against possible evils, ready to lament their failures with an abundance of tears.[31]

Guerric knew the tension between the active and contemplative lives,[32] the call to service of the brethren and the desire to sit quietly at the feet of the Lord. But he does not record this as a cause of personal stress in the way some of the other Cistercian Fathers have.[33] Perhaps this is so because he is less idealistic, more comfortable in dealing with everyday reality as it unfolds, perhaps because he is more humble, ready to identify and take hope with the brothers to whom he has said:

> Therefore, my brothers, if you long for the high spring, your desire is certainly to be praised. But if you have not yet attained to that, to send out your roots meanwhile to the waters that are below is a wholesome medicine. Whoever then is not successful in capturing the joys of the contemplative life, let him consider the holiness of the active life. And so let him enlarge the roots of his good desires, make his conduct more agreeable and control every circumstance of his life. . .whose words bring grace to the listener and whose actions bring life to him performing them.[34] . . . If anyone feels a desire for that best part which is praised in Mary, he may know that this is the reward of the man who cannot be reproached for failing to do Martha's part: it is not right that reward should be sought before merit.[35]

Yet Guerric does not hold that one way is essentially superior to the other. The goal is union with Christ Jesus, to know him and experience his love and presence; and this is granted to the busy as well as to the contemplative: ". . .Jesus deigns to meet and manifest himself not only to those who devote themselves to contemplation but also to those who quietly and devoutly walk the ways of action.[36] . . . Others may fly by contemplation; you at least do so by love."[37]

However, it is true, as we have seen in the text from the All Saints' Day sermon quoted above, Guerric does see the service of the spiritual father as a fruit of contemplation, and overflowing from its fullness. In this he is in accord with the teaching he received at Clairvaux in Bernard's first sermons on the Song of Songs.[38] And in this service he found a model in Mary, the Mother of the Word Incarnate.

> She showed herself to be a Martha in her care for the Child's rearing in such a way that nonetheless she fulfilled the part of Mary in her application to knowledge of the Word.[39]

For Guerric Mary is the New Eve, the Type of the Church, the truest of spiritual mothers. And it is in the consideration of his teaching on the spiritual mother that we will find, as we indicated at the beginning of this paper, those feminine complements which bring Guerric's understanding of the role of spiritual paternity to its fullness.

MOTHERING THE CHRIST

In the opening paragraph of this paper we quoted a significant passage from Guerric's third Christmas sermon. The abbot is to "show himself a mother by love and anxious care," to have "maternal solicitude and devotion."[40] As he goes on to apply the same text to his disciples, he charges them: "Keep watch then, holy mother, keep watch in your care for the new born child until Christ is formed in you...."[41] If this is true of the monk, *a fortiori* is the abbot to keep a watchful care that is directed toward the formation of Christ in his sons.

It is in his first sermon for the feast of the Assumption that Guerric speaks most fully of Mary's spiritual maternity:

> Then the blessed Mother of Christ, knowing that she is the mother of all Christians by reason of this mystery [being the New Eve, Type of the Church, Mother of Life], shows herself a mother by her care and loving attention. For her heart is not hardened against these children as if they were not her own; her womb...remains ever fruitful, never ceasing to bring forth the fruits of her motherly compassion...pregnant with inexhaustible tenderness.
> He was born of you once and for all, yet he remains in you always, making you ever fruitful. Within the locked garden of your chastity he makes the sealed well-spring of charity always abundant.
> ... If the Servant of Christ by his care and heartfelt tenderness bears his little children again and again until Christ be formed in them, how much more is this true of the very Mother of Christ? Paul begot his children by preaching the word of truth through which they were born again, but Mary in a manner far more holy and like to God...so that first

and foremost in all their needs and dangers they run to call upon her....[42]

Here we see then in Mary, the model, many of the qualities to be cultivated in the spiritual father: care, loving attention, soft-heartedness, fidelity, compassion, inexhaustible heartfelt tenderness, abundant charity, evangelical teaching, a fruitfulness that comes from Christ's abiding presence. He is to be such a person that his sons instinctively turn to him in their needs.

Anyone familiar with Guerric will not be surprised to find St. Paul coming to mind here; indeed, it is almost to be expected. Guerric's love and admiration for Paul is all but boundless.[43] But by evoking the Apostle here he not only introduces another quality of the spiritual father, but shows the scriptural basis for attributing maternal qualities to the pastoral office.

As Guerric goes on in the sermon to extol Mary's virtues: her chastity, humility, faithfulness, charity, prudence, and poverty, he clearly implies that these same must be what Christ can find in the one he will make a fruitful spiritual father.

Guerric speaks again of Mary's spiritual motherhood in the second sermon for her birthday, indicating the source and goal of their maturity and the mother's role of desire and loyal care:

> For she desires to form her Only-begotten in all her sons by adoption.
> Although they have been brought to birth by the word of truth, never
> theless she brings them forth every day by desire and loyal care until
> they reach the stature of the perfect man, the maturity of her Son....[44]

The Church, too, is a spiritual mother, and in Guerric's consideration of this reality, we find yet another type for the service of spiritual father, one closer, for it is actually through the spiritual fathers and mothers that the Church fulfills her maternal duty. In his third sermon for the Annunciation Guerric touches on some of the more painful aspects of his service that every spiritual father must sooner or later face:

> The Church is pregnant, brethren, not as Mary was, with Jesus alone,
> but as Rebecca was with Jacob and Esau,[45] that is, not only with those
> who are good and well-behaved, but also with those who are ill-tempered
> and undisciplined. However, these too, for the sake of Jesus, or perhaps
> because they possess the principle by which they are grounded in him,
> the womb of the Church receives and enfolds. But when the two infants
> struggled and fought in Rebecca's womb she, who previously had prayed
> to conceive, was grieved that her womb ached with pain, trouble, and
> sorrow. She was almost sorry that she had conceived. "If it was to be thus
> with me," she said, "why should I have conceived?" If it should happen,

brethren, that the bowels of our mother should complain thus of any one of us, I am afraid that it would have been better if that man had not been conceived, except that even for such we are not allowed to despair. He who even from stones raises up sons to Abraham will not allow it. If there be any such, may he soften the stony heart in them so that their mother's womb will not ache, and may he comfort their mother's womb so that she will not grow weary carrying them, however ill-behaved they may be, until Christ is formed in them. . . . [46]

In spite of the rich biblical imagery the passage is all too transparent to miss the open-hearted sharing of the spiritual father. Even the Golden-Age knew the "ill-tempered and undisciplined," and the abbot who eagerly welcomed them to the cloister as an answer to his prayer for fruitfulness, is now tempted to wish they had never been admitted. Yet love of Christ and faith in him demands another response, one of hope and not despair. The unruly ones have the principle of Christ's life in them and it will in time come to full life in them. In the meantime the spiritual father needs strengthening lest weariness lead him to fail to carry out his pastoral duties.

CONCLUSION

It would be impossible to summarize in a really adequate way this very rich teaching which, in fact, has already been presented in very summary fashion. It needs and can only be digested in that patristic fashion of circling about it and bit by bit entering into each of its facets till it becomes a living synthesis within the receiver. It is more than obvious, especially from the way in which Guerric, following St. Paul and the Gospels themselves, has integrated the feminine and masculine, that this teaching is equally a teaching on spiritual maternity—the office of spiritual generation and education depends in no wise on sex but on fullness of life. Also, as we have already mentioned, although Guerric, as an abbot, couching his teaching in the literary genre of sermons to his monks, expresses his teaching in a monastic frame, it is equally applicable to those who find themselves called to this ministry of spiritual paternity in other contexts, institutional or not. While an ecclesial office such as abbot, superior, or pastor might call for one who has this kind of spiritual fullness, the bearers of such life-giving spirit cannot be limited to office holders. Indeed, Guerric makes it clear in his central teaching on the Beatitudes that growing to such fullness and entering upon the service of spiritual paternity has its place in the normal development of the Christian life. Indeed, the problem that often confronts institutional monasticism is how to make it possible for the monk or nun who is not called to the abbatial office to exercise such paternity when they arrive at spiritual maturity. Certainly all should strive after such fullness, and when it is attained its energies should not be dissipated but employed as

fully as possible for the total growth of the whole Christ. These considerations could lead to another paper, so let us leave them for now and rather
seek to simply absorb as completely as we can the full richness of the
teaching of Guerric of Igny on the spiritual father.

NOTES

[1]*Exordium Magnum Cisterciense sive narratio de initia Cisterciensis Ordinis* (ed. Bruno
Griesser; Rome: Editiones Cistercienses, 1961) Dist. III, c. 9, p. 166.

[2]Guerric d'Igny, *Sermons,* ed. J. Morson and H. Costello; *Sources Chrétiennes* 166, 202
(Paris: Cerf, 1970, 1973) 1:22, 69-77.

[3]3 Christmas 4-5. Where no author is indicated the citation refers to the Sermons
of Guerric. The English translations used in this paper are taken from Guerric of
Igny, *Liturgical Sermons,* trans. Monks of Mount St. Bernard Abbey, CF 8, 32 (Spencer,
MA: Cistercian Publications, 1970-1971).

[4]*Ibid.*

[5]3 Peter and Paul 1.

[6]For example, Epistles 201:1, 233:3, 258, etc.

[7]Rogation 1-2.

[8]For example, CF 8:XVII; D. de Wilde, *De Beatu Guerrico abbate Igniacensi eiusque
doctrina de formatione Christi in nobis* (Westmalle: Typei Abbatiae, 1935) pp. 16-17.

[9]R. Milcomps, "Le Bienheureux Guerric. Sa vie—son oeuvre" in *Collectanea Cister-
ciensia* 19 (1957) 209, n. 1.

[10]See above "A Way to Holiness," pp. 35-47.

[11]All Saints 2.

[12]John 15:19.

[13]1 St. Benedict.

[14]*Ibid.,* n. 6.

[15]2 St. Benedict 5f.

[16]3 St. Benedict 3ff.

[17]2 St. Benedict 5.

[18]3 St. Benedict 2f.

[19]*Ibid.,* 5.

[20]*Ibid.*

[21]*Ibid.*

[22]*Ibid.*

[23]2 St. Benedict 7.

[24]4 St. Benedict. There are two places in his sermons where Guerric speaks with
unaccustomed zeal that approaches harshness—and even apologizes for it; these are
the places where he denounces detraction: 1 Pentecost, 5; 3 John Baptist 5.

[25]For example, 3 Annunciation 5: "You have shared your experience with me and
told me..."; 1 Epiphany 4; 2 Purification 7; 5 Purification 5; 1 St. Benedict 5;
1 Annunciation 5; 3 Easter 4; 3 Peter and Paul 1, 2, 6.

[26]Advent 4.

[27]*Ibid.,* n. 5.

[28]3 Advent 4.

[29]For example, 4 Advent, 1, 3; 5 Advent 1; etc.

[30]For example, 1 Epiphany 5-7; 2 Epiphany 5; 3 Epiphany 4; 5 Purification 6; 3 Easter 5; 4 John Baptist 3; 1 Nativity BVM 4; 2 Nativity BVM 4; All Saints 1.

[31]3 St. Benedict 6.

[32]1 Advent 3; 2 Peter and Paul 3; 4 Assumption 3.

[33]For example, Bernard of Clairvaux, *Sermons on the Song of Songs* 12:9, 30:7, 52:5f., 53:1ff.; William of St. Thierry, *On Contemplating God* 1, 12; *Meditations* 11:8f.; *The Nature and Dignity of Love* 8; *Exposition on the Song of Songs* 52.

[34]2 St. Benedict 6.

[35]4 Assumption 4.

[36]3 Easter 4.

[37]Ascension 5.

[38]Bernard of Clairvaux, *Sermons on the Song of Songs* 12. See above, "Three Stages of Spiritual Growth according to St. Bernard," pp. 82-93.

[39]4 Assumption 3.

[40]3 Christmas 5.

[41]*Ibid.*

[42]1 Assumption 2-4.

[43]See, for example, 2 Easter 3; 2 Pentecost 1; 2 John Baptist 1; 1 Peter and Paul; 1 Assumption 3; 2 Nativity BVM 1; On Psalmody 4.

[44]2 Nativity BVM 3.

[45]See Gen. 25:24ff.

[46]3 Annunciation 7.

Saint Aelred of Rievaulx

A Primer of the School of Love

The Cistercian scholar is not a scholar for scholarship's sake. He does not devote his consecrated hours to research and writing primarily because he wants to further studies in one or another particular field. Certainly, he does not write because he wants to see his name in print. Like his Fathers, his aim, while always ultimately the glory of the God he loves and serves, is primarily pragmatic. The early Cistercian Fathers, goaded on by St. Benedict's admonition to look to the "holy Catholic Fathers" and to the Sacred Scriptures,[1] endeavored to get the most authentic texts and then studied them with unflagging fidelity. Their research extended to other areas as well, such as the Gregorian chant.[2] Their aim in all: to enter into and live as fully as possible the heritage that was theirs, to live an authentic Benedictine life. Today's Cistercian scholar seeks to emulate his Fathers in this and, in turn, to study deeply the heritage as it has been incarnated in the Cistercian Fathers themselves, so that the fullness of this rich tradition can be lived today and handed on to tomorrow.

The true monk is a student all his life. He is ever listening to the precepts and teachings of his Master.[3] This begins for him as a work in the novitiate. Here he is to receive those initial formative lessons that will set the course he will follow as a Cistercian student, a disciple in the School of Love. He may go on to serve others as a senior or father in the school, but he will ever remain himself a student, learning from the Fathers under the guidance of the Holy Spirit, the supreme Master in this school, the one who taught the Fathers and made their teaching so life-giving. This initial formation of the novitiate is then extremely important. And it is important that it be in line with that imparted by the first Fathers who formed the monks of the golden age. How did the novice masters of that age inform their candidates? What were the initial lessons they imparted in the School of Love? We are most fortunate in that the great Master of the Cistercian School, the Theologian of Cistercian Life,[4] foresaw the need, for his own time and ours, to leave a clear and quite full presentation of the matter. Using his authority as a Father Immediate,[5] St. Bernard called upon the most outstanding novice master in the Clairvaux line and probably in the whole Order, and commanded him to provide for this need. In Aelred of Rievaulx's *Mirror of Charity*⁶ we have an authenticated presentation of the basic teaching given in the *Schola Caritatis*. It is an extensive work. Already in his own times, monks found it useful to make summations to capture the medulla of his teaching.⁷

I do not intend here to make a summation of the teaching of the *Speculum Caritatis,* the *Mirror of Charity*, but rather, after briefly placing it in its historical context, I want to highlight the significant elements which today's Cistercian novice master or novice mistress will want to be sure to make part of their formative teaching, to provide their novices with a full, living knowledge of their heritage.

AELRED OF RIEVAULX⁸

Aelred was still quite young—only 32—and young in the Order—seven years professed—when he was sent on an important mission to Rome in 1142. The controversy over the bishopric of York greatly interested Bernard of Clairvaux, so this reason, as well as the fact that Bernard was the Father Immediate or higher superior and canonical visitor for Rievaulx, made it fitting that the emissary stop at Clairvaux both on his way to Rome and on his return.

These were probably the first meetings Bernard had with the exceptional young monk, who was gifted with a rich and varied background. To Bernard, who had been abbot since he was twenty-five, after only two years of professed life, Aelred did not appear so young, and certainly not inexperienced. The former courtier was ready to serve as novice master of a rapidly growing abbey—founded but ten years ealier, it already housed some three hundred monks and lay-brothers—and soon thereafter to be sent to head one of Rievaulx's early foundations.

What Bernard did see in the young monk was that he had a thorough and clear grasp of the basic teaching of the School of Love. And so, employing his authority to overcome an understandable diffidence, Bernard required of the young novice master a *Mirror of Charity,* and personally outlined the form the treatise was to take.⁹

THE MIRROR OF CHARITY

We do not find in Aelred's *Speculum* an altogether orderly treatise. There is a basic order, that given him by Bernard: "What charity is, how its possession brings delight, and how its contrary vice, cupidity, imposes nothing but tyranny; how false it is to hold that charity is lessened by a life of austerity, and that in fact austerity increases charity; how charity must be exercised and manifested in our conduct."¹⁰ Aelred does adopt certain paradigms, notably St. John's lust of the flesh, lust of the eyes, and pride of life (1 Jn. 2:16), and Leviticus' three Sabbaths (Lev. 23-25). Yet he comes at the magnificent many-faceted gem of charity from many directions and uses many modes of approach: the rich typology of the Old Testament, exegesis of the New, the wisdom of the Fathers, the tight, precise definition and distinction of the scholastics, and open and often times very humble personal sharing. All of this adds up to an immensely rich and varied treatise, a teacher's manual for the novice master and novice mistress that can provide the basis for a most solid, stimulating and inspiring formation program and course of instruction.

THREE WAYS OF LIFE

Aelred sees three ways of life: the basic order of nature, the order of necessity, and the monastic order.[11] It is to the last that he addresses his treatise, but it is important that the candidate be fully cognizant of the first two so that he can embrace the third with true freedom. This is important for Aelred.

The first order is the order we are born into. As Aelred speaks of it we can appreciate his full humanism and basically positive approach to life.

> The things which God allows us in this life are all pure to the pure, and none of them are to be rejected. All are to be accepted with gratitude. These are things like the use of marriage, eating meat, drinking wine, possessing wealth.[12]

Aelred lists here things which the monk specifically gives up. The point is, he is not to give them up as bad things, but as good things, goods which he should be grateful God has given to his people. But, as Aelred goes on to point out, in their use, circumstances of time and place and varying modes of life are to be considered. Moderation is always to be observed. In actual fact, all of us, except the holy Virgin and her Son, have failed in our excesses. And so there is a second way of life, that "by means of which we make reparation for the abuse of what is allowed us in our natural way of life by restraining our appetites and abstaining from what is licit."[13] This restraint is not only necessary to make satisfaction for our past failures, but also to diminish and quiet our passions and forestall repeated excesses.

Beyond the 'order of necessity' there is the 'life of free sacrifice.'[14] Monastic life is a sacrifice we make of our own free will. We leave behind us the use of what is allowed in normal life to follow the precepts of Our Lord in the Gospel. After indicating the Gospel texts involved, Aelred goes on to stress the care one should take in committing oneself to such a way of life, for "once we have taken on the hard life of the monastery, our salvation is in peril if we leave it."[15] This does not make the willing sacrifice a thing of

coercion—Aelred is here answering an argument that would later be prominent among the Protestant Reformers and which we hear in our own
days—since in the first place no one is forced to take on the austere life. But
it is imperative that "before deciding we will take the hard road, we think
over what we are doing and what we propose to do. We must consider all
that the monastic life involves, and whether we have sufficient physical
strength to withstand the daily assaults of temptation."[16]

THE BASIC MONASTIC OBSERVANCES

There were those in Aelred's times—as in our own—who, out of a false
humanism, were attacking the austere ways—the "negative spirituality,"
one might say today—of the traditional Benedictine monasticism. Bernard,
in his prefatory letter, called upon Aelred to show "how false it is to think
that charity is lessened by a life of austerity."[17] In the course of his defense,
and at other points in his treatise, Aelred lists what he considers the basic
austerities or observances of the monastic life: vigils—the best corrective to
a light and wandering temperament, daily manual labor, poor food, rough
clothes, fast—the best weapon to fight lust, silence—the sword against
anger, recollection, patience, bearing temptations, turning from the world
and the things of the world, and walking in the way of obedience.[18]

Aelred does not develop his teaching on these for the most part. He
directs his readers to Benedict's *Rule for Monasteries,* Cassian's *Institutes*[19] and
the Fathers in general. He gives very balanced instruction on the importance of maintaining the observance and the due use of dispensations.[20]
Aelred presupposes in the men he is concerned with that basic attitude
called for by St. Benedict: that they truly seek God.[21] Or, as he spells it out
more concretely: I am speaking of those who labor seriously at the profession of being Christ's followers, who examine their consciences to the very
depths, and spare themselves nothing of the truth of self-knowledge.[22]

For Aelred, the inner attitude is the important thing. This is what gives
the observances their meaning and desirability. The monastic observances
are good and useful for the person who wants the freedom of Christ's yoke
and wishes to be freed from the yoke of the lust of the flesh, the lust of the
eyes, and the pride of life.[23] Herein lies Aelred's true humanism. A large
segment of the treatise is given to showing practically how this freedom is
achieved.

THE FULL CONTEXT

A larger part of the treatise, though, is dedicated to putting all this and
man himself in a larger context, his true context, the one that proclaims his
true dignity and meaning. The *Speculum* opens with a cosmic vision and it is

important that this be conveyed to the novice, for it is the only context within which the life of a contemplative monk can have its true meaning.

In presenting this Aelred does not hesitate to employ a profound and well developed theology that is not only cosmic but Trinitarian and anthropological. He presupposes in his reader an extensive familiarity with Sacred Scripture, with the Old Testament and the New. His references are many, his exegesis at times incisive. He constantly resorts to Scripture for images and illustrations.

While Aelred's approach is primarily patristic and his dependence on the Fathers extensive, he is not afraid of the clarity of the scholastics. He defines and distinguishes, and distinguishes his distinctions. For example, as he tries to establish a clear norm for helping the novice distinguish between true charity and natural feelings, he goes through a whole series of such distinctions:

Love
  I. Instinct—good in itself
  II. Act—
    A. By reason of its morality
      1. good—charity—helped by grace—good use of love
      2. bad—cupidity—unaided by grace—abuse of love
    B. By reason of the nature of the act
      1. choice of object—reason
      2. pursuit of the object
        a. inward—desire
          1.1. rational
          1.2. attraction—spontaneous inclination
            a.1. spiritual
              2.1. good—Holy Spirit
              2.2. bad—devil
            a.2. human
              2.1. according to virtue
                b.1. rational—example of good men
                b.2. irrational—fascination of evil men
              2.2. according to relation
                b.1. friendship
                b.2. kindred
                b.3. carnal
                  3.1. external appearance alone
                  3.2. as container of virtue
        b. outward—actions
      3. enjoyment of the object—term

All of Aelred's theologizing is ever in the service of practical living, of helping the novice to clearly discern his proper response to God, himself, his fellows, the whole of the creation. And love, charity, remains ever the central consideration.

> We who seek the heights of perfection by giving our will to God in a life dedicated to the pursuit of holiness, must, above all, keep charity in our mind's eye as the goal of our endeavor. Charity draws us to God. Charity makes us cleave to God by conforming us to Him. In charity all the fullness of perfection is contained.[24]

SOME PARTICULAR POINTS

In the course of his very rich treatise, Aelred touches upon an amazingly large number of concerns and meets each with some very practical instruction and pastoral advice.

Considering the extensive amount of attention he gives to it, Aelred considered the question of feelings, consolations, emotions a very important one for the novice. And today I think this is equally so. To a great extent the beginner's faith rests on feelings and the intensity of love is judged by them. If Aelred's *Speculum* was to reflect the true image of charity, which must be guided by faith, it was absolutely essential to give the novice the means of sorting this out. In the outline presented above we indicated the extent to which Aelred went to do this. He sums up his teaching:

> The visitations of God's grace that come to us in the form of feelings and emotions are for God to bestow when and where and to whom he wills. It is not for us to seek them, or even to ask for them, and if God should suddenly remove them from us, our wills must be in agreement with his. For the man who loves God is the man who bears patiently with all that God does to him, and who is zealous in carrying out God's precepts.[25]

Aelred is very frank and concrete in speaking about the temptations the novice will have to face. At times he will be burdened by the weight of his natural desires for earthly things.[26] When life is hard and wearisome he will be tempted to lose himself in a world of wishful thinking, looking forward to the time when he will be in a position to command rather than to obey, and presuming liberties that are not his to take.[27] He might even be beset with the "blasphemous thought" that the service of God is all in vain and there is no reward for those who keep his commandments.[28]

Aelred sees, then, the importance of encouragement, of helping the novice to see his present life in contrast to his past,[29] of giving him a true norm to judge his spiritual growth. For this last, Aelred draws extensively from Scripture,[30] and later sums it up in these words: "The quality of our will can be judged by two things, namely by the way we bear with whatever

God sends us in the way of sufferings and by the way we fulfill his commands."[31]

In the light of his later writings it is not surprising to find that Aelred gives relatively extensive teaching on friendship in this treatise on love. It certainly is important that today's novice benefit by balanced teaching in this regard. Aelred's approach is realistic: "I take it for granted that we cannot all enjoy each other."[32] His cautions are many, summed up in this strong statement: "Friendship is the most dangerous of all our affections."[33] These cautions should be carefully pondered, for they protect a most precious reality:

> It is such a great joy to have the consolation of someone's affection—someone to whom we are deeply united by the bonds of love, someone in whom our weary spirit may find rest, and to whom we may pour out our souls... someone whose conversation is as sweet as a song in the tedium of our daily life. He must be someone whose soul will be to us a refuge to creep into when the world is altogether too much for us, someone to whom we can confide all our thoughts. His spirit will give us the comforting kiss that heals all the sickness of our preoccupied hearts. He will weep with us when we are troubled, and rejoice with us when we are happy; he will always be there to consult when we are in doubt. We will be so deeply bound to him in our hearts that even when he is far away, we shall find him together with us in the spirit, together and alone. The world will fall asleep around us, we will find, and our souls will be at rest, embraced in absolute peace. Our two hearts will be quiet together, united as if they were one, as the grace of the Holy Spirit flows over us both.[34]

Related with this theme of friendship, but in some ways going beyond it, is the consideration of fraternal correction. Aelred gives very practical and concise instruction on this, considering not only the need of the brothers to help each other in this and the role of superiors, but also the need sometimes of the brethren to correct the superior.[35]

Aelred in his instruction of the novices does not forget that they will some day, please God, be responsible leaders in the community. If as novices they are not at least opened to the monastic values involved in all the aspects of community life, when will they be? So we find him considering matters such as the kind of music monks should employ—along with considerations on the role of song in prayer which the novice can immediately profit by,[36] monastic architecture and furnishings,[37] and even finances, "since even the management of money comes within the scope of charity."[38]

Aelred does not believe that the problems and abuses that exist in monastic communities should be hidden from the new men. He accepts the idealism, the enthusiasm that is proper to the beginner, but warns them, "Be careful to remember that there is no perfection in this life that may not be closely aped by people who are insincere. And I don't want you to be put off by them, when you discover frauds in religious life, as you certainly will."[39] He repeatedly points out monastic failings and even makes this rather caustic statement: "In fact it happens only too often that those most ill-suited to govern are put in positions of power simply to keep them quiet, and to stop their getting completely out of hand—a lamentable state of affairs."[40]

Aelred does not give any specific instruction on the sacramental life. Concern for the liturgy of the hours, the work of God, is prevalent. Confession was probably seen very much in the context of the novice's relationship with and openness to his novice master. The frequent allusions to the Eucharist give strong witness to the very significant place this had in the monk's life.[41] Certainly there can be no doubt about the importance Aelred placed on devotion to Jesus in his human life and Passion.

Scattered throughout the treatise are gems of practical advice, real *verba senioris*. I cannot resist the temptation to share just a few more of them:

> The human person is made up of body and soul, and our actions must be performed in regard to these two.[42]
> Too much concentration on one fault may blind us to the fact that we have others which also need to be dealt with.[43]
> We must guard against impatience at not being able to do all we would like to do, and also guard against doing too much of the things we like doing.[44]
> We must seek to enjoy one another in God, and at the same time enjoy God in each other.[45]

THE TREATISE

Aelred is a very good teacher. His conferences to his novices must have been as interesting as they were effective. He often resorts to tripartition to clarify and summarize his teaching and engrave it in memories. Take this example from the second book: We are roused by God's mercy, seeking the lost; purified by his kindness, helping the struggler; given rest by his justice, crowning the victor.[46] He then goes on to develop the three stages of conversion, mortification of the passions and self-will, and perfect happiness.[47] He spices his teaching with zesty examples: A monk who demands from his superiors as many dishes at meals as he sings nocturns in choir;[48] those who exercise their stomach muscles more than their brains,[49] or whose tears of devotion are but the result of over-eating.[50]

We cannot help but be deeply touched by Aelred's personal sharing in regard to his friend Simon and their relationship.[51] But perhaps the most effective section in the whole treatise is where Aelred records for us an interview with a novice which sums up an important part of his teaching.[52]

One of the qualities which marks the teaching of the treatise throughout and on several occasions becomes the explicit matter of the teaching is that of moderation.[53] This man, whose own life was to be total gift, yet called for the gift of self in wholehearted love to be given in a moderate way. As he approaches the conclusion of his treatise, Aelred sums up the matter himself:

> We have spoken of the due measure to be observed in various situations in life, and these situations are, after all, only so many steps whereby we rise up to the One who is to be loved above all else. And as we climb up toward the contemplation of God, we are at the same time looking after the salvation of our souls and taking care of our bodies, which they need. Since God has taught us that we must love our fellows and ourselves, it is first of all necessary that we should know how to go about obeying these two commandments. Then we have to see to it that we put the commandment into effect without sinning by excess on one side or the other.[54]

SABBATH REST

For Aelred, all is ordered to a contemplative union with God. To bring this out in his third part he employs a typology drawn from the Book of Leviticus: the three Sabbaths.[55] The Sabbath was for Aelred tranquillity of mind, peace and rest in the heart. There is the Sabbath day found when one is at peace with himself; the Sabbath year when one is at peace with his neighbor—his own family and house, his friends, all Christians, all Jews, all non-believers, and all enemies; and the Sabbath of Sabbaths, the Jubilee Year, when one enters into the rest of God, into "the greatest of all joys, which is found only in the contemplation of God."[56]

Aelred's concern here is with unity, and with the monk being who he is supposed to be: *monos*—one. This is the ultimate meaning, the perfect imaging or mirroring of charity; perfect unity of being and action in him who is one and one love. To conclude in Aelred's own words:

> And since there is no division in true unity, we must take care not to let our minds and hearts be distracted by this or that, but simply to be at one in God who is One. Let all be in him, and about him, through him, and with him. Let us know him alone, and enjoy him alone, and being always one in him, we shall always be at rest in him, celebrating our perpetual Sabbath.[57]

NOTES

[1]St. Benedict, *Rule for Monasteries* (hereafter RB) 73:3-4, ed. J. Neufville with introduction, translations and notes by A. de Vogüé, *La Règle de saint Benoît,* Sources Chrétiennes (hereafter SC) 181-6 (Paris: Les editions du Cerf, 1972) p. 672.

[2]For some interesting insights into this quest for authenticity, especially in the area of Gregorian Chant, but having a broader relevance, see C. Waddell's Introduction to the English Translation of the Prologue to the Cistercian Antiphonary in *The Works of Bernard of Clairvaux,* vol. 1, CF 1: *Treatise I,* (Spencer, MA: Cistercian Publications, 1970) pp. 153-160, especially pp. 156f., and his article in *The Cistercian Spirit. A Symposium in Memory of Thomas Merton,* CS 3 (Spencer, MA: Cistercian Publications, 1973) pp. 190-223: "The Origin and Early Evolution of the Cistercian Antiphonary: Reflections on Two Cistercian Chant Reforms."

[3]RB, Prol. 1; SC 181-412.

[4]This title has been rightly attributed to St. Bernard of Clairvaux by the scholar who knows him best and has done the most to make him known, Dom Jean Leclercq. See his article, "The Intentions of the Founders of the Cistercian Order" CS 3:88-133, especially pp. 101f.

[5]"Father Immediate"—this is the title Cistercians give to the abbot of the monastery which was or serves as the 'motherhouse' or community of origin of a monastery. According to the Cistercian law and practice, he visits the 'daughter house' regularly and at that time and others exercises some carefully circumscribed jurisdiction therein.

[6]*Liber De Speculo Caritatis* (hereafter Spec) ed. A. Hoste and C. H. Talbot, *Aelredi Rievallensis opera omnia,* 1 Opera ascetica, Corpus christianorum continuatio mediaevalis (hereafter CCM) 1 (Turnholt: Brepols, 1971) pp. 1-161. At the time of this writing there is no complete translation of the *Mirror of Charity* available in English. One will shortly be published in CF.

[7]See *Compendium speculi caritatis,* ed. R. Vonder Plaetse, CCM 1:163-240, especially the Preface.

[8]The best modern biographical study of Aelred is that of A. Squire, *Aelred of Rievaulx, A Study,* CS 50 (Kalamazoo, MI: Cistercian Publications, 1981). One should also see A. Hallier, *The Monastic Theology of Aelred of Rievaulx,* CS 2 (Spencer, MA: Cistercian Publications, 1969).

[9]See the prefatory letter of St. Bernard, CCMI: 3-4.

[10]*Ibid.*

[11]Spec. 3:76.

[12]Spec. 3:77.

[13]Spec. 3:79.

[14]Spec. 3:80.

[15]*Ibid.*

[16]Spec. 3:81.

[17]CCM 1:4.

[18]Spec. 2:8, 59, 63; 3:79, 102.

[19]Spec. 3:79. The references to RB are frequent.

[20]Spec. 3:96f., 102.
[21]RB 58:7.
[22]Spec. 2:3.
[23]Spec. 2:7.
[24]Spec. 3:96.
[25]Spec. 2:55.
[26]Spec. 2:64.
[27]Spec. 2:32.
[28]Spec. 2:36.
[29]Spec. 2:41ff.
[30]Spec. 2:33f.
[31]Spec. 2:54.
[32]Spec. 3:108.
[33]Spec. 3:57.
[34]Spec. 3:109.
[35]Spec. 3:98.
[36]Spec. 2:67ff.
[37]Spec. 2:70.
[38]Spec. 1:96.
[39]Spec. 2:44.
[40]Spec. 2:77.
[41]E.g., Spec. 1:1, 16; 2:68; 3:64, 77.
[42]Spec. 3:52.
[43]Spec. 3:79.
[44]Spec. 3:97.
[45]Spec. 3:52.
[46]Spec. 2:26.
[47]Spec. 2:27ff.
[48]Spec. 2:7.
[49]Spec. 2:35.
[50]*Ibid.*
[51]Spec. 1:98ff.
[52]Spec. 2:41ff.
[53]E.g., Spec. 3:54, 75, 79, 81, 97.
[54]Spec. 3:98.
[55]Spec. 3:1f.
[56]Spec. 3:5.
[57]Spec. 3:1.

Saint Aelred's Sermons
for the Feast of Saint Benedict

Introduction

Although not the best known of the Cistercian Fathers, Aelred of Rievaulx[1] with his true humanness is one of the most loved. In these days when our common concern is turned towards the renewal of Christian life in all its aspects and when there is such emphasis placed upon the full development of human potentialities and values, the frank and not untraditional statement of monastic values by a true Christian humanist[2] has a bracing effect. This gifted, sensitive monk entered the Cistercian Order while the last of the original Founders was probably still living.[3] He knew personally and perhaps intimately the great theologian of the Cistercian life, Bernard of Clairvaux. He therefore gives a very valuable witness to the spirit and aims that must stand as principles for authentic Cistercian renewal.

One readily recognizes the common traits of the Cistercian school in these three sermons of St. Aelred. The usual sources are used at great length. The same clear, logical order prevails. However, as one approaches these sermons seeking insights, it must be kept in mind that no one sermon or group of sermons reveals the total outlook of a preacher. To share the full insight of Aelred into the monastic way of life, it would be necessary to study all his sermons in connection with his other writings and, most important, his own way of life. We must remember, too, that in a sermon a preacher has a definite view, a particular concern, and he emphasizes what will support it. He does not seek a balanced portrayal of the whole.

We cannot include here a sketch of the life of St. Aelred. For this, we would direct the reader to F. M. Powicke's edition of Walter Daniel's *Life of Aelred*.[4] What St. Gregory the Great said of St. Benedict, "He could not teach other than he lived,"[5] undoubtedly can be applied also to St. Aelred. In the portrait which he draws of St. Benedict as abbot—the good Shepherd, the loving Father, the wise Master (I, 20)[6]—we can see the ideal which he lived so successfully as Abbot of Rievaulx.

A Cistercian abbot for over twenty-four years, Aelred must have preached at least three hundred sermons to his monks in Chapter.[7] To date, no comprehensive and scientific endeavor has been undertaken to compile and edit all his sermons. The largest collection we have is that published in 1855 in Volume 195 of the Migne Edition of the Latin Fathers. Here we find, besides Aelred's thirty-two sermons on Isaiah (the *Sermones de Oneribus*), twenty-five others for different seasons and feasts of the ecclesiastical calendar. In 1952 another collection of twenty-six sermons was published under the editorship of C. H. Talbot.[8] The three sermons for the Feast of St. Benedict which we present here, for the first time in English translation, are taken from the Migne Collection.[9] It would be difficult to give a more precise date than to place them sometime during the period in which Aelred was abbot, i.e., 1143 to 1166.[10]

Aelred's sources in composing these sermons are those we would expect from a member of the Cistercian School.[11] The predominating source is Sacred Scripture. In these three relatively brief sermons Aelred quotes the Sacred Text over fifty times (the largest number of quotations being, not surprisingly, from the Psalter) and he includes countless allusions. Aelred uses Scripture in all the ways that were typical of contemporary preachers following the patristic tradition. Sometimes a text is used in its full literal, historical sense, but more often it is used in an allegorical, tropological or (and especially) anagogical way.[12]

Aelred's second great source, not surprising in sermons for the Feast of St. Benedict, is the *Rule* and *Life* of Benedict himself.[13]

There are at least eight quotations from the *Rule*, and several references to the *Life* of Benedict by St. Gregory the Great.[14] Indeed, it is the spiritual doctrine of St. Benedict that informs the whole doctrine presented in the sermons.

We find no direct quotation of the Fathers apart from the few citations from St. Gregory, but the whole flavor of the sermons is certainly that of the patristic tradition. What Aelred says of St. Benedict can be applied to his own writing, "in his Rule, the gold of the Blessed Augustine shines, the silver of Jerome, the double-dyed purple of Gregory, the jewel-like sayings of the Fathers. . . ." (III, 3).

As is usual with the Cistercian Fathers, Aelred's concern is with the moral life. The whole aim of his sermons is to edify and instruct in the way of the Spirit.[15] His descriptions of human endeavor and human weakness are graphic and true to life (cf., e.g., I, 8; III, 5). He has an insight into fallen human nature ruled by passion, and the effects of this rule on man's whole life and relations with other men. (Perhaps in this Aelred is drawing on his own experience at the court of Scotland.) If we feel that he presents too negative a view of human life in the third paragraph of the second sermon, we have to admit it is wholly and solidly based on Revelation; it is Christian realism. Aelred, like Benedict, accepts with full human sympathy the fact that beginnings are difficult when fallen human nature tries to rise to its transcendent dignity in Christ. But he holds out the encouraging promise that life, even here, can be one of "untold sweetness and delights" (II, 6).[16] It would be a travesty of Aelred's outlook if we were to take the image of human life presented in one paragraph as his total outlook. He sees in St. Benedict the realization of the full potential, natural and supernatural, of a man called to be a master of creation and an intimate of God.[17]

These three sermons of Aelred's might give the impression that he thought that a man could be converted from a life of sin only by entering upon the monastic life. It is true that he did not think of monasticism as something for an exclusive few, but he certainly would not have considered it the only way to salvation. In studying and applying the doctrinal content of these sermons we must keep in mind the audience to whom they were addressed, namely, his monks at Rievaulx. Again, it might be thought that their doctrine is rather pedestrian. This is so because Aelred is concerned here with the beginnings of monastic life, with monastic conversion. He speaks of the first three days of the journey into the desert, just to Sinai, not the rest of the journey to the Promised Land. He is concerned with the first four steps of humility and does not take us up the whole ladder.[18]

Towards the ultimate goal there are only the forward glances of hope. We are there where Benedict has already gone (II, 2, 4) because we have placed our hearts upon it (II, 2), "for where your treasure is, there will be your heart also" (Mt. 6:21). The whole purpose of following the way of the *Rule* is to attain to that vision of love (II, 8). *Lectio,*[19] prayer and meditation are for us sinners "cities of refuge" within the very Land of Promise (III, 12) where we will at length find "a twofold rest, a twofold perfection: immortality for the body, beatitude for the soul" (III, 6).

The place of Christ is central in the *précis* of monastic spirituality which Aelred offers us in these sermons, as it was with St. Benedict. The way, the whole way, is Christ, and the goal is Christ (II, 4). The *Rule* teaches us to build a tabernacle for Christ in our hearts (I, 5); Christ is to reign in us; Christ is to be a pilgrim in us; Christ is to be identified with us, hungering in us, thirsting in us (III, 4). We are to be united with Christ in his death. We are to be renewed in his Resurrection (III, 15). And "when Christ our life appears, we will appear with him in glory" (III, 15). All of this is to be accomplished in us through the grace of our Redeemer, Jesus Christ, one with the Father and the Spirit (II, 8).

The monk's first step along the way that is Christ is to withdraw from the world, not only in body but also in mind and heart (I, 10). This is the monastic conversion. It is an intensely personal thing. By his own good will, his good desires, the good thoughts sown in him by the grace of God, a man turns from his sinful ways (I, 7). He is open to all sorts of rationalizations

(I, 8) but by God's grace he goes forth into the desert, into solitude. "And what does it mean to go into solitude? It means to consider this whole world as a desert, to desire the Fatherland, to have only as much of this world as is necessary to accomplish the journey" (I, 9).

Having entered the desert, the monk must follow the steps of humility and the exercises of monastic life (I, 12ff.; III, 12). Fear of the Lord, the beginning of humility, led the monk to give up the things that this world values. He must now seek to mortify the desires of the flesh that have come with him into the desert. For this Aelred prescribes what he considers the three basic corporal exercises of the monastic life: work, watching and fasting (I, 1, 10, 13, 15; III, 7, 12). Only when these exercises effectively achieve their aim will the monk become a spiritual man and be able to enjoy those spiritual exercises, *lectio,* prayer and meditation, which are for him "cities of refuge" in the Promised Land itself (III, 12). All these exercises are means to create a deep sense of compunction, true poverty and profound humility, the dispositions which will leave the monk wholly open to the divine goodness and mercy (I, 15).

But the fullness of this attitude is not yet achieved. The monk must take a further step on the way of humility, namely, he must subject himself, obey, give up his own likings, the *voluntas propria.* Only then is he totally open to the divine movement and ready to follow it into the fullness of divine love. There is here the negative element of self-sacrifice, leaving oneself totally, *ex toto relinquit seipsum* (I, 14); he must go out of himself—in love. The positive element is this total donation to God, "for love of God he subjects himself" (I, 14). The concern here, as with St. Benedict, is not primarily hierarchical obedience but the gift of oneself to others (III, 5) to the point of accepting "with a quiet mind" hard things and even injuries (I, 17). This is the simple Gospel teaching: "When they are struck on one cheek they offer the other. When they are forced to go one mile they go two. They sustain false brethren and persecution" (Mt. 5:39ff.). But there is another aspect to be considered in this question of giving up one's own will. The *voluntas propria* stands in opposition to the *voluntas communis.*[20]

Perhaps one of the more valuable contributions Aelred makes to our present-day concern is his teaching here on the full Christian dimension of community. The man who seeks his own quickly becomes envious of his brother, and this leads to suspicion. These are the flies in the sweet oil of brotherly love which destroy all its beauty (I, 9); and it is this oil which gives true sweetness to community life. For Aelred, community is no mere living together, no shallow communication. It is above all a deep sharing of life, of the Christ-life. It is being members of Christ and members, therefore, of one another (III, 8). In this true oneness there is a realization that whatever each one has received, he has received not for himself alone but for all his brothers (III, 7). His total sharing of life and all its joys and sorrows does not deny in any way the uniqueness of each individual (III, 7). "Each one has his proper gift from God" (1 Cor. 7:7). Each brings his particular gift, his talent, to the community (III, 7). There is a deep appreciation of the unique contribution of each and at the same time a very valuable sense of need, a realization that we do need our brother in order to realize fully our own potential in Christ (III, 7). This, of course, is simply Paul's doctrine of the Mystical Body,[21] very beautifully and very humanly expressed here by Aelred in the context of the daily monastic life so well known to his hearers.

A corollary of this appreciation and full respect for the total sharing yet particular functioning of the different members of the one body is the realization that each one in the community will have and should have a different measure in his practice of the various exercises of the monastic life. To those accustomed to thinking of early Citeaux as a rather mono-lithic structure of uniform monastic practices it comes as a surprise to hear this early Cistercian Father say to his community: "It must be realized that no one has the same grace in all these exercises [work, watching, fasting, *lectio,* prayer, meditation]...each one should take refuge in that practice in which he finds greater help" (III, 13).

Aelred draws in these sermons a close analogy between the law of Moses and the law of Benedict. Can he be suggesting that the latter, just like the former, may become obsolete in its particular observances, or rather, may find fulfillment in the all-embracing new law of love?

Another valuable contribution that these sermons of Aelred's make to our present-day concern is the witness they give of the attitude of the early Cistercians toward St. Benedict and his *Rule*. Aelred repeatedly speaks of St. Benedict as "our Father." He uses St. Paul's analogy to explain in what this paternity consists. It is Benedict's wisdom (I, 3; III, 2), teaching (I, 1, 20; II, 8), and doctrine (I, 4; II, 8) that engender spiritual life in his followers. But his example (II, 2, 4) and his intercessory care (I, 3, 20; II, 8; II, 2) are not lacking. Above all, he has given a *Rule* of life which will lead surely to the Vision (I, 5; II, 8). For Aelred, Benedict was a true Moses (I, 3; III, 2, 10): "Filled with the spirit of Moses" (III, 3), a legislator (III, 2, 7) who "established a law for us by which, if we observe it, we will enter heaven itself, the land of the living, and possess it forever" (I, 5). Aelred had a very great appreciation of the *Rule*. For him it was a spiritual tabernacle, a heavenly edifice. It was adorned with "the gold of the blessed Augustine, the silver of Jerome, the double-dyed purple of Gregory, the jewel-like sayings of the Fathers" (III, 4). Above all it enshrined the spirit of Benedict, who was "filled with the spirit of all the just" (III, 3). For Aelred, the *Rule* was "a most direct way" by which we may arrive at the Vision of Love (II, 8). But he certainly did not have in mind any mere external observance of it.

Another note in these sermons that rings true to our modern concern is the great insistence on interiority. Deeds are certainly important. It is not enough for a monk to withdraw from the world in spirit only (I, 10). One has actually to leave the world, leaving behind riches and honors. But what one does once in an exterior way, one has to do daily from the depths of one's heart (I, 10, 12, 15). With Benedict, Aelred taught that it is not enough to give up one's own likings, to be obedient, to suffer injuries and contradictions. To reap the fruit of all this it is necessary to be able to do it all with "a quiet mind" (I, 17). Only then has one truly embraced the monastic way of life. When outer actions reflect deep inner convictions of mind and heart, then will the monk truly have gone forth from Egypt, from the world of frivolity and sin, and be ready to offer a sacrifice pleasing to the Lord (I, 15). When he loves to be what he is for Christ's sake, the monk will be a true follower of St. Benedict and worthy through his intercession "to come to the pastures of eternal happiness, to the inheritance of the servants of God, to the joy of the disciples of Christ" (I, 19, 20).

NOTES

[1]A.D. 1110-1167.

[2]On Aelred's eminent qualities as a humanist, cf. Amedée Hallier, *The Monastic Theology of Aelred of Rievaulx,* trans. C. Heaney (Spencer, MA: Cistercian Publications, 1968), Conclusion.

[3]Since the exact date on which Aelred entered Rievaulx is not certain, it is possible that he entered shortly after rather than before the death of St. Stephen.

[4]F. M. Powicke, ed., *Walter Daniel's Life of Aelred* (London: Thomas Nelson & Sons, 1950).

[5]*The Four Books of the Dialogues of St. Gregory the Pope Concerning the Eternity of the Soul* (hereafter, *Dialogues*), bk. II, ch. 35.

[6]References in parentheses refer to the Sermons, the Roman numeral indicating the Sermon, the Arabic, the paragraph.

[7]According to the *Customary* in force at that time the abbot was expected to preach to the community on at least twelve special days in the year: the Feasts of Christmas, Epiphany, Easter, Ascension, Pentecost, Assumption of the Blessed Virgin, Nativity of St. John the Baptist, Sts. Peter and Paul, St. Benedict, and the Dedication of the Abbatial Church, and also the First Sunday of Advent and Palm Sunday. Cf. Guignard, *Les Monuments Primitifs de la Règle Cistercienne* (Dijon, 1878), p. 161. On other days, undoubtedly the abbot spoke to the community, giving them simple instruction on the *Rule.* Over and above these talks to the community it is certain that Aelred preached other sermons outside the monastery, a few of which have been recorded for us. Cf. *Life,* pp. 99f.

[8]*Sermones Inediti B. Aelredi Abbatis Rievallensis,* ed. C. H. Talbot (Rome: Curia S. O. Cisterciensis, 1952).

[9]Sermons 5-7: PL 195, 238D-251A.

[10]Since Aelred died on January 12, 1167, the last of these sermons was preached at the latest in the previous year.

[11]For a fuller treatment of the sources of St. Aelred, cf. Hallier, *op. cit.,* ch. 4 and Conclusion.

[12]Cf. Talbot, *op. cit.,* pp. 12ff.

[13]The *Life* as well as the *Rule* of St. Benedict was the norm for the early Cistercians. Cf. *The Little Exordium,* ch. 15, trans. R. Larkin, in L. Lekai, *The White Monks* (Okauchee, WI: Cistercian Fathers, 1953), pp. 262ff.

[14]This is the *Life* as it is found in the Second Book of the *Dialogues,* cf. *supra,* n. 5.

[15]Cf. Talbot, *op. cit.,* p. 2.

[16]Cf. *St. Benedict's Rule for Monasteries,* Prologue, 48f. (For citations of RB we use the division of chapter and verse of E. Manning [Westmalle, 1862], who follows Lentini): " . . . the way of salvation, whose entrance cannot but be narrow. For as we advance in the religious life and in faith, our hearts expand and we run the way of God's commandments with unspeakable sweetness and love." Trans. L. Doyle (Collegeville, MN: Liturgical Press, 1948), p. 5.

[17]To realize that Aelred's outlook is basically very positive we need only to call to mind a passage such as this, from the *Mirror of Charity:* "The beauty and goodness of creatures, with all their different functions, serve rather to help man to find happiness and love" (I, 1). His outlook on life is well summed up by G. Webb and A. Walker: "He shares with his master, St. Bernard, a deep compassion for fallen mankind, when his thoughts turn to the weighty matter of the soul's responsibility for sin. But he shares, too, the mentality of William of St. Thierry, who sought in his meditations for the Face of God and found it shining through the faces of the pure of heart." (Aelred of Rievaulx, *The Mirror of Charity,* trans. G. Webb and A. Walker [London: Mowbrays, 1962], p. xl).

[18]For a full treatment of Aelred's monastic spirituality, cf. Hallier, *op. cit.,* ch. 3.

[19]It is difficult to find a suitable English equivalent for the word *lectio* as it is understood in monastic tradition. It is not simply reading. Its nature may vary from quite serious study to little more than holding an open book in one's hand. What is distinctive about it is that it is directly ordered to and wholly impregnated by the quest for God, contact with him, experience of him. Sometimes it is rendered in English as "sacred reading" but this still needs explanation.

[20]Cf. St. Bernard of Clairvaux, *Sermons for the Easter Season,* II, 8: ed. J. Mabillon, vol. I (Paris: Gaume, 1839), col. 1967A, trans. A. Luddy, *Sermons for the Seasons and Principal Feasts,* (Westminster, MD: Newman, 1950), vol. 2, p. 193; III, 3: col. 1971C, Luddy, p. 201.

[21]Cf. Rom. 14:4; 1 Cor. 12:12ff.; Eph. 4:4-16.

Saint Aelred's
First Sermon for the
Feast of Saint Benedict

1. I know that you are accustomed to welcome with joy the feast days of the saints whenever they come, and that you increase your fervor by recalling and meditating on their lives and perfections. But I think that this feast of our holy Father Benedict means more to you than others and is in some way more welcome. This is not so because it is a greater feast than all others but because he, our Father, is closer to us than the other saints, for in Christ Jesus through the Gospel he has given us birth.[1] Whatever purity you have achieved through chastity, all the spiritual joy you have found in love, all the glory that is yours through a good conscience in despising worldliness, in labors, vigils, fasts, and voluntary poverty, all this comes from his teaching. Whatever progress you have made in meditation, prayer, compunction, devotion, and the rest of the spiritual life, has not all of this been brought about in you by God's grace through his ministry and example? Therefore he is closer to you than the rest of the saints, so that his feast ought rightly to be for you a day of greater joy.

2. Consider Israel of the flesh, the Jews. By origin they sprang from the great Fathers, Abraham, Isaac, and Jacob, concerning whom the Lord said: "I am the God of Abraham, the God of Isaac, and the God of Jacob";[2] which, indeed, the Lord said because of their excellence. Nevertheless, the Jews themselves glory more in Moses, saying: "We are the disciples of Moses."[3] As the Apostle James says in the Acts: "Moses has those who preach him every Sabbath in the synagogue."[4] Why do the Jews have such an affection for Moses? I think it is because the Lord, through the ministry of Moses, led them out of the land of Egypt, across the Red Sea; because through his prayers they received the manna from heaven, water from the rock; because by his prayers they overcame their enemies; because they received from his hand the Law, which, if observed, would allow them to receive and possess the Land of Promise.

3. Certainly, my brothers, if we see clearly and understand the benefits which the Lord has given us through our holy Father Benedict, we will see very clearly that monks ought not to love him any less than the Jews loved

Moses. Through the ministry of Moses, the Lord led the Jews out of Egypt. Through the ministry of St. Benedict he has led us out of the world. They were under the domination of a very cruel king, Pharaoh; we were under the domination of the devil. They were the slaves of the Egyptians; we, of our vices. The servants of Pharaoh spurred them on with whips, demanding bricks from mud. Perhaps you have forgotten the whipping you suffered in the world. One man sought after worldly honors and riches. What stripes he suffered from these desires; how he was beaten about by fear, by envy; how he was plagued by fear lest he lose it, and by sorrow when he did lose it! Another was driven on, wholly intent on satisfying his own wants and desires. How such a man was beaten about by erotic love, envy, suspicions! And what happened when these vices were discovered? How he suffered! How downcast he was in spirit! And, over and above all this, how his conscience beat him! And what happened when each one began to think on his life and his sins? How often, because of these blows of his conscience, did he not resolve and say: "I will never do that again. Never again will I get bogged down in that vice." And nevertheless the servants of Pharaoh, that is, the unclean spirits, pressed upon us in our hestitations to make bricks from mud, that is, to do sordid and foul things. And so we built the city of Pharaoh, the devil, in our hearts.

4. Each one can recall the violence which he suffered from his own evil habits and see how, by the grace of God and the doctrine of St. Benedict, he is now free. He sees that God has given us greater things through St. Benedict than he gave to the Jews through Moses. If you compare the spiritual joy which you often experience in savoring Christ, with the manna which the Jews ate in the desert, if you compare the victories which you often gain over your spiritual enemies through the merits and doctrine of St. Benedict with the Jews' victories over men, you will see indeed that the things which you have received are much greater because they are spiritual.

5. Moses established a law for the Jews and instructed them so that they might enter the Land of Promise and possess it till the end of the world. St. Benedict established a law for us by which, if we observe it, we will enter heaven itself, the Land of the Living, and possess it forever. This law, my brothers, is his *Rule*. In this *Rule* he teaches us to offer God spiritual sacrifices, to celebrate the Sabbath spiritually, to build in our hearts a spiritual tabernacle for Christ. If we observe this law we will be, as he himself says, heirs of the Kingdom of Heaven.[5]

6. But since we have mentioned Moses and Pharaoh, let us say something about their words for our edification on this feast of our Father. As you know, when the sons of Israel were captive under the domination of Pharaoh in Egypt, Moses was sent in God's name to demand that the impious king set his people free. When he contemptuously refused to do

this, he and his people were afflicted with many great plagues. Finally, because of these, Pharaoh said to Moses: "Go and offer sacrifice to the Lord your God, but in this country."[6] Moses replied: "That would not be right." And he gave the reason: "We shall sacrifice to our God offerings abominable to the Egyptians."[7] They could not offer sacrifice to God in Egypt because they ought to sacrifice what the Egyptians thought to be an abomination. Although this might be read as a question: "Can we offer to our God what is abominable to the Egyptians?" the meaning is the same. For when Moses said to Pharaoh: "Can we offer to our God what is abominable to the Egyptians?" there is understood, "in this land," and also, "It cannot be done in this way." However, Moses indicates where this ought to be carried out, for he adds, "We must go three days' journey into the wilderness to sacrifice to the Lord."[8]

7. You know, my brothers, what is signified by Egypt, who Pharaoh is, and who the Egyptians are. Nevertheless, I will say briefly, Egypt is the world; Pharaoh, the devil; the Egyptians, vice and sin. So understood, you were in that Egypt, under those Egyptians, under that Pharaoh. The devil held you captive through love of the world, through love of kinsfolk. You were held in bondage by your own passions and evil habits. When would he have let you go, my brothers, if the Lord had not struck him down? And how did the Lord do this? Indeed, by your own good will which he gave you, by the good desires which he inspired in you, and the good thoughts which he sowed in your hearts. By all these things the Lord struck down the devil. By all of these, the forces of Egypt—your vices and sins—were worn away. Nevertheless, Pharaoh had a hold on you through your evil habits and he did not let you quickly break these bonds of habit.

8. When he saw that your good intention was going to win out, what did he say? "Go and offer sacrifice to your Lord, but in this country." I wonder if all of you have not heard this voice of the devil, either secretly in the depths of your own hearts or openly in the voice of one of his members. "Do you wish," he says, "to serve God? Good! But is it necessary to give up your possessions, your churches, your riches? Serve God here. Do penance here. Serve God with these possessions of yours. Give alms." I think you will recognize what I am saying. How many, my brothers, have been deceived by this voice! Of this fact we have both knowledge and experience. We know some who have formed a good intention, firmly promised to leave the world, and almost did. But then they heard the voice of Pharaoh; they heard and they agreed. They began to wish to live as quasi-religious in the world, but they were deceived. For they fell again into their former vices and added, moreover, that of hypocrisy. No wonder! Great my brothers, great indeed was their presumption in wishing to do penance in the midst of riches, pleasures, and honors, when it was through riches, pleasures, and honors that they had fallen into such horrible sins.

9. Not so with us, my brothers, not so with us. We must go three days' journey into solitude so that we can offer to the Lord our God in sacrifice that which is abominable to the Egyptians. Perhaps penance itself is abominable to the Egyptians and therefore we cannot offer this sacrifice in their midst. But first let us see what are these three days of journey.

10. The first day's journey is to leave the world. The second is to leave our vices and sins and to turn ourselves to better ways of living. The third is to leave the doing of our own will. Whoever has made this journey of three days can sacrifice to the Lord that which is abominable to the Egyptians. Note well, my brothers, there are many who have given up the riches and honors of the world and have gone, as it were, one day's journey from the world. But because they do not yet wish to give up their evil habits but are as proud as before, as lustful as before, as bitter and angry as before, they have not made the second day's journey; and therefore they are not worthy to sacrifice to God. There are others who do both these things, that is, they give up riches and honors and they abstain from their former sins. But because they go apart by themselves into some forest or some other place, and eat when they want, fast when they want, watch when they want, sleep when they want, labor and rest when they want, without doubt they have not completed the third day's journey. And those who live in community and seem to have left doing their own will, if they still seek certain freedoms so that they can go out when they want, speak when they want, work when they want, read when they want, do whatever they want as much as possible according to their own likings, they have not completed the third day's journey either. I do not say this of all those who have this freedom, but of those who seek this freedom and take pleasure in it. For some go out sometimes and speak and do these things, all of which are more of a burden than a delight to them. Gladly would they remain in quiet repose. Therefore only he who has made the three days' journey has fully left Egypt. First of all, just as he once left behind him the riches of the world in an exterior way, so daily, constantly, he rejects them from the depths of his heart. He must always stand before the Lord with a spirit free from all cupidity and ambition, saying with St. Peter: "Behold, we have left all things."[9] And then, correcting his ways, he manfully resists those vices which dominated him in the world. Finally, he mortifies all his willful desires, depending on the counsel of his spiritual father for whatever he has to do.

11. Certainly, my brothers, Moses taught the sons of Israel that they had literally to take a three-day journey at the end of which they would come to the place where they would actually offer sacrifices to God. Our Father St. Benedict has taught you, however, of the spiritual journey of three days, and has shown you clearly enough the way through which you can com-

plete this three-day journey. For it seems to me that the first day's journey is accomplished through the way of fear of the Lord, the second through the way of mortification, and the third through the way of obedience.[10] Listen to St. Benedict as he shows us this way.

12. "The first degree of humility is fear of the Lord."[11] And, it seems to me, the first judgment of humility is contempt for riches and temporal goods. For as long as a man seeks the riches and honors of this world, he can perhaps be humble, but certainly his humility is not apparent. And therefore, through the first degree of humility a man comes to the first sign of humility. Indeed, each one of you can see this from his own experience. For how could you have divested yourself of your riches, your possessions, how could you have made this journey, unless the fear of the Lord urged you on? Therefore the fear of the Lord is the way in which this first day's journey is accomplished. But, someone might say, how can I who have left nothing make this first day's journey? Because I had nothing in the world, I left nothing. Whoever thinks this, let him answer me. When he was in the world did he not desire riches? Did he not do his best to acquire what he could? If, therefore, he has given up his cupidity, he has, indeed, completed the first day's journey well.

13. Now let us see the path of the second day's journey, that we may willingly run along it. It is the mortification of our flesh. St. Benedict says: "The second step in humility is that a man does not love his own will, does not delight in satisfying the desires of the flesh."[12] This is clearly the way by which we can make the second day's journey. We will avoid our former vices if we mortify the desires of our flesh through vigils and fasts and labor. Let no one say: "I am strong. I am chaste. I am wise. I do not need to work, to watch, to fast." Is he wiser than Paul? Is he stronger than St. Benedict? St. Paul chastised his body that he might keep it in subjection, as he himself said, "in hunger and thirst, in toil and hardship."[13] Nevertheless, he saw in his flesh another law fighting the law in his spirit.[14] St. Benedict, too, for a number of years lived on bread and water and nevertheless he was not able to escape the temptations of lust. As you heard in the readings at Vigils this morning, he was almost overcome by them.[15] So it was with him, and you who have been intent on I know not what pleasures and vanities, do you think that you can escape the corruption of the flesh? Therefore the man who wishes to make this day's journey of self-denial does not take pleasure in satisfying the desires of his flesh.

14. Now let us hear what St. Benedict has to say of the third day's journey. "The third step in humility is that one, for the love of God, subjects himself to his senior in all obedience."[16] In this way, indeed, a man wholly sacrifices himself and gives himself to God. In all obedience he subjects himself to another so that he cannot eat as he likes, nor fast nor labor when

he wishes, but when the other commands; and so in all things he follows not his own likings but the will of another.

15. The man who has made these three days' journeys must offer a sacrifice of what is abominable to the Egyptians, that is, those things which the Egyptians abominate. For the Egyptians are lovers of the world, worldlings, and libertines. "They rejoice when they do evil and are happy in the most depraved things."[17] And when they have satisfied their evil desires they rejoice, are proud, and know no shame; they do not wish to repent. Therefore, abominable to the Egyptians are the bitterness of penance, the tears of sorrow, voluntary poverty, and a humble estimation of self.[18] These things, abominable to the Egyptians, we ought to offer to the Lord, our God. Let us repent of our sins. Let us mourn and weep for the sins which we have committed and are committing, so that our sins and our vices may be drowned in the tears of penitence as if in the bitter and salty waters of Egypt and thus perish and be wiped out. Let us embrace poverty. Let us be vile and despicable in our own eyes. And thus having truly gone forth from Egypt, we will offer to the Lord our God what is abominable to the Egyptians, and our sacrifice will be pleasing to him.

16. There are some indeed who after they have left the world continue to take pride in their rank or their clerical status or even in the riches and pomp of the nobility which they have left behind. They think that they should be more honored than others. They want their superiors to call them to their councils and to honor them more than others. They want to have a role to play in all his doings. If something is arranged or done without their advice they become indignant and angry and think that the superior is contemning them out of envy. Such men as these have not yet offered to the Lord the abominations of the Egyptians.

17. See how St. Benedict teaches us to offer those things which are abominable to the Egyptians. After he has taught us by the first three degrees of humility the way through which we can make the three days' journey, he immediately continues concerning the abominations of the Egyptians. "The fourth degree is to follow patiently, with a quiet mind, in the way of obedience even in hard and contrary things, even in the face of injuries."[19] He goes on to quote: "When they are struck on one cheek they offer the other. When they are forced to go one mile they go two. They sustain false brethren and persecution."[20] These things are clearly the abominations of the Egyptians because all these things are abhorred by them, that is, by the worldly minded. For they think it is a great disgrace, not only if they suffer injuries patiently but even if they do not vindicate themselves and take revenge insofar as they are able. But these sacrifices are pleasing to God. In them are slain those things which the world cultivates and loves.

18. Rightly did holy Moses say: "If we immolate in their presence those things which the Egyptians worship, they will stone us."[21] What do the Egyptians worship? Riches and honor, gold and silver, the delights of the belly and gluttonous living. These things the Egyptians worship. Whatever Egyptian has them is proud and exalts himself above the others. And those who do not have them venerate and honor and even, as it were, adore those who have. Whence it is said in the psalm: "May their sheep be fruitful, abounding in their pastures. May their cattle be fat. May there be no breach in their wall, nor exile, nor outcries in their streets."[22] This is the happiness of the Egyptians. And other Egyptians who do not have these things call those who have them blessed, and say, as the Prophet adds: "Happy are the people for whom things are thus."[23] Whoever wishes to sacrifice these things in his heart while still living among worldly men, that is, whoever wishes to contemn riches, honors, and pleasures, and live simply, soberly, chastely, and religiously, is immediately stoned by the Egyptians, that is, he is abused by his hard-hearted fellow citizens. One calls him a deceiver; another, hypocrite. Therefore, you have wisely gone out of Egypt and come three days' journey into solitude.

19. But what does it mean, to come into solitude? It means to consider this whole world as a desert, to desire the Fatherland, to have only as much of this world as is necessary to accomplish the journey, not as much as the flesh desires. Therefore, offer sacrifices to God. Put to death within yourselves those things which the world loves. Love to be of little worth for Christ's sake, to be poor for Christ, to be despised for Christ.

20. This our blessed Father Benedict teaches us. Follow his footsteps, his doctrine, so that he may recognize you among his own as the shepherd does his sheep, the father his sons, the master his disciples. And thus by his intercession may you come to the pasture of eternal happiness, to the inheritance of the servants of God, to the joy of the disciples of Christ, through the goodness of our Lord Jesus Christ, who, as God, lives and reigns with the Father and the Holy Spirit for ever and ever. Amen.

NOTES

[1] Cf. 1 Cor. 4:15.
[2] Ex. 3:8.
[3] Jn. 9:29.
[4] Acts 15:21.
[5] RB, Prol. 39.
[6] Ex. 8:25.
[7] Ex. 8:26.
[8] Ex. 8:27.
[9] Mt. 19:27.

[10]In the text we have there seems to be a missing element which we have supplied in view of what is to follow. The text has *nam sicut mihi videtur prima dieta perficitur per viam mortificationis, tertia per viam obedientiae.*

[11]RB 7:10.

[12]RB 7:31.

[13]2 Cor. 11:27.

[14]Cf. Rom. 7:23.

[15]*Dialogues,* bk. II, ch. 2.

[16]RB 7:34.

[17]Prov. 2:14.

[18]St. Bernard uses the same text of Exodus in the same accommodated sense in his *Second Sermon for the Feast of Sts. Peter and Paul.*

[19]RB 7:35.

[20]RB 7:42f. Cf. Mt. 5:39ff.

[21]Ex. 8:26.

[22]Ps. 143:13f. (The Vulgate enumeration of the Psalms is used throughout.)

[23]Ps. 143:15.

Saint Aelred's
Second Sermon for the
Feast of Saint Benedict

1. As today we celebrate the passage of our holy Father Benedict, I must say something about him, especially since I see that you are eager that I should. Like good sons you have come together to hear about your Father who, in Christ Jesus, gave birth to you in the Gospel.[1]

2. Because we know that he has passed beyond, let us see where he came from and where he has gone. True, he came from here where we still are, and he has gone on to that place to which we have not yet come. We are not corporally where he has gone, but we are there in hope and love, as our Redeemer has told us: "Where your treasure is, there also is your heart."[2] Thus the Apostle said: "For us, our homeland is in heaven."[3] Indeed, St. Benedict himself, while he lived corporally in this world, dwelt in thought and desire in the heavenly Fatherland. So today our Father has passed from earth to heaven, from prison to the Kingdom, from death to life, from misery to glory; from this life which can rather be called death, he has happily passed on to the Land of the Living.

3. I say he has passed on to the Land of the Living, because this life is not that of the living but of the dying. All the things which I have mentioned: death, prison, and misery are found in this life. Indeed, all these things *are* this present life. For if it were not death, the Apostle Paul would never have said: "Daily I die for your glory, my brothers,"[4] and again: "What a wretched man I am! Who will rescue me from the body of this death?"[5] Very clearly he calls this life death, and to live in the body, to be dead. The Psalmist gives witness that this life is to be called a prison, as he says: "Bring my soul out of this prison."[6] That this life is miserable, indeed misery itself, daily experience of our own miseries teaches each one of us. But we also have the witness of David, who calls it a miserable pit and a muddy swamp. With undisguised joy he proclaimed himself to have been free from it (because he knew he would be free): "He heard my prayers and drew me out of this pit of misery and the mire of the swamp."[7]

4. Since we know now where St. Benedict came from and where he has

gone, let us see how he went. For it would be of no profit to those wishing to follow him if they knew only where he came from and where he went, and not how he went. Truly, he went through Christ, to Christ. Through faith in Jesus Christ, which worked in him through love, he passed to the vision and contemplation of Jesus Christ, by which every good desire is satisfied. So his way was Christ, who said of himself in the Gospel: "I am the Way, the Truth, and the Life."[8] Through him he passed to him because he is Life itself, and also the Way. A most direct way was the wonderful way of life of our Father, for it was holy.

5. As St. Gregory has said, this present life is nothing other than a way. He who lives well and praiseworthily passes to God, and to life eternal. But the man who lives an evil life is journeying towards hell and eternal death. This is the way of sinners. David speaks of it in the first psalm: "Happy the man who never follows the advice of the wicked, or loiters on the way that sinners take."[9] Through this evil way one comes to the sinners' wretched death. As the Prophet said: "The death of sinners is the worst."[10] Very logically, indeed, he says the death of sinners is the worst because their way is evil. And as the Apostle says: "Evil men go from bad to worse; erring themselves, they lead others into error."[11] The death of sinners therefore is said to be the "worst," because as long as they live they become more and more evil, until, having reached the depths, they merit to be cut off and thrown into the fire.

6. But our blessed Father Benedict did not follow this way. He did not lead an evil life but held fast to the way of which it is said: "The way of the just is straight."[12] Although narrow, it leads to life. The beginning of this way is narrow but afterwards, as St. Benedict himself teaches us in his *Rule*, one runs in the way of God's commandments with untold sweetness and delight.[13] For those who are beginning, it is indeed narrow, as it was for David when he said: "Because of the words of your mouth I have followed difficult ways."[14] But did this prophet ever say that because he found it difficult in the beginning he left or he thought he should leave it? God forbid! Rather, he held fast until he could make this very different statement: "I have run in the way of your commandments because you have enlarged my heart."[15] St. Benedict also found the way narrow at the beginning of his conversion. But in the end he found it wide open. Was not the way difficult for him? As we read in his *Life*, in order not to consent to lust, he threw himself into a thorn bush.[16] But when he found the way difficult, what did he do? He did not depart from it; rather he held fast and manfully stood his ground. He first did what he later taught, so that he might teach his followers what he himself did. Thus Pope St. Gregory said of him: "Just as he lived, so he taught. He could not teach other than he lived."[17] That he stood manfully in the way of God we can learn from his

own words, since in his *Rule* he warns one shaken by fear not to depart from the way of salvation.

7. Experience itself had taught him that one could begin only by the narrow way. But he knew that however narrow it might be, it nevertheless led to life as our Lord himself had said: "Narrow is the way which leads to life and few they are who walk in it."[18] To what life this way leads, our Lord himself in another place teaches us, saying: "This is eternal life, to know you, the only true God, and Jesus Christ whom you have sent."[19] This is the way which leads to the well of seeing and living, through which, we read, Isaac was made perfect.[20] Concerning this way, the Book of Wisdom says: "The path of the virtuous is like the light of dawn, its brightness growing to the fullness of day."[21] A servile fear of hell makes this way narrow. Perfect love makes it broad. As long as anyone fears, he suffers difficulty in the way of God, and experiences hardship. When, however, he comes to that love which completely casts out fear, with unmingled joy he cries out with the Apostle: "I have fought a good fight, I have run the race to the finish. I have kept the faith."[22] With David he sings: "I have run in the way of your commandments because you have enlarged my heart."[23] Indeed, one who so loves Christ desires, like Paul, to be dissolved and to be with him.[24] Indeed he finds it most painful to be separated from him any longer, and daily with tears he repeats those words of the Psalmist: "How much longer will you forget me, O Lord? For ever?"[25] And with Habacuc: "How long, Lord, am I to cry for help while you will not listen; to cry, 'Oppression!' and you will not save?"[26]

8. St. Benedict passed along this way, as we have said, from death to life, from Egypt to the Promised Land, that is, from the darkness of this world to that Jerusalem which is a vision of peace. And certainly he passed along happily, because he lived praiseworthily. He passed along this way like Moses, so that he merited to see a great vision: not how a bush burned and yet was not consumed,[27] but how the blessed angels and their equals, the saints of God, always burn with love, and that love in them never grows cold. Let us, my dearest ones, so pass through this life that we see that great vision. Let us follow the footsteps of our blessed Father Benedict. We have a most direct way by which we may arrive, namely, his *Rule* and his doctrine. If we hold on to this, as we ought, and persevere in it, without doubt we will come to where he is. Through the merits and intercession of St. Benedict, may this be accomplished in us through the grace of our Redeemer, Jesus Christ, who lives and reigns with the Father and the Holy Spirit, God, for ever and ever. Amen.

NOTES

[1]Cf. 1 Cor. 4:15.
[2]Mt. 6:21.
[3]Phil. 3:20.
[4]1 Cor. 15:31.
[5]Rom. 7:24.
[6]Ps. 141:7.
[7]Ps. 39:2.
[8]Jn. 14:6.
[9]Ps. 1:1.
[10]Ps. 33:22.
[11]2 Tm. 3:13.
[12]Is. 26:7.
[13]RB, Prol. 49.
[14]Ps. 16:4.
[15]Ps. 118:32.
[16]*Dialogues,* bk. II, ch. 2.
[17]*L. c.,* ch. 35.
[18]Mt. 7:14.
[19]Jn. 17:3.
[20]Cf. Gen. 25:11 (Vulgate).
[21]Prov. 4:18.
[22]2 Tm. 4:7.
[23]Ps. 118:32.
[24]Cf. Phil. 1:23.
[25]Ps. 12:1.
[26]Hab. 1:2.
[27]Cf. Ex. 3:3.

Saint Aelred's
Third Sermon for the
Feast of Saint Benedict

1. You have often heard, my dearest brothers, that Moses, after he led the sons of Israel from Egypt, built a tabernacle in the desert, using the offerings of the sons of Israel.[1] Some gave him gold; some, silver; some, precious stones; and some, animals. It is not necessary to list all of them now. But we should reflect on this, for as the Apostle said: "All this was done in figure."[2]

2. We were in a sense in a spiritual Egypt when we were living a worldly life, for Egypt may be interpreted as "darkness." Evil conduct and sin, and obstinacy in these, are real darkness. At one time we were in this darkness, for by participating in these things we ourselves were made darkness; as the Apostle says: "You were at one time darkness."[3] However, in order that we might be light in the Lord, he gave us a certain Moses, a certain legislator, namely, our holy Father Benedict, whose feast we celebrate today. By his wisdom and care we pass through the desert of this world, to come to the Land of Promise: not that one which the carnal sons of Israel carnally desired, but that which the Prophet hoped for when he said: "I believe I will see the good things of the Lord in the Land of the Living."[4] Of it the Lord said: "Blessed are the meek for they shall possess the land."[5]

3. Benedict was not only filled with the spirit of Moses; he was also, in a sense, filled with the spirit of all the just. He built a spiritual tabernacle from the offerings of the sons of Israel. In his Rule the gold of the blessed Augustine shines, the silver of Jerome, the double-dyed purple of Gregory,[6] the jewel-like sayings of the Fathers; with all these this heavenly edifice is adorned.

4. You, my brothers, are the tabernacle of God; you, the temple of God. As the Apostle says: "Holy is the temple of God which you are."[7] A temple, because the Lord will reign forever in you. And yet a tabernacle, because he is on pilgrimage in you, he hungers in you, he thirsts in you.

5. This tabernacle is still borne along by the ministry of the Levites. Some carry it on their shoulders, others with the aid of oxen and wagons. They carry the tabernacle who attentively fulfill the precept of our Moses: "Let

them most patiently bear one another's infirmities, whether of body or of mind. Let them vie with one another in obedience."[8] Those carry it on their shoulders, who, expecting no earthly reward, constantly reflect on what follows in the same chapter: "Let them prefer absolutely nothing to Christ."[9] Those do not carry it on their own shoulders, who do indeed guard the prescriptions of the *Rule*, but hope for some passing thing: dignities, honors, or something of that sort. When they are frustrated in this hope, in this help of wagons (for by wagons, temporal honors are signified), they put aside the tabernacle and depart. Others also carry it, not on their own shoulders, but with the help of oxen, that is, superiors. For they always wish to be praised by their superiors and to have some passing favor shown to them. So that if perchance they receive some harsh word from them, it is as if they have lost all help, and they lay aside the tabernacle altogether or carry it only with murmuring. It is concerning them that the Apostle said: "There will be a time when they will not bear with sound doctrine, but each with itching ears will seek teachers to suit his own likings."[10] Just as the adulterer seeks the stimulus of lust, so they seek the stimulus of adulation.

6. But this, my brothers, this is what becomes of this tabernacle if it is carried through the desert of this world until it is brought into the land of promise: it becomes a temple, dedicated by the true Solomon for seven days and seven days;[11] that is, by a twofold rest, a twofold perfection: immortality for the body, beatitude for the soul.

7. But now we, my brothers, if we are spiritual sons of Israel, if spiritually we go forth from the land of Egypt, each and all of us must make our offering for the construction of this tabernacle. Each of us from that in which he abounds: "For each one has his proper gift from God; one this and indeed another that."[12] One can offer more work; another, more vigils; another, more fasting; another, more prayer; and another, more *lectio* or meditation. From all these offerings one tabernacle is made, so that, as our legislator declares, no one says or presumes that anything is his own, but all things are common to all.[13] This is to be understood, my brothers, not only of our cowls and robes but much more of our virtues and spiritual gifts. Therefore no one should glory on his own over any grace given him by God as if it were his own. No one should be envious of his brother because of some grace, as if it were exclusively his brother's. Whatever each one has he should consider as belonging to all his brothers, and whatever his brother has, he should not doubt that it is also his own. Indeed, almighty God can immediately bring to perfection anyone he pleases, and give each one all the virtues. But his loving provision for us is such that each one needs the other, and what anyone does not find in himself, he has in the other. Thus humility is preserved, love increased, and unity realized.

8. Therefore each belongs to all, and all belong to each. Each one has the benefit of the virtues of all, while his humility is preserved by the consciousness of his own personal weakness. Let not our lay brothers bewail that they do not sing or watch as much as the monks. Nor the monks, that they do not work as much as the lay brothers. For in very truth I say: whatever one does, this belongs to all; and whatever all do, this belongs to each. For just as the members of one body have not all the same function, yet, as the Apostle says: "The many are one body, each one a member of the other."[14] Therefore let the weak man say: I am strong; because, just as in him his brother has patience in infirmity, so he in his brother has strength in endurance.

9. Beware lest dying flies destroy the sweetness of the oil.[15] The sweetness of the oil is the sweetness of fraternal love; the flies, cupidity, envy, and suspicion, which destroy such love. For no one who sets his heart on anything of this world loves perfectly. And from this cupidity envy is born; for whatever one wants inordinately for oneself, one is envious of in others. And then one usually begins to be suspicious of the person envied.

10. But now let us compare certain prescriptions of the Moses of old with those of our own Moses.

11. Moses of old established six cities of refuge for the sons of Israel. Three were outside the Land of Promise, and three within. Whoever killed a man by chance would be safe if he fled to one of these.[16] There is a slaying of the body and there is a slaying of the spirit. For sin indeed is the death of the soul. And this is the worst kind of murder: to kill oneself by vice or another by bad example. The sons of Israel did not have cities of refuge as long as they were in Egypt; not because they did not kill, but because they did so more by pride than by mishap. And we, when we were in the spiritual Egypt, sinned, not because we were weak, but because we were proud. Sin delighted us, and therefore we had no cities of refuge. Now, although we have gone forth from Egypt, "if we say we have no sin, we deceive ourselves and the truth is not in us."[17] "In many things we all offend."[18] But it is important, whether it be from weakness and ignorance, or from pride. For as long as anyone lies proudly dead in some sin, even though he seems to have fled from Egypt, the city of refuge profits him not at all. As the Apostle says: "If we sin deliberately after receiving the knowledge of the truth, no victim for sin remains for us."[19]

12. It seems to me those six cities of refuge can signify the six general exercises that are prescribed for us. There are three corporal ones: work, watching, and fasting. These pertain especially to those who are still drawn by carnal passions and to this extent are still outside the Promised Land. They cannot say: "Our way of life is in heaven."[20] And there are three spiritual ones: *lectio*,[21] prayer, and meditation. These pertain especially to

those whose passions are now weakened and who have passed on to virtuous desires, tasting in these cities how sweet is the Lord,[22] the fruit of the Land of Promise.

13. Let us fly to these cities, taking refuge from those who pursue us because of our murders. Who are they? The devil and our own evil desires, for as the Apostle says: "Each one is tempted, lured and enticed by his own concupiscence."[23] The more one sins, the more one's desire to sin increases. Hear the Apostle who greatly feared this enemy: "I see," he says, "another law in my body, fighting against the law in my mind, and making me captive to the law of sin which is in my members."[24] Hear him fleeing to these cities: "I chastise my body, and bring it into service."[25] How? As he clearly said elsewhere: "In labors, in watching, in fasting."[26] Hear Peter calling us to these cities: "Be sober, and watch in prayer...."[27] What is said in the law: that one must flee to any one of these cities,[28] had thus to be commanded, so that it might be fulfilled literally. For it must be realized that no one has the same grace in all these exercises. In time of temptation each one should take refuge in that practice in which he finds greater help.

14. Now we must consider the further command: that from these cities one must not depart until the death of the high priest.[29] And who is our high priest, except Jesus?[30] Therefore, we must continue in labors, fasting and watching, until our earthly flesh is truly mortified, until we bear about in our bodies the death of Jesus,[31] so that we can say with the Apostle: "With Christ, I am nailed to the cross."[32] And also, "I carry the stigmata of the Lord Jesus Christ in my body."[33] But there is a mortification of the spirit just as of the flesh. Therefore it is written: "Sing to the Lord with harps and harps";[34] that is, with a twofold harp. And so, the same things must be insisted upon in regard to spiritual things. Just as the flesh is killed by evil passions, the spirit is killed by evil thoughts.

15. If, then, we are united with Christ in a death like his, we shall be his companions in the resurrection, walking in newness of life.[35] When Christ our life appears, we shall appear with him in glory.[36]

16. Through the merits and prayers of our blessed Father Benedict may this be granted to us by our Lord Jesus Christ himself, who lives and reigns with the Father and the Holy Spirit, for ever and ever. Amen.

NOTES

[1] Cf. Ex. 35:21ff.
[2] 1 Cor. 10:11.
[3] Eph. 5:8.
[4] Ps. 26:13.
[5] Mt. 5:5.
[6] We have a curious anachronism here, as Aelred is most probably thinking of Pope

St. Gregory. A reference to Gregory of Nyssa or Gregory of Nazianzus would be very unusual for him, whereas he has two references to Pope Gregory in the previous sermon, and it is more usual to associate this Gregory with Augustine and Jerome. Yet Pope Gregory was not yet born when Benedict was building his "tabernacle."

[7] 1 Cor. 3:17.

[8] RB 72:5f.

[9] *L. c.*, 11.

[10] 2 Tim. 4:3.

[11] 3 Kings 8:65 (Vulgate following the Greek).

[12] 1 Cor. 7:7; RB 40:1.

[13] RB 33:6.

[14] Rom. 12:4. Cf. 1 Cor. 12:12ff.; Eph. 4:4, 16.

[15] Cf. Eccl. 10:1.

[16] Cf. Nm. 35:9.

[17] 1 Jn. 1:8.

[18] Jas. 3:2.

[19] Heb. 10:26.

[20] Phil. 3:20.

[21] Cf. note 19 *supra*, Introduction p. 240.

[22] Cf. Ps. 33:9.

[23] Jas. 1:14.

[24] Rom. 7:23.

[25] 1 Cor. 9:27.

[26] 2 Cor. 6:5.

[27] 1 Pt. 4:7.

[28] Cf. Dt. 19:5.

[29] Cf. Jos. 20:6.

[30] Heb. 5:5.

[31] 2 Cor. 4:10.

[32] Gal. 2:20.

[33] Gal. 6:17.

[34] Ps. 97:5. Aelred's text, on which this accommodation rests, differs from the Vulgate. The Vulgate reads: *"Psallite Domino in cithara, in cithara et voce psalmi."* Aelred has, *"Psallite Deo in cithara et cithara."*

[35] Rom. 6:4.

[36] Col. 3:4.

Baptism of the Spirit

Many Catholics and others of traditional sacramental churches are uncomfortable, if not totally unhappy, with the terminology "Baptism of the Spirit." And I think many others would agree, humanly speaking, that it is not the most fortunate thing that this expression, commonly used by our classical Pentecostal friends, has been widely adopted by us in spite of the ambiguity it contains. The heresy of "re-baptism" long plagued the Church. We believe in "one Baptism." Moreover, in that one Baptism the Holy Spirit is surely received. No Catholic Pentecostal is denying or wants to deny these fundamental truths. No one favors the ambiguity, yet we are faced with the fact that the terminology is now widely used and will continue to be used. So let us try to understand it and appreciate it.

The term "Baptism of the Spirit" seeks to express an event, very real and very beautiful, which takes place in a Christian when he freely and fully opens himself to the Holy Spirit and allows Christ's promised Comforter to enter into his life to guide him freely into a life of love, praise, and joyous service. In a word, when he gives the Spirit a blank check and lets him write on it what he will. At that particular moment the newness of life, the new power to praise and love is such that it is as though there had been no life nor presence there before. This tremendous new impulse of life can find no better analogue than that mysterious event which first makes us divinized sons of God, living members of Christ, men capable of knowing and loving God as he knows and loves himself: Baptism into Christ Jesus.

This idea that there is a moment in the ordinary spiritual growth of the Christian when the Holy Spirit of Love comes in a very special new way into his life, is not a new one. It belongs to our Catholic tradition. As I believe it might be helpful, I would like to cite one witness to that tradition: the twelfth-century English saint and mystic, Aelred of Rievaulx. This Cistercian abbot was a disciple of Bernard of Clairvaux, the towering spiritual leader of that century. Bernard was the last great man of God who, as a man of God, was able to lead the whole of Western Christendom—a truly charismatic leader, guiding Church and State alike. And Aelred, in his own more modest way, served God's people in Great Britain as the "Bernard of the North." For over eight centuries now Christians have drawn guidance and nourishment from the spiritual writings of Aelred, and never has his orthodoxy been questioned or suspected.

In his Second Sermon for the Feast of Pentecost,[1] Aelred traces out the normal stages of spiritual growth for a Christian, drawing his model from events in Christ's life:

> Contemplate in Christ three stages, as it were, planned by his wonderful kindness, not for his own benefit but for ours. First he was baptized, then he was transfigured, finally he was glorified. He was baptized in the Jordan, transfigured on the mountain, and glorified at length in heaven. At Christ's baptism the Holy Spirit was shown as a dove, at his transfiguration as a cloud, but after his glorification as fire. Take these three stages to represent three stages in the soul's progress: purification, probation, and rewarding. Christ's baptism represents our purification, his transfiguration our probation, and his glorification our rewarding. We are purified by confession, we are proved by temptation, and we are rewarded by the fullness of charity. However, in all of these the Spirit must come to the aid of our weakness.

The Saint then goes on to develop each of the three stages. His description of the third is especially beautiful, and is the one we rejoice to see developing in our own lives and the lives of our communities:

> When, however, the Christian has been taken up into the lofty cenacle of charity and has entered into an abiding tranquillity of mind..., fear is driven out, toil is changed into rest, sorrow into joy, and it becomes certain that neither death nor life, neither angels nor archangels will separate him from the love of God. Here one tastes how good and how pleasant it is for brothers to live in unity. Here we are made truly disciples of Christ, "together in the same place."

Aelred then goes on to the passage that most interests us here:

> But from where do all these things come if not because "suddenly there came from the sky a noise..."? The love of God has flooded our hearts through the Holy Spirit who has been given to us. Certainly the Holy Spirit is given at the Jordan [first stage of spiritual growth, or conversion], but he is given with moaning, with tears, compunction, fear, and renunciation of the world, so that we may reject what is our own and take upon ourselves the common life. He is given on the mountain also [the second stage], to those who are wearied and tired out by many temptations, in order that they may be consoled and refreshed, that their flesh may glow white with chastity and their minds be enlightened by

discretion. In these places some part of the Spirit is given, if I may so express it. But in the cenacle, "in the same place," *the very plenitude of the Spirit is conceived.* It had not been given previously because Jesus had not yet been glorified. At the first stage the Lord Jesus is seen as humble and kind, at the second beneficent, at the third as glorious. He is kind to the man who seeks, beneficent to the man who is making progress, glorious for the man who has arrived at the summit of perfection. *Such great fullness of the Spirit is therefore given at this stage that in comparison it may be said neither to be given nor to be possessed at the others.* "For the Spirit had not been given previously because Jesus had not yet been glorified." [Italics added.]

I think Aelred here expresses very well the reality of the experience of many good traditional Christians who have been "baptized in the Spirit." The Holy Spirit has been present and active in their lives since their Baptism and conversion, and he has continued to abide with them and strengthen them all along the way. But there was that time when they were brought into the cenacle and received such a plenitude of the Spirit into their lives that it was, as it were, a wholly new beginning; they were "baptized in the Spirit." Aelred does not use our terminology, but he certainly expresses our experience.

I would like to add a further reflection or two. First of all, we must keep in mind the fact well expressed by another twelfth-century Cistercian, William of St. Thierry:

It must be remembered, however, that the stages of love are not like the rungs of a ladder. The soul does not leave the lesser loves behind as it moves onward to the more perfect love. All the degrees of love work together as one, and for this reason another soul's experience of the stages of growth may well follow an order which differs from the one described.[2]

Aelred has placed the "Baptism of the Spirit" on the summit of perfection. And, indeed, it is the perfect man who is least unworthy of the great gift of Love. But the Lord is limited by no scale of perfection or human calculation of merits. "In other words, when the Lord wants to show mercy, he does" (Rom. 9:18).

Note, however, that Aelred connects this Baptism or special outpouring of the Spirit with the glorification of Christ. In fact, a mark of "Baptism in the Spirit" is the desire and ability to praise and glorify Christ. Most Christians will attest that before being baptized in the Spirit their prayer was one of asking, repenting, and some thanking, but little or no praise; but with the Baptism, Christ was glorified in their lives, and now they cannot cease from praising and glorifying him in the Holy Spirit. Praise him!

NOTES

[1]Sermo "In die Pentecoste" in C. H. Talbot, ed., *Sermones inediti B. Aelredi Abbatis Rievallensis,* Series scriptorum S. Ordinis Cisterciensis, vol. 1 (Rome: Editiones Cistercienses, 1952), pp. 106-112. I am grateful to Fr. Theodore Berkeley, OCSO, of Mount St. Bernard's Abbey for allowing me to use here the translation he has prepared for publication in the Cistercian Fathers Series.

[2]William of St. Thierry, *On the Nature and Dignity of Love,* tr. G. Webb and A. Walker (London: Mowbrays, 1956), pp. 59-60.

The Later Fathers

Fasting
Some Thoughts from Isaac of Stella

I am afraid that we are painfully conscious that our abstinence can in no way compare with that of the Fathers. While they were able to content themselves with one lean meal taken late in the day, we find ourselves indulging in three rather well rounded meals and perhaps one or two "coffee breaks" for good measure. Here again we seem to be faced with a traditional observance which the times and in particular our own times have relentlessly worn away. We have indeed adapted, but have we kept the spirit? Hence there arises the question, what did fasting mean for the Cistercian Fathers, and how should we seek to live this meaning today.

In quest of some answer I turned to Isaac of Stella. If hiddenness is the mark of a good monk then indeed Isaac was a truly great monk, for not only do we not know in what year he died but we are not sure even in what abbey he died. As we read the sermons of Isaac we are indeed aware that he does differ from the other Cistercian Fathers. Yet it is perhaps more a difference of approach and style than of doctrine. The Scriptures are not woven as abundantly into his fabric, his style is less biblical and the influence of the schools is more in evidence. For example his long search into the mystery of predestination, which we find in his Sermons for the Second Sunday of Lent, savor much of the scholastic bent of mind.[1] Yet they are not without parallels in Augustine,[2] Bernard,[3] and William of St. Thierry.[4] Perhaps one of the more fascinating things in Isaac is the way he likes to do things with words.[5] This certainly makes reading him in the original Latin something of a challenge.

Isaac has three Sermons of the First Sunday of Lent, five for the Second Sunday and two for the Third Sunday. In each case they are a homily on the Gospel for the day. Undoubtedly, the sermons were written as a single unit rather than being sermons that come to us from different years. Isaac indicates this in the series for the Second Sunday of Lent.

As he says at the beginning of the Second Sermon, it is the next day at the rest period during work that he takes up the topic again in response to a question of one of his brethren.[6] But he went too long and the work did not get done. And so on the following evening, when the work was finished, as he indicates at the beginning of the Third Sermon, he goes on with his topic.[7] We find this same situation expressed at the beginning of the Fifth Sermon.[8] This may be indeed merely a literary device, yet it probably in some way reflects the reality.

A GOOD TEACHER

Isaac was indeed a very realistic and down to earth monk. In turning to him for guidance in fasting we need not be fearful of his expecting too much of us. In his First Sermon for the Second Sunday of Lent, speaking of the Canaanite woman he says:

> By the woman can be understood any soul which has been aided by the Lord so that it hates sin and desires justice but nevertheless has not the means to do easily what easily it desires to do. It has received the help to will to do good, but it cannot manage to carry through. It finds itself doing not the good it desires, but the evil it hates.[9]

And shortly before this he says to his monks quite tersely: "Do not wish to sin even though you cannot yet not sin."[10]

Indeed, in his First Sermon for the Third Sunday of Lent, where he is preaching on Christ's casting out the devil, he assures us that each one has his own personal devil:

> Let each one of you, my dearest ones, ask Jesus for himself, and this most earnestly, that he might wholly drive out the devil from him or he will again be oppressed by the demon. . . . Each one has his own personal demon who keeps a special eye on him, watching him everywhere and in all things. This is something no monk should be ignorant of. . . .[11]

Then he goes on to describe in a very self-revealing way his own relations with his own demon:

> I think mine knows me very well, and I know him. In fact, no one is better known to me because no one is more harmful to me. No one is more familiar, because no one is around me more. . . .[12]

We need not fear that such a man as this, so fully in contact with his own humanity and all its weaknesses, will be too exigent on us or not understand our weaknesses.

FASTING

Yet when he comes to speak of fasting, he puts things right on the line:

> Spiritual men who have left off the ways of flesh and blood, who have forgotten their people and the house of the flesh and have gone out into

the solitude of the spirit, have not in one step escaped all the needs of flesh and blood.[13]

They are still subject to the imperious demands of nature. It is a little thing to cut off all that is superfluous if they don't also cut back on their needs. If they do not dare to slay in one fell swoop the animal part of man and the weak body, nonetheless they will indulge it only late in the day with a sparing meal and then only grudgingly. "The man who eats whenever he is hungry doesn't have any idea what a fast is. The virtue and merit of fasting begin only when one is hungry."[14] Fasting really counts only when one hungers, and the longer this endures, the more the fast counts.

That is Isaac's brief word on fasting, at least physical fasting, and it is scant comfort for us. But he immediately goes on to say: "There is another more sacred and higher type of fasting."[15] Those who have entered into the way of the spirit are to carefully and diligently observe it, and constantly too, all the days of their lives, in times of prosperity and in times of adversity, whether one be a superior or a subject, engaged in contemplation or activity. And this fast is the fast from the delights and consolations of this world.[16]

In the previous sermon he spoke of another kind of spiritual fast: "This is the fast which the Lord chooses: to abstain from all evil, not only in external works, but also interiorly from evil desires."[17] But there he was speaking to all. Here it is a question of a spiritual man, from whom a more exigent fast is to be expected.

However, even as he sets before us the ideal, Isaac is not lacking in that full Christian humanism, the true incarnationalism that marks the whole Cistercian school. He readily sees and openly declares—man cannot live without pleasure. "Deprived of all consolation, the soul can in no wise hope to survive.... Can you live without the consolation of some pleasure? Not at all."[18] But the spiritual man is to find his delight and consolation in the Lord. "I remembered God and I was filled with joy."[19] His delightful nourishment is found in meditations, prayer, communion with the Lord.

We ought to imitate Christ. He went out into the desert to fast so that he might "meditate on the law of the Lord day and night."[20]

THE DESERT

For Isaac the desert is not only a place.[21] Though it is this in the sense that physical solitude is important to him. The humble receive God's grace whereby "They despise the world, flee from it, conquer the devil, go apart from the crowd whose evil talk destroys virtue; they seek the desert and a hidden place where they can be free for God."[22] In their sweet silence monks speak to the Lord "mouth to mouth" and thus they come to have "clean lips." It is because of their desire for this cleanness that "they do withdraw from the midst of people with unclean lips, fly from all the attractions of this world and remain purified in solitude."[23] And Isaac says very frankly (using a very up to date expression): "I, my dearest ones, find my thing (*meam rem*) here, nor is it easy for me to find anything else which interests me more. By the grace of God I am saved not only from sin, but from every occasion of sin, indeed, as it is evident I have withdrawn with a contrite heart from all the doings of society and the common world of men into this desolate and arid desert."[24]

But more important is a desert of the spirit and above all the desert of God.[25] We enter these deserts when, following Christ's example, we go out of ourselves and, as the angels, meditate constantly on the divine law, the law which is to be found not only in the written letter, but in our own natures, in the world about us, and above all in the Wisdom of God who is "the Eternal Law and the Law of laws."[26]

I think the point in all of this is that one cannot succeed in fasting, the true fast of the spirit, nor even corporal fasting, if he or she does not turn to something positive—if his search is not essentially positive. There can be no voids. The human person must be filled. He needs satisfaction. The true purpose of fasting is to give him greater freedom to turn to something else, to be freer from lower needs and providing for them. And conversely, the desire to reach after higher things, to find delight in them, postulates fasting. He cannot at one and the same time seek satisfaction, pleasure, delight in both ways. He has to give up the delights of this world if he wants the delights of God.

CHARITY

Though Isaac undoubtedly holds in high esteem what today some refer to as the negative virtues—fasting, silence, solitude—there is no doubt he has a firm grasp on the true hierarchy of values. Charity is supreme.

> For charity is the reason why in everything we ought to act or not act, change or not change. It is the principle which motivates us, the end toward which we ought to direct all things.[27] All these things (being, wisdom, virtue) make us good and religious men through our charity which has been formed in us by the love by which God loves us and turns us to himself.[28]

For Isaac charity was a very down to earth thing. It was reaching out to a brother in need, really conscious of his needs, the spiritual even more than the material. "Why are we less solicitous, brothers, to seek the moments of grace in each other, so that where we see a greater need, we help each other more and carry each other's fraternal burden?"[29] His doctrine of fraternal love was based on a deep appreciation of the reality of the mystical body which he presents with unsurpassable beauty. To give just a sample of it:

> Just as in the human body, while the acts of the members are different, they have nonetheless a beautiful need of each other, and supply each other with a most solicitous charity. So in the body of Christ. Each is necessary to the other, so that no one is superfluous just as no one is sufficient unto himself. The one who has more does not abound, the one who has less is not left short, but all give themselves to each other in love.[30]

But what perhaps makes even a deeper impression on the reader as he savors the Lenten sermons of Isaac is his deep personal love for Jesus Christ which so motivates all. It too is a very down to earth thing. The sacred humanity is no merely carnal thing to be transcended. Christ who is the sublime God over all[31] is yet the beloved, very human friend, master, and savior. Simple citations would not really convey this. The whole needs to be read. For Isaac, Christ's example is supreme.

And here perhaps we have the practical answer to our question as to what we should do about fasting today. Isaac opens his First Sermon with the exclamation: "My Lord, Jesus Christ, did all things as one led, sent, called, ordered; He did nothing of himself. . . . He was led by the Spirit into the desert. . . . Whoever acts in the Spirit of God are sons of God."[32] In imitation of Christ, we must simply do as the Spirit leads us.

Although our question has been a very particular one and our field of study very limited, yet I think it can give us a very real insight into the mind and heart of Isaac of Stella. He comes to us across the span of eight centuries as quite a person and a great monk, a man truly spiritual and truly human, one whom we could approach with confidence. His lofty monastic ideals are not divorced from a real understanding of human nature, weakened by sin, opposed by the forces of evil, yet meant to find strength in fraternal union and the inspiring love of Jesus Christ. Above all, Isaac loved Jesus Christ.

NOTES

[1]Take for example a passage such as this from the Second Sermon: "*Ejus itaque sempiterna ac incommutabili essentia, id est ipso qui est semper operante, sunt quecunque sunt, tantum, tunc ac tandiu, quantum, quando et quandiu ipse id operatur. Ejus aeterna sapientia, id est ipso qui est, quo sapiens est, semper operante, sapiunt, quicunque sapientes sunt, tantum, tunc, tandiu et taliter quantum, quando, quandiu et qualiter ipse id operatur. . .etc. . . .*" PL 194:1804DF. I know of no published English translation of the Lenten sermons of Isaac. An English translation is presently being prepared by Fr. Hugh McCaffery of Mount Melleray Abbey who is basing himself on the partially published critical edition of Isaac's Sermons (the first thirty-nine sermons have been published by Sources Chrétiennes, Vols.

130 and 207, prepared by Dom Anselm Hoste of Steenbrugge. Fr. McCaffery's translation will appear in the Cistercian Fathers Series.

²Indeed Isaac depends a good bit on Augustine for his thought and even explicitly quotes him in the course of his Fourth Sermon for the Second Sunday of Lent.

³The way Isaac uses words not infrequently reminds one of some passages of St. Bernard.

⁴See especially William's First Meditation where he himself struggles with the problem of predestination: trans. Sr. Penelope in *The Works of William of St. Thierry,* vol. 1, in the Cistercian Fathers Series, 3 (Spencer, MA: Cistercian Publications, 1970).

⁵A good example is found in the Fourth Sermon for the Second Sunday of Lent: *"Nec omne quod alicui bonum, simpliciter bonum esse, sicut nec omne quod alicui malum statim malum. Sunt etenim bona bonis bona, sicut mala malis mala. Et sunt bona malis mala, sicut mala bonis bona. Nec tamen unquam mala bona, aut bona mala. Sunt et fortasse bona bonis mala, sicut et mala malis bona."* PL 194:1811B.

⁶"Well, my brothers, our manual labor is wearying us. Let us pause a little while I respond to the question of this brother concerning the end of yesterday's sermon." PL 194:1800C.

⁷"It was necessary, my dearest ones, that today's sweat make up for the loss of yesterday's labor. For yesterday's sermon was overly long, as you know, and stole from us as it were the work time. As someone said: 'He detained the day with a word (*sermone*) but we, detained by a *sermon* (*sermone*), lost the day.' [The reference is to Joshua 10:12f.]. Therefore since there is now practically no time left, and we have fulfilled our full measure of labor, let us say very little." PL 194:1806A.

⁸PL 194:1812D.

⁹PL 194:1799Af.

¹⁰PL 194:1798D.

¹¹PL 194:1818D.

¹²*Ibid.*

¹³PL 194:1794A.

¹⁴*Ibid.,* B.

¹⁵*Ibid.*

¹⁶*Ibid.*

¹⁷PL 194:1791A.

¹⁸PL 194:1796D.

¹⁹*Ibid.,* Ps. 76:4.

²⁰Ps. 1:2.

²¹Third Sermon for the First Sunday of Lent, PL 194:1797A.

²²First Sermon for the First Sunday of Lent, PL 194:1788B.

²³Fifth Sermon for the Second Sunday of Lent, PL 194:1815A.

²⁴First Sermon for the Second Sunday of Lent, PL 194:1799D.

²⁵Third Sermon for the First Sunday of Lent, PL 194:1797A.

²⁶*Ibid.*

²⁷Second Sermon for the First Sunday of Lent, PL 194:1793C.

²⁸Second Sermon for the Second Sunday of Lent, PL 194:1805C.

²⁹Second Sermon for the First Sunday of Lent, PL 194:1792Df.

[30]Second Sermon for the Second Sunday of Lent, PL 194:1801Df.
[31]First Sermon for the Second Sunday of Lent, PL 194:1797C.
[32]First Sermon for the First Sunday of Lent, PL 194:1787Cf.

Saint Peter of Tarentaise
(1174-1974)

St. Peter II of Tarentaise is virtually unknown today. Especially is this true in the English-speaking world, where only one significant article has been published on him.[1] He is quite apt to be confused with his predecessor, St. Peter I of Tarentaise,[2] also a Cistercian, or a later thirteenth-century Dominican, also called Peter of Tarentaise, who became Blessed Pope Innocent V.[3] Yet an outstanding contemporary Cistercian historian, Dom Anselm Dimier, does not hesitate to affirm that, in his own times and after, Peter enjoyed "a notoriety, a glory equal to that of a St. Bernard."[4]

Almost all of what is known about Peter has been made readily available through the patient labors of Dom Anselm, who not only has published the most complete biographical study (just cited) but also has prepared two volumes of documents (*Recueil de textes pour servir a l'histoire de s. Pierre II de Tarentaise* and *Recueil de documents pour servir a l'histoire des reliques de s. Pierre II de Tarentaise [Tamïe, 1941]*) which contain almost all the known sources for such a study.

We find testimony in support of this statement in a rather surprising source contemporary to the Saint himself. Walter Map, the Oxford protege of Henry II of England, a man not noted, certainly, for his love of the Cistercians, speaks of meeting and ministering to St. Peter when the latter came to Limoges to mediate between the Kings of England and France. Walter does not hesitate to say that the Archbishop of Tarentaise was "a man of such virtue and of such outstanding miracles that he can most justly be said to be equal in merits to the ancient Fathers who are venerated in the Church."[5]

The action of Peter's own Cistercian Order likewise confirms this. According to the dating of Dom Dimier, the General Chapter of the Order, within days of Peter's demise, wrote to the Pope to ask his canonization[6] and got Louis VII of France to do the same.[7] When the canonization was finally obtained—and it was obtained even more quickly than that of Bernard of Clairvaux,[8] the Order gave his feast special rank,[9] and this was constantly raised until, like Bernard's feast, it was set at the highest: a feast of sermon with a procession through the cloisters.[10]

At Citeaux, on profession days it was the relics of Peter and St. William of Bourges, the only two Cistercians who enjoyed with Bernard the honor of formal canonization, that were, according to the ritual, exposed on the high altar.[11]

Dom Anselm Dimier's comparison is not inept. There is far more than the mere coincidence that Bernard's canonization falls in the year of Peter's death to link the two saints. For one thing, they were personally acquainted. For nine years they sat together in the General Chapter as brother abbots.[12] And even after his election as Archbishop, he had the right to come to the Chapter and probably did so at times.[13] In 1135, as Bernard was returning from Italy he took the pass through the Alps that brought him to the gates of Tamié and, as was his wont in traveling, he stopped to visit his brother Cistercians.[14] This was not Bernard's only trip across the Alps, and probably on other journeys he found his way to the same mountain refuge.[15]

In 1141 the electors of Tarentaise chose for themselves a very reluctant pastor. In the face of strong pressure, Peter finally agreed to abide by the decision of the General Chapter and he and his electors went thither. The Acts of the Chapter tell us that "there by the authority of the whole Order, especially indeed that of Bernard of Clairvaux, for whom he had always shown a singular reverence, he [Peter] was compelled to accept the election."[16]

As Peter's life unfolded, it was indeed similar to Bernard's in many respects. Both were about the same age[17] when they entered small Cistercian communities that were to develop rapidly.[18] Both knew the formative influence of St. Stephen Harding; Bernard directly, Peter through his abbot, John of Valence, who was formed at Citeaux.[19] Both saw much of their family follow in their footsteps.[20] They were both called upon at a relatively young age to lead a new foundation.[21] Their succeeding years saw mounting fame, numerous miracles, extensive travels and missions of reconciliation. In time of schism both stood forcefully and courageously at the side of the man who in the end was acknowledged to be the true Vicar of Christ.[22] Both were respected by high and low alike,[23] not excluding the grateful Roman Pontiffs.[24] And in the midst of all this activity, both longed to be free of it, to hide themselves in the cloister and live the regular life.[25] Peter's prolonged visits to the Carthusians in the last years of his life call to mind Bernard's intimate friend, William of St. Thierry and his visit to Mount Dieu.[26]

Shortly after Bernard's canonization on January 18, 1174, Peter consecrated an altar in honor of the new saint at the Abbey of Longuay near Langres[27] and then quickly went to join him in glory.[28] When the Fathers of the Order sought to promote Peter's canonization they were asked to provide a *Life* of the saint.[29] Without hesitation they turned to the same abbot who had prepared the *Life* of Bernard to promote his cause, Geoffrey of Auxerre, Bernard's one time secretary and later his successor, who had taken up the pen where William of St. Thierry had left off.[30] Later Geoffrey moved south and became more intimate with Peter. He had accompanied him on some of his journeys and had first-hand knowledge of his miraculous powers.[31] In the course of the *Life*, Geoffrey puts words in the mouth of Peter that are strikingly reminiscent of Bernard of Clairvaux.[32] It would be impossible to ascertain whether these are more Peter's words or more Geoffrey's. But we can recall Bernard's words to William of St. Thierry: "...to use the same language indicates a oneness of soul. If our words are common it is because our hearts are close."[33]

If there are many points of contact and similarity between the two saints, there are yet striking differences. On the abbatiate of St. Peter, Anselm Dimier tells us that "During the ten years St. Peter spent at Tamié his life was primarily that of a monk: a life in solitude, a life of prayer."[34] Although this might be said of the first ten years of Bernard's abbatial career, it could hardly be said of the greater part of it when he spent at least a third of the time on the road.

In all, the missions of Bernard as a peacemaker were more significant and more successful than those of Peter. While we have record of six papal missions[35] and about ten others,[36] the only truly significant one was Peter's mission to reconcile the Kings of England and France. And here he was not successful. The King of England returned home with the French wives of the alienated princes and the war was resumed after Easter.[37]

As we mentioned, like Bernard, Peter took his stand with the true Pope when a schism arose, and it was a courageous one. He was the only, or almost the only,[38] vassal of the Emperor who opposed him in his creation and support of the anti-pope. And Peter traveled abroad, outside his own diocese, in the Empire, seeking to win loyalty and support for Alexander III. Although he did not convert the Emperor, the latter did not dare to inhibit him[39] and he had some real effect on the outcome. But it was Henry of Beauvais, the Cistercian brother of King Louis, who more closely approximated the role of Bernard in rallying support for the true Pontiff and healing the schism.[40]

In that Peter's impact on the ecclesiastical and political world was considerably more restrained than that of Bernard, to that extent he can perhaps be considered as a more typical example of the gifted and holy men who were drawn to Citeaux in its first flowering. Those men who enjoyed the peace of the life of a simple monk for only a short time, then were set over one of the rapidly multiplying foundations, and then elected to an episcopal see. To mention only a few of these, some of those figuring in the life of St.

Peter, there are St. Peter I of Tarentaise, the first Cistercian abbot to become a bishop. He had been in the original Molesme group and was the founding abbot of La Ferté. John, Peter's own father abbot, was sent out from Cîteaux to start Bonnevaux, where Peter entered in 1122. He was later elected Bishop of Valence. Amedeus of Lausanne had first entered at Bonnevaux and later became abbot of Hautecombe before being elected to the see of Lausanne. Peter's neighbor, Warren (Guerin) of Alps was elected to Sion. And his successor as abbot of Tamié, Bernard, became Bishop of Maurienne. We have already mentioned his more successful collaborator in healing the schism, Henry of Beauvais, who had been at Clairvaux. And the Peter who was abbot of Cîteaux at the time of Peter's death and who first promoted his cause for canonization was soon made bishop of Auterbach.[41]

Many of these were men of preeminent sanctity who have been honored with the title of saint or blessed and have received liturgical cult at least locally or within the Cistercian Order.[42] But it is only Peter, along with Bernard and William of Bourges, the former abbot of Chalis, who were formally canonized.[43] It may seem strange that only three Cistercians were ever formally canonized. This was not because the Cistercian Order was wholly indifferent about the matter. These three causes, along with that of St. Malachy, were strenuously promoted.[44] The General Chapter of 1220 sought to promote the cause of Hugh of Bonnevaux and Robert of Molesme, but Rome never carried through; nevertheless they received a full cult in the Cistercian Order.[45] This perhaps underlines again the significance of St. Peter in the eyes of his contemporaries.

One interesting thing about this lover of solitude, this contemplative become archbishop, was his great practicality. As abbot of Tamié he had set up a system of granges and water works that still call forth admiration.[46] As archbishop he quickly put his house in order, replacing the canons by regulars with whom he lived and shared the common choral life. He energetically restored the fabric and furnishings of his own cathedral church and then set out to bring about the same in the parishes. Where the people were poor he organized a collection of an egg a week to pay for new chalices and things like that.[47] The people of his territory often suffered in the spring when the previous year's harvest ran out and there was as yet no new growth. So St. Peter established the "Pain de Mai," a food distribution scheme that continued in regular practice down to the French Revolution.[48] When he fled from his diocese to hide in an unknown German monastery, he carefully changed his guise several times and thus covered all his tracks.[49] Finally, in the last years of his life, after taking the advice of neighboring bishops and various communities of canons, he personally drafted a very clear and detailed document to provide for the division of income and goods between his cathedral canons and the episcopal see so that there would be no confusion or dissension when he died.⁵⁰ He was a "Mary" who fulfilled "Martha's" role well enough during his ten years as abbot and thirty-three years as archbishop.

We can see then how accurate Dom Anselm Dimier's statement is. Known from Oxford to Rome, reverenced by pope and emperor, St. Peter of Tarentaise was a powerful wonderworker and a humble, loving pastor who made Christ visibly present.

We might well ask, then, why the memory of this man, so acclaimed in his own day, has all but disappeared? The fact that his major relics are all but hidden away in the little abbey he founded high in the Alps⁵¹ contributes to his oblivion. The fact that he left virtually no literary heritage is still more significant.⁵² I think the secular historian might well be forgiven for passing him over in silence. In his most important missions to the mighty of the world he was apparently ineffectual. Barbarossa respected him, the Kings of England and France venerated him, but none of them heeded his admonitions, at least not until after he was laid to rest. His support for Alexander III was significant, but its efficacy seems to be eclipsed by that of the brother of the King of France.

But the monastic historian, the Cistercian, cannot be so easily excused. Of course such a historian might point out that Peter's career as a Cistercian, more particularly as a Cistercian abbot, was relatively brief in comparison to his long years as an active and leading metropolitan. But such detachment hardly affected the outlook of Peter's contemporary Cistercians who were the ones who energetically promoted his cause of canonization. St. Peter was, and should still be, a glory of the Cistercian Order. Even as a prelate he exemplified in a most striking way some of the most fundamental monastic virtues in his great love of retirement and solitude, of poverty and simplicity, of obedience and humility, of love and care for the poor. Let us hope that the years intervening between the centenary of his death and that of his canonization will see a renewed interest in, reverence for, and study of this great Cistercian saint.

NOTES

[1]L. F. Barmann, "Peter of Tarentaise: A Biographical Study of the Twelfth Century" in *Revue de l'Université Ottawa* 31 (1961) 96-125.

[2]Peter I, never formally canonized, was the first Cistercian to be elected bishop. He had been a monk at Molesme and was among the founders of Citeaux. He was sent as the founding abbot of the first daughter house of Citeaux, La Ferté.

[3]H. K. Mann, *The Lives of the Popes of the Middle Ages,* 18 vols. (St. Louis: Herder, 1902-1932) 16:1-22.

4[A. Dimier], *St. Pierre de Tarentaise* (Poitiers: Renault, 1935), p. I.

5*Monumenta Germaniae historica, Scriptores,* 27:67.

6Dom Dimier (*Textes de s. Pierre,* p. 129) dates the letter of the Cistercian abbots to the Pope 1174, although with a question mark. Peter died the day the General Chapter opened, September 14th. So the assembled Chapter, which lasted only a few days, must have acted almost as soon as they received news of the death. The text of the letter can be found in *Acta Sanctorum* [AA. SS.], Maii t. 2 (Rome: Palme, 1866), pp. 318-319.

7AA. SS., Maii t. 2:319.

8Bernard died in 1153 and was canonized only in 1174, while Peter was canonized less than eighteen years after his death.

9J. M. Canivez, *Statuta Capitulorum Generalium Ordinis Cisterciensis ab anno 1116 ad annum 1786,* 8 vols. (Louvain: *Revue d'Histoire Ecclesiastique,* 1933-1941), (hereafter cited as *Statuta*), 1:146; 1196:2, 86.

10*Statuta,* 4:488; 1439:97. Dom Dimier questions whether the feast actually ever truly enjoyed this rank in practice, for it is not so described in any surviving breviaries. After the dispersal of the relics the feast was reduced to one of the lowest ranks.

11"A la profession des religieux nous mettons sur l'autel devant lequel elle se fait quatre reliques dont deux sont des bras de saint Pierre de Tarentaise, et de saint Guillaume de Bourges, à cause qu'ils ont été religieux de notre ordre."—*Rituel propre de l'abbaye de Cîteaux* (1724) Dijon Mss. 119 (86), pp. 49-50.

12Peter was appointed abbot of Tamié in 1132, where he served until he was elected Archbishop of Tarentaise in 1141. During all this time Bernard was abbot of Clairvaux.

13We have in fact documentation for only one such appearance, in 1170, when Peter appeared to sponsor Hugh of Burgundy's petition for affiliation. A. Manrique, *Annales Cistercienses,* 1170 V, 7-10, 2:50. Also, *Statuta,* 1:78f.

14Dimier, *St. Pierre,* p. 44.

15*Ibid.*

16*Statuta,* 1:34f., 1141.

17Bernard was about 22 when he entered Citeaux, Peter about 20 when he first made Bonnevaux his home.

18The growth of Citeaux, the motherhouse, was much greater than that of Bonnevaux, yet the latter did see a progeny of twelve during Peter's lifetime.

19John of Valence was among the original founders and was chosen by Stephen to be the first abbot of Bonnevaux. He was later elected Bishop of Valence.

20Peter's older brother, Lambert, followed him almost at once to Bonnevaux. His younger brother, André, like Bernard's Nivard, came later and then his father, as did Bernard's. His mother as well as his sister first went to a Benedictine (if we may use such an expression for that period) nunnery and were later installed in a new Cistercian foundation by the Saint, who constituted his mother abbess. Dimier, *Saint Pierre,* p. 8.

21Bernard was sent out as the head of Citeaux's third foundation at the age of 25; Peter was about 30 when he led Bonnevaux's third daughter house.

22Bernard stood by Innocent II against Pierleone and was very influential in winning others to his side. Peter stood with Alexander III against Barbarossa's creations.

[23] Peter's biographer tells us of the almost exaggerated homage paid to him by the King of England (AA. SS. Maii t. 2:330) and constantly relates how he was mobbed by the people.

[24] After his courageous attempts to bring Barbarossa around, Peter was summoned to Rome where the Pope received him with great marks of friendship. Dimier, *Saint Pierre*, pp. 121-123.

[25] The delightful vignette of the Archbishop's flight to an unknown Cistercian monastery, which a modern French biographer cannot resist comparing with the flights of the Curé d'Ars (H. Riguet, *Printemps en chrétienté: L'Aventure spirituelle de Saint Pierre de Tarentaise* [Mercury: Tamié, 1967], pp. 87ff.), provides one of the most refreshing interludes in the *Vita*, p. 325f.

[26] Dimier, *Saint Pierre*, pp. 138-142; J. M. Déchanet, *William of St. Thierry: The Man and His Work*, CS 10 (Spencer, MA: Cistercian Publications, 1972), pp. 95-96. It was during these visits that Peter and St. Hugh, later bishop of Lincoln, became intimate friends.

[27] Dimier, *Saint Pierre*, p. 200.

[28] Peter died on Sept. 14, 1174 at the Abbey of Bellevaux in Franche-Comté.

[29] Letter of Lucius III to Peter of Citeaux and Peter of Clairvaux, AA. SS. Maii t. 2:319-320.

[30] PL 185:301-368. William died before he got very far in describing Bernard's very active career and his many miracles, but he did describe with adulation what most interested him, Bernard the monk, the man of God (PL 185:225-268). Geoffrey then took up the task. For a detailed discussion of the significance of Geoffrey's precise contribution see A. H. Bredero, "The Canonization of Bernard of Clairvaux" in *Bernard of Clairvaux: Studies Commemorating the Eight-Hundredth Anniversary of His Canonization*, CS 28 (Washingtion, DC: Cistercian Publications, 1974).

[31] He certainly describes enough of them in the *Life*, but we must remember he is responding to a certain *stylus curiae* in writing a *Vita* for canonization and he does document his information with considerable care. In the correspondence relative to the *Life* and in the edition, Geoffrey is referred to as Geoffrey of Hautecombe, for at the time of the writing he was abbot of that monastery. Auxerre was his native place. He was successively abbot of Igny, Clairvaux, Fossanova and Hautecombe. One should reflect on the very interesting life of this monk who lived in a relatively more stable time and in a closely organized order, before criticizing the "instability" of Robert of Molesme or any other monastic reformer of the previous century.

[32] See Dimier, *Saint Pierre*, pp. 68-69 and the notes there.

[33] Ep. 86, PL 182:210; tr. Bruno Scott James, *The Letters of St. Bernard of Clairvaux* (London: Burns & Oates, 1953), Letter 88, p. 127.

[34] Dimier, *Saint Pierre*, p. 44.

[35] In 1155 Adrian IV sent Peter to mediate between two religious houses in the diocese of Lausanne. Eugene III had used him to mediate between the Bishop of Maurienne and the Lords of Chambre (1153). In 1164 he was sent to arbitrate between a saint, Anthelme of Belley, and a blessed, Humbert III, Count of Savoie. In 1173, Alexander III sent him to try to bring together the Kings of England and

France—Henry II and Louis VII. And death caught him abroad because he had been sent on a mission. But just before this he had reconciled the monks of his old abbey, Bonnevaux, and his cherished retreat, Grande Chartreuse (1174).

36Peter acted as mediator between Guerin of Sion and Count Amedeus; Betton, the abbey he founded and over which he set his mother to rule, and the Bishop of Maurienne (deciding in favor of the Bishop); the monks of St. Chaffre and the canons of Maurienne (1153); the canons of St. Maurice d'Agaune and the Cistercians of Hautcrêt (1157); the Bishop of Geneve and the Count of the Genevois (1156); Barbarossa and the city of Milan (1159); the canons of Abondance and their daughter house of Sixt (1161); the parties of the civil war in Vercelli (1165); Alphonsus of Toulouse and Humbert III of Savoie (1167); the Church of Lyons and the Count of Forez (1167); and the Chartreuse of Reposoir and Turumbert of Brême (1168).

37Dimier, *Saint Pierre,* pp. 155ff.

38*Ibid.,* p. 114. Eberhard of Salzburg also stood firm.

39When Peter's adversaries urged the Emperor to squelch the outspoken Archbishop as he had others, the Emperor is reported to have replied: "If I repress men, as they deserve, all right; but do not expect me to oppose God himself."—AA. SS. Maii t. 2:327.

40Dimier, *Saint Pierre,* pp. 117f.

41We could also mention Othon of Friesing, former abbot of Morimond; Guichard of Lyons from Potigny; Hugh of Macon, bishop of Auxerre, also formerly abbot of Pontigny; Ponce of Clermont, formerly of Clairvaux, etc., etc.

42This would include the first four mentioned above. We might note in passing that Peter's brother Lambert became abbot of Chezery and is honored as a saint; his father and other brother, André, are honored as blessed.

43As mentioned, Bernard was canonized the year Peter died. William of Bourges was canonized in 1217, only eight years after his death. There was evidently a growing proficiency in promoting causes! In the Cistercian *Litany of Saints,* Peter is the first Cistercian prelate mentioned, after Augustine of Hippo and before St. Malachy, St. Edmund of Canterbury (whose relics were in the Cistercian abbey of Pontigny) and St. William.

44For the canonization of Bernard see A. H. Bredero, art. cit., note 30 above; for Peter see Dimier, *Saint Pierre,* pp. 181-184 and the documents in AA. SS. Maii t. 2:318-319, 342-344; for William see the three *Vitae* in AA. SS. Jan. 1:628-639, especially pp. 637-638; for St. Malachy see C. Waddell, "The Two Saint Malachy Offices from Clairvaux" in *Bernard of Clairvaux: Studies Presented to Dom Jean Leclercq,* CS 23 (Washington: Cistercian Publications, 1973), pp. 123-160.

45*Statuta,* 1:526f., 1220:48, 53. See also, A Monk of Tamié (A. Dimier), *Saint Hughes de Bonnevaux de l'Ordre de Cîteaux. 1120-1194* (Grenoble: St. Bruno, 1941), pp. 213-214.

46F. Bernard, *L'Abbaye de Tamié, ses granges* (Grenoble: Allier, 1967) and his article, "L'Abbaye de Tamié et ses nombreuses granges de frères convers, des régions d'Albertville, de Pontcharra-sur-Bréda et du Pont-de-Beauvoisin" in *Revue Savoisienne* (1963): 39-75.

47Barmann, *op. cit.,* p. 107.

48H. Riguet, *op. cit.,* pp. 31-33.

[49]AA. SS. Maii t. 2:326.

[50]Dimier, *Textes,* pp. 96-102.

[51]Dimier, *Saint Pierre,* pp. 186-194.

[52]The only text we have written by Peter himself is the document dividing the goods of the See of Tarentaise, which is a sort of spiritual testament; see above, note 50.

Appendix

Getting Acquainted with the Cistercian Fathers

I have often been asked how to go about studying the Cistercian Fathers. This will be an attempt to respond to this question.

St. Bernard

St. Bernard is undoubtedly the center of the Cistercian school, the master and guide who profoundly influenced all the others. This is not to deny that there was not some reciprocal influence on him, especially in the case of William of St. Thierry.[1] However, I do not think Bernard is the Father with whom to begin getting acquainted with the Cistercian Fathers. His thought is generally quite developed and complex; his style very cultivated; his writings carefully edited for publication. He makes a very difficult starting place for most. So that he might not seem to be neglected in the first years, around his feast we might begin to get acquainted with him[2] and a couple of his earlier, simpler, and more enjoyable works, such as the *Steps of Humility and Pride*[3] and the treatise *On Loving God*[4], might be studied.

Liturgical Context

The whole life of the Christian should flow out of the liturgy and flow back into it, should flow along in harmony with it. The reliving of the Christ-life, which is the Church's in the course of the year, should also be the life of each Christian. That is why I said, "around his feast." Indeed, in general, I like to tie in the study of the Cistercian Fathers with the liturgy. They themselves presented much of their doctrine in the context of the occurring liturgy; much of what we have of their writings is liturgical sermons.[5]

Guerric of Igny

The Father I think best to begin with is Guerric of Igny, and this for several reasons. For one thing, in some respects he is truly in the middle of things. He is the favored disciple of Bernard of Clairvaux. Later, Guerric had Bernard as his Father Immediate while at the same time he himself was the Father Immediate of William of St. Thierry. Guerric entered Clairvaux probably around 1123, before Bernard had as yet been catapulted into his worldwide role and still was able to spend considerable time at home with his community. Bernard took special interest in the young men in formation[6] and there is good reason to believe that Guerric in a very particular way claimed his attention.[7] The choice of Guerric as Abbot of Igny undoubtedly came about in part through the influence of Bernard,[8] which would indicate that the Abbot of Clairvaux saw in him a man who had grasped well the spirituality he sought to impart and would be able to pass it on to others. For his part, Guerric, on his regular visits to his daughter house, Signy, because of his love for his Master,[9] would have sought out his Master's closest friend[10] and would have tried to learn from him all he could about their beloved Bernard. It was perhaps William's Father Immediate, just as it was Aelred's[11] who encouraged him to edit some of his past jottings and also to put on paper what may be his finest work.[12]

Another consideration in choosing to do Guerric first is the limits of his corpus. We have only fifty-three Liturgical Sermons and one Sermon from his commentary on the Song of Songs. The whole can be readily grasped and worked with.

More significant, though, is the simplicity, clarity, and practicality of Guerric's Sermons. They are, perhaps, among the least edited of the writings that have come down to us from our Fathers; the closest to what the monks might have actually heard as they sat in chapter. Guerric's Sermons are full of good, down-to-earth, practical teaching. There is a complete though concise theology of work, of poverty, of silence, etc. And yet his doctrine is not pedestrian. It is truly Cistercian—the ideal of contemplative union with God is always present, Guerric makes no bones about it—all are called to this and many of his monks are having experience of it.[13]

In reading the Fathers, I think the first thing we have to do is to meet them as real, living, actual persons, as spiritual men with whom we can converse, in a living way, as we move through their writings. For Guerric, fairly sufficient biographical data can be found in the "Introduction" to the English translation of his Liturgical Sermons.[14] But this should be brought alive in the context of the real concrete Cistercian life. The *Exordium Magnum* is a help here.[15] Although its historicity leaves something to be desired by current standards of historical study, this twelfth-century version of our modern serious comic books gives us much of the color and flavor of the time. It should be used for each Father where it can be used. In this task of bringing the Fathers concretely to life, those who have been in the Order for some time have a distinct advantage. Not only have they gained a certain connaturality with the same life, had the same Cistercian charism grow and develop within them, but the usages lived prior to the 1960's, and especially before 1955, were in may details those codified in 1132. Thus from lived experience they are able to flesh out the life of the Fathers.

Undoubtedly, it is helpful if the student has had an opportunity to study the general history of the period, secular and ecclesial. The more immediate context is greatly illuminated by Father Bede Lackner's *The Eleventh-Century Background of Cîteaux*[16] and the study of a general history of Citeaux like the *Compendium of the History of the Cistercian Order*[17] or Father Louis Lekai's *The Cistercians*.[18] It is also invaluable to have some grasp of the Scriptural and Patristic background of our Fathers. Father Henri de Lubac's *Exégèse Médiévale*[19] is most precious here. But even if the student lacked all of these he could still draw very great fruit from the Cistercian Fathers. After all, the monks who first received the substance of this doctrine from the Fathers probably did not have all that background or foreground. In any case, we certainly do not have to wait till we do have all this background study before getting acquainted with the Fathers and letting them speak to our hearts.

After we have gotten to know the man so that we can really communicate with him, it is time to survey his works, to see the whole so we can more fully appreciate the significance of each part. When Guerric died in 1156 he was in the process of editing his Sermons for publication.[20] He had a definite theme in mind, that of the Beatitudes. These were seen by all the Fathers as summing up the Cistercian way to holiness.[21] The theme is first found in the Advent Sermons and reaches its climax in the All Saints' Day Sermon, where he explicitly traced out this ascent and was developing it. He completed only the First Sermon with its development of the first Beatitude. In the course of his eighteen years as abbot he would have preached almost that many times for each feast. For his collection he was choosing five Sermons for each, and these five formed in themselves a little treatise. Each Sermon begins with a verse or a line from the liturgy of the day, but often this is only a taking-off point. The development of the ideas is not always logical (though some sets of Sermons can be outlined in almost scholastic form) but rather it is through the association of ideas, especially Scriptural words and themes. It is really a delight to follow this weave of thought that always ends up at the contemplative heart of things.

With this background we are ready to go through the year with Guerric to study him and to lay the foundation for using him more fruitfully for spiritual reading and *lectio*.

Study—Spiritual Reading—Lectio Divina

I like to distinguish—at least in theory, not so much in practice—between sacred study, spiritual reading, and *lectio divina*. What we have been talking about up to now is primarily study. Study is concerned immediately with acquiring ideas and understanding. If there is question of sacred study, it is of a matter directly related to God, his revelation, theology, our quest for God. All study, of course, can have a sacred character about it, and can be made a prayer, but of its nature study seeks to acquire conceptual knowledge.

Spiritual reading also has as its immediate aim the acquiring of knowledge, of ideas, but now their relevance to our spiritual life, our search for God, is definitely to the fore. We want knowledge that will flow into act, that will motivate us. For example, I am having trouble with silence, keeping it, seeing the sense of it, or using it well. So I turn to Guerric. With the Analytic Index at the end of his Sermons[22] it is easy to trace a theme in his writings. I quickly find many beautiful and strongly motivating thoughts on silence.[23]

But in *lectio divina* we are no longer in search of knowledge or ideas, but of the reality. We want the Word to come into us and come alive in us. When we sit down to *lectio*, after having implored the activity of the Spirit, we begin to read without any concern whatsoever for progress through the text. If the first word comes alive in us, we abide in it for how ever long the Word speaks to us in and through it. Some days our whole *lectio* can be but a word. Other days many words and paragraphs have to wash through us and cleanse us before a word can become effectively sacramental of the Word. As Guerric points out, some days it may happen that the Word remains silent throughout our *lectio*, but later he meets us on the way as we go about our work.[24] *Lectio* is prayer. And if I were to call any particular thing the Cistercian-Benedictine "technique," it is this.

So, having come to know Guerric personally, we are ready to walk through the liturgical year with him. I suggest, if it is possible, that we spend two years with him: the first year, trying to see the Five Sermons for each feast as a whole little treatise with the unfolding of its theme. The second year, the concentration can be on the various doctrinal and moral themes and the other precious nuggets. With all this behind us we are ready for a lifetime of fruitful *lectio* with Guerric. And we will find, year after year, as the feasts come around, we return again and again to Guerric and each time derive more from our contact with him.

But the year is not all feasts. So as we go through the two years with Guerric we can begin, between the feasts, to get acquainted with another Father. The second Father I would suggest is William of St. Thierry.

William of St. Thierry

I have come to really love William, and I think any modern will. He speaks so openly and personally. He is a man of our times. It is not surprising that the last few years have seen at least six students devoting their doctoral years to him.[25] What is especially fascinating for us is that we can see the

contemplative vocation grow and develop in William and share this with
him in his writings.

William had been a good scholarly Black Monk for some years, a highly
respected monk, probably prior of his monastery, when in company with
his abbot he visited Bernard of Clairvaux. The visit made a profound impact
on him. Thirty years later he would still write of it in awed terms, using
exalted liturgical analogy.[26] It was an hour of conversion. He wanted to
become what young Bernard was. At almost the same hour he himself was
chosen to be an abbot. And so he had a community with whom to share his
new quest. Many of his treatises, I believe, are edited from conferences he
gave his communities.

First William explored what contemplation is and how one can hope to
acquire it. This is his treatise *On Contemplating God.*[27] The way is love, and so
he turns his considerations to love: *On the Nature and Dignity of Love.*[28] Then, in
the true Cistercian way, he knew he had to get to know the lover and his
power at work in him—grace. Like so many of the other Fathers, he then
produced his treatise on man: *On the Nature of the Body and the Soul.*[29] His
treatises on grace, which followed, took the form of a *Commentary on the Epistle
to the Romans,*[30] which is largely drawn from St. Augustine. William relied
very heavily on the Fathers and did not hesitate to use their very texts and
words. Now that he was ready to turn his attention to the text that was at
the heart of all Cistercian mystical doctrine, the Song of Songs, he did not
immediately launch out on his own. He had begun an explanation with
Bernard which he published as the *Brevis Commentatio.*[31] Next he searched
through all of Ambrose of Milan and Gregory the Great and drew out all
they had to say, verse by verse, on the great love song.[32] With all this behind
him, he was ready to begin his own commentary, his *Exposition on the Song of
Songs.*[33]

Rich additional light is thrown upon this whole development by William's
very personal *Meditations,* which were written through these same years.[34]
We have from this same period, too, a letter or rather a treatise on the
Eucharist,[35] a response to a request, which indicates, as do many other
incidental writings, how important a place the Eucharist held in the Fathers'
lives.[36]

As one grows in union with Christ, one comes to have his mind and heart,
to share all his loves and concerns. The Fathers were men of the Church. As
much as they longed for Mary's part, for Rachel's embraces, they accepted
Martha's role when such was demanded and became fruitful like Lia.[37]
When Abelard imperiled the true faith and true theology, William forsook
his holy leisure and his love song and spoke out on the true nature of faith
and its content, for the sake of the young monks in his community and all
who were being influenced and confused by the subtle dialectic of this cocky

genius.[38] After the battle was over, William sought deeper solitude for a time with the nearby Carthusians. And to express his fraternal gratitude to them and again to help the young, he wrote his magnificent synthesis, *The Golden Epistle*.[39] Finally, as life drew to a close he began to paint an idealized icon of all this in the biography of his idol and lifelong inspiration, the incarnation of all he strove for, his beloved friend, the Abbot of Clairvaux.[40]

To get to know William we have the invaluable help of a monk who lived with him in love. Dom Jean-Marie Déchanet's *William of Saint Thierry: the Man and His Work*[41] may not meet with the unanimous approval of later scholarship on every point, but its inner feel for William can hardly be surpassed.[42] Father Déchanet's "Introduction" to *Meditation Thirteen* is also important.[43] And the *Vita antiqua*[44] serves much the same role as the *Exordium Magnum*. But William will best be known through his writings. This is, of course, true for all the Fathers, but most especially for William.

I have chosen to take William in the second place not only because he is so actual but also because, as had been pointed out, he often wrote for the young, for beginners. He himself said that his *Meditations* were "not entirely useless for forming novices' minds to prayer."[45] After getting acquainted with the man and surveying his works, I would spend most of the two years we are studying Guerric for the feasts, studying William in between. This will hardly do him justice but will lay some foundation for a lifetime of *lectio* as we go back to him again and again.

In studying William I would follow the chronological order basically, with some variations and various emphasis. I think the treatises *On Contemplating God* and *On the Nature and Dignity of Love*[46] should be done thoroughly. They are basic and very rich. Rather summarily, the treatise on man and the *Commentary on Romans;*[47] more at length, the *Meditations*.[48] It is worthwhile looking at the tract *On the Sacrament of the Altar*.[49] Summarily, the *Commentaries on the Song of Songs* from Ambrose and Gregory[50] as a preparation for a thorough study of the *Exposition on the Song of Songs*.[51] But before going into his treatment of the Song I like to do the treatises on faith. *The Mirror of Faith*[52] should really be studied. It can be a great help when the challenges to faith come in life. *The Enigma of Faith*[53] again could be treated rather summarily. Its solid doctrine will be the source of much fruitful *lectio* later.

Theology

I might make an observation here. If the study of the Cistercian Fathers is going to be a basic source for formation and there is not going to be any other formal course in theology, we would do well to develop more carefully and at greater length William's doctrine on grace in the *Commentary on Romans,* on the Eucharist, and on the content of faith, the Trinity, in the

Enigma. The same would hold true later on in treating of Bernard's dogmatic treatises.

With all this background one is ready to appreciate more fully why William's synthesis is called *The Golden Epistle.*[54] It is deserving of being treated as gold. Our novice master told me he spent eight months on it with his novices. One might want to spend three years with Guerric for the feasts in order to have more time to spend with William.

I would put off a study of William's *Life of Bernard* (although it probably tells more about its author than its subject) till later when I meet Bernard, and in the last months of the second or third liturgical year with Guerric I would begin another Cistercian Father. This time it would be Aelred of Rievaulx.

Aelred of Rievaulx

To get to know Aelred we are most fortunate in having the very excellent study of Aelred Squire.[55] The author places each of Aelred's works fully in the context of his life. Hallier's study is also helpful.[56] And, of course, color and life are added by the idolizing biography of Aelred's friend and infirmarian, Walter Daniel.[57] Aelred, like William, is a person easy to get to know and popular in our times.

After introducing the man, I would give a general introduction to Aelred's Liturgical Sermons,[58] so that as we finish the second or third year with Guerric's Sermons we could take up Aelred's for the next two years. In between the feasts I would survey his treatises[59] and historical studies[60] in basically chronological order, giving the bulk of the time to the spiritual treatises and adding little to Squire's treatment of the historical works. Obviously, his *Pastoral Prayer*[61] is of capital importance and the *Sermons on Isaiah*[62] are especially rich. It is very important to tie the *Spiritual Friendship*[63] into its proper context in the *Mirror of Charity.*[64] These two treatises bring together Aelred's whole life[65] and only then is it clear how spiritual friendship, as Aelred understood it, is the ultimate climax of a truly contemplative life. Unfortunately, Aelred's treatise on man[66] was not completed at his death and so is not as helpful as it might have been in forming a synthesis of his teaching.

In the last months of the second (or third) year with Aelred, we are ready to move on to Bernard.

Saint Bernard

The pattern is the same. In the last months of the liturgical year we meet Bernard in earnest[67] and generally introduce his Liturgical Sermons.[68] Then in the following years as we study his Sermons with the feasts, and Bernard has a much richer collection of them, we also study his other works. I would suggest doing the *Letters*[69] before going on to the treatises. They will enrich our feel for this wonderful, alive, human, yet in some ways superhuman, and terribly attractive person. Then the *Occasional Sermons*, the *Sentences*, and the *Parables*[70] could be enjoyed. Then the treatises.[71] As I mentioned above, the earliest ones might be studied earlier in the course. I would present the treatises in chronological order leading up to the five books *On Consideration*. Finally I would come to his masterpiece, the *Sermons on the Song of Songs*.[72] Actually, the brief beautiful treatise on prayer to be found in the first twelve Sermons[73] might have been treated some earlier year in the course for the Saint's feast.

At least three years could be spent with Bernard. Longer, certainly, if one is going to use this course to supply for theology and to draw from it a study of the attributes of God, the nature of the Trinity and the Incarnation, the Redemption, Mariology, Ecclesiology, and the nature of sin and grace. In this case all of this should be complemented by earlier Patristic background and modern Scriptural exegesis and theological development and insight. But even without all this sophistication of learning, just listening to Bernard as a Spiritual Father will take time and deeply enrich one's whole life and movement in God.

As we draw near the end of the third or fourth year with Bernard, we can begin to get acquainted with Isaac of Stella. The first chapter of Professor McGinn's book, *The Golden Chain*,[74] is useful here. Then we can go on through the next liturgical year(s) with his Sermons for the Liturgical Year[75] and his treatises[76] and also reach out to some of the lesser Fathers and the precious treatises they have left us. I think of Baldwin of Ford's treatise, *On the Sacrament of the Altar*[77] and his lovely little work, *On the Common Life*.[78] And there is Hugh of Barzelle's *Brothers Living Together*.[79]

The basic foundations have been laid. Each one can now be left free to go ahead according to his own attraction. There is a lifetime to go back to the rich pastures in the four Evangelists of Citeaux[80] or to go ahead. Years can be spent with Gilbert's and John of Ford's continuation of St. Bernard's Commentary on the *Song of Songs*.[81] There is Stephen of Salley's *Mirror for Novices* and his treatise on psalmody,[82] Amedeus of Lausanne's *Homilies on Mary*,[83] Hugh of Pontigny's Liturgical Sermons,[84] and those of Helinand of Froidmont.[85] And one must not forget the delightful little *Lives*[86] that give so much insight into the times and their ideals. Here we will find something about the first Mothers of the Order,[87] and their writings should not be wholly neglected.[88]

The Cistercian well is so extremely rich and plentiful, and all of it is so seasoned with the Scriptures, the living Word of God, that if we would have it so, we would never need drink from any other source. At least let us not fail to taste these waters and lead our young to taste them, and be ready to serve them to those who come seeking Cistercian spirituality. It takes time to develop a taste for good wine, but once one does, he always longs for more.

A Possible Schedule for a Program Such as Has Been Described

FIRST YEAR

August	Bernard's *Steps of Humility*
September	Introducing Guerric of Igny
	*Liturgical Sermons of Guerric**
December	Introducing William of St. Thierry
	On Contemplating God
	Nature and Dignity of Love
	(Nature of the Body and Soul)
	(Commentary on Romans)
	Meditations

SECOND YEAR

August	Bernard's *Apology*
September	*Sacrament of the Altar*
	Mirror of Faith
	(Enigma of Faith)
	Exposition on the Song of Songs
	The Golden Epistle

THIRD YEAR

August	Bernard's *On Loving God*
September	Introducing Aelred of Rievaulx
	*Liturgical Sermons of Aelred**
	Mirror of Charity
	Pastoral Prayer
	On Jesus at Twelve Years of Age
	Rule of Life for a Recluse

FOURTH YEAR

August	[Bernard's *Knights of the Temple*]

*The Liturgical Sermons are read through the course of the year at the time of the respective season or feast.

September   Homilies on Isaiah
                       (On the Soul)
                       (Historical Works)
                     Spiritual Friendship

FIFTH YEAR

August   [Bernard's On the Song of Songs, Sermons 1-12]
September   Introducing Bernard of Clairvaux
                       Liturgical Sermons of Bernard*
                       Letters
                       Occasional Sermons
                       Sentences
                       Parables

SIXTH YEAR

                     On the Song of Songs
                     Treatises: On Grace and Free Will
                                 Precepts and Dispensation
                                 Life of Saint Malachy
                                 On Consideration

SEVENTH YEAR

September   Introducing Isaac of Stella
                       Liturgical Sermons of Isaac*
                       On the Soul
                       On the Mass
                     Other Cistercian Fathers

NOTES

[1]See above, "Two Treatises on Love."

[2]Perhaps the best volume presently available to introduce St. Bernard is Jean Leclercq's *Saint Bernard and the Cistercian Spirit*, CS 16. The *Vita prima* helps give flavor and color; an English translation of William's part of this was published under the title *St. Bernard of Clairvaux*, tr. G. Webb and A. Walker (Westminster, MD: Newman Press, 1960).

[3]*S. Bernard opera*, ed. J. Leclercq, C. H. Talbot, H. Rochais (Rome: Editiones Cistercienses, 1957-) (hereafter referred to as OB) 3:13-59; tr. Ambrose Conway in *The Works of Bernard of Clairvaux*, vol. 5, CF 13.

[4]OB 3:119-154; CF 13.

[5]E.g., *The Liturgical Sermons of Guerric of Igny*, PL 185:11-214, CF 8 and 32, also in Sources Chrétiennes 166 and 202; Bernard's *Sermons Through the Year*, OB 4 and 5; Aelred's *Sermons for the Liturgical Year*, PL 195 and *Sermones inediti*, ed. C. H. Talbot, Series Scriptorum S. Ordinis Cisterciensis (Rome: Editiones Cistercienses, 1952); Isaac of Stella's *Sermons*, PL 194:1689-1876; Helinand of Froidmont, *Sermons*, PL 212:477 ff. Translations of all of these will be appearing in CF.

[6]See J. Leclercq, "Saint Bernard and the Contemplative Community" in *Contemplative Community: A Symposium*, CS 21, section "Formation," pp. 103-107.

[7]See *The Letters of St. Bernard of Clairvaux*, tr. B. S. James (London: Burns & Oates, 1953), Letters 92 and 93, pp. 137ff. In Migne these are Letters 89 and 90, PL 182:220-222.

[8]See J. Morson and H. Costello, "Introduction," in *The Liturgical Sermons of Guerric of Igny*, vol. 1 (Spencer, MA: Cistercian Publications, 1970), CF 8, pp. xviiff.

[9]Guerric speaks of Bernard as "our Master, the exegete of the Holy Spirit," *Third Sermon for the Feast of Pentecost*, CF 32:160f.

[10]See Bernard's Letters to William of St. Thierry, Ep. 85 and 86, PL 182:206-210; tr. James, Letters 87 and 88, pp. 124-128, where we read such passages as: "I love you as much as I can according to the power that has been given me." "It was you who gave me this formula of greeting when you wrote 'To his friend all that a friend could wish.' Receive back what is your own, and in doing so realize that my soul is not far from one with whom I share a common language."

[11]See the Introductory letter to the *Mirror of Charity* where Bernard says: "I asked you as a brother, or, I should say, I enjoined and charged you by the blessed name of God, to write. . . . To satisfy your modesty, you will preface the work with this letter so that if anything in the *Mirror of Charity* should offend the reader, he shall blame me who forced you to produce it. . . ."

[12]It seems that it was while he was at Signy that William edited his *Meditations* and *Commentaries* from previously written notes. And it was here that he wrote his *Exposition on the Song of Songs* (ed. J.-M. Déchanet, Sources chrétiennes 82, Paris: Cerf, 1962; tr. Columba Hart, CF 6, 1969). I personally believe that this treatise flows out of conferences which he gave to the community at Signy.

[13]See above, "Together unto God: Contemplative Community in the Sermons of Guerric of Igny."

[14]CF 8:vii-xxviii.

15*Exordium Magnum Cisterciense sive narratio di initio Cisterciensis Ordinis,* ed. Bruno Griesser, Series Scriptorum S. Ordinis Cisterciensis, vol. 2 (Rome: Editiones Cistercienses, 1961). English trans. in preparation.

16CS 8 (Washington, DC: Cisterican Publications, 1972).

17By a Father of the Abbey of Gethsemani (A. Wulff), *Compendium of the History of the Cistercian Order* (Trappist, KY: Gethsemani, 1944).

18Louis J. Lekai, *The Cistercians: Ideals and Reality* (Kent, OH: Kent State U. Press, 1977).

19Henri de Lubac, *Exégèse médiévale,* 4 vols. (Paris: Aubier, 1959-1964).

20*Exordium Magnum,* p. 166.

21See above, "A Way to Holiness."

22CF 32:219-230.

23I think Guerric's sublime yet practical and realistic theology of silence is one of the most beautiful and useful contributions he makes as a Cistercian Father, although I would not want in any way to slight his magnificent Mariology.

24*The Third Sermon for Easter* 35:4, CF 32:95.

25John D. Anderson, Catholic University of America, *The Enigma fidei of William of Saint Thierry: A Translation and Commentary* (Washington, DC: Cistercian Publications, 1974). Stanislaus Ceglar, Catholic University of America, *William of Saint Thierry: The Chronology of His Life with a Study of His Treatise* On the Nature of Love, *his Authorship of the* Brevis Commentatio, *the* In Lacu *and the* Reply to Cardinal Matthew (1971). E. Rozanne Elder, The University of Toronto, *The Image of Invisible God: The Evolving Christology of William of Saint Thierry* (1972). Rita Riccio, Catholic University of Milan, *L' "Epistola ad fratres de Monte Dei" di Guielmo di St. Thierry* (1969). Louis M. Savary, Catholic University of America, *Psychological Themes in the Golden Epistle of William of Saint Thierry to the Carthusians of Mont-Dieu, Analecta Cartusiana* 8 (1973). Thomas Michael Tomasic, Fordham University, *The Three Theological Virtues as Modes of Intersubjectivity in the Thought of William of St. Thierry* (1970).

26"Going into the hovel which had become a palace by his presence in it, and thinking what a wonderful person dwelt in such a despicable place, I was filled with such awe of the hut itself that I felt as if I were approaching the very altar of God. And the sweetness of his character so attracted me to him and filled me with desire to share his life amid such poverty and simplicity, that if the chance had then been given to me I should have asked nothing more than to be allowed to remain with him always, looking after him and ministering to his needs."—*St. Bernard of Clairvaux: The Story of His Life as recorded in the* Vita Prima Bernardi, tr. G. Webb and A. Walker (Westminster, MD: 1960), p. 56.

27In *The Works of William of Saint Thierry,* vol. 1, tr. Penelope Lawson, CF 3 (Spencer, MA: Cistercian Publications, 1971), pp. 36-64.

28Tr. Thomas X. Davis, CF 30 (Kalamazoo, MI: Cistercian Publications, 1981).

29In *Three Treatises on the Soul: A Cistercian Anthology,* ed. B. McGinn, CF 24 (Washington, DC: Cistercian Publications, 1974). See G. Webb, *An Introduction to the Cistercian De Anima,* Aquinas Paper 36 (London: Aquinas, 1961).

30In *The Works of William of Saint Thierry,* vol. 9, tr. John Anderson, CF 27 (Kalamazoo, MI: Cisterican Publications, 1979).

31PL 184:407. See also, Ceglar, *op. cit.,* supra note 25; and Jacques Hourlier,

"Guillaume de Saint Thierry et la *'Brevis Commentatio in Cantica,' " Analecta SOC* 12 (1956) 105-114.

[32]*Commentarium in Cantica Canticorum ex scriptis Sti Ambrosii* PL 15:1947-2060; *Excerpta ex libris Sti Gregorii papae super Cantica Canticorum,* PL 180:441-474.

[33]Tr. Columba Hart in *The Works of William of Saint Thierry,* vol. 2, CF 6.

[34]Tr. Penelope Lawson in *The Works of William of Saint Thierry,* vol. 1, CF 3:89-190.

[35]*De sacramento altaris,* PL 180:345-366. A tr. is being prepared for publication in CF Series.

[36]To indicate a few of the other specifically Eucharistic texts: Isaac of Stella, *Epistola de officio Missae,* PL 194:1880-1896; Ogerius of Locedio, *Sermones in coena Domini,* PL 184:879-950; Baldwin of Ford, *Liber de sacramento altaris,* ed. J. Morson, Sources Chrétiennes 93-94 (1963). But there are besides innumerable rich and beautiful passages on the Eucharist in their other writings.

[37]William expresses this tension between activity and contemplation in *On Contemplating God,* 1, CF 3:36-37; *Meditations* 11:13, CF 3:164-165; *Golden Epistle,* Introduction 18, CF 12:15.

[38]*The Mirror of Faith,* tr. G. Webb and A. Walker, Fleur de Lys Series (London: Mowbrays, 1959); *The Enigma of Faith,* tr. J. Anderson, CF 9 (Washington, DC: Cistercian Publications, 1974).

[39]In *The Works of William of Saint Thierry,* vol. 4, tr. Theodore Berkeley, CF 12 (Spencer, MA: Cistercian Publications, 1971).

[40]See note 26 above.

[41]CS 10 (Spencer, MA: Cistercian Publications, 1972).

[42]The new information offered by Ceglar in his thesis (see note 25 above) should be considered in evaluating Déchanet's chronology.

[43]CF 3:181-185.

[44]Published with notes and introduction by A. Poncelet in *Mélanges Godefroid Kurth,* vol. I (Liege, 1908) pp. 85-96. English translation David N. Bell, *Cisterican Studies* 11 (1976) 246-255.

[45]In his introduction to the *Golden Epistle,* CF 12:6.

[46]See notes 27 and 28 above.

[47]See notes 29 and 30 above.

[48]See note 34 above.

[49]See note 35 above.

[50]See note 32 above.

[51]See note 33 above.

[52]See note 38 above.

[53]*Ibid.*

[54]See note 39 above.

[55]Aelred Squire, *Aelred of Rievaulx: A Study,* CS 50 (Kalamazoo, MI: Cistercian Publications, 1981).

[56]Amedée Hallier, *The Monastic Theology of Aelred of Rievaulx,* CS 2 (Spencer, MA: Cistercian Publications, 1969).

[57]Walter Daniel, *Life of Aelred, Abbot of Rievaulx,* ed. F. M. Powicke (London: Nelson, 1950).

[58]PL 194:209-360. A translation has been prepared by Theodore Berkeley for

publication in the Cistercian Fathers Series as soon as it can be checked with the new critical edition to be published shortly by Corpus Christianorum (CCM).

[59]*Mirror of Charity*, CCM 1:3-161; *Jesus at the Age of Twelve*, CCM 1:249-278, CF 2:1-39; *Spiritual Friendship*, CCM 1:287-350, CF 5; *A Rule of Life for a Recluse*, CCM 1:637-682, CF 2:41-102; *Homilies on the Burdens of Isaiah*, PL 195:363-500; *Dialogue on the Soul*, CCM 1:685-754, CF 22; *Pastoral Prayer*, CCM 1:757-763, CF 2:103-118. Translations of all of these have appeared or will appear in the CF Series.

[60]*History of the Kings*, PL 195:711-738: *Battle of the Standard*, PL 195:701-712; *Life of St. Edward*, PL 195:737-790; *On the Miracles of the Holy Fathers who rest in Hexham Church*, Acta sanctorum Ordinis Sancti Benedicti, saec. tertia, pars prima (Paris, 1672); *Life of Saint Ninian* in *Lives of the English Saints* (London, 1845).

[61]See note 59 above.

[62]*Ibid.*

[63]*Ibid*

[64]*Ibid*. In the last part of the Third Book, Aelred places spiritual friendship in the context of the whole of the way to God.

[65]*The Mirror of Charity* is Aelred's first published work; the *Spiritual Friendship* developed over the years.

[66]Aelred of Rievaulx, *De anima*, ed. C. H. Talbot (London: Warburg Institute, 1952); tr. C. H. Talbot, *Dialogue on the Soul*, CF 22 (Kalamazoo, MI: Cistercian Publications, 1981).

[67]Vacandard, (*Vie de saint Bernard*, 2 vols. [Paris: Lecoffre, 1895]) is still the best standard biography of St. Bernard although it is dated. The same is true of Jean Leclercq's *S. Bernard mystique* (Paris: Desclée de Brouwer, 1948) and Etienne Gilson's *The Mystical Theology of Saint Bernard*, tr. A. H. C. Downes (New York: Sheed and Ward, 1955). But there are innumerable supplementary studies to draw from. For the most recent, see Eugene Manning, *Bibliographie Bernardine (1957-1970)*, Documentation Cistercienne 6 (1972). William of St. Thierry's *Life*, as mentioned above, as well as the other primitive *Lives*, should be employed for the color and actuality they bring to the picture.

[68]OB 4-5.

[69]*The Letters of St. Bernard of Clairvaux*, tr. B. S. James (London: Burns & Oates, 1953).

[70]OB 6-7.

[71]Leclercq has included eight treatises in the third volume of his critical edition.

[72]OB 1-2, CF 4, 7.

[73]See above, "Three Stages of Spiritual Growth according to St. Bernard."

[74]Bernard McGinn, *The Golden Chain: A Study in the Theological Anthropology of Isaac of Stella*, CS 15 (Washington, DC: Cistercian Publications, 1972).

[75]PL 194:1749-1876. There is a new critical edition available for the sermons: ed. A. Hoste, Sources Chrétiennes 130 and 207 (Paris: Cerf, 1967 and 1974), tr. Hugh McCaffery, CF 11 (Kalamazoo, MI: Cistercian Publications, 1979).

[76]*On the Soul*, PL 194:1875-1890, CF 24:153-178; *On the Mass*, PL 194:1889-1895.

[77]See note 36 above.

[78]PL 204:540-562.

[79]John Morson, "The *Cohabitatione Fratrum* of Hugh of Barzelle," *Studia Anselmiana* 41 (1957) 119-140.

[80]Thus Gilson called Bernard, Aelred, William of St. Thierry and Guerric of Igny.

[81]Gilbert of Hoyland, *Sermones in Canticum,* PL 184:11-252, CF 14 (1978), 20, 26 (1979); John of Ford, *Super extremam partem cantici canticorum sermones CXX,* ed. E. Mikkers and H. Costello, CCM 17 and 18 (1970), CF 29 (1977), 36 (1980).

[82]E. Mikkers, "Un *Speculum novitii* inédit d'Etienne de Salley," *Collectanea* OCR 8 (1946) 17-68; idem, "Un traité inédit d'Etienne de Salley sur la psalmodie," *Cîteaux* 23 (1972) 245-288.

[83]Sources Chrétiennes 72, ed. Deshusses (1960), CF 18 (1979).

[84]These are presently being edited by Nicolas Groves of the University of Chicago, who will then prepare an English translation for the CF Series. Translations of all the aforementioned have been or are being prepared for that series.

[85]PL 212:477ff.

[86]E.g., *Das Leben des hl. Robert von Molesme,* ed. C. Spahr (Fribourg, 1944); "Vita Venerabilis Amedaei Altae Ripae († c. 1150)" ed. M. Anselm Dimier, *Studia Monastica* 5 (1963) 265-304; "Vita B. Davidis Monachi Hemmenrodinsis," ed. B. Schneider, *Analecta SOC* 11 (1955) 27-44; "Vita Venerabilis Lukardis Monialis Ordinis Cisterciensis in Superior Wimaria," *Analecta Bollandiana* 18 (1899) 305-367; "Vita S. Roberti Novi Monasterii in Anglia Abbatis," *ibid.,* 56 (1938) 334-360 (there is a substantial English translation of this in *The Lives of English Saints* [London, 1865]) "Le texte Complet de la vie de Christian de l'Aumone," ed. Jean Leclercq, *ibid.,* 71 (1953), 21-52.

[87]See in particular the *Life of Lutgard* mentioned in the previous note. Also L. Reypens, *Vita Beatrici* (Antwerp: Ruusbroec-Genootschap, 1963).

[88]I think of Beatrice of Nazareth, Gertrude of Helfta, Hildegard of Bingen, Lutgard, etc. The only work readily available in English is *The Exercises of Saint Gertrude,* tr. Benedictine Nun of Regina Laudis (Columba Hart) (Westminster, MD: Newman, 1956). I do hope the Cistercian nuns will soon begin to collaborate in the work of Cistercian Publications by translating the works of the Cistercian Mothers.